M000281768

Mystical Paths to God:
Three Journeys

Mystical Paths to God: Three Journeys

The Practice of the Presence of God
Interior Castle
Dark Night of the Soul
by Brother Lawrence, St. Teresa of Avila, and
St. John of the Cross

©2008 Wilder Publications

This book is a product of its time and does not reflect the same values as it would if it were written today. Parents might wish to discuss with their children how views on race have changed before allowing them to read this classic work.

All rights reserved. Printed in the United States of America. No part of this book may be used or reproduced in any manner without written permission except for brief quotations for review purposes only.

Wilder Publications, LLC.
PO Box 3005
Radford VA 24143-3005

ISBN 10: 1-60459-265-6
ISBN 13: 978-1-60459-265-8

The Practice of the Presence of God
by Brother Lawrence

Preface

This book consists of notes of several conversations had with, and letters written by Nicholas Herman, of Lorraine, a lowly and unlearned man, who, after having been a footman and soldier, was admitted a Lay Brother among the barefooted Carmelites at Paris in 1666, and was afterwards known as "Brother Lawrence."

His conversion, which took place when he was about eighteen years old, was the result, under God, of the mere sight in midwinter, of a dry and leafless tree, and of the reflections it stirred respecting the change the coming spring would bring. From that time he grew eminently in the knowledge and love of GOD, endeavoring constantly to walk *as in His presence*. No wilderness wanderings seem to have intervened between the Red Sea and the Jordan of his experience. A wholly consecrated man, he lived his Christian life through as a pilgrim—as a steward and not as an owner, and died at the age of eighty, leaving a name which has been as "ointment poured forth."

The "Conversations" are supposed to have been written by M. Beaufort, Grand Vicar to M. de Chalons, formerly Cardinal de Noailles, by whose recommendation the letters were first published.

The book has, within a short time, gone through repeated English and American editions, and has been a means of blessing to many souls. It contains very much of that wisdom which only lips the Lord has touched can express, and which only hearts He has made teachable can receive.

May this edition also be blessed by GOD, and redound to the praise of the glory of His grace.

First Conversation

The first time I saw *Brother Lawrence*, was upon the 3d of August, 1666. He told me that GOD had done him a singular favor, in his conversion at the age of eighteen.

That in the winter, seeing a tree stripped of its leaves, and considering that within a little time the leaves would be renewed and after that the flowers and fruit appear, he received a high view of the Providence and Power of GOD, which has never since been effaced from his soul. That this view had perfectly set him loose from the world, and kindled in him such a love for GOD, that he could not tell whether it had increased during the more than forty years he had lived since.

That he had been footman to M. Fieubert, the treasurer, and that he was a great awkward fellow who broke everything.

That he had desired to be received into a monastery, thinking that he would there be made to smart for his awkwardness and the faults he should commit, and so he should sacrifice to GOD his life, with its pleasures: but that God had disappointed him, he having met with nothing but satisfaction in that state.

That we should establish ourselves in a sense of GOD'S Presence, by continually conversing with Him. That it was a shameful thing to quit His conversation, to think of trifles and fooleries.

That we should feed and nourish our souls with high notions of GOD; which would yield us great joy in being devoted to Him.

That we ought to *quicken*, i.e., *to enliven, our faith*. That it was lamentable we had so little; and that instead of taking *faith* for the rule of their conduct, men amused themselves with trivial devotions, which changed daily. That the way of Faith was the spirit of the Church, and that it was sufficient to bring us to a high degree of perfection.

That we ought to give ourselves up to GOD, with regard both to things temporal and spiritual, and seek our satisfaction only in the fulfilling of His will, whether he lead us by suffering or by consolation, for all would lie equal to a soul truly resigned. That there needed fidelity in those dryness, or insensibilities and irksomenesses in prayer, by which GOD tries our love to him; that *then* was the time for us to make good and effectual acts of resignation, whereof one alone would oftentimes very much promote our spiritual advancement.

That as for the miseries and sins he heard of daily in the world, he was so far from wondering at them, that, on the contrary, he was surprised that there were not more, considering the malice sinners were capable of; that for his part he prayed for them; but knowing that GOD could remedy the mischiefs they did when He pleased, he gave himself no farther trouble.

That to arrive at such resignation as GOD requires, we should watch attentively over all the passions which mingle as well in spiritual things as in those of a grosser nature; that GOD would give light concerning those passions to those who truly desire to serve Him. That if this was my design, viz., sincerely to serve GOD, I might come to him (B. Lawrence) as often as I pleased, without any Fear of being troublesome; but if not, that I ought no more to visit him.

Second Conversation

That he had always been governed by love, without selfish views; and that having resolved to make the love of GOD the *end* of all his actions, he had found reasons to be well satisfied with his method. That he was pleased when he could take up a straw from the ground for the love of GOD, seeking Him only, and nothing else, not even His gifts.

That he had been long troubled in mind from a certain belief that he should be damned; that all the men in the world could not have persuaded him to the contrary; but that he had thus reasoned with himself about it: *I engaged in a religious life only for the love of* GOD, *and I have endeavored to act only for Him; whatever becomes of me, whether I be lost or saved, I will always continue to act purely for the love of* GOD. *I shall have this good at least, that till death I shall have done all that is in me to love Him.* That this trouble of mind had lasted four years; during which time he had suffered much. But that at last he had seen that this trouble arose from want of faith; and that since then he had passed his life in perfect liberty and continual joy. That he had placed his sins betwixt him and GOD, as it were, to tell Him that he did not deserve His favors, but that GOD still continued to bestow them in abundance.

That in order to form a habit of conversing with GOD continually, and referring all we do to Him, we must at first apply to Him with some diligence: but that after a little care we should find His love inwardly excite us to it without any difficulty.

That he expected after the pleasant days GOD had given him, he should have his turn of pain and suffering; but that he was not uneasy about it, knowing very well, that as he could do nothing of himself, GOD would not fail to give him the strength to bear it.

That when an occasion of practicing some virtue offered, he addressed himself to GOD, saying, LORD, *I cannot do this unless Thou enablest me*: and that then he received strength more than sufficient.

That when he had failed in his duty, he only confessed his fault, saying to GOD, *I shall never do otherwise, if You leave me to myself; it is You who must hinder my falling, and mend what is amiss.* That after this, he gave himself no further uneasiness about it.

That we ought to act with GOD in the greatest simplicity, speaking to Him frankly and plainly, and imploring His assistance in our affairs, just as they happen. That GOD never failed to grant it, as he had often experienced.

That he had been lately sent into Burgundy, to buy the provision of wine for the society, which was a very unwelcome task for him, because he had no turn for business, and because he was lame and could not go about the boat but by rolling himself over the casks. That however he gave himself no uneasiness about it, nor about the purchase of the wine. That he said to GOD, *It was His business he was about,* and that he afterwards found it very well performed. That he had been sent into Auvergne, the year before, upon the same account; that he could not tell how the matter passed, but that it proved very well.

So, likewise, in his business in the kitchen (to which he had naturally a great aversion), having accustomed himself to do everything there for the love of GOD, and with prayer, upon all occasions, for His grace to do his work well, he had found everything easy, during fifteen years that he had been employed there.

That he was very well pleased with the post he was now in; but that he was as ready to quit that as the former, since he was always pleasing himself in every condition, by doing little things for the love of GOD.

That with him the set times of prayer were not different from other times; that he retired to pray, according to the directions of his Superior, but that he did not want such retirement, nor ask for it, because his greatest business did not divert him from GOD.

That as he knew his obligation to love GOD in all things, and as he endeavored so to do, he had no need of a director to advise him, but that he needed much a Confessor to absolve him. That he was very sensible of his faults, but not discouraged by them; that he confessed them to GOD, but did not plead against Him to excuse them. When he had so done, he peaceably resumed his usual practice of love and adoration.

That in his trouble of mind, he had consulted nobody, but knowing only by the light of faith that GOD was present, he contented himself with directing all his actions to Him, *i.e.,* doing them with a desire to please Him, let what would come of it.

That useless thoughts spoil all: that the mischief began there; but that we ought to reject them, as soon as we perceived their impertinence to the matter in hand, or our salvation; and return to our communion with GOD.

That at the beginning he had often passed his time appointed for prayer, in rejecting wandering thoughts, and falling back into them. That he could never regulate his devotion by certain methods as some do. That nevertheless, at first he had *meditated* for some time, but afterwards that went off, in a manner he could give no account of.

That all bodily mortifications and other exercises are useless, except as they serve to arrive at the union with GOD by love; that he had well considered this, and found it the shortest way to go straight to Him by a continual exercise of love, and doing all things for His sake.

That we ought to make a great difference between the acts of the *under-standing* and those of the *will*: that the first were comparatively of little value, and the others, all. That our only business was to love and delight ourselves in GOD.

That all possible kinds of mortification, if they were void of the love of GOD, could not efface a single sin. That we ought, without anxiety, to expect the pardon of our sins from the Blood of JESUS CHRIST, only endeavoring to love

Him with all our hearts. That GOD seemed to have granted the greatest favors to the greatest sinners, as more signal monuments of his mercy.

That the greatest pains or pleasures of this world, were not to be compared with what he had experienced of both kinds in a spiritual state: so that he was careful for nothing and feared nothing, desiring only one thing of GOD, viz., that he might not offend Him.

That he had no scruples; for, said he, when I *fail* in my duty, I readily acknowledge it, saying, *I am used to do so: I shall never do otherwise, if I am left to myself.* I fail not, then I give GOD thanks, acknowledging the strength comes from Him.

Third Conversation

He told me that the *foundation of the spiritual life* in *him*, had been a high notion and esteem of GOD in faith; which when he had once well conceived, he had no other care at first, but faithfully to reject every other thought, *that he might perform all his actions for the love of* GOD. That when sometimes he had not thought of GOD for a good while, he did not disquiet himself for it; but after having acknowledged his wretchedness to GOD, he returned to Him with so much the greater trust in Him, as he had found himself wretched through forgetting Him.

That the trust we put in GOD, honors Him much, and draws down great graces.

That it was impossible, not only that GOD should deceive, but also that He should long let a soul suffer which is perfectly resigned to Him, and resolved to endure everything for His sake.

That he had so often experienced the ready succors of Divine Grace upon all occasions, that from the same experience, when he had business to do, he did not think of it beforehand; but when it was time to do it, he found in GOD, as in a clear mirror, all that was fit for him to do. That of late he had acted thus, without anticipating care; but before the experience above mentioned, he had used it in his affairs.

When outward business diverted him a little from the thought of GOD, a fresh remembrance coming from GOD invested his soul, and so inflamed and transported him that it was difficult for him to contain himself.

That he was more united to GOD in his outward employments, than when he left them for devotion in retirement.

That he expected hereafter some great pain of body or mind; that the worst that could happen to him was, to lose that sense of GOD which he had enjoyed so long; but that the goodness of GOD assured him He would not forsake him utterly, and that He would give him strength to bear whatever evil He permitted to happen to him; and therefore that he feared nothing, and had no occasion to consult with anybody about his state. That when he had attempted to do it, he had always come away more perplexed; and that as he was conscious of his readiness to lay down his life for the love of GOD, he had no apprehension of danger. That perfect resignation to GOD was a sure way to heaven, a way in which we had always sufficient light for our conduct.

That in the beginning of the spiritual life, we ought to be faithful in doing our duty and denying ourselves; but after that, unspeakable pleasures followed; that in difficulties we need only have recourse to JESUS CHRIST, and beg his grace; with that everything became easy.

That many do not advance in the Christian progress because they stick in penances, and particular exercises, while they neglect the love of GOD, which is the *end*. That this appeared plainly by their works, and was the *reason* why we see so little solid virtue.

That there needed neither art nor science for going to GOD, but only a heart resolutely determined to apply itself to nothing but Him, or for *His* sake, and to love him only.

Fourth Conversation

He discoursed with me very frequently, and with great openness of heart concerning his manner of *going* to GOD, whereof some part is related already.

He told me that all consists *in one hearty renunciation* of everything which we are sensible does not lead to GOD; that we might accustom ourselves to a continual conversation with Him, with freedom and in simplicity. That we need only to recognize GOD intimately present with us, to address ourselves to Him every moment, that we may beg His assistance for knowing His will in things doubtful, and for rightly performing those which we plainly see he requires of us, offering them to Him before we do them, and giving Him thanks when we have done.

That in this conversation with God, we are also employed in praising, adoring and loving Him incessantly, for His infinite goodness and perfection.

That, without being discouraged on account of our sins, we should pray for His grace with a perfect confidence, as relying upon the infinite merits of our LORD JESUS CHRIST. That GOD never failed offering us His grace at each action; that he distinctly perceived it, and never failed of it, unless when his thoughts had wandered from a sense of GOD'S Presence, or he had forgotten to ask His assistance.

That GOD always gave us light in our doubts, when we had no other design but ask to please Him.

That our sanctification did not depend upon *changing* our works, but in doing that for GOD's sake, which we commonly do for our own. That it was lamentable to see how many people mistook the means for the end, addicting themselves to certain works, which they performed very imperfectly, by reason of their human or selfish regards.

That the most excellent method he had found of going to GOD, was that of doing our common business without any view of pleasing men,[1] and (as far as we are capable) purely for the love of GOD.

That it was a great delusion to think that the times of prayer ought to differ from other times: that we are as strictly obliged to adhere to GOD by action in the time of action, as by prayer in the season of prayer.

That his prayer was nothing else but a sense of the presence of GOD, his soul being at that time insensible to everything but Divine love: and that when the appointed times of prayer were past, he found no difference, because he still continued with GOD, praising and blessing Him with all his might, so that he passed his life in continual joy; yet hoped that GOD would give him somewhat to suffer, when he should grow stronger.

That we ought, once for all, heartily to put our whole trust in GOD, and make a total surrender of ourselves to Him, secure that He would not deceive us.

That we ought not to be weary of doing little things for the love of GOD, who regards not the greatness of the work, but the love with which it is performed. That we should not wonder if, in the beginning, we often failed in our endeavors, but that at last we should gain a habit, which will naturally produce its acts in us, without our care, and to our exceeding great delight.

That the whole substance of religion was faith, hope and charity; by the practice of which we become united to the will of GOD: that all besides is indifferent, and to be used as a means that we may arrive at our end, and be swallowed up therein, by faith and charity.

That all things are possible to him who *believes*—that they are less difficult to him who *hopes*—that they are more easy to him who *loves*, and still more easy to him who perseveres in the practice of these three virtues.

That the end we ought to propose to ourselves is to become, in this life, the most perfect worshippers of GOD we can possibly be, as we hope to be through all eternity.

That when we enter upon the spiritual life, we should consider, and examine to the bottom, what we are. And then we should find ourselves worthy of all contempt, and not deserving indeed the name of Christians: subject to all kinds of misery and numberless accidents, which trouble us and cause perpetual vicissitudes in our health, in our humors, in our internal and external dispositions; in fine, persons whom GOD would humble by many pains and labors, as well within as without. After this we should not wonder that troubles, temptations, oppositions and contradictions happen to us from men. We ought, on the contrary, to submit ourselves to them, and bear them as long as GOD pleases, as things highly advantageous to us.

That the greater perfection a soul aspires after, the more dependent it is upon Divine grace.

[2]Being questioned by one of his own society (to whom he was obliged to open himself) by what means he had attained such an habitual sense of GOD, he told him that, since his first coming to the monastery, he had considered GOD as the end of all his thoughts and desires, as the mark to which they should tend, and in which they should terminate.

That in the beginning of his noviciate, he spent the hours appointed for private prayer in thinking of GOD, so as to convince his mind of, and to impress deeply upon his heart, the Divine existence, rather by devout sentiments, and submission to the lights of faith, than by studied reasonings and elaborate meditations. That by this short and sure method, he exercised himself in the knowledge and love of GOD, resolving to use his utmost endeavor to live, in a continual sense of His Presence, and if possible, never to forget Him more.

That when he had thus in prayer filled his mind with great sentiments of that infinite Being, he went to his work appointed in the kitchen (for he was cook to the society); there having first considered severally the things his office required, and when and how each thing was to be done, he spent all the intervals of his time, as well before as after his work, in prayer.

That when he began his business, he said to GOD, with a filial trust in Him, "O my GOD, since Thou art with me, and I must now, in obedience to Thy commands, apply my mind to these outward things, I beseech Thee to grant me the grace to continue in Thy Presence; and to this end do Thou prosper me with Thy assistance, receive all my works, and possess all my affections."

As he proceeded in his work, he continued his familiar conversation with his Maker,—imploring His grace, and offering to Him all his actions.

When he had finished, he examined himself how he had discharged his duty; if he found *well*, he returned thanks to GOD; if otherwise, he asked pardon; and without being discouraged, he set his mind right again, and continued his exercise of the *presence* of GOD, as if he had never deviated from it. "Thus," said he, "by rising after my falls, and by frequently renewed acts of faith and love, I am come to a state wherein it would be as difficult for me not to think of GOD as it was at first to accustom myself to it."

As brother Lawrence had found such an advantage in walking in the presence of GOD, it was natural for him to recommend it earnestly to others; but his example was a stronger inducement than any arguments he could propose. His very countenance was edifying, such a sweet and calm devotion appearing in it as could not but effect the beholders. And it was observed that in the greatest hurry of business in the kitchen, he still preserved his recollection and heavenly-mindedness. He was never hasty nor loitering, but did each thing in its season, with an even, uninterrupted composure and tranquility of spirit. "The time of business," said he, "does not with me differ from the time of prayer; and in the noise and clatter of my kitchen, while several persons are at the same time calling for different things, I possess GOD in as great tranquility as if I were upon my knees at the blessed sacrament."

First Letter

Since you desire so earnestly that I should communicate to you the method by which I arrived at that *habitual sense of* GOD'S *Presence*, which our LORD, of His mercy, has been pleased to vouch-safe to me, I must tell you that it is with great difficulty that I am prevailed on by your importunities; and now I do it only upon the terms that you show my letter to nobody. If I knew that you should let it be seen, all the desire that I have for your advancement would not be able to determine me to it. The account I can give you is:

Having found in many books different methods of going to GOD, and divers practices of the spiritual life, I thought this would serve rather to puzzle me than facilitate what I sought after, which was nothing but how to become wholly GOD'S. This made me resolve to give the all for the all; so after having given myself wholly to GOD, that He might take away my sin, *I renounced, for the love of Him, everything that was not He; and I began to live as if there was none but He and I in the world.* Sometimes I considered myself before Him as a poor criminal at the feet of his judge; at other times I beheld Him in my heart as my FATHER, as my GOD: I worshipped Him the oftenest that I could, keeping my mind in His holy Presence, and recalling it as often as I found it wandered from Him. I found no small pain in this exercise, and yet I continued it, notwithstanding all the difficulties that occurred, without troubling or disquieting myself when my mind had wandered involuntarily. I made this my business as much all the day long as at the appointed times of prayer; for at all times, every hour, every minute, even in the height of my business, I drove away from my mind everything that was capable of interrupting my thought of GOD.

Such has been my common practice ever since I entered in religion; and, though I have done it very imperfectly, yet I have found great advantages by it. These, I well know, are to be imputed to the mere mercy and goodness of GOD, because we can do nothing without Him; and *I* still less than any. But when we are faithful to keep ourselves in His holy Presence, and set Him always before us, this not only hinders our offending Him, and doing anything that may displease Him, at least wilfully, but it also begets in us a holy freedom, and, if I may so speak, a familiarity with GOD, wherewith we ask, and that successfully, the graces we stand in need of. In fine, by often repeating these acts, they become *habitual*, and the presence of GOD rendered as it were *natural to* us Give Him thanks, if you please, with me, for His great goodness towards me, which I can never sufficiently admire, for the many favors He has done to so miserable a sinner as I am. May all things praise Him. Amen.

I am, in our LORD, yours, etc.

Second Letter

To the Reverend _____
Not finding my manner of life in books, although I have no difficulty about it, yet, for greater security, I shall be glad to know your thoughts concerning it.

In a conversation some days since with a person of piety, he told me the spiritual life was a life of grace, which begins with servile fear, which is increased by hope of eternal life, and which is consummated by pure love. That each of these states had its different stages, by which one arrives at last at that blessed consummation.

I have not followed all these methods. On the contrary, from I know not what instincts, I found they discouraged me. This was the reason why, at my entrance into religion, I took a resolution to give myself up to GOD, as the best return I could make for His love; and, for the love of Him, to renounce all besides.

For the first year I commonly employed myself during the time set apart for devotion with the thought of death, judgment, heaven, hell, and my sins, Thus continued some years, applying my mind carefully the rest of the day, and even in the midst of my business, *to the presence of* GOD, whom I considered always as *with* me, often as *in* me.

At length I came insensibly to do the same thing during my set time of prayer, which caused in me great delight and consolation. This practice produced in me so high an esteem for GOD, that *faith* alone was capable to satisfy me in that point.[3]

Such was my beginning; and yet I must tell you that for the first ten years I suffered much: the apprehension that I was not devoted to GOD as I wished to be, my past sins always present to my mind, and the great unmerited favors which GOD did me, were the matter and source of my sufferings. During this time I fell often, and rose again presently. It seemed to me that all creatures, reason, and GOD Himself were against me; and *faith* alone for me. I was troubled sometimes with thoughts that to believe I had received such favors was an effect of my presumption, which pretended to be *at once* where others arrive with difficulty; at other times that it was a wilful delusion, and that there was no salvation for me.

When I thought of nothing but to end my days in these troubles (which did not at all diminish the trust I had in GOD, and which served only to increase my faith), I found myself changed all at once; and my soul, which, till that time, was in trouble, felt a profound inward peace, as if she were in her centre and place of rest.

Ever since that time I walk before GOD simply, in faith, with humility and with love; and I apply myself diligently to do nothing and think nothing which may displease Him. I hope that when I have done what I can, He will do with me what He pleases.

As for what passes in me at present, I cannot express it. I have no pain or difficulty about my state, because I have no will but that of GOD, which I endeavor to accomplish in all things, and to which I am so resigned that I would not take up a straw from the ground against His order, or from any other motive than purely that of love to Him.

I have quitted all forms of devotion and set prayers but those to which my state obliges me. And I make it my business only to persevere in His holy presence, wherein I keep myself by a simple attention, and a general fond regard to GOD, which I may call an *actual presence of* GOD; or, to speak better, an habitual, silent and secret conversation of the soul with GOD, which often causes me joys and raptures inwardly, and sometimes also outwardly, so great, that I am forced to use means to moderate them and prevent their appearance to others.

In short, I am assured beyond all doubt that my soul has been with GOD above these thirty years. I pass over many things that I may not be tedious to you, yet I think it proper to inform you after what manner I consider myself before GOD, whom I behold as my King.

I consider myself as the most wretched of men, full of sores and corruption, and who has committed all sorts of crimes against his King; touched with a sensible regret, I confess to him all my wickedness, I ask His forgiveness, I abandon myself in His hands that He may do what he pleases with me. The King, full of mercy and goodness, very far from chastising me, embraces me with love, makes me eat at His table, serves me with His own hands, gives me the key of His treasures; He converses and delights Himself with me incessantly, in a thousand and a thousand ways, and treats me in all respects as His favorite. It is thus I consider myself from time to time in His holy presence.

My most useful method is this simple attention, and such a general passionate regard to GOD; to whom I find myself often attached with greater sweetness and delight than that of an infant at the mother's breast; so that, if I dare use the expression, I should choose to call this state the bosom, of GOD, for the inexpressible sweetness which I taste and experience there.

If sometimes my thoughts wander from it by necessity or infirmity, I am presently recalled by inward motions so charming and delicious that I am ashamed to mention them. I desire your reverence to reflect rather upon my great wretchedness, of which you are fully informed, than upon the great favors which GOD does me, all unworthy and ungrateful as I am.

As for my set hours of prayer, they are only a continuation of the same exercise. Sometimes I consider myself there as a stone before a carver, whereof he is to make a statue; presenting myself thus before GOD, I desire Him to form His perfect image in my soul, and make me entirely like Himself.

At other times, when I apply myself to prayer, I feel all my spirit and all my soul lift itself up without any care or effort of mine, and it continues as it were suspended and firmly fixed in GOD, as in its centre and place of rest.

I know that some charge this state with inactivity, delusion and self-love. I confess that it is a holy inactivity, and would be a happy self-love, if the soul in that state were capable of it; because, in effect, while she is in this repose, she cannot be disturbed by such acts as she was formerly accustomed to, and which were then her support, but which would now rather hinder than assist her.

Yet I cannot bear that this should be called delusion; because the soul which thus enjoys GOD desires herein nothing but Him. If this be delusion in me, it belongs to GOD to remedy it. Let Him do what He pleases with me; I desire only Him, and to be wholly devoted to Him. You will, however, oblige me in sending me your opinion, to which I always pay a great deference, for I have a singular esteem for your reverence, and am in our LORD,

Yours, etc.

Third Letter

We have a GOD who is infinitely gracious and knows all our wants. I always thought that He would reduce you to extremity. He will come in His own time, and when you least expect it. Hope in Him more than ever; thank Him with me for the favors he does you, particularly for the fortitude and patience which He gives you in your afflictions. It is a plain mark of the care He takes of you. Comfort yourself, then, with Him, and give thanks for all.

I admire also the fortitude and bravery of Mr. ____. God has given him a good disposition and a good will; but there is in him still a little of the world, and a great deal of youth. I hope the affliction which GOD has sent him will prove a wholesome remedy to him, and make him enter into himself. It is an accident which should engage him to put all his trust in *Him* who accompanies him everywhere. Let him think of Him as often as he can, especially in the greatest dangers. A little lifting up of the heart suffices. A little remembrance of GOD, one act of inward worship, though upon a march, and a sword in hand, are prayers, which, however short, are nevertheless very acceptable to GOD; and far from lessening a soldier's courage in occasions of danger, they best serve to fortify it.

Let him then think of GOD the most he can. Let him accustom himself, by degrees, to this small but holy exercise. No one will notice it, and nothing is easier than to repeat often in the day these little internal adorations. Recommend to him, if you please, that he think of GOD the most he can, in the manner here directed. It is very fit and most necessary for a soldier, who is daily exposed to the dangers of life. I hope that GOD will assist him and all the family, to whom I present my service, being theirs and Yours, etc.

Fourth Letter

I have taken this opportunity to communicate to you the sentiments of one of our society, concerning the admirable effects and continual assistances which he receives from *the presence of* GOD. Let you and me both profit by them.

You must know his continual care has been, for about forty years past that he has spent in religion, to be *always with* GOD, and to do nothing, say nothing, and think nothing which may displease Him; and this without any other view than purely for the love of Him, and because he deserves infinitely more.

He is now so accustomed to that *Divine Presence*, that he receives from it continual succors upon all occasions. For about thirty years, his soul has been filled with joys so continual, and sometimes so great, that he is forced to use means to moderate them, and to hinder their appearing outwardly.

If sometimes he is a little too much absent from that *Divine Presence*, GOD presently makes Himself to be felt in his soul to recall him, which often happens when he is most engaged in his outward business. He answers with exact fidelity to these inward drawings, either by an elevation of his heart towards GOD, or by a meek and fond regard to Him, or by such words as love forms upon these occasions, as for instance, *My God, here I am all devoted to Thee*: LORD, *make me according to Thy heart*. And then it seems to him (as in effect he feels it) that this GOD of love, satisfied with such few words, reposes again, and rests in the fund and centre of his soul. The experience of these things gives him such an assurance that GOD is always in the fund or bottom of his soul, that it renders him incapable of doubting it upon any account whatever.

Judge by this what content and satisfaction he enjoys while he continually finds in himself so great a treasure. He is no longer in an anxious search after it, but has it open before him, and may take what he pleases of it.

He complains much of our blindness, and cries often that we are to be pitied who content ourselves with so little. GOD, saith he, *has infinite treasure to bestow, and we take up with a little sensible devotion, which passes in a moment. Blind as we are, we hinder GOD, and stop the current of His graces. But when He finds a soul penetrated with a lively faith, He pours into it His graces and favors plentifully: there they flow like a torrent, which, after being forcibly stopped against its ordinary course, when it has found a passage, spreads itself with impetuosity and abundance.*

Yes, we often stop this torrent by the little value we set upon it. But let us stop it no more; let us enter into ourselves and break down the bank which hinders it. Let us make way for grace; let us redeem the lost time, for perhaps we have but little left. Death follows us close; let us be well prepared for it: for we die but once; and a miscarriage *there* is irretrievable.

I say again, let us enter into ourselves. The time presses, there is no room for delay: our souls are at stake. I believe you have taken such effectual measures that you will not be surprised. I commend you for it; it is the one thing necessary. We must, nevertheless, always work at it, because not to advance in the spiritual life is to go back. But those who have the gale of the HOLY SPIRIT go forward even in sleep. If the vessel of our soul is still tossed with winds and storms, let us awake the LORD, who reposes in it, and He will quickly calm the sea.

I have taken the liberty to impart to you these good sentiments, that you may compare them with your own. It will serve again to kindle and inflame them, if by misfortune (which GOD forbid, for it would be indeed a great misfortune) they should be, though never so little, cooled. Let us then *both* recall our first fervors. Let us profit by the example and the sentiments of this brother, who is little known of the world, but known of GOD, and extremely caressed by Him. I will pray for you; do you pray instantly for me, who am, in our LORD.

Yours, etc.

Fifth Letter

I received this day two books and a letter from Sister ____, who is preparing to make her profession, and upon that account desires the prayers of your holy society, and yours in particular. I perceive that she reckons much upon them; pray do not disappoint her. Beg of GOD that she may make her sacrifice in the view of His love alone, and with a firm resolution to be wholly devoted to Him. I will send you one of these books which treat of *the presence of* GOD; a subject which, in my opinion, contains the whole spiritual life; and it seems to me that whoever duly practices it will soon become spiritual.

I know that for the right practice of it, the heart must be empty of all other things; because GOD will possess the heart *alone*; and as He cannot possess it *alone* without emptying it of all besides, so neither can He act *there*, and do in it what He pleases, unless it be left vacant to Him.

There is not in the world a kind of life more sweet and delightful than that of a continual conversation with GOD. Those only can comprehend it who practice and experience it; yet I do not advise you to do it from that motive. It is not pleasure which we ought to seek in this exercise; but let us do it from a principle of love, and because GOD would have us.

Were I a preacher, I should, above all other things, preach the practice of *the presence of* GOD; and, were I a director, I should advise all the world to do it, so necessary do I think it, and so easy too.

Ah! knew we but the want we have of the grace and assistance of GOD, we should never lose sight of Him, no, not for a moment. Believe me; make immediately a holy and firm resolution never more wilfully to forget Him, and to spend the rest of your days in His sacred presence, deprived for the love of Him, if He thinks fit, of all consolations.

Set heartily about this work, and if you do it as you ought, be assured that you will soon find the effects of it. I will assist you with my prayers, poor as they are. I recommend myself earnestly to yours and those of your holy society being theirs, and more particularly

Yours, etc.

Sixth Letter

To the Same.

I have received from Mrs. ____, the things which you gave her for me. I wonder that you have not given me your thoughts of the little book I sent to you, and which you must have received. Pray set heartily about the practice of it in your old age: it is better late than never.

I cannot imagine how religious persons can live satisfied without the practice of *the presence of* GOD. For my part. I keep myself retired with Him in the fund or centre of my soul as much as I can; and while I am so with Him I fear nothing, but the least turning from Him is insupportable.

This exercise does not much fatigue the body; it is, however, proper to deprive it sometimes, nay often; of many little pleasures which are innocent and lawful, for GOD will not permit that a soul which desires to be devoted entirely to Him should take other pleasures than with Him: that is more than reasonable.

I do not say that therefore we must put any violent constraint upon ourselves. No, we must serve GOD in a holy freedom; we must do our business faithfully; without trouble or disquiet, recalling our mind to GOD mildly, and with tranquility, as often as we find it wandering from Him.

It is, however, necessary to put our whole trust in GOD, laying aside all other cares, and even some particular forms of devotion, though very good in themselves, yet such as one often engages in unreasonably, because these devotions are only means to attain to the end. So when by this exercise of *the presence of* GOD we are *with Him* who is our end, it is then useless to return to the means; but we may continue with Him our commerce of love, persevering in His holy presence, one while by an act of praise, of adoration or of desire; one while by an act of resignation or thanksgiving; and in all the ways which our spirit can invent.

Be not discouraged by the repugnance which you may find in it from nature; you must do yourself violence. At the first one often thinks it lost time, but you must go on, and resolve to persevere in it to death, notwithstanding all the difficulties that may occur. I recommend myself to the prayers of your holy society, and yours in particular. I am, in our LORD,

Yours, etc.

Seventh Letter

I pity you much. It will be of great importance if you can leave the care of your affairs to ____, and spend the remainder of your life only in worshiping GOD. He requires no great matters of us; a little remembrance of Him from time to time; a little adoration; sometimes to pray for His grace, sometimes to offer Him your sufferings, and sometimes to return Him thanks for the favors He has given you, and still gives you, in the midst of your troubles, and to console yourself with Him the oftenest you can. Lift up your heart to Him, sometimes even at your meals, and when you are in company: the least little remembrance will always be acceptable to Him. You need not cry very loud; He is nearer to us than we are aware of.

It is not necessary for being with GOD to be always at church: we may make an oratory of our heart wherein to retire from time to time to converse with Him in meekness, humility and love. Every one is capable of such familiar conversation with GOD, some more, some less: He knows what we can do. Let us begin, then. Perhaps He expects but one generous resolution on our part. Have courage. We have but little time to live; you are near sixty-four, and I am almost eighty. Let us live and die with GOD. Sufferings will be sweet and pleasant to us while we are with Him; and the greatest pleasures will be, without Him, a cruel punishment to us. May He be blessed for all. Amen.

Accustom yourself, then, by degrees thus to worship Him, to beg His grace, to offer Him your heart from time to time in the midst of your business, even every moment, if you can. Do not always scrupulously confine yourself to certain rules, or particular forms of devotion, but act with a general confidence in GOD, with love and humility. You may assure — of my poor prayers, and that I am their servant, and particularly

Yours in our LORD, etc.

Eighth Letter

(Concerning wandering thoughts in Prayer.)

You tell me nothing new; you are not the only one that is troubled with wandering thoughts. Our mind is extremely roving; but, as the will is mistress of all our faculties, she must recall them, and carry them to GOD as their last end.

When the mind, for want of being sufficiently reduced by recollection at our first engaging in devotion, has contracted certain bad habits of wandering and dissipation, they are difficult to overcome, and commonly draw us, even against our wills, to the things of the earth.

I believe one remedy for this is to confess our faults, and to humble ourselves before GOD. I do not advise you to use multiplicity of words in prayer: many words and long discourses being often the occasions of wandering. Hold yourself in prayer before GOD, like a dumb or paralytic beggar at a rich man's gate. Let it be *your* business to keep your mind in the presence of the LORD. If it sometimes wander and withdraw itself from Him, do not much disquiet yourself for that: trouble and disquiet serve rather to distract the mind than to re-collect it: the will must bring it back in tranquility. If you persevere in this manner, GOD will have pity on you.

One way to re-collect the mind easily in the time of prayer, and preserve it more in tranquility, is *not to let it wander too far at other times*: you should keep it strictly in the presence of GOD; and being accustomed to think of Him often, you will find it easy to keep your mind calm in the time of prayer, or at least to recall it from its wanderings.

I have told you already at large, in my former letters, of the advantages we may draw from this practice of the presence of GOD: let us set about it seriously, and pray for one another.

Yours, etc.

Ninth Letter

The enclosed is an answer to that which I received from ____; pray deliver it to her. She seems to me full of good will, but she would go faster than grace. One does not become holy all at once. I recommend her to you: we ought to help one another by our advice, and yet more by our good examples. You will oblige me to let me hear of her from time to time, and whether she be very fervent and very obedient.

Let us thus think often that our only business in this life is to please GOD, and that all besides is but folly and vanity. You and I have lived about forty years in religion (*i.e.*, a monastic life). Have we employed them in loving and serving GOD, who by His mercy has called us to this state and for that very end? I am filled with shame and confusion when I reflect on one hand upon the great favors which GOD has done, and incessantly continues to do me; and on the other, upon the ill use I have made of them, and my small advancement in the way of perfection.

Since by His mercy He gives us still a little time, let us begin in earnest: let us repair the lost time: let us return with a full assurance to that FATHER of mercies, who is always ready to receive us affectionately. Let us renounce, let us generously renounce, for the love of Him, all that is not Himself; He deserves infinitely more. Let us think of Him perpetually. Let us put all our trust in Him. I doubt not but we shall soon find the effects of it in receiving the abundance of His grace, with which we can do all things, and without which we can do nothing but sin.

We cannot escape the dangers which abound in life without the actual and *continual* help of GOD: let us then pray to Him for it *continually.* How can we pray to Him without being with Him? How can we be with Him but in thinking of Him often? And how can we often think of Him, but by a holy habit which we should form of it? You will tell me that I am always saying the same thing. It is true, for this is the best and easiest method I know; and as I use no other, I advise all the world to do it. We must *know* before we can *lore.* In order to *know* GOD, we must often *think* of Him; and when we come to *love* Him, we shall then also think of Him often, for our heart will be with our treasure. This is an argument which well deserves your consideration.

I am, Yours, etc.

Tenth Letter

I have had a good deal of difficulty to bring myself to write to Mr. ____, and I do it now purely because you and Madam ____ desire me. Pray write the directions and send it to him. I am very well pleased with the trust which you have in GOD: I wish that He may increase it in you more and more. We cannot have too much in so good and faithful a Friend, who will never fail us in this world nor in the next.

If Mr. ____ makes his advantage of the loss he has had, and puts all his confidence in GOD, He will soon give him another friend, more powerful and more inclined to serve him. He disposes of hearts as He pleases. Perhaps Mr. ____ was too much attached to him he has lost. We ought to love our friends, but without encroaching upon the love due to GOD, which must be the principal.

Pray remember what I have recommended to you, which is, to think often on GOD, by day, by night, in your business, and even in your diversions. He is always near you and with you: leave Him not alone. You would think it rude to leave a friend alone who came to visit you: why then must GOD be neglected? Do not then forget Him, but think on Him often, adore Him continually, live and die with Him; this is the glorious employment of a Christian. In a word, this is our profession; if we do not know it, we must learn it. I will endeavor to help you with my prayers, and am, in our LORD, Yours, etc.

Eleventh Letter

I do not pray that you may be delivered from your pains, but I pray GOD earnestly that He would give you strength and patience to bear them as long as He pleases. Comfort yourself with Him who holds you fastened to the cross. He will loose you when He thinks fit. Happy those who suffer with Him: accustom yourself to suffer in that manner, and seek from Him the strength to endure as much, and as long, as He shall judge to be necessary for you. The men of the world do not comprehend these truths, nor is it to be wondered at, since they suffer like what they are, and not like Christians. They consider sickness as a pain to nature, and not as a favor from GOD; and seeing it only in that light, they find nothing in it but grief and distress. But those who consider sickness as coming from the hand of GOD, as the effect of His mercy, and the means which He employs for their salvation—such, commonly find in it great sweetness and sensible consolation.

I wish you could convince yourself that GOD is often (in some sense) nearer to us, and more effectually present with us, in sickness than in health. Rely upon no other Physician; for, according to my apprehension, He reserves your cure to Himself. Put, then, all your trust in Him, and you will soon find the effects of it in your recovery, which we often retard by putting greater confidence in physic than in GOD.

Whatever remedies you make use of, they will succeed only so far as He permits. When pains come from GOD, He only can cure them. He often sends diseases of the body to cure those of the soul. Comfort yourself with the sovereign Physician both of the soul and body.

Be satisfied with the condition in which GOD places you: however happy you may think me, I envy you. Pains and sufferings would be a paradise to me while I should suffer with my GOD; and the greatest pleasures would be hell to me if I could relish them without Him. All my consolation would be to suffer something for His sake.

I must, in a little time, go to GOD. What comforts me in this life is, that I now see Him *by faith*; and I see Him in such a manner as might make me say sometimes, *I believe no more, but I see.* I feel what faith teaches us, and in that assurance and that practice of faith, I will live and die with Him.

Continue then always with GOD: it is the only support and comfort for your affliction. I shall beseech Him to be with you. I present my service.

Yours, etc.

Twelfth Letter

If we were well accustomed to the exercise of *the presence of* GOD, all bodily diseases would be much alleviated thereby. GOD often permits that we should suffer a little to purify our souls and oblige us to continue *with* Him.

Take courage: offer Him your pains incessantly: pray to Him for strength to endure them. Above all, get a habit of entertaining yourself often with GOD, and forget Him the least you can. Adore Him in your infirmities, offer yourself to Him from time to time, and in the height of your sufferings, beseech Him humbly and affectionately (as a child his father) to make you conformable to His holy-will. I shall endeavor to assist you with my poor prayers.

GOD has many ways of drawing us to Himself. He sometimes hides Himself from us, but *faith* alone, which will not fail us in time of need, ought to be our support, and the foundation of our confidence, which must be all in GOD.

I know not how GOD will dispose of me. I am always happy. All the world suffer; and I, who deserve the severest discipline, feel joys so continual and so great that I can scarce contain them.

I would willingly ask of GOD a part of your sufferings, but that I know my weakness, which is so great, that if He left me one moment to myself I should be the most wretched man alive. And yet I know not how He can leave me alone, because faith gives me as strong a conviction as sense can do, that He never forsakes us until we have first forsaken Him. Let us fear to leave Him. Let us be always with Him. Let us live and die in His presence. Do you pray for me, as I for you.

I am, Yours, etc.

Thirteenth Letter

To the Same .

I am in pain to see you suffer so long. What gives me some ease and sweetens the feelings I have for your griefs is, that they are proofs of GOD'S love towards you. See them in that view and you will bear them more easily. As your case is, it is my opinion that you should leave off human remedies, and resign yourself entirely to the providence of GOD: perhaps He stays only for that resignation and a perfect trust in Him to cure you. Since, notwithstanding all your cares, physic has hitherto proved unsuccessful, and your malady still increases, it will not be tempting GOD to abandon yourself in His hands, and expect all from Him.

I told you in my last that He sometimes permits bodily diseases to cure the distempers of the soul. Have courage then: make a virtue of necessity. Ask of GOD, not deliverance from your pains, but strength to bear resolutely, for the love of Him, all that He should please, and as long as He shall please.

Such prayers, indeed, are a little hard to nature, but most acceptable to GOD, and sweet to those that love Him. Love sweetens pains; and when one loves GOD, one suffers for His sake with joy and courage. Do you so, I beseech you: comfort yourself with Him, who is the only Physician of all our maladies. He is the FATHER of the afflicted, always ready to help us. He loves us infinitely more than we imagine. Love Him, then, and seek no consolation elsewhere. I hope you will soon receive it. Adieu. I will help you with my prayers, poor as they are, and shall always be, in our LORD Yours, etc.

Fourteenth Letter

To the Same

I render thanks to our LORD for having relieved you a little, according to your desire. I have been often near expiring, but I never was so much satisfied as then. Accordingly, I did not pray for any relief, but I prayed for strength to suffer with courage, humility and love. Ah, how sweet it is to suffer with GOD! However great the sufferings may be, receive them with love. It is paradise to suffer and be with Him; so that if in this life we would enjoy the peace of paradise we must accustom ourselves to a familiar, humble, affectionate conversation with Him. We must hinder our spirits wandering from Him upon any occasion. We must make our heart a spiritual temple, wherein to adore Him incessantly. We must watch continually over ourselves, that we may not do, nor say, nor think anything that may displease Him. When our minds are thus employed about GOD, suffering will become full of unction and consolation.

I know that to arrive at this state the beginning is very difficult, for we must act purely in faith. But though it is difficult, we know also that we can do all things with the grace of GOD, which He never refuses to them who ask it earnestly. Knock, persevere in knocking, and I answer for it that He will open to you in His due time, and grant you all at once what He has deferred during many years. Adieu! Pray to Him for me, as I pray to Him for you. I hope to see Him quickly.

I am, Yours, etc.

Fifteenth Letter

GOD knoweth best what is needful for us, and all that He does is for our good. If we knew how much He loves us, we should always be ready to receive equally and with indifference from His Hand the sweet and the bitter: all would please that came from Him. The sorest afflictions never appear intolerable, except when we see them in the wrong light. When we see them as dispensed by the hand of GOD, when we know that it is our loving FATHER who abases and distresses us, our sufferings will lose their bitterness, and become even matter of consolation.

Let all our employment be to *know* GOD: the more one *knows* Him, the more one *desires* to know Him. And as *knowledge* is commonly the measure of *love* , the deeper and more extensive our *knowledge* shall be, the greater will be our *love* : and if our love of GOD were great, we should love Him equally in pains and pleasures.

Let us not content ourselves with loving GOD for the mere sensible favors, how elevated soever, which he has done, or may do us. Such favors, though never so great, cannot bring us so near to Him as faith does in one simple act. Let us seek Him often by faith. He is within us: seek Him not elsewhere. If we do love Him alone, are we not rude, and do we not deserve blame, if we busy ourselves about trifles which do not please and perhaps offend Him. It is to be feared these *trifles* will one day cost us dear.

Let us begin to be devoted to Him in good earnest. Let us cast everything besides out of our hearts. He would possess them alone. Beg this favor of Him. If we do what we can on our parts, we shall soon see that change wrought in us which we aspire after. I cannot thank Him sufficiently for the relaxation He has vouchsafed you. I hope from His mercy the favor to see Him within a few days.[4] Let us pray for one another.

I am, in our LORD, Yours, etc.

Notes:

[1]: Gal. i, 10; Eph. vi, 5, 6.

[2]: The particulars which follow are collected from other accounts of Brother Lawrence.

[3]: *I suppose he means* that all distinct notions he could form of GOD, were unsatisfactory, because he perceived them to be unworthy of GOD; and therefore his mind was not to be satisfied but by the views of *faith* , which apprehend GOD as infinite and incomprehensible, as He is in Himself, and not as He can be conceived by human ideas.

[4]: He took to his bed two days after, and died within the week.

Interior Castle
by St. Teresa of Avila
translated by E. Allison Peers

"I Began to Think of the Soul as If it Were a Castle Made of a Single Diamond..."

Interior Castle is one of the most celebrated books on mystical theology in existence. It is the most sublime and mature of Teresa of Avila's works, and expresses the full flowering of her deep experience in guiding souls toward spiritual perfection. In addition to its profound mystical content, it is also a treasury of unforgettable maxims on such ascetic subjects as self-knowledge, humility, detachment, and suffering. But above all, this account of a soul's progress in virtue and grace is the record of a life — of the interior life of Teresa of Avila, whose courageous soul, luminous mind, and endearingly human temperament hold so deep an attraction for the modern mind.

In its central image and style, *Interior Castle*, like so many works of genius, is extremely simple. Teresa envisioned the soul as "a castle made of a single diamond . . . in which there are many rooms, just as in Heaven there are many mansions." She describes the various rooms of this castle — the degrees of purgation and continual strife — through which the soul in its quest for perfection must pass before reaching the innermost chamber, the place of complete transfiguration and communion with God.

Teresa was an incredibly gifted teacher whose devotion to the sublimest task — the guidance of others toward spiritual perfection — has resulted in the widespread fame of her writings. There is no life more real than the interior life, and few persons have had such an extraordinarily rich experience of that reality as has Teresa. In *Interior Castle*, she exhorts and inspires her readers to participate in the search for this ultimate spiritual reality, the source of her own profound joy.

Probably no other books by a Spanish author have received such wide popular acclaim as the Life and Interior Castle of St. Teresa of Avila. It is remarkable that a woman who lived in the sixteenth century, who spent most of her life in an enclosed convent, who never had any formal schooling and never aspired to any public fame, should have won such an extraordinary reputation, both among scholars and among the people.

There can be little doubt that her popularity has been due, in large measure, to Divine Grace, which first inspired her at an early age to put aside every aim but the quest for God and then enabled her to attain a degree of fervor in her love for Him which sustained her and impelled her to perform prodigious works in His name. She established new foundations for her order, carried on the spiritual direction of souls given into her care, wrote brilliant treatises for the edification of her fellow nuns, and reached the very summit of personal sanctity through a life of prayer, humility, and charity. Before everything else, it is the intense fervor of her spirituality which speaks to readers everywhere, just as it is the determination and courage of her soul which inspires those who want to be more courageous and determined than they are. But, next to this, it is the purely human quality of her writings that makes so wide an appeal. Her writing is characterized by a liveliness of thought, rich imagination, spontaneity of expression, and a structural "sweet disorder" that many readers find attractive and illuminating.

When it is remembered that she wrote at the command of her superiors — that is, under obedience — and that her writing was done in haste during brief periods, snatched, as it were, from the duties of the religious life, and that she herself thought her writings of so little importance that she never even reread what she had written, is it any wonder that the ordinary man and woman finds her efforts irresistibly attractive?

It is truly amazing, too, to ponder the depths of humility that prompted this remarkably gifted woman to answer those who commanded her to write: "For the love of God, let me work at my spinning wheel and go to choir and perform the duties of the religious life, like the other sisters. I am not meant to write: I have neither the health nor the wits for it."

It must be to those superiors, then, that generations of appreciative readers must render their thanks for the masterful books — outstanding among them, the Interior Castle — through which the teachings of St. Teresa survive to instruct, inspire, and delight.

Interior Castle by St. Teresa of Avila translated and edited by E. Allison Peers

From the Critical Edition of P. Silverio de Stanta Teresa, C.D. To the Gracious Memory of P. Edmund Gurdon Sometime Prior of the Carthusian Monastery of Miraflores a Man of God

Principal Abbreviations

A.V. — Authorized Version of the Bible (1611).

D.V. — Douai Version of the Bible (1609).

Letters — Letters of St. Teresa. Unless otherwise stated, the numbering of the Letters follows Vols. VII-IX of P. Silverio. Letters (St.) indicates the translation of the Benedictines of Stanbrook (London, 1919-24, 4 vols.).

Lewis — The Life of St. Teresa of Jesus, etc., translated by David Lewis, 5th ed., with notes and introductions by the Very Rev. Benedict Zimmerman, O.C.D., London, 1916.

P. Silverio — Obras de Santa Teresa de Jesús, editadas y anotadas por el P. Silverio de Santa Teresa, C.D., Durgos, 1915-24, 9 vols.

Ribera — Francisco de Ribera, Vida de Santa Teresa de Jesús, Nueva ed. aumentada, con introducción, etc., por el P. Jaime Pons, Barcelona, 1908.

S.S.M. — E. Allison Peers, Studies of the Spanish Mystics, London, 1927-30, 2 vols.

St. John of the Cross — The Complete Works of Saint John of the Cross, Doctor of the Church, translated from the critical edition of P. Silverio de Santa Teresa, C.D., and edited by E. Allison Peers, London, 1934-35, 3 vols.

Yepes — Diego de Yepes, Vida de Santa Teresa, Madrid, 1615.

Introduction: (The Mansions)[1]

Towards the end of her life, probably near the end of the year 1579, St. Teresa was travelling with three of her nuns from Medina del Campo, across the bleak Castilian plateau, on her way to St. Joséph's, Avila. Accidentally (or, as it would be more accurate to say, providentially) she fell in with an old friend, a Hieronymite, Fray Diego de Yepes. Their meeting took place at an inn in the town of Arévalo, where he had arrived some time previously, and, as was fitting, he had been given the most comfortable room. When the little party of nuns, half frozen but still cheerful, reached the inn, there was mutual delight at the encounter; and Fray Diego not only gave up his room to them but appointed himself their personal servant for the period of their stay. They spent, so he tells us, "a very great part of the night" in conversation about their Divine Master. On the next day it was snowing so hard that no one could leave. So Fray Diego said Mass for the four nuns and gave them Communion, after which they spent the day "as recollectedly as if they had been in their own convent". In the evening, however, St. Teresa had a long conversation with her former confessor, who later was to become her biographer, and in the course of this she recounted to him the story of how she came to write the Interior Castle. The report of this narrative may suitably be given in the words of Fray Diego himself, taken from a letter which he wrote to Fray Luis de León about nine years later.[2]

"This holy Mother," he writes, "had been desirous of obtaining some insight into the beauty of a soul in grace. Just at that time she was commanded to write a treatise on prayer, about which she knew a great deal from experience. On the eve of the festival of the Most Holy Trinity she was thinking what subject she should choose for this treatise, when God, Who disposes all things in due form and order, granted this desire of hers, and gave her a subject. He showed her a most beautiful crystal globe, made in the shape of a castle, and containing seven mansions, in the seventh and innermost of which was the King of Glory, in the greatest splendour, illumining and beautifying them all. The nearer one got to the centre, the stronger was the light; outside the palace limits everything was foul, dark and infested with toads, vipers and other venomous creatures.

"While she was wondering at this beauty, which by God's grace can dwell in the human soul, the light suddenly vanished. Although the King of Glory did not leave the mansions, the crystal globe was plunged into darkness, became as black as coal and emitted an insufferable odour, and the venomous creatures outside the palace boundaries were permitted to enter the castle.

"This was a vision which the holy Mother wished that everyone might see, for it seemed to her that no mortal seeing the beauty and splendour of grace, which sin destroys and changes into such hideousness and misery, could possibly have the temerity to offend God. It was about this vision that she told me on that day, and she spoke so freely both of this and of other things that she realized herself that she had done so and on the next morning remarked to me: 'How I forgot myself last night! I cannot think how it happened. These desires and this love of mine made me lose all sense of proportion. Please God they may have done me some good!' I promised her not to repeat what she had said to anyone during her lifetime."

Some days before she was granted this marvellous vision, St. Teresa had had a very intimate conversation on spiritual matters with P. Jerónimo Gracián; the upshot of this was that she undertook to write another book in which she would expound afresh the teaching on perfection to be found in her Life, at that time in the hands of the Inquisitors.[3] This we learn from a manuscript note, in Gracián's hand, to the sixth chapter of the fourth book of Ribera's biography of St. Teresa:

What happened with regard to the Book of the Mansions is this. Once, when I was her superior, I was talking to her about spiritual matters at Toledo, and she said to me: "Oh, how well that point is put in the book of my life, which is at the Inquisition!" "Well," I said to her, "as we cannot get at that, why not recall what you can of it, and of other things, and write a fresh book and expound the teaching in a general way, without saying to whom the things that you describe have happened." It was in this way that I told her to write this Book of the Mansions, telling her (so as to persuade her the better) to discuss the matter with Dr. Velázquez, who used sometimes to hear her confessions; and he told her to do so too.[4]

Although she did as she was instructed, however, P. Gracián tells us that she made various objections, all of them dictated by her humility. "Why do they want me to write things?" she would ask. "Let learned men, who have studied, do the writing; I am a stupid creature and don't know what I am saying. There are more than enough books written on prayer already. For the love of God, let me get on with my spinning and go to choir and do my religious duties like the other sisters. I am not meant for writing; I have neither the health nor the wits for it."[5]

Such was the origin of the Interior Castle, one of the most celebrated books on mystical theology in existence. It is the most carefully planned and arranged of all that St. Teresa wrote. The mystical figure of the Mansions gives it a certain unity which some of her other books lack. The lines of the fortress of the soul are clearly traced and the distribution of its several parts is admirable in proportion and harmony. Where the book sometimes fails to maintain its precision of method, and falls into that "sweet disorder" which in St. Teresa's other works makes such an appeal to us, is in the secondary themes which it treats — in the furnishing of the Mansions, as we might say, rather than in their construction. A scholastic writer, or, for that matter, anyone with a scientific mind, would have carried the logical arrangement of the general plan into every chapter. Such a procedure, however, would have left no outlet for St. Teresa's natural spontaneity: it is difficult, indeed, to say how far experiential mysticism can ever lend itself to inflexible scientific rule without endangering its own spirit. Since God is free to establish an ineffable communion with the questing soul, the soul must be free to set down its experiences as they occur to it.

In its language and style, the Interior Castle is more correct, and yet at the same time more natural and flexible, than the Way of perfection. Its conception, like that of so many works of genius, is extremely simple. After a brief preface, the author comes at once to her subject:

I began to think of the soul as if it were a castle made of a single diamond or of very clear crystal, in which there are many rooms, just as in Heaven there are many mansions.

These mansions are not "arranged in a row one behind another" but variously — "some above, others below, others at each side; and in the centre and midst of them all is the chiefest mansion, where the most secret things pass between God and the soul."

The figure is used to describe the whole course of the mystical life — the soul's progress from the First Mansions to the Seventh and its transformation from an imperfect and sinful creature into the Bride of the Spiritual Marriage. The door by which it first enters the castle is prayer and meditation. Once inside, "it must be allowed to roam through these mansions" and "not be compelled to remain for a long time in one single room". But it must also cultivate self-knowledge and "begin by entering the room where humility is acquired rather than by flying off to the other rooms. For that is the way to progress".

How St. Teresa applies the figure of the castle to the life of prayer (which is also the life of virtue — with her these two things go together) may best be shown by describing each of the seven stages in turn.[6]

FIRST MANSIONS. This chapter begins with a meditation on the excellence and dignity of the human soul, made as it is in the image and likeness of God: the author laments that more pains are not taken to perfect it. The souls in the First Mansions are in a state of grace, but are still very much in love with the venomous creatures outside the castle — that as, with occasions of sin — and need a long and searching discipline before they can make any progress. So they stay for a long time in the Mansions of Humility, in which, since the heat and light from within reach them only in a faint and diffused form, all is cold and dim.

SECOND MANSIONS. But all the time the soul is anxious to penetrate farther into the castle, so it seeks every opportunity of advancement — sermons, edifying conversations, good company and so on. It is doing its utmost to put its desires into practice: these are the Mansions of the Practice of Prayer. It is not yet completely secure from the attacks of the poisonous reptiles which infest the courtyard of the castle, but its powers of resistance are increasing. There is more warmth and light here than in the First Mansions.

THIRD MANSIONS. The description of these Mansions of Exemplary Life begins with stern exhortations on the dangers of trusting to one's own strength and to the virtues one has already acquired, which must still of necessity be very weak. Yet, although the soul which reaches the Third Mansions may still fall back, it has attained a high standard of virtue. Controlled by discipline and penance and disposed to performing acts of charity toward others, it has acquired prudence and discretion and orders its life well. Its limitations are those of vision: it has not yet experienced to the full the inspiring force of love. It has not made a full self-oblation, a total self-surrender. Its love is still governed by reason, and so its progress is slow. It suffers from aridity, and is given only occasional glimpses into the Mansions beyond.

FOURTH MANSIONS. Here the supernatural element of the mystical life first enters: that is to say, it is no longer by its own efforts that the soul is acquiring what it gains. Henceforward the soul's part will become increasingly less and God's part increasingly greater. The graces of the Fourth Mansions, referred to as "spiritual consolations", are identified with the Prayer of Quiet, or the Second Water, in the Life. The soul is like a fountain built near its source and the water of life flows into it, not through an aqueduct, but directly from the spring. Its love is now free from servile fear: it has broken all the bonds which previously hindered its progress; it shrinks from no trials and attaches no importance to anything to do with the world. It can pass rapidly from ordinary to infused prayer and back again. It has not yet, however, received the highest gifts of the Spirit and relapses are still possible.

FIFTH MANSIONS. This is the state described elsewhere as the Third Water, the Spiritual Betrothal, and the Prayer of Union — that is, incipient Union. It marks a new degree of infused contemplation and a very high one. By means of the most celebrated of all her metaphors, that of the silkworm, St. Teresa explains how far the soul can prepare itself to receive what is essentially a gift from God. She also describes the psychological conditions of this state, in which, for the first time, the faculties of the soul are "asleep". It is of short duration, but, while it lasts, the soul is completely possessed by God.

SIXTH MANSIONS. In the Fifth Mansions the soul is, as it were, betrothed to its future Spouse; in the Sixth, Lover and Beloved see each other for long periods at a time, and as they grow in intimacy the soul receives increasing favours, together with increasing afflictions. The afflictions which give the description of these Mansions its characteristic colour are dealt with in some detail. They may be purely exterior — bodily sickness; misrepresentation, backbiting and persecution; undeserved praise; inexperienced, timid or over-scrupulous spiritual direction. Or they may come partly or wholly from within — and the depression which can afflict the soul in the Sixth Mansions, says St. Teresa, is comparable only with the tortures of hell. Yet it has no desire to be freed from them except by entering the innermost Mansions of all.

SEVENTH MANSIONS. Here at last the soul reaches the Spiritual Marriage. Here dwells the King — "it may be called another Heaven": the two lighted candles join and become one, the falling rain becomes merged in the river. There is complete transformation, ineffable and perfect peace; no higher state is conceivable, save that of the Beatific Vision in the life to come.

While each of these seven Mansions is described with the greatest possible clarity, St. Teresa makes it quite plain that she does not regard her description as excluding others. Each of the series of moradas (the use of the plural throughout, especially in the title of each chapter, is noteworthy) may contain as many as a million rooms; all matters connected with spiritual progress are susceptible of numerous interpretations, for the grace of God knows no limit or measure. Her description is based largely on her own experience; and, though this has been found to correspond very nearly with that of most other great mystics, there are various divergences on points of detail. She never for a moment intended her path to be followed undeviatingly and step by step, and of this she is careful frequently to remind us.

At the end of this last, most mystical and most mature of her books, St. Teresa invites all her daughters to enter the Interior Castle, drawing a picturesque contrast between the material poverty of the convents of the Reform and the spiritual luxuriance and beauty of the Mansions — where, as she delightfully puts it, they can go as often as they please without needing to ask the permission of their superiors. There is no doubt whatever that she considered mystical experience to be within the reach of all her daughters: we find this conviction enunciated in the nineteenth chapter of the Way of perfection and repeated so frequently in the Interior Castle that it is needless to give references. She does not, of course, mean that every one of her nuns who prepares herself as far as she can to receive mystical favours does in fact receive them: she could not presume to pronounce upon the secret judgments of God. But she evidently believes that, generally speaking, infused contemplation is accessible to any Christian who has the resolution to do all that in him lies towards obtaining it.

It must not be forgotten that, notwithstanding the mystical character of the greater part of the Interior Castle, it is also a treasury of unforgettable maxims on such ascetic themes as self-knowledge, humility, detachment and suffering. The finest of these maxims alone would fill a book, and it would be as invidious as self-indulgent to quote any of them here. Yet many have supposed the Interior Castle to be concerned solely with raptures, ecstasies and visions, with Illumination and Union; or to be a work created by the imagination, instead of the record of a life. There is no life more real than the interior life of the soul; there is no writer who has a firmer hold on reality than St. Teresa.

Sublime as is the Interior Castle, it would be difficult for any conscientious student who practised what it taught to lose his way in it. St. Teresa did not write it in any sense as a spiritual autobiography or an account of the wonders which God's Spirit had wrought in her soul — still less as a literary work, a storehouse of spiritual maxims or a treatise on psychology. She intended it for the instruction of her own daughters and of all other souls who, either in her own day or later, might have the ambition to penetrate either the outer or the inner Mansions. At all times in the history of Christian perfection there has been a dearth of persons qualified to guide souls to the highest states of prayer: the Interior Castle will both serve as an aid to those there are and to a great extent supply the need for more.

The autograph of the Interior Castle is to be found in the convent of the Discalced Carmelite nuns of Seville. When the book was first written its author's intention was to divide it only into seven main sections, or "Mansions", and not to make any subdivision of these into chapters. But by the time the manuscript was completed she had changed her mind, and, utilizing her margins, she was able to subdivide each of the seven parts of the book as she thought best. The titles of these sub-divisions she wrote on a separate sheet and they have unfortunately been lost. During her own lifetime, however, the nuns of her Toledo convent made a copy of the book, including these titles, which me so Teresan in style that their authenticity cannot for a moment be doubted.[7]

From the note already referred to written by Gracián in Ribera's biography of St. Teresa we learn that the Interior Castle, on its completion, was submitted to the closest scrutiny by himself and a Dominican theologian, P. Yanguas, in the presence of the author. The picture which he draws of these sessions is a memorable one.

I would take up numerous phrases in the book, saying that they did not sound well to me, and Fray Diego would reply, while she (St. Teresa) would tell us to expunge them. And we did expunge a few, not because there was any erroneous teaching in them, but because many would find them too advanced and too difficult to understand; for such was the zeal of my affection for her that I tried to make certain that there should be nothing in her writings which could cause anyone to stumble.

These meetings took place in the parlour of the Discalced Carmelite convent at Segovia during June and July 1580. It is regrettable that Gracián should not have described them in greater detail, for, as she knew both her critics well enough to be quite frank with them, and as her command of mystical theology was stronger than theirs on the experiential side and weaker only on the theoretical, many of her comments must have been well worthy of preservation.

Few corrections, in actual fact, were made in the autograph and none of them has any great doctrinal significance. It is a striking thing that, at a time when such care had perforce to be taken by writers on mystical theology, when false mystics of all kinds were springing up continually and when the Inquisition was therefore maintaining a greatly increased vigilance, so important and so ambitious a work as this should need modifying only here and there, merely to avoid the risk of misinterpretation by the ill-informed or the hypercritical.

A few of the corrections, together with some erasures and marginal additions, are in the hand of St. Teresa herself; the remainder, including a few which have been incorrectly attributed to P. Yanguas, were made by P. Gracián. It would seem that Gracián, besides being the critic at these Segovian sessions, was also the committee's secretary: that is to say, when the three had come to an agreement about some alteration that had to be made, it was he who would actually make it.

Some years later, the work of this committee was examined by another critic, who took objection to many of the corrections, including all those made by Gracián, and restored the original readings, adding to the first page of St. Teresa's manuscript a short note which will be found on the corresponding page of this edition.[8] Both early and recent editors, without exception, have believed this critic to have been Fray Luis de León: its style and content could not be more like that of St. Teresa's first editor as we have it, for example, in the famous letter to the Carmelite nuns of Madrid which he prefixed to his edition, but the handwriting is certainly not that of Fray Luis. The note and the additions are in fact the work of St. Teresa's biographer P. Francisco de Ribera, whose concern for the fidelity with which her writings should be reproduced we learn from the letter which he wrote to M. María de Cristo, Vicaress of the Carmelite nuns at Valladolid. As we have already said, Ribera had himself projected a collected edition of St. Teresa's works, for which purpose he borrowed the autographs of the Way of perfection and the Interior Castle. There would therefore be no improbability in the assumption of his having made these corrections; and a comparison of them with manuscripts known to be his at the University of Salamanca, the Royal Academy of History and elsewhere seems to put the matter beyond doubt.

St. Teresa began the Interior Castle, as she herself tells us, on Trinity Sunday (June 2), 1577. She was then in Toledo, where she had been staying for nearly a year, but in July she left for St. Joséph's, Avila, and it was there that she completed the book on November 29 of the same year. When we remember the difficult times through which the Reform was passing, the preoccupations of a practical kind with which the Mother Foundress was continually being assailed, and the large amount of time taken up by other activities, and by the daily observance of her Rule, we may well marvel at the serenity of mind which in so short a period could produce a work of this length, containing some of the very finest pages she ever wrote.

During the space of less than six months which elapsed between the beginning of the book and its completion took place that change of Nuncios which was so disastrous for the Reform, the transference of St. Joséph's, Avila, from the jurisdiction of the Ordinary to that of the Order and that stormy scene at the Incarnation when the nuns endeavoured vainly to elect St. Teresa as their Prioress. So it is not surprising that, as we learn from the fourth chapter of the Fifth Mansions, "almost five months"[9] out of the six had gone by before she reached that chapter. As a Toledo nun copied the book while the Saint wrote it, and had reached the second chapter of the Fifth Mansions before she left for Avila, she would seem to have worked hard at the book for the month or six weeks which she spent at Toledo after beginning it and then to have done nothing further unto late in October. This meant that the time actually spent in writing was not six months, but less than three.

There is ample evidence as to the intensity with which St. Teresa worked at the Interior Castle. It will suffice to quote one witness. "At the time when our holy Mother was writing the book of the Mansions at Toledo," deposed M. María del Nacimiento, "I often saw her as she wrote, which was generally after Communion. She was very radiant and wrote with great rapidity, and as a rule she was so absorbed in her work that even if we made a noise she would never stop, or so much as say that we were disturbing her."[10] The same nun, according to M. Mariana de los Angeles, once saw St. Teresa caught in a rapture while she was writing the book and is reported as asserting that she wrote a portion of it while in this condition.[11] This, however, is second-hand evidence, though it tends to confirm the direct evidence. Not that even this can always be trusted. Ana de la Encarnación, for example, declares that she saw St. Teresa writing the Interior Castle at Segovia, which is next to impossible, for we know a great deal about the Saint's movements during these years and there is no record of her having been at Segovia in 1577.

When the book was written, St. Teresa entrusted it to the keeping of P. Gracián, who in his turn gave it for a time to M. María de San José, Prioress of the Sevilian convent and a close friend of the writer. In November 1581, we find her authorizing M. María to read the chapters on the Seventh Mansions, under the seal of confession, to a former confessor of her own, P. Rodrigo Alvarez. "Read him the last Mansion," the letter runs, "and tell him that that person (i.e., herself) has reached that point and has the peace which goes with it".[12] As we shall see, P. Alvarez left a note on the manuscript attesting that the chapters in question had been duly read to him and declaring that they were entirely orthodox and in conformity with the teaching of the Saints.

Eventually P. Gracián took back the manuscript, and, except for short periods when it was lent to V. Ana de Jesús for the preparation of Luis de León's edition, and, as already related, to P. Ribera, he retained it for long after St. Teresa's death, presenting it finally to a Sevilian gentleman who had been a great benefactor of the Reform, Don Pedro Cerezo Pardo. When, in 1617, this gentleman's daughter Catalina took the habit in the Sevilian convent of the Reform, she brought the highly-prized manuscript as part of her dowry. Thus by a strange concatenation of events the autograph returned to the Sevilian house, where it has remained ever since.

A few words may be added on the copies and editions of the Interior Castle. The Toledo copy seems to be the oldest. It bears the date 1577 — which may refer to the year of the book's composition but is generally supposed to indicate the year in which the copy was made. The copyists were four nuns, one of whom, as has been said, went as far as the second chapter of the Fifth Mansions, the remainder of the work being shared by the other three. The title given to the book by St. Teresa is placed at the end of the fourth chapter and the copy ends with the table of chapters and the summary of the contents of each chapter of which the original is now lost. It is noteworthy that the first amanuensis made no chapter-divisions, presumably because at that time the autograph had none. Some of St. Teresa's additions are not included and none of the corrections and glosses made by P.

Gracián — again, it must be supposed, because they were not then in the autographs. All these facts point to the conclusion that this copy was made as St. Teresa wrote, and that, when she left Toledo for Avila, taking the unfinished autograph with her, she left behind her an unfinished copy which was completed only at a later date. As the corrections in Gracián's hand were made in 1580 (Introduction, above), this date may be taken as falling between 1578 and 1580. Some critics believe that among the corrections in this copy are a number made by St. Teresa herself. [P. Silverio, however, does not share their opinion.]

An interesting copy, which belongs to the Discalced nuns of Córdoba, is that which was made by P. Gracián before he disposed of the autograph. The work is beautifully done in red and black ink and nowhere is Gracián's exquisite hand seen to better advantage: indeed, the calligraphy rivals that of any professional monastic copyist of the Middle Ages. The prologue and the epilogue are omitted, the former possibly because of its allusive reference to Gracián himself. The titles given to the chapters by St. Teresa are included. The copy makes a good many alterations, mainly verbal, in the text, due probably to the repeated requests of St. Teresa that, if it should ever be decided to print her writings, he would polish and revise them.

The copy now in the University of Salamanca was made in 1588 by P. Ribera and a Brother Antonio Arias at the College of the Society of Jesus in that city. The date suggests that the autograph was passed on to him after Luis de León had finished with it. Of the numerous other copies to be found in Carmelite houses the most noteworthy are two which were made from the autograph by a Discalced Carmelite, P. Tomás de Aquino, in the eighteenth century. One of these, used by La Fuente for his edition of 1861, in the "Biblioteca de Autores Españoles", contains a critical study from which the editor quotes.

Two editions — one early and one comparatively recent — merit remark. The earliest of all the editions, Luis de León's (1588), rejects Gracián's emendations and respects only those in the handwriting of St. Teresa. It makes, however a great many changes of its own, mainly of a verbal kind, though such an omission as the reference in Mansions V, iv to St. Ignatius of Loyola and the Society of Jesus is a striking exception to this rule. The majority of Luis de León's modifications have not been adopted in this edition; a few are referred to in the notes. Until La Fuente went to P. Tomás de Aquino's copy, the text of 1588 was followed by later editors with but few modifications.

In commemoration of the third centenary of St. Teresa's death, the Cardinal-Archbishop of Seville, a Carmelite of the Observance, Fray Joaquín Lluch, published a photo-lithography edition of the autograph which did a good deal to restore the respect due to it. [P. Silverio's edition, however, is based on the autograph itself, which he was able to study at Seville, so that past neglect of it is now fully atoned for.]

Interior Castle[13]
JHS.

Few tasks which I have been commanded to undertake by obedience have been so difficult as this present one of writing about matters relating to prayer: for one reason, because I do not feel that the Lord has given me either the spirituality or the desire for it; for another, because for the last three months I have been suffering from such noises and weakness in the head that I find it troublesome to write even about necessary business. But, as I know that strength arising from obedience has a way of simplifying things which seem impossible, my will very gladly resolves to attempt this task alhough the prospect seems to cause my physical nature great distress; for the Lord has not given me strength enough to enable me to wrestle continually both with sickness and with occupations of many kinds without feeling a great physical strain. May He Who has helped me by doing other and more difficult things for me help also in this: in His mercy I put my trust.

I really think I have little to say that I have not already said in other books which I have been commanded to write; indeed, I am afraid that I shall do little but repeat myself, for I write as mechanically[14] as birds taught to speak, which, knowing nothing but what is taught them and what they hear, repeat the same things again and again. If the Lord wishes me to say anything new, His Majesty will teach it me or be pleased to recall to my memory what I have said on former occasions; and I should be quite satisfied with this, for my memory is so bad that I should be delighted if I could manage to write down a few of the things which people have considered well said, so that they should not be lost. If the Lord should not grant me as much as this, I shall still be the better for having tried, even if this writing under obedience tires me and makes my head worse, and if no one finds what I say of any profit.

And so I begin to fulfil my obligation on this Day of the Holy Trinity, in the year MDLXXVII,[15] in this convent of St. Joseph of Carmel in Toledo, where I am at this present, submitting myself as regards all that I say to the judgment of those who have commanded me to write, and who are persons of great learning. If I should say anything that is not in conformity with what is held by the Holy Roman Catholic Church,[16] it will be through ignorance and not through malice. This may be taken as certain, and also that, through God's goodness, I am, and shall always be, as I always have been, subject to her. May He be for ever blessed and glorified. Amen.

I was told by the person who commanded me to write that, as the nuns of these convents of Our Lady of Carmel need someone to solve their difficulties concerning prayer, and as (or so it seemed to him) women best understand each other's language, and also in view of their love for me, anything I might say would be particularly useful to them. For this reason he thought that it would be rather important if I could explain things clearly to them and for this reason it is they whom I shall be addressing in what I write — and also because it seems ridiculous to think that I can be of any use to anyone else. Our Lord will be granting me a great favour if a single one of these nuns should find that my words help her to praise Him ever so little better. His Majesty well knows that I have no hope of doing more, and, if I am successful in anything that I may say, they will of course understand that it does not come from me. Their only excuse for crediting me with it could be their having as little understanding as I have ability in these matters if the Lord of His mercy does not grant it me.

First Mansions:
In which there are Two Chapters

Chapter 1

Treats of the beauty and dignity of our souls; makes a comparison by the help of which this may be understood; describes the benefit which comes from understanding it and being aware of the favours which we receive from God; and shows how the door of this castle is prayer.

While I was beseeching Our Lord to-day that He would speak through me, since I could find nothing to say and had no idea how to begin to carry out the obligation laid upon me by obedience, a thought occurred to me which I will now set down, in order to have some foundation on which to build. I began to think of the soul as if it were a castle made of a single diamond or of very clear crystal, in which there are many rooms,[17] just as in Heaven there are many mansions.[18] Now if we think carefully over this, sisters, the soul of the righteous man is nothing but a paradise, in which, as God tells us, He takes His delight.[19] For what do you think a room will be like which is the delight of a King so mighty, so wise, so pure and so full of all that is good? I can find nothing with which to compare the great beauty of a soul and its great capacity. In fact, however acute our intellects may be, They will no more be able to attain to a comprehension of this than to an understanding of God; for, as He Himself says, He created us in His image and likeness.[20] Now if this is so — and it is — there is no point in our fatiguing ourselves by attempting to comprehend the beauty of this castle; for, though it is His creature, and there is therefore as much difference between it and God as between creature and Creator, the very fact that His Majesty says it is made in His image means that we can hardly form any conception of the soul's great dignity and beauty.[21]

It is no small pity, and should cause us no little shame, that, through our own fault, we do not understand ourselves, or know who we are. Would it not be a sign of great ignorance, my daughters, if a person were asked who he was, and could not say, and had no idea who his father or his mother was, or from what country he came? Though that is great stupidity, our own is incomparably greater if we make no attempt to discover what we are, and only know that we are living in these bodies, and have a vague idea, because we have heard it and because our Faith tells us so, that we possess souls. As to what good qualities there may be in our souls, or Who dwells within them, or how precious they are — those are things which we seldom consider and so we trouble little about carefully preserving the soul's beauty. All our interest is centred in the rough setting of the diamond, and in the outer wall of the castle — that is to say, in these bodies of ours.

Let us now imagine that this castle, as I have said, contains many mansions,[22] some above, others below, others at each side; and in the centre and midst of them all is the chiefest mansion where the most secret things pass between God and the soul. You must think over this comparison very carefully; perhaps God will be pleased to use it to show you something of the favours which He is pleased to grant to souls, and of the differences between them, so far as I have understood this to be possible, for there are so many of them that nobody can possibly understand them all, much less anyone as stupid as I. If the Lord grants you these favours, it will be a great consolation to you to know that such things are possible; and, if you never receive any, you can still praise His great goodness. For, as it does us no harm to think of the things laid up for us in Heaven, and of the joys of the blessed, but rather makes us rejoice and strive to attain those joys ourselves, just so it will do us no harm to find that it is possible in this our exile for so great a God to commune with such malodorous worms, and to love Him for His great goodness and boundless mercy. I am sure that anyone who finds it harmful to realize that it is possible for God to grant such favours during this our exile must be greatly lacking in humility and in love of his neighbour; for otherwise how could we help rejoicing that God should grant these favours to one of our brethren when this in no way hinders Him from granting them to ourselves, and that His Majesty should bestow an understanding of His greatness upon anyone soever? Sometimes He will do this only to manifest His power, as He said of the blind man to whom He gave his sight, when the Apostles asked Him if he were suffering for his own sins or for the sins of his parents.[23] He grants these favours, then, not because those who receive them are holier than those who do not, but in order that His greatness may be made known, as we see in the case of Saint Paul and the Magdalen, and in order that we may praise Him in His creatures.

It may be said that these things seem impossible and that it is better not to scandalize the weak. But less harm is done by their disbelieving us than by our failing to edify those to whom God grants these favours, and who will rejoice and will awaken others to a fresh love of Him Who grants such mercies, according to the greatness of His power and majesty. In any case I know that none to whom I am speaking will run into this danger, because they all know and believe that God grants still greater proofs of His love. I am sure that, if any one of you does not believe this, she will never learn it by experience. For God's will is that no bounds should be set to His works. Never do such a thing, then, sisters, if the Lord does not lead you by this road.

Now let us return to our beautiful and delightful castle and see how we can enter it. I seem rather to be talking nonsense, for, if this castle is the soul, there can clearly be no question of our entering it. For we ourselves are the castle: and it would be absurd to tell someone to enter a room when he was in it already! But you must understand that there are many ways of "being" in a place. Many souls remain in the outer court of the castle, which is the place occupied by the guards; they are not interested in entering it, and have no idea what there is in that wonderful place, or who dwells in it, or even how many rooms it has. You will have read certain books on prayer which advise the soul to enter within itself: and that is exactly what this means.

A short time ago I was told by a very learned man that souls without prayer are like people whose bodies or limbs are paralysed: they possess feet and hands but they cannot control them. In the same way, there are souls so infirm and so accustomed to busying themselves with outside affairs that nothing can be done for them, and it seems as though they are incapable of entering within themselves at all. So accustomed have they grown to living all the time with the reptiles and other creatures to be found in the outer court of the castle that they have almost become like them; and although by nature they are so richly endowed as to have the power of holding converse with none other than God Himself, there is nothing that can be done for them. Unless they strive to realize their miserable condition and to remedy it, they will be turned into pillars of salt for not looking within themselves, just as Lot's wife was because she looked back.[24]

As far as I can understand, the door of entry into this castle is prayer and meditation: I do not say mental prayer rather than vocal, for, if it is prayer at all, it must be accompanied by meditation. If a person does not think Whom he is addressing, and what he is asking for, and who it is that is asking and of Whom he is asking it, I do not consider that he is praying at all even though he be constantly moving his lips. True, it is sometimes possible to pray without paying heed to these things, but that is only because they have been thought about previously; if a man is in the habit of speaking to God's Majesty as he would speak to his slave, and never wonders if he is expressing himself properly, but merely utters the words that come to his lips because he has learned them by heart through constant repetition, I do not call that prayer at all — and God grant no Christian may ever speak to Him so! At any rate, sisters, I hope in God that none of you will, for we are accustomed here to talk about interior matters, and that is a good way of keeping oneself from falling into such animal-like habits.[25]

Let us say no more, then, of these paralysed souls, who, unless the Lord Himself comes and commands them to rise, are like the man who had lain beside the pool for thirty years:[26] they are unfortunate creatures and live in great peril. Let us rather think of certain other souls, who do eventually enter the castle. These are very much absorbed in worldly affairs; but their desires are good; sometimes, though infrequently, they commend themselves to Our Lord; and they think about the state of their souls, though not very carefully. Full of a thousand preoccupations as they are, they pray only a few times a month, and as a rule they are thinking all the time of their preoccupations, for they are very much attached to them, and, where their treasure is, there is their heart also.[27] From time to time, however, they shake their minds free of them and it is a great thing that they should know themselves well enough to realize that they are not going the right way to reach the castle door. Eventually they enter the first rooms on the lowest floor, but so many reptiles get in with them that they are unable to appreciate the beauty of the castle or to find any peace within it. Still, they have done a good deal by entering at all.

You will think this is beside the point, daughters, since by the goodness of the Lord you are not one of these. But you must be patient, for there is no other way in which I can explain to you some ideas I have had about certain interior matters concerning prayer. May it please the Lord to enable me to say something about them; for to explain to you what I should like is very difficult unless you have had personal experience; and anyone with such experience, as you will see, cannot help touching upon subjects which, please God, shall, by His mercy, never concern us.

Chapter II

Describe the hideousness of a soul in mortal sin, some part of which God was pleased to manifest to a certain person. Says something also of self-knowledge. This chapter is profitable, since it contains some noteworthy matters. Explains in what sense the Mansions are to be understood.

Before passing on, I want you to consider what will be the state of this castle, so beautiful and resplendent this Orient pearl, this tree of life, planted in the living waters of life[28] — namely, in God — when the soul falls into a mortal sin. No thicker darkness exists, and there is nothing dark and black which is not much less so than this. You need know only one thing about it — that, although the Sun Himself, Who has given it all its splendour and beauty, is still there in the centre of the soul, it is as if He were not there for any participation which the soul has in Him, though it is as capable of enjoying Him as is the crystal of reflecting the sun. While in a state like this the soul will find profit in nothing, and hence, being as it is in mortal sin, none of the good works it may do will be of any avail[29] to win it glory; for they will not have their origin in that First Principle, which is God, through Whom alone our virtue is true virtue. And, since this soul has separated itself from Him, it cannot be pleasing in His eyes; for, after all, the intention of a person who commits a mortal sin is not to please Him but to give pleasure to the devil; and, as the devil is darkness itself, the poor soul becomes darkness itself likewise.

I know of a person[30] to whom Our Lord wished to show what a soul was like when it committed mortal sin. That person says that, if people could understand this, she thinks they would find it impossible to sin at all, and, rather than meet occasions of sin, would put themselves to the greatest trouble imaginable. So she was very anxious that everyone should realize this. May you be no less anxious, daughters, to pray earnestly to God for those who are in this state and who, with all their works, have become sheer darkness. For, just as all the streamlets that flow from a clear spring are as clear as the spring itself, so the works of a soul in grace are pleasing in the eyes both of God and of men, since they proceed from this spring of life, in which the soul is as a tree planted. It would give no shade and yield no fruit if it proceeded not thence, for the spring sustains it and prevents it from drying up and causes it to produce good fruit. When the soul, on the other hand, through its own fault, leaves this spring and becomes rooted in a pool of pitch-black, evil-smelling water, it produces nothing but misery and filth.

It should be noted here that it is not the spring, or the brilliant sun which is in the centre of the soul, that loses its splendour and beauty, for they are always within it and nothing can take away their beauty. If a thick black cloth be placed over a crystal in the sunshine, however, it is clear that, although the sun may be shining upon it, its brightness will have no effect upon the crystal.

O souls redeemed by the blood of Jesus Christ! Learn to understand yourselves and take pity on yourselves! Surely, if you understand your own natures, it is impossible that you will not strive to remove the pitch which blackens the crystal? Remember, if your life were to end now, you would never enjoy this light again.

O Jesus! How sad it is to see a soul deprived of it! What a state the poor rooms of the castle are in! How distracted are the senses which inhabit them! And the faculties, which are their governors and butlers and stewards — how blind they are and how ill-controlled! And yet, after all, what kind of fruit can one expect to be borne by a tree rooted in the devil?

I once heard a spiritual man say that he was not so much astonished at the things done by a soul in mortal sin as at the things not done by it. May God, in His mercy, deliver us from such great evil, for there is nothing in the whole of our lives that so thoroughly deserves to be called evil as this, since it brings endless and eternal evils in its train. It is of this, daughters, that we should walk in fear, and this from which in our prayers we must beg God to deliver us; for, if He keep not the city, we shall labour in vain,[31] since we are vanity itself. That person to whom I referred just now said that the favour which God had granted her had taught her too things: first, she had learned to have the greatest fear of offending Him, for which reason she continually begged Him not to allow her to fall, when she saw what legible consequences a fall could bring; secondly, she had found it a mirror of humility, for it had made her realize that any good thing we do has its source, not in ourselves but rather in that spring where this tree, which is the soul, is planted, and in that sun which sheds its radiance on our works. She says that she saw this so clearly that, whenever she did any good thing, or saw such a thing done, she betook herself straightway to its Source, realizing that without His help we are powerless. She then went on at once to praise God; and, as a rule, when she did any good action, she never gave a thought to herself at all.

If we can remember these two things, sisters, the time you have spent in reading all this, and the time I have spent in writing it, will not have been lost. Wise and learned men know them quite well, but we women are slow and need instruction in everything. So perhaps it may be the Lord's will that these comparisons shall be brought to our notice. May He be pleased of His goodness to give us grace to understand them.

These interior matters are so obscure to the mind that anyone with as little learning as I will be sure to have to say many superfluous and even irrelevant things in order to say a single one that is to the point. The reader must have patience with me, as I have with myself when writing about things of which I know nothing; for really I sometimes take up my paper, like a perfect fool, with no idea of what to say or of how to begin. I fully realize how important it is for you that I should explain certain interior matters to the best of my ability; for we continually hear what a good thing prayer is, and our Constitutions oblige us to engage in it for so many hours daily, yet they tell us nothing beyond what we ourselves have to do and say very little about the work done by the Lord in the soul — I mean, supernatural work. As I describe the things He does, and give various explanations of them, it will be very helpful for us to think of this celestial building which is within us and is so little understood by mortals, although many of them frequent it. And although the Lord has thrown some light upon many matters of which I have written, I do not think I have understood some of them, especially the most difficult, as well as I do now. The trouble, as I have said, is that, before I can get to them, I shall have to explain many things that are well known — it is bound to be so when a person is as stupid as I.

Let us now turn to our castle with its many mansions. You must not imagine these mansions as arranged in a row, one behind another, but fix your attention on the centre, the room or palace occupied by the King. Think of a palmito,[32] which has many outer rinds surrounding the savoury part within, all of which must be taken away before the centre can be eaten. Just so around this central room are many more, as there also are above it. In speaking of the soul we must always think of it as spacious, ample and lofty; and this can be done without the least exaggeration, for the soul's capacity is much greater than we can realize, and this Sun, Which is in the palace, reaches every part of it. It is very important that no soul which practises prayer, whether little or much, should be subjected to undue constraint or limitation. Since God has given it such dignity, it must be allowed to roam through these mansions — through those above, those below and those on either side. It must not be compelled to remain for a long time in one single room — not, at least, unless it is in the room of self-knowledge.[33] How necessary that is (and be sure you understand me here) even to those whom the Lord keeps in the same mansion in which He Himself is! However high a state the soul may have attained, self-knowledge is incumbent upon it, and this it will never be able to neglect even should it so desire. Humility must always be doing its work like a bee making its honey in the hive: without humility all will be lost. Still, we should remember that the bee is constantly flying about from flower to flower, and in the same way, believe me, the soul must sometimes emerge from self-knowledge and soar aloft in meditation upon the greatness and the majesty of its God. Doing this will help it to realize its own baseness better than thinking of its own nature, and it will be freer from the reptiles which enter the first rooms — that is, the rooms of self-knowledge. For although, as I say, it is through the abundant mercy of God that the soul studies to know itself, yet one can have too much of a good thing, as the saying goes,[34] and believe me, we shall reach much greater heights of virtue by thinking upon the virtue of God than if we stay in our own little plot of ground and tie ourselves down to it completely.

I do not know if I have explained this clearly: self-knowledge is so important that, even if you were raised right up to the heavens, I should like you never to relax your cultivation of it; so long as we are on this earth, nothing matters more to us than humility. And so I repeat that it is a very good thing — excellent, indeed — to begin by entering the room where humility is acquired rather than by flying off to the other rooms. For that is the way to make progress, and, if we have a safe, level road to walk along, why should we desire wings to fly? Let us rather try to get the greatest possible profit out of walking. As I see it, we shall never succeed in knowing ourselves unless we seek to know God: let us think of His greatness and then come back to our own baseness; by looking at His purity we shall see our foulness; by meditating upon His humility, we shall see how far we are from being humble.

There are two advantages in this. First, it is clear that anything white looks very much whiter against something black, just as the black looks blacker against the white. Secondly, if we turn from self towards God, our understanding and our will become nobler and readier to embrace all that is good: if we never rise above the slough of our own miseries we do ourselves a great disservice. We were saying just now how black and noisome are the streams that flow from souls in mortal sin. Similarly, although this is not the same thing — God forbid! It is only a comparison — so long as we are buried in the wretchedness of our earthly nature these streams of ours will never disengage themselves from the slough of cowardice, pusillanimity and fear. We shall always be glancing around and saying: "Are people looking at me or not?" "If I take a certain path shall I come to any harm?" "Dare I begin such and such a task?" "Is it pride that is impelling me to do so?" "Can anyone as wretched as I engage in so lofty an exercise as prayer?" "Will people think better of me if I refrain from following the crowd?" "For extremes are not good," they say, "even in virtue; and I am such a sinner that if I were to fail I should only have farther to fall; perhaps I shall make no progress and in that case I shall only be doing good people harm; anyway, a person like myself has no need to make herself singular."

Oh, God help my daughters, how many souls the devil must have ruined in this way! They think that all these misgivings, and many more that I could describe, arise from humility, whereas they really come from our lack of self-knowledge. We get a distorted idea of our own nature, and, if we never stop thinking about ourselves, I am not surprised if we experience these fears and others which are still worse. It is for this reason, daughters, that I say we must set our eyes upon Christ our Good, from Whom we shall learn true humility, and also upon His saints. Our understanding, as I have said, will then be ennobled, and self-knowledge will not make us timorous[35] and fearful; for, although this is only the first Mansion, it contains riches of great price, and any who can elude the reptiles which are to be found in it will not fail to go farther. Terrible are the crafts and wiles which the devil uses to prevent souls from learning to know themselves and understanding his ways.

With regard to these first Mansions I can give some very useful information out of my own experience. I must tell you, for example, to think of them as comprising not just a few rooms, but a very large number.[36] There are many ways in which souls enter them, always with good intentions; but as the devil's intentions are always very bad, he has many legions of evil spirits in each room to prevent souls from passing from one to another, and as we, poor souls, fail to realize this, we are tricked by all kinds of deceptions. The devil is less successful with those who are nearer the King's dwelling-place; but at this early stage, as the soul is still absorbed in worldly affairs, engulfed in worldly pleasure and puffed up with worldly honours and ambitions, its vassals, which are the senses and the faculties given to it by God as part of its nature, have not the same power, and such a soul is easily vanquished, although it may desire not to offend God and may perform good works. Those who find themselves in this state need to take every opportunity of repairing to His Majesty, and to make His blessed Mother their intercessor, and also His saints, so that these may do battle for them, since their own servants have little strength for defending themselves. In reality it is necessary in every state of life for our help to come from God. May His Majesty grant us this through His mercy. Amen.

How miserable is this life which we live! As I have said a great deal elsewhere, daughters, about the harm which comes to us through our not properly understanding this matter of humility and self-knowledge, I am not saying more to you here, though it is a matter of the greatest importance to us. May the Lord grant that something I have said will be of use to you.

You must note that the light which comes from the palace occupied by the King hardly reaches these first Mansions at all; for, although they are not dark and black, as when the soul is in a state of sin, they are to some extent darkened, so that they cannot be seen (I mean by anyone who is in them); and this not because of anything that is wrong with the room, but rather (I hardly know how to explain myself) because there are so many bad things — snakes and vipers and poisonous creatures — which have come in with the soul that they prevent it from seeing the light. It is as if one were to enter a place flooded by sunlight with his eyes so full of dust[37] that he could hardly open them. The room itself is light enough, but he cannot enjoy the light because he is prevented from doing so by these wild beasts and animals, which force him to close his eyes to everything but themselves. This seems to me to be the condition of a soul which, though not in a bad state, is so completely absorbed in things of the world and so deeply immersed, as I have said, in possessions or honours or business, that, although as a matter of fact it would like to gaze at the castle and enjoy its beauty, it is prevented from doing so, and seems quite unable to free itself from all these impediments. Everyone, however, who wishes to enter the second Mansions, will be well advised, as far as his state of life permits, to try to put aside all unnecessary affairs and business. For those who hope to reach the principal Mansion, this is so important that unless they begin in this way I do not believe they will ever be able to get there. Nor, indeed, even though it has entered the castle, is the soul free from great peril in the Mansion which it actually inhabits; for, being among such poisonous things, it cannot, at some time or another, escape being bitten by them.

What would happen, then, daughters, if those who, like ourselves, are free from these obstacles, and have already entered much farther into other secret mansions of the castle, should, through their own fault, go out again into this hurly-burly? Our sins must have led many people whom God has granted favours to relapse through their faults into this wretched state. We here, so far as outward things are concerned, are free; may it please the Lord to make us free as regards inward things as well and to deliver us from evil. Beware, my daughters, of cares which have nothing to do with you. Remember that in few of the mansions of this castle are we free from struggles with devils. It is true that in some of them, the wardens, who, as I think I said, are the faculties, have strength for the fight; but it is most important that we should not cease to be watchful against the devil's wiles, lest he deceive us in the guise of an angel of light. For there are a multitude of ways in which he can deceive us, and gradually make his way into the castle, and until he is actually there we do not realize it.

As I told you before, he works like a noiseless file, and we must be on the look-out for him from the beginning. In order to explain this better I want to give you several illustrations. He inspires a sister with yearnings to do penance, so that she seems to have no peace save when she is torturing herself. This, in itself, is good; but, if the prioress has ordered that no penance is to be done without leave, and yet the sister thinks that she can venture to persist in so beneficial a practice, and secretly orders her life in such a way that in the end she ruins her health and is unable to do what her Rule demands, you see what this apparently good thing has led to. Another sister is inspired with zeal for the greatest possible perfection. This, again, is a very good thing; but the result of it might be that she would think any little fault on the part of the sisters a serious failure, and would always be looking out for such things and running to the prioress about them; sometimes she might even be so zealous about religious observances as to be unable to see her own faults; and this the others, observing only her zeal about their misdeeds and not understanding the excellence of her intentions, might well take none too kindly.

The devil's aim here must not be made light of, for he is trying to bring about a cooling of charity and love among the sisters, and if he could do this he would be working a great deal of harm. Let us realize, my daughters, that true perfection consists in the love of God and of our neighbour, and the more nearly perfect is our observance of these two commandments, the nearer to perfection we shall be. Our entire Rule and Constitutions are nothing but means which enable us to do this the more perfectly. Let us refrain from indiscreet zeal, which may do us great harm: let each one of you look to herself. As I have said a great deal to you about this elsewhere[38] I will not enlarge on it further.

This mutual love is so important for us that I should like you never to forget it; for if the soul goes about looking for trifling faults in others (which sometimes may not be imperfections at all, though perhaps our ignorance may lead us to make the worst of them) it may lose its own peace of mind and perhaps disturb that of others. See, then, how dearly perfection can be bought. The devil might also use this temptation in the case of a prioress, and then it would be more dangerous still. Much discretion is necessary here; for, if it were a question of her contravening the Rule and Constitutions, it would not always do to take a lenient view of the matter — she would have to be spoken to about it; and, if she did not then amend, the prelate would have to be told: to do this would be a charity. This would also apply to the sisters, where the fault was a grave one: to say nothing through fear that taking the matter up would be yielding to temptation would itself be to yield to temptation. However, to prevent deception by the devil, it should be strongly stressed that no sister must discuss such things with any other, for from this practice the devil can pluck great advantage and start habits of slander; these matters must be discussed, as I have said, only with the person whose concern they are. Here, glory be to God, we keep almost continuous silence, so that the opportunity does not arise; none the less, it is well that we should be on our guard.

Second Mansions:
In which there is One Chapter only[39]

Treats of the great importance of perseverance if we are to reach the final Mansions and of the fierce war which the devil wages against us. Tells how essential it is, if we are to attain our goal, not to miss our way at the beginning. Gives a method which has proved very efficacious.

Let us now come to consider who the souls are that enter the second Mansions and what they do there. I want to say very little to you about this, because elsewhere I have written of it at length,[40] and it will be impossible for me to avoid repeating a great deal of this, because I cannot remember anything of what I said. If it could be arranged[41] in a different form, I am quite sure you would not mind, as we are never tired of books that treat of this, numerous though they are.

This chapter has to do with those who have already begun to practise prayer and who realize the importance of not remaining in the first Mansions, but who often are not yet resolute enough to leave those Mansions, and will not avoid occasions of sin, which is a very perilous condition. But it is a very great mercy that they should contrive to escape from the snakes and other poisonous creatures, if only for short periods and should realize that it is good to flee from them. In some ways, these souls have a much harder time than those in the first Mansions; but they are in less peril, for they seem now to understand their position and there is great hope that they will get farther into the castle still. I say they have a harder time because the souls in the first Mansions are, as it were, not only dumb, but can hear nothing, and so it is not such a trial to them to be unable to speak; the others, who can hear and not speak, would find the trial much harder to bear. But that is no reason for envying those who do not hear, for after all it is a great thing to be able to understand what is said to one.

These souls, then, can understand the Lord when He calls them; for, as they gradually get nearer to the place where His Majesty dwells, He becomes a very good Neighbour to them. And such are His mercy and goodness that, even when we are engaged in our worldly pastimes and businesses and pleasures and hagglings, when we are falling into sins and rising from them again (because these creatures are at once so venomous and so active and it is so dangerous for us to be among them that it will be a miracle if we escape stumbling over them and falling) — in spite of all that, this Lord of ours is so anxious that we should desire Him and strive after His companionship that He calls us ceaselessly, time after time, to approach Him; and this voice of His is so sweet that the poor soul is consumed with grief at being unable to do His bidding immediately, and thus, as I say, it suffers more than if it could not hear Him.

I do not mean by this that He speaks to us and calls us in the precise way which I shall describe later; His appeals come through the conversations of good people, or from sermons, or through the reading of good books; and there are many other ways, of which you have heard, in which God calls us. Or they come through sicknesses and trials, or by means of truths which God teaches us at times when we are engaged in prayer; however feeble such prayers may be God values them highly. You must not despise this first favour, sisters, nor be disconsolate, even though you have not responded immediately to the Lord's call; for His Majesty is quite prepared to wait for many days, and even years, especially when He sees we are persevering and have good desires. This is the most necessary thing here; if we have this we cannot fail to gain greatly. Nevertheless, the assault which the devils now make upon the soul, in all kinds of ways, is terrible; and the soul suffers more than in the preceding Mansions; for there it was deaf and dumb, or at least it could hear very little, and so it offered less resistance, like one who to a great extent has lost hope of gaining the victory. Here the understanding is keener and the faculties are more alert, while the clash of arms and the noise of cannon are so loud that the soul cannot help hearing them. For here the devils once more show the soul these vipers — that is, the things of the world — and they pretend that earthly pleasures are almost eternal: they remind the soul of the esteem in which it is held in the world, of its friends and relatives, of the way in which its health will be endangered by penances (which the soul always wants to do when it first enters this Mansion) and of impediments of a thousand other kinds.

Oh, Jesus! What confusion the devils bring about in the poor soul, and how distressed it is, not knowing if it ought to proceed farther or return to the room where it was before! On the other hand, reason tells the soul how mistaken it is in thinking that all these earthly things are of the slightest value by comparison with what it is seeking, faith instructs it in what it must do to find satisfaction; memory shows it how all these things come to an end, and reminds it that those who have derived so much enjoyment from the things which it has seen have died. Sometimes they have died suddenly and been quickly forgotten by all: people whom we once knew to be very prosperous are now beneath the ground, and we trample upon their graves, and often, as we pass them, we reflect that their bodies are seething with worms — of these and many other things the soul is reminded by memory. The will inclines to love One in Whom it has seen so many acts and signs of love, some of which it would like to return. In particular, the will shows the soul how this true Lover never leaves it, but goes with it everywhere and gives it life and being. Then the understanding comes forward and makes the soul realize that, for however many years it may live, it can never hope to have a better friend, for the world is full of falsehood and these pleasures which the devil pictures to it are accompanied by trials and cares and annoyances; and tells it to be certain that outside this castle it will find neither security nor peace: let it refrain from visiting one house after another when its own house is full of good things, if it will only enjoy them. How fortunate it is to be able to find all that it needs, as it were, at home, especially when it has a Host Who will put all good things into its possession, unless, like the Prodigal Son, it desires to go astray and eat the food of the swine![42]

It is reflections of this kind which vanquish devils. But, oh, my God and Lord, how everything is ruined by the vain habits we fall into and the way everyone else follows them! So dead is our faith that we desire what we see more than what faith tells us about — though what we actually see is that people who pursue these visible things meet with nothing but ill fortune. All this is the work of these poisonous creatures which we have been describing. For, if a man is bitten by a viper, his whole body is poisoned and swells up; and so it is in this case, and yet we take no care of ourselves. Obviously a great deal of attention will be necessary if we are to be cured and only the great mercy of God will preserve us from death. The soul will certainly suffer great trials at this time, especially if the devil sees that its character and habits are such that it is ready to make further progress: all the powers of hell will combine to drive it back again.

Ah, my Lord! It is here that we have need of Thine aid, without which we can do nothing. Of Thy mercy, allow not this soul to be deluded and led astray when its journey is but begun. Give it light so that it may see how all its welfare consists in this and may flee from evil companionship. It is a very great thing for a person to associate with others who are walking in the right way: to mix, not only with those whom he sees in the rooms where he himself is, but with those whom he knows to have entered the rooms nearer the centre, for they will be of great help to him and he can get into such close touch with them that they will take him with them. Let him have a fixed determination not to allow himself to be beaten, for, if the devil sees that he has firmly resolved to lose his life and his peace and everything that he can offer him rather than to return to the first room, he will very soon cease troubling him. Let him play the man and not be like those who went down on their knees in order to drink when they went to battle — I forget with whom[43] — but let him be resolute, for he is going forth to fight with all the devils and there are no better weapons than the Cross.

There is one thing so important that, although I have said it on other occasions,[44] I will repeat it once more here: it is that at the beginning one must not think of such things as spiritual favours, for that is a very poor way of starting to build such a large and beautiful edifice. If it is begun upon sand, it will all collapse:[45] souls which build like that will never be free from annoyances and temptations. For it is not in these Mansions, but in those which are farther on, that it rains manna; once there, the soul has all that it desires, because it desires only what is the will of God. It is a curious thing: here we are, meeting with hindrances and suffering from imperfections by the thousand, with our virtues so young that they have not yet learned how to walk — in fact, they have only just been born: God grant that they have even been born at all! — and yet we are not ashamed to be wanting consolations in prayer and to be complaining about periods of aridity. This must not be true of you, sisters: embrace the Cross which your Spouse bore upon His shoulders and realize that this Cross is yours to carry too: let her who is capable of the greatest suffering suffer most for Him and she will have the most perfect freedom. All other things are of quite secondary importance: if the Lord should grant them to you, give Him heartfelt thanks.

You may think that you will be full of determination to resist outward trials if God will only grant you inward favours. His Majesty knows best what is suitable for us; it is not for us to advise Him what to give us, for He can rightly reply that we know not what we ask.[46] All that the beginner in prayer has to do — and you must not forget this, for it is very important — is to labour and be resolute and prepare himself with all possible diligence to bring his will into conformity with the will of God. As I shall say later, you may be quite sure that this comprises the very greatest perfection which can be attained on the spiritual road. The more perfectly a person practises it, the more he will receive of the Lord and the greater the progress he will make on this road; do not think we have to use strange jargon or dabble in things of which we have no knowledge or understanding, our entire welfare is to be found in what I have described. If we go astray at the very beginning and want the Lord to do our will and to lead us just as our fancy dictates, how can this building possibly have a firm foundation? Let us see that we do as much as in us lies and avoid these venomous reptiles, for often it is the Lord's will that we should be persecuted and afflicted by evil thoughts, which we cannot cast out, and also by aridities; and sometimes He even allows these reptiles to bite us, so that we may learn better how to be on our guard in the future and see if we are really grieved at having offended Him.

If, then, you sometimes fail, do not lose heart, or cease striving to make progress, for even out of your fall God will bring good, just as a man selling an antidote will drink poison before he takes it in order to prove its power. If nothing else could show us what wretched creatures we are and what harm we do to ourselves by dissipating our desires, this war which goes on within us would be sufficient to do so and to lead us back to recollection. Can any evil be greater than the evil which we find in our own house? What hope can we have of being able to rest in other people's homes[47] if we cannot rest in our own? For none of our friends and relatives are as near to us as our faculties, with which we have always to live, whether we like it or not, and yet our faculties seem to be making war upon us, as if they were resentful of the war made upon them by our vices. "Peace, peace," said the Lord, my sisters, and many a time He spoke words of peace to His Apostles.[48] Believe me, unless we have peace, and strive for peace in our own home, we shall not find it in the homes of others. Let this war now cease. By the blood which Christ shed for us, I beg this of those who have not begun to enter within themselves; and those who have begun to do so must not allow such warfare to turn them back. They must realize that to fall a second time is worse than to fall once. They can see that it will lead them to ruin: let them place their trust, not in themselves, but in the mercy of God, and they will see how His Majesty can lead them on from one group of Mansions to another and set them on safe ground where these beasts cannot harass or hurt them, for He will place the beasts in their power and laugh them to scorn; and then they themselves — even in this life, I mean — will enjoy many more good things than they could ever desire.

As I said first of all, I have already written to you about how you ought to behave when you have to suffer these disturbances with which the devil torments you;[49] and about how recollection cannot be begun by making strenuous efforts, but must come gently, after which you will be able to practise it for longer periods at a time. So I will say no more about this now, except that it is very important for you to consult people of experience; for otherwise you will imagine that you are doing yourselves great harm by pursuing your necessary occupations. But, provided we do not abandon our prayer, the Lord will turn everything we do to our profit, even though we may find no one to teach us. There is no remedy for this evil of which we have been speaking except to start again at the beginning; otherwise the soul will keep on losing a little more every day — please God that it may come to realize this.

Some of you might suppose that, if it is such a bad thing to turn back, it would have been better never to have begun, but to have remained outside the castle. I told you, however, at the outset, and the Lord Himself says this, that he who goes into danger shall perish in it,[50] and that the door by which we can enter this castle is prayer. It is absurd to think that we can enter Heaven without first entering our own souls — without getting to know ourselves, and reflecting upon the wretchedness of our nature and what we owe to God, and continually imploring His mercy. The Lord Himself says: "No one will ascend to My Father, but by Me"[51] (I am not sure if those are the exact words, but I think they are)[52] and "He that sees Me sees My Father."[53] Well, if we never look at Him or think of what we owe Him, and of the death which He suffered for our sakes, I do not see how we can get to know Him or do good works in His service. For what can be the value of faith without works, or of works which are not united with the merits of our Lord Jesus Christ? And what but such thoughts can arouse us to love this Lord? May it please His Majesty to grant us to understand how much we cost Him, that the servant is not greater than his Lord,[54] that we must needs work if we would enjoy His glory, and that for that reason we must perforce pray, lest we enter continually into temptation.[55]

Third Mansions:
In which there are Two Chapters

Chapter 1

Treats of the insecurity from which we cannot escape in this life of exile, however lofty a state we may reach, and of how good it is for us to walk in fear. This chapter contains several good points.

TO those who by the mercy of God have overcome in these combats, and by dint of perseverance have entered the third Mansions, what shall we say but "Blessed is the man that feareth the Lord"?[56] As I am so stupid in these matters, it has been no small thing that His Majesty should have enabled me to understand the meaning of this verse in the vernacular. We shall certainly be right in calling such a man blessed, for, unless he turns back, he is, so far as we can tell, on the straight road to salvation. Here, sisters, you will see the importance of having overcome in your past battles; for I am convinced that the Lord never fails to give a person who does this security of conscience, which is no small blessing. I say "security", but that is the wrong word, for there is no security in this life, so, whenever I use it, you must understand the words "unless he strays from the path on which he has set out".

It is really a perfect misery to be alive when we have always to be going about like men with enemies at their gates, who cannot lay aside their arms even when sleeping or eating, and are always afraid of being surprised by a breaching of their fortress in some weak spot. Oh, my Lord and my God! How canst Thou wish us to desire such a miserable life as that? It would be impossible to refrain from wishing and begging Thee to take us from it, were it not for our hope that we may lose it for Thy sake, or spend it wholly in Thy service — and, above all, for the realization that it is Thy will for us. If that is indeed so, my God, let us die with Thee, as Saint Thomas said,[57] for life without Thee is nothing but death many times over and constant dread at the possibility of losing Thee for ever. So I think, daughters, that the happiness we should pray for is to enjoy the complete security of the blessed;[58] for what pleasure can anyone have when beset by these fears if his only pleasure consists in pleasing God? Remember that all this, and much more, could be said of some of the saints, and yet they fell[59] into grave sins, and we cannot be certain that God will give us His hand and help us to renounce them[60] and do penance for them. (This refers to particular help.)[61]

Truly, my daughters, I am so fearful as I write this that, when it comes to my mind, as is very often the case, I hardly know how to get the words down, or how to go on living. Beseech His Majesty, my daughters, always to live within me, for otherwise what security can there be in a life as misspent as mine? And do not let it depress you to realize that I am like that — I have sometimes seen you depressed when I have told you so. The reason it affects you in that way is that you would like to think I had been very holy. That is quite right of you: I should like to think so myself. But what can I do about it when I have lost so much through my own fault? I shall not complain that God ceased giving me all the help

I needed if your wishes were to be fulfilled: I cannot say this without tears and great confusion when I realize that I am writing for those who are themselves capable of teaching me. Rigorous has been the task that obedience has laid upon me![62] May it please the Lord that, as it is being done for His sake, you may gain some profit from it and may ask Him to pardon this wretched and foolhardy woman. But His Majesty well knows that I can count only upon His Mercy, and, as I cannot help having been what I have, there is nothing for me to do but approach God and trust in the merits of His Son, and of the Virgin, His Mother, whose habit both you and I unworthily wear. Praise Him, my daughters, for you are really the daughters of Our Lady, and when you have as good a Mother as that there is no reason for you to be scandalized at my unworthiness. Imitate Our Lady and consider how great she must be and what a good thing it is that we have her for our Patroness; even my sins and my being what I am have not been sufficient to bring any kind of tarnish upon this sacred Order.

But of one thing I must warn you: although you are in this Order, and have such a Mother, do not be too sure of yourselves; for David was a very holy man, yet you know what Solomon[63] became. Nor must you set store by the fact that you are cloistered and lead lives of penitence. Nor must you become confident because you are always talking about God, continually engaging in prayer, withdrawing yourselves completely from the things of this world and (to the best of your belief) abhorring them. All that is good, but, as I have said, it is not enough to justify us in laying aside our fears. So you must repeat this verse and often bear it in mind: Beatus vir, qui timet Dominum.64

And now I forget what I was saying — I have been indulging in a long digression. Whenever I think of myself I feel like a bird with a broken wing and I can say nothing of any value. So I will leave all this for now and return to what I had begun to explain concerning the souls that have entered the third Mansions. In enabling these souls to overcome their initial difficulties, the Lord has granted them no small favour, but a very great one. I believe that, through His goodness, there are many such souls in the world: they are most desirous not to offend His Majesty; they avoid committing even venial sins;[65] they love doing penance, they spend hours in recollection; they use their time well; they practise works of charity toward their neighbours; and they are very careful in their speech and dress and in the government of their household if they have one. This is certainly a desirable state and there seems no reason why they should be denied entrance to the very last of the Mansions; nor will the Lord deny them this if they desire it, for their disposition is such that He will grant them any favour.

Oh, Jesus! How could anyone ever say that he has no desire for such a wonderful thing, especially when he has got over the most troublesome stages leading to it? Surely no one could do so. We all say we desire it; but if the Lord is to take complete possession of the soul more than that is necessary. Words are not enough, any more than they were for the young man when the Lord told him what to do if he wished to be perfect.[66] Ever since I began to speak of these Mansions I have had that young man in mind, for we are exactly like him; and this as a rule is the origin of our long periods of aridity in prayer, although these have other sources as well. I am saying nothing here of interior trials, which vex many good souls to an intolerable degree, and through no fault of their own, but from which the Lord always rescues them, to their great profit, as He does also those who suffer from melancholy and other infirmities. In all things we must leave out of account the judgments of God.

Personally, I think that what I have said is the most usual thing. These souls know that nothing would induce them to commit a sin — many of them would not intentionally commit even a venial sin — and they make good use of their lives and their possessions. So they cannot be patient when the door is closed to them and they are unable to enter the presence of the King, Whose vassals they consider themselves, and in fact are. Yet even on earth a king may have many vassals and they do not all get so far as to enter his chamber. Enter, then, enter within yourselves, my daughters; and get right away from your own trifling good works, for these you are bound, as Christians, to perform, and, indeed, many more. It will be enough for you that you are vassals of God; do not try to get so much that you achieve nothing. Look at the saints who have entered the King's chamber and you will see the difference between them and ourselves. Do not ask for what you have not deserved. For we have offended God, and, however faithfully we serve Him, it should never enter our heads that we can deserve anything.

Oh, humility, humility! I do not know why I have this temptation, but whenever I hear people making so much of their times of aridity, I cannot help thinking that they are somewhat lacking in it. I am not, of course, referring to the great interior trials of which I have spoken, for they amount to much more than a lack of devotion. Let us test ourselves, my sisters, or allow the Lord to test us; for He knows well how to do it, although often we refuse to understand Him. And now let us return to these carefully-ordered souls and consider what they do for God, and we shall then see how wrong we are to complain of His Majesty. For, if, when He tells us what we must do in order to be perfect, we turn our backs upon Him and go away sorrowfully, like the young man in the Gospel,[67] what do you expect His Majesty to do, for the reward which He is to give us must of necessity be proportionate with the love which we bear Him? And this love, daughters, must not be wrought in our imagination but must be proved by works. Yet do not suppose God has any need of our works; what He needs is the resoluteness of our will.

It may seem to us that we have done everything — we who wear the religious habit, having taken it of our own will and left all the things of the world and all that we had for His sake (for although, like Saint Peter, we may have left only our nets, yet He esteems a person who gives all that he has as one who gives in fullest measure).[68] This is a very good beginning; and, if we persevere in it, instead of going back, even if only in desire, to consort with the reptiles in the first rooms, there is no doubt that, by persevering in this detachment and abandonment of everything, we shall attain our object. But it must be on this condition — and note that I am warning you of this — that we consider ourselves unprofitable servants, as we are told, either by Saint Paul or by Christ,[69] and realize that we have in no way obliged Our Lord to grant us such favours; but rather that, the more we have received of Him, the more deeply do we remain in His debt. What can we do for so generous a God, Who died for us and created us and gives us being, without counting ourselves fortunate in being able to repay Him something of what we owe Him for the way He has served us[70] (I write this word reluctantly, but it is the truth,[71] for all the time He lived in the world He did nothing but serve) without asking Him once more for gifts and favours?

Consider carefully, daughters, these few things which have been set down here, though they are in rather a jumbled state, for I cannot explain them better; the Lord will make them clear to you, so that these periods of aridity may teach you to be humble, and not make you restless, which is the aim of the devil. Be sure that, where there is true humility, even if God never grants the soul favours, He will give it peace and resignation to His will, with which it may be more content than others are with favours. For often, as you have read, it is to the weakest that His Divine Majesty gives favours, which I believe they would not exchange for all the fortitude given to those who go forward in aridity. We are fonder of spiritual sweetness than of crosses. Test us, O Lord, Thou Who knowest all truth, that we may know ourselves.

Chapter II

Continues the same subject and treats of aridities in prayer and of what the author thinks may result from them; and of how we must test ourselves; and of how the Lord proves those who are in these Mansions.

I have known a few souls who have reached this state — I think I might even say a great many — and who, as far as we can see, have for many years lived an upright and carefully ordered life, both in soul and in body and then, after all these years, when it has seemed as if they must have gained the mastery over the world, or at least must be completely detached from it, His Majesty has sent them tests which have been by no means exacting and they have become so restless and depressed in spirit that they have exasperated me,[72] and have even made me thoroughly afraid for them. It is of no use offering them advice, for they have been practising virtue for so long that they think they are capable of teaching others and have ample justification for feeling as they do.

Well, I cannot find, and have never found, any way of comforting such people, except to express great sorrow at their trouble, which, when I see them so miserable, I really do feel. It is useless to argue with them, for they brood over their woes and make up their minds that they are suffering for God's sake, and thus never really understand that it is all due to their own imperfection. And in persons who have made so much progress this is a further mistake; one cannot be surprised if they suffer, though I think this kind of suffering ought to pass quickly. For often it is God's will that His elect should be conscious of their misery and so He withdraws His help from them a little — and no more than that is needed to make us recognize our limitations very quickly. They then realize that this is a way of testing them, for they gain a clear perception of their shortcomings, and sometimes they derive more pain from finding that, in spite of themselves, they are still grieving about earthly things, and not very important things either, than from the matter which is troubling them. This, I think, is a great mercy on the part of God, and even though they are at fault they gain a great deal in humility.

With those other persons of whom I am speaking it is different: they consider they have acted in a highly virtuous way, as I have said, and they wish others to think so too. I will tell you about some of them so that we may learn to understand and test ourselves before we are tested by the Lord — and it would be a very great advantage if we were prepared and had learned to know ourselves first.

A rich man, who is childless and has no one to leave his money to, loses part of his wealth; but not so much that he has not enough for himself and his household — he still has enough and to spare. If he begins to get restless and worried, as though he had not a crust of bread left to eat, how can Our Lord ask him to leave all for His sake? It may be, of course, that he is suffering because he wants to give the money to the poor. But I think God would rather I were resigned to what His Majesty does, and kept my tranquillity of soul, than that I should do such acts of charity as these. If this man cannot resign himself, because the Lord has not led him thus far, well and good; but he ought to realize that he lacks this freedom of spirit and in that case he will pray for it and prepare himself for the Lord to give it to him.

Another person, who has means enough to support himself, and indeed an excess of means, sees an opportunity of acquiring more property. Let him take such an opportunity, certainly, if it comes to him; but if he strives after it, and, on obtaining it, strives after more and more, however good his intention may be (and good it must be, because, as I have said, these are all virtuous people and given to prayer), he need not be afraid that he will ever ascend[73] to the Mansions which are nearest the King.

It is much the same thing if such people are despised in any way or lose some of their reputation. God often grants them grace to bear this well, for He loves to help people to be virtuous in the presence of others, so that the virtue itself which they possess may not be thought less of, or perhaps He will help them because they have served Him, for this our God is good indeed. And yet they become restless, for they cannot do as they would like to and control their feelings all at once. Yet oh, dear me! Are not these the same persons who some time ago were meditating upon how the Lord suffered, and upon what a good thing it is to suffer, and who were even desiring to suffer? They would like every one else to live as well-ordered a life as they do themselves; all we can hope is that they will not begin to imagine that the trouble they have is somebody else's fault and represent it to themselves as meritorious.

You will think, sisters, that I am wandering from the point, and am no longer addressing myself to you, and that these things have nothing to do with us, as we own no property and neither desire it nor strive after it and nobody ever slights us. It is true that these examples are not exactly applicable to us, but many others which are can be deduced from them, though it is unnecessary, and would be unseemly, for me to detail them. From these you will find out if you are really detached from the things you have abandoned, for trifling incidents arise, though not precisely of this kind, which give you the opportunity to test yourselves and discover if you have obtained the mastery over your passions. And believe me, what matters is not whether or no we wear a religious habit; it is whether we try to practise the virtues, and make a complete surrender of our wills to God and order our lives as His Majesty ordains: let us desire that not our wills, but His will, be done.[74] If we have not progressed as far as this, then, as I have said, let us practise humility, which is the ointment for our wounds; if we are truly humble, God, the Physician,[75] will come in due course, even though He tarry, to heal us.

The penances done by these persons are as carefully ordered as their lives. They have a great desire for penance, so that by means of it they may serve Our Lord — and there is nothing wrong in that — and for this reason they observe great discretion in their penances, lest they should injure their health. You need never fear that they will kill themselves: they are eminently reasonable folk! Their love is not yet ardent enough to overwhelm their reason. How I wish ours would make us dissatisfied with this habit of always serving God at a snail's pace! As long as we do that we shall never get to the end of the road. And as we seem to be walking along and getting fatigued all the time — for, believe me, it is an exhausting road — we shall be very lucky if we escape getting lost. Do you think, daughters, if we could get from one country to another in a week, it would be advisable, with all the winds and snow and floods and bad roads, to take a year over it? Would it not be better to get the journey over and done with? For there are all these obstacles for us to meet and there is also the danger of serpents. Oh, what a lot I could tell you about that! Please God I have got farther than this myself—though I often fear I have not!

When we proceed with all this caution, we find stumbling-blocks everywhere; for we are afraid of everything, and so dare not go farther, as if we could arrive at these Mansions by letting others make the journey for us! That is not possible, my sisters; so, for the love of the Lord, let us make a real effort: let us leave our reason and our fears in His hands and let us forget the weakness of our nature which is apt to cause us so much worry. Let our superiors see to the care of our bodies; that must be their concern: our own task is only to journey with good speed so that we may see the Lord. Although we get few or no comforts here, we shall be making a great mistake if we worry over our health, especially as it will not be improved by our anxiety about it — that I well know. I know, too, that our progress has nothing to do with the body, which is the thing that matters least. What the journey which I am referring to demands is great humility, and it is the lack of this, I think, if you see what I mean, which prevents us from making progress. We may think we have advanced only a few steps, and we should believe that this is so and that our sisters' progress is much more rapid; and further we should not only want them to consider us worse than anyone else, but we should contrive to make them do so.

If we act thus, this state is a most excellent one, but otherwise we shall spend our whole lives in it and suffer a thousand troubles and miseries. Without complete self-renunciation, the state is very arduous and oppressive, because, as we go along, we are labouring under the burden of our miserable nature, which is like a great load of earth and has not to be borne by those who reach the later Mansions. In these present Mansions the Lord does not fail to recompense us with just measure, and even generously, for He always gives us much more than we deserve by granting us a spiritual sweetness much greater than we can obtain from the pleasures and distractions of this life. But I do not think that He gives many consolations, except when He occasionally invites us to see what is happening in the remaining Mansions, so that we may prepare to enter them.

You will think that spiritual sweetness and consolations are one and the same thing: why, then, this difference of name? To me it seems that they differ a very great deal, though I may be wrong. I will tell you what I think about this when I write about the fourth Mansions, which will follow these, because, as I shall then have to say something about the consolations which the Lord gives in those Mansions, it will come more appropriately. The subject will seem an unprofitable one, yet none the less it may be of some use, for, once you understand the nature of each, you can strive to pursue the one which is better. This latter is a great solace to souls whom God has brought so far, while it will make those who think they have everything feel ashamed; and if they are humble they will be moved to give thanks. Should they fail to experience it, they will feel an inward discouragement — quite unnecessarily, however, for perfection consists not in consolations, but in the increase of love; on this, too, will depend our reward, as well as on the righteousness and truth which are in our actions.

If this is true — and it is — you will wonder what is the use of my discussing these interior favours, and explaining what they are. I do not know: you must ask the person who commanded me to write, for I am under an obligation not to dispute with my superiors, but to obey them, and it would not be right for me to dispute with them. What I can tell you truly is that, when I had had none of these favours, and knew nothing of them by experience, and indeed never expected to know about them all my life long (and rightly so, though it would have been the greatest joy for me to know, or even to conjecture, that I was in any way pleasing to God), none the less, when I read in books of these favours and consolations which the Lord grants to souls that serve Him, it would give me the greatest pleasure and lead my soul to offer fervent praises to God. Now if I, who am so worthless a person, did that, surely those who are good and humble will praise Him much more. If it only enables a single person to praise Him once, I think it is a good thing that all this should be said, and that we should realize what pleasure and what delights we lose through our own fault. All the more so because, if they come from God, they come laden with love and fortitude, by the help of which a soul can progress with less labour and grow continually in good works and virtues. Do not suppose that it matters little whether or no we do what we can to obtain them. But if the fault is not yours, the Lord is just, and what His Majesty denies you in this way He will give you in other ways — His Majesty knows how. His secrets are hidden deep; but all that He does will be best for us, without the slightest doubt.

What I think would be of the greatest profit to those of us who, by the goodness of the Lord, are in this state — and, as I have said, He shows them no little mercy in bringing them to it, for, when here, they are on the point of rising still higher — is that they should be most studious to render ready obedience. Even though they be not in a religious Order, it would be a great thing for them to have someone to whom they could go, as many people do, so that they might not be following their own will in anything, for it is in this way that we usually do ourselves harm. They should not look for anyone (as the saying has it) cast in the same mould as themselves[76] who always proceeds with great circumspection; they should select a man who is completely disillusioned with the things of the world. It is a great advantage for us to be able to consult someone who knows us, so that we may learn to know ourselves. And it is a great encouragement to see that things which we thought impossible are possible to others, and how easily these others do them. It makes us feel that we may emulate their flights and venture to fly ourselves, as the young birds do when their parents teach them; they are not yet ready for great flights but they gradually learn to imitate their parents. This is a great advantage, as I know. However determined such persons may be not to offend the Lord, they will do well not to run any risk of offending Him; for they are so near the first Mansions that they might easily return to them, since their fortitude is not built upon solid ground like that of souls who are already practised in suffering. These last are familiar with the storms of the world, and realize how little need there is to fear them or to desire worldly pleasures. If those of whom I am speaking, however, had to suffer great persecutions, they might well return to such pleasures and the devil well knows how to contrive such persecutions in order to do us harm; they might be pressing onward with great zeal, and trying to preserve others from sin, and yet be unable to resist any temptations which came to them.

Let us look at our own shortcomings and leave other people's alone; for those who live carefully ordered lives are apt to be shocked at everything and we might well learn very important lessons from the persons who shock us. Our outward comportment and behaviour may be better than theirs, but this, though good, is not the most important thing: there is no reason why we should expect everyone else to travel by our own road, and we should not attempt to point them to the spiritual path when perhaps we do not know what it is. Even with these desires that God gives us to help others, sisters, we may make many mistakes, and thus it is better to attempt to do what our Rule tells us — to try to live ever in silence and in hope, and the Lord will take care of His own. If, when we beseech this of His Majesty, we do not become negligent ourselves, we shall be able, with His help, to be of great profit to them. May He be for ever blessed.

Fourth Mansions:
In which there are Three Chapters

Chapter 1

Treats of the difference between sweetness or tenderness in prayer and consolations, and tells of the happiness which the author gained from learning how different thought is from understanding. This chapter is very profitable for those who suffer greatly from distractions during prayer.

Before I begin to speak of the fourth Mansions, it is most necessary that I should do what I have already done — namely, commend myself to the Holy Spirit, and beg Him from this point onward to speak for me, so that you may understand what I shall say about the Mansions still to be treated. For we now begin to touch the supernatural[77] and this is most difficult to explain unless His Majesty takes it in hand, as He did when I described as much as I understood of the subject, about fourteen years ago.[78] Although I think I have now a little more light upon these favours which the Lord grants to some souls, it is a different thing to know how to explain them. May His Majesty undertake this if there is any advantage to be gained from its being done, but not otherwise.

As these Mansions are now getting near to the place where the King dwells, they are of great beauty and there are such exquisite things to be seen and appreciated in them that the understanding is incapable of describing them in any way accurately without being completely obscure to those devoid of experience. But any experienced person will understand quite well, especially if his experience has been considerable. It seems that, in order to reach these Mansions, one must have lived for a long time in the others; as a rule one must have been in those which we have just described, but there is no infallible rule about it, as you must often have heard, for the Lord gives when He wills and as He wills and to whom He wills, and, as the gifts are His own, this is doing no injustice to anyone.

Into these Mansions poisonous creatures seldom enter, and, if they do, they prove quite harmless — in fact they do the soul good. I think in this state of prayer it is much better for them to enter and make war upon the soul, for, if it had no temptations, the devil might mislead it with regard to the consolations which God gives, and do much more harm than he can when it is being tempted. The soul, too, would not gain so much, for it would be deprived of all occasions of merit and be living in a state of permanent absorption. When a soul is continuously in a condition of this kind I do not consider it at all safe, nor do I think it possible for the Spirit of the Lord to remain in a soul continuously in this way during our life of exile.

Returning to what I was saying I would describe here — namely, the difference between sweetness in prayer and spiritual consolations — it seems to me that we may describe as sweetness what we get from our meditations and from petitions made to Our Lord. This proceeds from our own nature, though, of course, God plays a part in the process (and in everything I say you must understand this, for we can do nothing without Him). This spiritual sweetness arises from the actual virtuous work which we perform, and we think we have acquired it by our labours. We are quite right to feel satisfaction[79] at having worked in such a way. But, when we come to think of it, the same satisfaction[80] can be derived from numerous things that may happen to us here on earth. When, for example, a person suddenly acquires some valuable property; or equally suddenly meets a person whom he dearly loves; or brings some important piece of business or some other weighty matter to a successful conclusion, so that everyone speaks well of him; or when a woman has been told that her husband or brother or son is dead and he comes back to her alive. I have seen people shed tears over some great joy[81]; sometimes, in fact, I have done so myself.

It seems to me that the feelings[82] which come to us from Divine things are as purely natural as these, except that their source is nobler, although these worldly joys are in no way bad. To put it briefly, worldly joys have their source in our own nature and end in God, whereas spiritual consolations have their source in God, but we experience them in a natural way and enjoy them as much as we enjoy those I have already mentioned, and indeed much more. Oh, Jesus! How I wish I could make myself clear about this! For I think I can see a very marked difference between these two things and yet I am not clever enough to make my meaning plain: may the Lord explain it for me!

I have just remembered a verse which we say at the end of the last psalm at Prime. The last words of the verse are Cum dilatasti cor meum.83 To anyone who has much experience, this will suffice to explain the difference between the two; though, to anyone who has not, further explanation is necessary. The spiritual sweetness which has been described does not enlarge the heart; as a rule, it seems to oppress it somewhat. The soul experiences a great happiness[84] when it realizes what it is doing for God's sake; but it sheds a few bitter tears which seem in some way to be the result of passion[85]. I know little about these passions of the soul; if I knew more, perhaps I could make the thing clear, and explain what proceeds from sensuality and what from our own nature. But I am very stupid; I could explain this state if only I could understand my own experience of it. Knowledge and learning are a great help in everything.

My own experience of this state — I mean of these favours and this sweetness in meditation — was that, if I began to weep over the Passion, I could not stop until I had a splitting headache; and the same thing happened when I wept for my sins. This was a great grace granted me by Our Lord, and I will not for the moment examine each of these favours and decide which is the better of the two; I wish, however, that I could explain the difference between them. In the state I am now describing, the tears and longings sometimes arise partly from our nature and from the state of preparedness we are in;[86] but nevertheless, as I have said, they eventually lead one to God. And this is an experience to be greatly prized, provided the soul be humble, and can understand that it does not make it any the more virtuous; for it is impossible to be sure that these feelings are effects of love, and, even so, they are a gift of God. Most of the souls which dwell in the Mansions already described are familiar with these feelings of devotion, for they labour with the understanding almost continuously, and make use of it in their meditations. They are right to do this, because nothing more has been given them; they would do well, however, to spend short periods in making various acts, and in praising God and rejoicing in His goodness and in His being Who He is, and in desiring His honour and glory. They should do this as well as they can, for it goes a long way towards awakening the will. But, when the Lord gives them this other grace, let them be very careful not to reject it for the sake of finishing their customary meditation.

As I have written about this at great length elsewhere,[87] I will not repeat it here. I only want you to be warned that, if you would progress a long way on this road and ascend to the Mansions of your desire, the important thing is not to think much, but to love much; do, then, whatever most arouses you to love. Perhaps we do not know what love is: it would not surprise me a great deal to learn this, for love consists, not in the extent of our happiness, but in the firmness of our determination to try to please God in everything, and to endeavour, in all possible ways, not to offend Him, and to pray Him ever to advance the honour and glory of His Son and the growth of the Catholic Church. Those are the signs of love; do not imagine that the important thing is never to be thinking of anything else and that if your mind becomes slightly distracted all is lost.

I have sometimes been terribly oppressed by this turmoil of thoughts and it is only just over four years ago that I came to understand by experience that thought (or, to put it more clearly, imagination[88]) is not the same thing as understanding. I asked a learned man about this and he said I was right, which gave me no small satisfaction. For, as the understanding is one of the faculties of the soul, I found it very hard to see why it was sometimes so timid[89]; whereas thoughts, as a rule, fly so fast that only God can restrain them; which He does by uniting us in such a way that we seem in some sense to be loosed from this body.[90] It exasperated me[91] to see the faculties of the soul, as I thought, occupied with God and recollected in Him, and the thought, on the other hand, confused and excited.

O Lord, do Thou remember how much we have to suffer on this road through lack of knowledge! The worst of it is that, as we do not realize we need to know more when we think about Thee, we cannot ask those who know; indeed we have not even any idea what there is for us to ask them. So we suffer terrible trials because we do not understand ourselves; and we worry over what is not bad at all, but good, and think it very wrong. Hence proceed the afflictions of many people who practise prayer, and their complaints of interior trials — especially if they are unlearned people — so that they become melancholy, and their health declines, and they even abandon prayer altogether, because they fail to realize that there is an interior world close at hand. Just as we cannot stop the movement of the heavens, revolving as they do with such speed, so we cannot restrain our thought. And then we send all the faculties of the soul after it, thinking we are lost, and have misused the time that we are spending in the presence of God. Yet the soul may perhaps be wholly united with Him in the Mansions very near His presence, while thought remains in the outskirts of the castle, suffering the assaults of a thousand wild and venomous creatures and from this suffering winning merit. So this must not upset us, and we must not abandon the struggle, as the devil tries to make us do. Most of these trials and times of unrest come from the fact that we do not understand ourselves.

As I write this, the noises in my head are so loud that I am beginning to wonder what is going on in it.[92] As I said at the outset, they have been making it almost impossible for me to obey those who commanded me to write. My head sounds just as if it were full of brimming rivers, and then as if all the water in those rivers came suddenly rushing downward; and a host of little birds seem to be whistling, not in the ears, but in the upper part of the head, where the higher part of the soul is said to be; I have held this view for a long time, for the spirit seems to move upward with great velocity. Please God I may remember to explain the cause of this when I am writing of the later Mansions: here it does not fit in well. I should not be surprised to know that the Lord has been pleased to send me this trouble in my head so that I may understand it better, for all this physical turmoil is no hindrance either to my prayer or to what I am saying now, but the tranquillity and love in my soul are quite unaffected, and so are its desires and clearness of mind.

But if the higher part of the soul is in the upper part of the head, how is it that it experiences no disturbance? That I do not know, but I do know that what I say is true. I suffer when my prayer is not accompanied by suspension of the faculties, but, when the faculties are suspended, I feel no pain until the suspension is over; it would be a terrible thing if this obstacle forced me to give up praying altogether. It is not good for us to be disturbed by our thoughts or to worry about them in the slightest; for if we do not worry and if the devil is responsible for them they will cease, and if they proceed, as they do, from the weakness which we inherit from the sin of Adam, and from many other weaknesses, let us have patience and bear everything for the love of God. Similarly we are obliged to eat and sleep, and we cannot escape from these obligations, though they are a great burden to us.

Let us recognize our weakness in these respects and desire to go where nobody will despise us. I sometimes recall words I have heard, spoken by the Bride in the Canticles,[93] and really I believe there is no point in our lives at which they can more properly be used, for I do not think that all the scorn and all the trials which we may have to suffer in this life can equal these interior battles. Any unrest and any strife can be borne, as I have already said, if we find peace where we live; but if we would have rest from the thousand trials which afflict us in the world and the Lord is pleased to prepare such rest for us, and yet the cause of the trouble is in ourselves, the result cannot but be very painful, indeed almost unbearable. For this causes Lord, do Thou take us to a place where these weaknesses, which sometimes seem to be making sport of the soul, do not cause us to be despised. Even in this life the Lord will free the soul from this, when it has reached the last Mansion, as, if it please God, we shall explain.

These weaknesses will not give everyone so much trouble, or assail everyone as violently, as for many years they troubled and assailed me. For I was a wicked person and it seemed as though I were trying to take vengeance on myself. As it has been such a troublesome thing for me, it may perhaps be so for you as well, so I am just going to describe it, first in one way and then in another, hoping that I may succeed in making you realize how necessary it is, so that you may not grow restless and distressed. The clacking old mill must keep on going round and we must grind our own flour: neither the will nor the understanding must cease working.

This trouble will sometimes be worse, and sometimes better, according to our health and according to the times and seasons. The poor soul may not be to blame for this, but it must suffer none the less, for, as we shall commit other faults, it is only right that we should have patience. And as we are so ignorant that what we read and are advised — namely, that we should take no account of these thoughts — is not sufficient to teach us, it does not seem to me a waste of time if I go into it farther and offer you some consolation about it; though this will be of little help to you until the Lord is pleased to give us light. But it is necessary (and His Majesty's will) that we should take proper measures and learn to understand ourselves, and not blame our souls for what is the work of our weak imagination and our nature and the devil.

Chapter 11

Continues the same subject and explains by a comparison what is meant by consolations and how we must obtain them without striving to do so.

God help me in this task which I have embarked upon.[94] I had quite forgotten what I was writing about, for business matters and ill-health forced me to postpone continuing it until a more suitable time, and, as I have a poor memory, it will all be very much confused, for I cannot read it through again. It may even be that everything I say is confused; that, at least, is what I am afraid of. I think I was talking about spiritual consolations and explaining how they are sometimes bound up with our passions. They often cause fits of sobbing; I have heard, indeed, that some persons find they produce constrictions of the chest and even exterior movements, which cannot be controlled, and which are violent enough to make blood gush from the nose and produce similar disconcerting symptoms. About this I can say nothing, for I have not experienced it, but there must be some cause for comfort in it, for, as I say, it all leads to a desire to please God and to have fruition of His Majesty.

What I call consolations from God, and elsewhere have termed the Prayer of Quiet, is something of a very different kind, as those of you will know who by the mercy of God have experienced it. To understand it better, let us suppose that we are looking at two fountains, the basins of which can be filled with water. There are certain spiritual things which I can find no way of explaining more aptly than by this element of water; for, as I am very ignorant, and my wits give me no help, and I am so fond of this element, I have observed it more attentively than anything else. In all the things that have been created by so great and wise a God there must be many secrets by which we can profit, and those who understand them do profit by them, although I believe that in every little thing created by God there is more than we realize, even in so small a thing as a tiny ant.

These two large basins can be filled with water in different ways: the water in the one comes from a long distance, by means of numerous conduits and through human skill; but the other has been constructed at the very source of the water and fills without making any noise. If the flow of water is abundant, as in the case we are speaking of, a great stream still runs from it after it has been filled; no skill is necessary here, and no conduits have to be made, for the water is flowing all the time. The difference between this and the carrying of the water by means of conduits is, I think, as follows. The latter corresponds to the spiritual sweetness which, as I say, is produced by meditation. It reaches us by way of the thoughts; we meditate upon created things and fatigue the understanding; and when at last, by means of our own efforts, it comes, the satisfaction which it brings to the soul fills the basin, but in doing so makes a noise, as I have said.

To the other fountain the water comes direct from its source, which is God, and, when it is His Majesty's will and He is pleased to grant us some supernatural favour, its coming is accompanied by the greatest peace and quietness and sweetness within ourselves — I cannot say where it arises or how. And that content and delight are not felt, as earthly delights are felt, in the heart — I mean not at the outset, for later the basin becomes completely filled, and then this water begins to overflow all the Mansions and faculties, until it reaches the body. It is for that reason that I said it has its source in God and ends in ourselves — for it is certain, and anyone will know this who has experienced it, that the whole of the outer man enjoys this consolation and sweetness.

I was thinking just now, as I wrote this, that a verse which I have already quoted, Dilatasti cor meum,95 speaks of the heart's being enlarged. I do not think that this happiness has its source in the heart at all. It arises in a much more interior part, like something of which the springs are very deep; I think this must be the centre of the soul, as I have since realized and as I will explain hereafter. I certainly find secret things in ourselves which often amaze me — and how many more there must be! O my Lord and my God! How wondrous is Thy greatness! And we creatures go about like silly little shepherd-boys, thinking we are learning to know something of Thee when the very most we can know amounts to nothing at all, for even in ourselves there are deep secrets which we cannot fathom. When I say "amounts to nothing at all" I mean because Thou art so surpassingly great, not because the signs of greatness that we see in Thy works are not very wonderful, even considering how very little we can learn to know of them.

Returning to this verse, what it says about the enlargement of the heart may, I think, be of some help to us. For apparently, as this heavenly water begins to flow from this source of which I am speaking — that is, from our very depths — it proceeds to spread within us and cause an interior dilation and produce ineffable blessings, so that the soul itself cannot understand all that it receives there. The fragrance it experiences, we might say, is as if in those interior depths there were a brazier on which were cast sweet perfumes; the light cannot be seen, nor the place where it dwells, but the fragrant smoke and the heat penetrate the entire soul, and very often, as I have said, the effects extend even to the body. Observe — and understand me here — that no heat is felt, nor is any fragrance perceived: it is a more delicate thing than that; I only put it in that way so that you may understand it. People who have not experienced it must realize that it does in very truth happen; its occurrence is capable of being perceived, and the soul becomes aware of it more clearly than these words of mine can express it. For it is not a thing that we can fancy, nor, however hard we strive, can we acquire it, and from that very fact it is clear that it is a thing made, not of human metal, but of the purest gold of Divine wisdom. In this state the faculties are not, I think, in union, but they become absorbed and are amazed as they consider what is happening to them.

It may be that in writing of these interior things I am contradicting what I have myself said elsewhere. This is not surprising, for almost fifteen years have passed since then,96 and perhaps the Lord has now given me a clearer realization of these matters than I had at first. Both then and now, of course, I may be mistaken in all this, but I cannot lie about it: by the mercy of God I would rather die a thousand deaths: I am speaking of it just as I understand it.

The will certainly seems to me to be united in some way with the will of God; but it is by the effects of this prayer and the actions which follow it that the genuineness of the experience must be tested and there is no better crucible for doing so than this. If the person who receives such a grace recognizes it for what it is, Our Lord is granting him a surpassingly great favour, and another very great one if he does not turn back. You will desire, then, my daughters, to strive to attain this way of prayer, and you will be right to do so, for, is I have said, the soul cannot fully understand the favours which the Lord grants it there or the love which draws it ever nearer to Himself, it is certainly desirable that we should know how to obtain this favour. I will tell you what I have found out about it.

We may leave out of account occasions when the Lord is pleased to grant these favours for no other reason than because His Majesty so wills. He knows why He does it and it is not for us to interfere. As well as acting, then, as do those who have dwelt in the Mansions already described, have humility and again humility! It is by humility that the Lord allows Himself to be conquered so that He will do all we ask of Him, and the first way in which you will see if you have humility is that if you have it you will not think you merit these favours and consolations of the Lord or are likely to get them for as long as you live. "But how," you will ask, "are we to gain them if we do not strive after them?" I reply that there is no better way than this one which I have described. There are several reasons why they should not be striven for. The first is because the most essential thing is that we should love God without any motive of self-interest. The second is because there is some lack of humility in our thinking that in return for our miserable services we can obtain anything so great. The third is because the true preparation for receiving these gifts is a desire to suffer and to imitate the Lord, not to receive consolations; for, after all, we have often offended Him. The fourth reason is because His Majesty is not obliged to grant them to us, as He is obliged to grant us glory if we keep His commandments, without doing which we could not be saved, and He knows better than we what is good for us and which of us truly love Him. That is certain truth, as I know; and I also know people who walk along the road of love, solely, as they should, in order to serve Christ crucified, and not only do they neither ask for consolations nor desire them, but they beg Him not to give them to them in this life. The fifth reason is that we should be labouring in vain; for this water does not flow through conduits, as the other does, and so we gain nothing by fatiguing ourselves if it cannot be had at the source. I mean that, however much we may practise meditation, however much we do violence to ourselves,[97] and however many tears we shed, we cannot produce this water in those ways; it is given only to whom God wills to give it and often when the soul is not thinking of it at all.

We are His, sisters; may He do with us as He will and lead us along whatever way He pleases. I am sure that if any of us achieve true humility and detachment (I say "true" because it must not be in thought alone, for thoughts often deceive us; it must be total detachment) the Lord will not fail to grant us this favour, and many others which we shall not even know how to desire. May He be for ever praised and blessed. Amen.

Chapter III

Describes what is meant by the Prayer of Recollection, which the Lord generally grants before that already mentioned. Speaks of its effects and of the remaining effects of the former kind of prayer, which had to do with the consolations given by the Lord.

The effects of this kind of prayer are numerous; some of them I shall explain. First of all, I will say something (though not much, as I have dealt with it elsewhere)[98] about another kind of prayer, which almost invariably begins before this one. It is a form of recollection which also seems to me supernatural for it does not involve remaining in the dark, or closing the eyes, nor is it dependent upon anything exterior. A person involuntarily closes his eyes and desires solitude; and, without the display of any human skill there seems gradually to be built for him a temple in which he can make the prayer already described; the senses and all external things seem gradually to lose their hold on him, while the soul, on the other hand, regains its lost control.

It is sometimes said that the soul enters within itself and sometimes that it rises above itself;[99] but I cannot explain things in that kind of language, for I have no skill in it. However, I believe you will understand what I am able to tell you, though I may perhaps be intelligible only to myself. Let us suppose that these senses and faculties (the inhabitants, as I have said, of this castle, which is the figure that I have taken to explain my meaning) have gone out of the castle, and, for days and years, have been consorting with strangers, to whom all the good things in the castle are abhorrent. Then, realizing how much they have lost, they come back to it, though they do not actually re-enter it, because the habits they have formed are hard to conquer. But they are no longer traitors and they now walk about in the vicinity of the castle. The great King, Who dwells in the Mansion within this castle, perceives their good will, and in His great mercy desires to bring them back to Him. So, like a good Shepherd, with a call so gentle that even they can hardly recognize it, He teaches them to know His voice and not to go away and get lost but to return to their Mansion; and so powerful is this Shepherd's call that they give up the things outside the castle which had led them astray, and once again enter it.

I do not think I have ever explained this before as clearly as here. When we are seeking God within ourselves (where He is found more effectively and more profitably than in the creatures, to quote Saint Augustine, who, after having sought Him in many places, found Him within)[100] it is a great help if God grants us this favour. Do not suppose that the understanding can attain to Him, merely by trying to think of Him as within the soul, or the imagination, by picturing Him as there. This is a good habit and an excellent kind of meditation, for it is founded upon a truth — namely, that God is within us. But it is not the kind of prayer that I have in mind, for anyone (with the help of the Lord, you understand) can practise it for himself. What I am describing is quite different. These people are sometimes in the castle before they have begun to think about God at all. I cannot say where they entered it or how they heard their Shepherd's call: it was certainly not with their ears, for outwardly such a call is not audible. They become markedly conscious that they are gradually retiring[101] within themselves; anyone who experiences this will discover what I mean: I cannot explain it better. I think I have read that they are like a hedgehog or a tortoise withdrawing into itself[102]; and whoever wrote that must have understood it well. These creatures, however, enter within themselves whenever they like; whereas with us it is not a question of our will — it happens only when God is pleased to grant us this favour. For my own part, I believe that, when His Majesty grants it, He does so to people who are already leaving the things of the world. I do not mean that people who are married must actually leave the world — they can do so only in desire: His call to them is a special one and aims at making them intent upon interior things. I believe, however, that if we wish to give His Majesty free course, He will grant more than this to those whom He is beginning to call still higher.

Anyone who is conscious that this is happening within himself should give God great praise, for he will be very right to recognize what a favour it is; and the thanksgiving which he makes for it will prepare him for greater favours. One preparation for listening to Him, as certain books tell us, is that we should contrive, not to use our reasoning powers, but to be intent upon discovering what the Lord is working in the soul; for, if His Majesty has not begun to grant us absorption, I cannot understand how we can cease thinking in any way which will not bring us more harm than profit, although this has been a matter of continual discussion among spiritual persons. For my own part, I confess my lack of humility, but their arguments have never seemed to me good enough to lead me to accept what they say. One person told me of a certain book by the saintly Fray Peter of Alcántara (for a saint I believe he is), which would certainly have convinced me, for I know how much he knew about such things; but we read it together, and found that he says exactly what I say, although not in the same words; it is quite clear from what he says that love must already be awake.[103] It is possible that I am mistaken, but I base my position on the following reasons.

First, in such spiritual activity as this, the person who does most is he who thinks least and desires to do least:[104] what we have to do is to beg like poor and needy persons coming before a great and rich Emperor and then cast down our eyes in humble expectation. When from the secret signs He gives us we seem to realize that He is hearing us, it is well for us to keep silence, since He has permitted us to be near Him and there will be no harm in our striving not to labour with the understanding — provided, I mean, that we are able to do so. But if we are not quite sure that the King has heard us, or sees us, we must not stay where we are like ninnies, for there still remains a great deal for the soul to do when it has stilled the understanding; if it did nothing more it would experience much greater aridity and the imagination would grow more restless because of the effort caused it by cessation from thought. The Lord wishes us rather to make requests of Him and to remember that we are in His presence, for He knows what is fitting for us. I cannot believe in the efficacy of human activity in matters where His Majesty appears to have set a limit to it and to have been pleased to reserve action to Himself. There are many other things in which He has not so reserved it, such as penances, works of charity and prayers; these, with His aid, we can practise for ourselves, as far as our miserable nature is capable of them.

The second reason is that all these interior activities are gentle and peaceful, and to do anything painful brings us harm rather than help. By "anything painful" I mean anything that we try to force ourselves to do; it would be painful, for example, to hold our breath. The soul must just leave itself in the hands of God, and do what He wills it to do, completely disregarding its own advantage and resigning itself as much as it possibly can to the will of God. The third reason is that the very effort which the soul makes in order to cease from thought will perhaps awaken thought and cause it to think a great deal. The fourth reason is that the most important and pleasing thing in God's eyes is our remembering His honour and glory and forgetting ourselves and our own profit and ease and pleasure. And how can a person be forgetful of himself when he is taking such great care about his actions that he dare not even stir, or allow his understanding and desires to stir, even for the purpose of desiring the greater glory of God or of rejoicing in the glory which is His? When His Majesty wishes the working of the understanding to cease, He employs it in another manner, and illumines the soul's knowledge to so much higher a degree than any we can ourselves attain that He leads it into a state of absorption, in which, without knowing how, it is much better instructed than it could ever be as a result of its own efforts, which would only spoil everything. God gave us our faculties to work with, and everything will have its due reward; there is no reason, then, for trying to cast a spell over them — they must be allowed to perform their office until God gives them a better one.

As I understand it, the soul whom the Lord has been pleased to lead into this Mansion will do best to act as I have said. Let it try, without forcing itself or causing any turmoil, to put a stop to all discursive reasoning, yet not to suspend the understanding, nor to cease from all thought, though it is well for it to remember that it is in God's presence and Who this God is. If feeling this should lead it into a state of absorption, well and good; but it should not try to understand what this state is, because that is a gift bestowed upon the will. The will, then, should be left to enjoy it, and should not labour except for uttering a few loving words, for although in such a case one may not be striving to cease from thought, such cessation often comes, though for a very short time.

I have explained elsewhere[105] the reason why this occurs in this kind of prayer (I am referring to the kind which I began to explain in this Mansion). With it I have included this Prayer of Recollection which ought to have been described first, for it comes far below the consolations of God already mentioned, and is indeed the first step towards attaining them. For in the Prayer of Recollection it is unnecessary to abandon meditation and the activities of the understanding. When, instead of coming through conduits, the water springs directly from its source, the understanding checks its activity, or rather the activity is checked for it when it finds it cannot understand what it desires, and thus it roams about all over the place, like a demented creature, and can settle down to nothing. The will is fixed so firmly upon its God that this disturbed condition of the understanding causes it great distress; but it must not take any notice of this, for if it does so it will lose a great part of what it is enjoying; it must forget about it, and abandon itself into the arms of love, and His Majesty will teach it what to do next; almost its whole work is to realize its unworthiness to receive such great good and to occupy itself in thanksgiving.

In order to discuss[106] the Prayer of Recollection I passed over the effects or signs to be observed in souls to whom this prayer is granted by God Our Lord. It is clear that a dilation or enlargement of the soul takes place, as if the water proceeding from the spring had no means of running away, but the fountain had a device ensuring that, the more freely the water flowed, the larger became the basin. So it is in this kind of prayer, and God works many more wonders in the soul, thus fitting and gradually disposing it to retain all that He gives it. So this gentle movement and this interior dilation cause the soul to be less constrained in matters relating to the service of God than it was before and give it much more freedom. It is not oppressed, for example, by the fear of hell, for, though it desires more than ever not to offend God (of Whom, however, it has lost all servile fear), it has firm confidence that it is destined to have fruition of Him. A person who used to be afraid of doing penance lest he should ruin his health now believes that in God he can do everything, and has more desire to do such things than he had previously. The fear of trials that he was wont to have is now largely assuaged, because he has a more lively faith, and realizes that, if he endures these trials for God's sake, His Majesty will give him grace to bear them patiently, and sometimes even to desire them, because he also cherishes a great desire to do something for God. The better he gets to know the greatness of God, the better he comes to realize the misery of his own condition; having now tasted the consolations of God, he sees that earthly things are mere refuse; so, little by little, he withdraws from them and in this way becomes more and more his own master. In short, he finds himself strengthened in all the virtues and will infallibly continue to increase in them unless he turns back and commits offenses against God — when that happens, everything is lost, however far a man may have climbed towards the crest of the mountain. It must not be understood, however, that all these things take place because once or twice God has granted a soul this favour; it must continue receiving them, for it is from their continuance that all our good proceeds.

There is one earnest warning which I must give those who find themselves in this state: namely, that they exert the very greatest care to keep themselves from occasions of offending God. For as yet the soul is not even weaned but is like a child beginning to suck the breast. If it be taken from its mother, what can it be expected to do but die? That, I am very much afraid, will be the lot of anyone to whom God has granted this favour if he gives up prayer; unless he does so for some very exceptional reason, or unless he returns to it quickly, he will go from bad to worse. I am aware how much ground there is for fear about this and I have been very much grieved by certain people I know, in whom I have seen what I am describing; they have left Him Who in His great love was yearning to give Himself to them as a Friend, and to prove His friendship by His works. I earnestly warn such people not to enter upon occasions of sin, because the devil sets much more store by one soul in this state than by a great number of souls to whom the Lord does not grant these favours. For those in this state attract others, and so they can do the devil great harm and may well bring great advantage to the Church of God. He may see nothing else in them except that His Majesty is showing them especial love, but this is quite sufficient to make him do his utmost to bring about their perdition. The conflict, then, is sterner for such souls than for others and if they are lost their fate is less remediable. You, sisters, so far as we know, are free from these perils. May God free you from pride and vainglory and grant that the devil may not counterfeit these favours. Such counterfeits, however, will be recognizable because they will not produce these effects, but quite contrary ones.

There is one peril of which I want to warn you, though I have spoken of it elsewhere; I have seen persons given to prayer fall into it, and especially women, for, as we are weaker than men, we run more risk of what I am going to describe. It is this: some women, because of prayers, vigils and severe penances, and also for other reasons, have poor health. When they experience any spiritual consolation, therefore, their physical nature is too much for them; and as soon as they feel any interior joy there comes over them a physical weakness and languor, and they fall into a sleep, which they call "spiritual", and which is a little more marked than the condition that has been described. Thinking the one state to be the same as the other, they abandon themselves to this absorption; and the more they relax, the more complete becomes this absorption, because their physical nature continues to grow weaker. So they get it into their heads that it is arrobamiento, or rapture. But I call it abobamiento, foolishness;[107] for they are doing nothing but wasting their time at it and ruining their health.

One person was in this state for eight hours; she was not unconscious, nor was she conscious of anything concerning God. She was cured by being told to take more food and sleep and to do less penance; for, though she had misled both her confessor and other people and, quite involuntarily, deceived herself, there was one person who understood her. I believe the devil would go to any pains to gain such people as that and he was beginning to make good progress with this one.

It must be understood that although, when this state is something that really comes from God, there may be languor, both interior and exterior, there will be none in the soul, which, when it finds itself near God, is moved with great joy. The experience does not last long, but only for a little while. Although the soul may become absorbed again, yet this kind of prayer, as I have said, except in cases of physical weakness, does not go so far as to overcome the body or to produce in it any exterior sensation. Be advised, then, and, if you experience anything of this kind, tell your superior, and relax as much as you can. The superior should give such persons fewer hours of prayer — very few, indeed — and should see that they sleep and eat well, until their physical strength, if it has become exhausted, comes back again. If their constitution is so weak that this does not suffice, they can be certain that God is not calling them to anything beyond the active life. There is room in convents for people of all kinds; let anyone of this type, then, be kept busy with duties, and let care be taken that she is not left alone very much, or her health will be completely ruined. This sort of life will be a great mortification to her, but it is here that the Lord wishes to test her love for Him by seeing how she bears His absence and after a while He may well be pleased to restore her strength; if He is not, her vocal prayer and her obedience will bring her as much benefit and merit as she would have obtained in other ways, and perhaps more.

There may also be some who are so weak in intellect and imagination — I have known such — that they believe they actually see all they imagine. This is highly dangerous and perhaps we shall treat of it later, but no more shall be said here; for I have written at great length of this Mansion, as it is the one which the greatest number of souls enter. As the natural is united with the supernatural in it, it is here that the devil can do most harm; for in the Mansions of which I have not yet spoken the Lord gives him fewer opportunities. May He be for ever praised. Amen.

Fifth Mansions:
In which there are Four Chapters

Chapter 1

Begins to explain how in prayer the soul is united with God. Describes how we may know that we are not mistaken about this.

Oh, sisters! How shall I ever be able to tell you of the riches and the treasures and the delights which are to be found in the fifth Mansions? I think it would be better if I were to say nothing of the Mansions I have not yet treated, for no one can describe them, the understanding is unable to comprehend them and no comparisons will avail to explain them, for earthly things are quite insufficient for this purpose. Send me light from Heaven, my Lord, that I may enlighten these Thy servants, to some of whom Thou art often pleased to grant fruition of these joys, lest, when the devil transfigures himself into an angel of light, he should deceive them, for all their desires are occupied in desiring to please Thee.

Although I said "to some", there are really very few who do not enter these Mansions that I am about to describe. Some get farther than others; but, as I say, the majority manage to get inside. Some of the things which are in this room, and which I will mention here, are, I am sure, attained by very few;[108] but, if they do no more than reach the door, God is showing them great mercy by granting them this; for, though many are called, few are chosen.[109] So I must say here that, though all of us who wear this sacred habit of Carmel are[110] called to prayer and contemplation — because that was the first principle of our Order and because we are descendent upon the line of those holy Fathers of ours from Mount Carmel who sought this treasure, this precious pearl of which we speak, in such great solitude and with such contempt for the world — few of us[111] prepare ourselves for the Lord to reveal it to us. As far as externals are concerned, we are on the right road to attaining the essential virtues; but we shall need to do a very great deal before we can attain to this higher state and we must on no account be careless. So let us pause here, my sisters, and beg the Lord that, since to some extent it is possible for us to enjoy Heaven upon earth, He will grant us His help so that it will not be our fault if we miss anything may He also show us the road and give strength to our souls so that we may dig until we find this hidden treasure, since it is quite true that we have it within ourselves. This I should like to explain if the Lord is pleased to give me the knowledge.

I said "strength to our souls", because you must understand that we do not need bodily strength if God our Lord does not give it us; there is no one for whom He makes it impossible to buy His riches; provided each gives what he has, He is content. Blessed be so great a God! But observe, daughters, that, if you are to gain this, He would have you keep back nothing; whether it be little or much, He will have it all for Himself, and according to what you know yourself to have given, the favours He will grant you will be small or great. There is no better test than this of whether or no our prayer attains to union. Do not think it is a state, like the last, in which we dream; I say "dream", because the soul seems to be, as it were, drowsy, so that it neither seems asleep nor feels awake. Here we are all asleep, and fast asleep, to the things of the world, and to ourselves (in fact, for the short time that the condition lasts, the soul is without consciousness and has no power to think, even though it may desire to do so). There is no need now for it to devise any method of suspending the thought. Even in loving, if it is able to love, it cannot understand how or what it is that it loves, nor what it would desire; in fact, it has completely died to the world so that it may live more fully in God. This is a delectable death, a snatching of the soul from all the activities which it can perform while it is in the body; a death full of delight, for, in order to come closer to God, the soul appears to have withdrawn so far from the body that I do not know if it has still life enough to be able to breathe.[112] I have just been thinking about this and I believe it has not; or at least, if it still breathes, it does so without realizing it. The mind would like to occupy itself wholly in understanding something of what it feels, and, as it has not the strength to do this, it becomes so dumbfounded that, even if any consciousness remains to it, neither hands nor feet can move; as we commonly say of a person who has fallen into a swoon, it might be taken for dead. Oh, the secrets of God! I should never weary of trying to describe them to you, if I thought I could do so successfully. I do not mind if I write any amount of nonsense, provided that just once in a way I can write sense, so that we may give great praise to the Lord.

I said that there was no question here of dreaming, whereas as in the Mansion that I have just described the soul is doubtful as to what has really happened until it has had a good deal of experience of it. It wonders if the whole thing was imagination, if it has been asleep, if the favour was a gift of God, or if the devil was transfigured into an angel of light. It retains a thousand suspicions, and it is well that it should, for, as I said, we can sometimes be deceived in this respect, even by our own nature. For, although there is less opportunity for the poisonous creatures to enter, a few little lizards, being very agile, can hide themselves all over the place; and, although they do no harm — especially, as I said, if we take no notice of them — they correspond to the little thoughts which proceed from the imagination and from what has been said it will be seen that they are often very troublesome. Agile though they are, however, the lizards cannot enter this Mansion, for neither imagination nor memory nor understanding can be an obstacle to the blessings that are bestowed in it. And I shall venture to affirm that, if this is indeed union with God,[113] the devil cannot enter or do any harm; for His Majesty is in such close contact and union with the essence of the soul[114] that he will not dare to approach, nor can he even understand this secret thing. That much is evident: for it is said that he does not understand our thoughts;[115] still less, therefore, will he understand a thing so secret that God will not even entrust our thoughts with it.[116] Oh, what a great blessing is this state in which that accursed one can do us no harm! Great are the gains which come to the soul with God working in it and neither we ourselves nor anyone else hindering Him. What will He not give Who so much loves giving and can give all that He will?

I fear I may be leaving you confused by saying "if this is indeed union with God" and suggesting that there are other kinds of union. But of course there are! If we are really very fond of vanities the devil will send us into transports over them; but these are not like the transports of God, nor is there the same delight and satisfaction for the soul or the same peace and joy. That joy is greater than all the joys of earth, and greater than all its delights, and all its satisfactions, so that there is no evidence that these satisfactions and those of the earth have a common origin; and they are apprehended, too, very differently, as you will have learned by experience. I said once*117* that it is as if the one kind had to do with the grosser part of the body, and the other kind penetrated to the very marrow of the bones; that puts it well, and I know no better way of expressing it.

But I fancy that even now you will not be satisfied, for you will think that you may be mistaken, and that these interior matters are difficult to investigate. In reality, what has been said will be sufficient for anyone who has experienced this blessing, for there is a great difference between the false and the true. But I will give you a clear indication which will make it impossible for you to go wrong or to doubt if some favour has come from God; His Majesty has put it into my mind only to-day, and I think it is quite decisive. In difficult matters, even if I believe I understand what I am saying and am speaking the truth, I use this phrase "I think", because, if I am mistaken, I am very ready to give credence to those who have great learning. For even if they have not themselves experienced these things, men of great learning have a certain instinct[118] to prompt them. As God uses them to give light to His Church, He reveals to them anything which is true so that it shall be accepted; and if they do not squander their talents, but are true servants of God, they will never be surprised at His greatness, for they know quite well that He is capable of working more and still more. In any case, where matters are in question for which there is no explanation, there must be others about which they can read, and they can deduce from their reading that it is possible for these first-named to have happened.

Of this I have the fullest experience; and I have also experience of timid, half-learned men whose shortcomings have cost me very dear. At any rate, my own opinion is that anyone who does not believe that God can do much more than this, and that He has been pleased, and is sometimes still pleased, to grant His creatures such favours, has closed the door fast against receiving them. Therefore, sisters, let this never be true of you, but trust God more and more, and do not consider whether those to whom He communicates His favours are bad or good. His Majesty knows all about this, as I have said; intervention on our part is quite unnecessary; rather must we serve His Majesty with humility and simplicity of heart, and praise Him for His works and wonders.

Turning now to the indication which I have described as[119] a decisive one: here is this soul which God has made, as it were, completely foolish in order the better to impress upon it true wisdom. For as long as such a soul is in this state, it can neither see nor hear nor understand: the period is always short and seems to the soul even shorter than it really is. God implants Himself in the interior of that soul in such a way that, when it returns to itself, it cannot[120] possibly doubt that God has been in it and it has been in God; so firmly does this truth remain within it that, although for years God may never grant it that favour again, it can neither forget it nor doubt that it has received it (and this quite apart from the effects which remain within it, and of which I will speak later). This certainty of the soul is very material.

But now you will say to me: How did the soul see it and understand it if it can neither see nor understand? I am not saying that it saw it at the time,[121] but that it sees it clearly afterwards, and not because it is a vision, but because of a certainty which remains in the soul, which can be put there only by God. I know of a person who had not learned that God was in all things by presence and power and essence; God granted her a favour of this kind, which convinced her of this so firmly[122] that, although one of those half-learned men whom I have been talking about, and whom she asked in what way God was in us (until God granted him an understanding of it he knew as little of it as she), told her that He was in us only by grace, she had the truth so firmly implanted within her that she did not believe him, and asked others, who told her the truth, which was a great consolation to her.[123]

Do not make the mistake of thinking that this certainty has anything to do with bodily form — with the presence of Our Lord Jesus Christ, for example, unseen by us, in the Most Holy Sacrament. It has nothing to do with this — only with His Divinity. How, you will ask, can we become so convinced of what we have not seen? That I do not know, it is the work of God. But I know I am speaking the truth; and if anyone has not that certainty, I should say that what he has experienced is not union of the whole soul with God but only union of one of the faculties or some one of the many other kinds of favour which God grants the soul. In all these matters we must stop looking for reasons why they happened; if our understanding cannot grasp them, why should we try to perplex it? It suffices us to know that He Who brings this to pass is all-powerful,[124] and as it is God Who does it and we, however hard we work, are quite incapable of achieving it, let us not try to become capable of understanding it either.

With regard to what I have just said about our incapability, I recall that, as you have heard, the Bride in the Songs says: "The King brought me" (or "put me", I think the words are) "into the cellar of wine."[125] It does not say that she went. It also says that she was wandering about in all directions seeking her Beloved.[126] This, as I understand it, is the cellar where the Lord is pleased to put us, when He wills and as He wills. But we cannot enter by any efforts of our own; His Majesty must put us right into the centre[127] of our soul, and must enter there Himself; and, in order that He may the better show us His wonders, it is His pleasure that our will, which has entirely surrendered itself to Him, should have no part in this. Nor does He desire the door of the faculties and senses, which are all asleep, to be opened to Him; He will come into the centre of the soul without using a door, as He did when He came in to His disciples, and said Pax vobis,128 and when He left the sepulchre without removing the stone. Later on you will see how it is His Majesty's will that the soul should have fruition of Him in its very centre, but you will be able to realize that in the last Mansion much better than here.

Oh, daughters, what a lot we shall see if we desire to see no more than our own baseness and wretchedness and to understand that we are not worthy to be the handmaidens of so great a Lord, since we cannot comprehend His marvels. May He be for ever praised. Amen.

Chapter II

Continues the same subject. Explains the Prayer of Union by a delicate comparison. Describes the effects which it produces in the soul. Should be studied with great care.

You will suppose that all there is to be seen in this Mansion has been described already, but there is much more to come yet, for, as I said, some receive more and some less. With regard to the nature of union, I do not think I can say any thing further; but when the soul to which God grants these favours prepares itself for them, there are many things to be said concerning what the Lord works in it. Some of these I shall say now, and I shall describe that soul's state. In order the better to explain this, I will make use of a comparison which is suitable for the purpose; and which will also show us how, although this work is performed by the Lord, and we can do nothing to make His Majesty grant us this favour, we can do a great deal to prepare ourselves for it.

You will have heard of the wonderful way in which silk is made — a way which no one could invent but God — and how it comes from a kind of seed which looks like tiny peppercorns[129] (I have never seen this, but only heard of it, so if it is incorrect in any way the Fault is not mine). When the warm weather comes, and the mulberry-trees begin to show leaf, this seed starts to take life; until it has this sustenance, on which it feeds, it is as dead. The silkworms feed on the mulberry-leaves until they are full-grown, when people put down twigs, upon which, with their tiny mouths, they start spinning silk, making themselves very tight little cocoons, in which they bury themselves. Then, finally, the worm, which was large and ugly, comes right out of the cocoon a beautiful white butterfly.

Now if no one had ever seen this, and we were only told about it as a story of past ages, who would believe it? And what arguments could we find to support the belief that a thing as devoid of reason as a worm or a bee could be diligent enough to work so industriously for our advantage, and that in such an enterprise the poor little worm would lose its life? This alone, sisters, even if I tell you no more, is sufficient for a brief meditation, for it will enable you to reflect upon the wonders and the wisdom of our God. What, then, would it be if we knew the properties of everything? It will be a great help to us if we occupy ourselves in thinking of these wonderful things and rejoice in being the brides of so wise and powerful a King.

But to return to what I was saying. The silkworm is like the soul which takes life when, through the heat which comes from the Holy Spirit, it begins to utilize the general help which God gives to us all, and to make use of the remedies which He left in His Church — such as frequent confessions, good books and sermons, for these are the remedies for a soul dead in negligences and sins and frequently plunged into temptation. The soul begins to live and nourishes itself on this food, and on good meditations, until it is full grown — and this is what concerns me now: the rest is of little importance.

When it is full-grown, then, as I wrote at the beginning, it starts to spin its silk and to build the house in which it is to die. This house may be understood here to mean Christ. I think I read or heard somewhere that our life is hid in Christ, or in God (for that is the same thing), or that our life is Christ.[130] (The exact form of this[131] is little to my purpose.)

Here, then, daughters, you see what we can do, with God's favour. May His Majesty Himself be our Mansion as He is in this Prayer of Union which, as it were, we ourselves spin. When I say He will be our Mansion, and we can construct it for ourselves and hide ourselves in it, I seem to be suggesting that we can subtract from God, or add to Him. But of course we cannot possibly do that! We can neither subtract from, nor add to, God, but we can subtract from, and add to, ourselves, just as these little silkworms do. And, before we have finished doing all that we can in that respect, God will take this tiny achievement of ours, which is nothing at all, unite it with His greatness and give it such worth that its reward will be the Lord Himself. And as it is He Whom it has cost the most, so His Majesty will unite our small trials with the great trials which He suffered, and make both of them into one.

On, then, my daughters! Let us hasten to perform this task and spin this cocoon. Let us renounce our self-love and self-will, and our attachment to earthly things. Let us practise penance, prayer, mortification, obedience, and all the other good works that you know of. Let us do what we have been taught; and we have been instructed about what our duty is. Let the silkworm die — let it die, as in fact it does when it has completed the work which it was created to do. Then we shall see God and shall ourselves be as completely hidden in His greatness as is this little worm in its cocoon. Note that, when I speak of seeing God, I am referring to the way in which, as I have said, He allows Himself to be apprehended in this kind of union.

And now let us see what becomes of this silkworm, for all that I have been saying about it is leading up to this. When it is in this state of prayer, and quite dead to the world, it comes out a little white butterfly. Oh, greatness of God, that a soul should come out like this after being hidden in the greatness of God, and closely united with Him, for so short a time — never, I think, for as long as half an hour! I tell you truly, the very soul does not know itself. For think of the difference between an ugly worm and a white butterfly; it is just the same here. The soul cannot think how it can have merited such a blessing — whence such a blessing could have come to it, I meant to say, for it knows quite well that it has not merited it at all.[132] It finds itself so anxious to praise the Lord that it would gladly be consumed and die a thousand deaths for His sake. Then it finds itself longing to suffer great trials and unable to do otherwise. It has the most vehement desires for penance, for solitude, and for all to know God. And hence, when it sees God being offended, it becomes greatly distressed. In the following Mansion we shall treat of these things further and in detail, for, although the experiences of this Mansion and of the next are almost identical, their effects come to have much greater power; for, as I have said, if after God comes to a soul here on earth it strives to progress still more, it will experience great things.

To see, then, the restlessness of this little butterfly — though it has never been quieter or more at rest in its life! Here is something to praise God for — namely, that it knows not where to settle and make its abode. By comparison with the abode it has had, everything it sees on earth leaves it dissatisfied, especially when God has again and again given it this wine which almost every time has brought it some new blessing. It sets no store by the things it did when it was a worm — that is, by its gradual weaving of the cocoon. It has wings now: how can it be content to crawl along slowly when it is able to fly? All that it can do for God seems to it slight by comparison with its desires. It even attaches little importance to what the saints endured, knowing by experience how the Lord helps and transforms a soul, so that it seems no longer to be itself, or even its own likeness. For the weakness which it used to think it had when it came to doing penance is now turned into strength. It is no longer bound by ties of relationship, friendship or property. Previously all its acts of will and resolutions and desires were powerless to loosen these and seemed only to bind them the more firmly; now it is grieved at having even to fulfil its obligations in these respects lest these should cause it to sin against God. Everything wearies it, because it has proved that it can find no true rest in the creatures.

I seem to be enlarging on this subject and there is much more that I could say: anyone to whom God has granted this favour will realize that I have said very little. It is not surprising, then, that, as this little butterfly feels a stranger to things of the earth, it should be seeking a new resting-place. But where will the poor little creature go? It cannot return to the place it came from, for, as has been said, however hard we try, it is not in our power to do that until God is pleased once again to grant us this favour. Ah, Lord! What trials begin afresh for this soul! Who would think such a thing possible after it had received so signal a favour? But, after all,[133] we must bear crosses in one way or another for as long as we live. And if anyone told me that after reaching this state he had enjoyed continual rest and joy, I should say that he had not reached it at all, but that if he had got as far as the previous Mansion, he might possibly have experienced some kind of consolation the effect of which was enhanced by physical weakness, and perhaps even by the devil, who gives peace to the soul in order later to wage a far severer war upon it.

I do not mean that those who attain to this state have no peace: they do have it, and to a very high degree, for even their trials are of such sublimity and come from so noble a source that, severe though they are, they bring peace and contentment. The very discontent caused by the things of the world arouses a desire to leave it, so grievous that any alleviation it finds can only be in the thought that its life in this exile is God's will. And even this is insufficient to comfort it, for, despite all it has gained, the soul is not wholly resigned to the will of God, as we shall see later. It does not fail to act in conformity with God's will, but it does so with many tears and with great sorrow at being unable to do more because it has been given no more capacity. Whenever it engages in prayer, this is a grief to it. To some extent, perhaps, it is a result of the great grief caused by seeing how often God is offended, and how little esteemed, in this world, and by considering how many souls are lost, both of heretics and of Moors; although its greatest grief is over the loss of Christian souls, many of whom, it fears, are condemned, though so great is God's mercy that, however evil their lives have been, they can amend them and be saved.

Oh, the greatness of God! Only a few years since — perhaps only a few days — this soul was thinking of nothing but itself. Who has plunged it into such grievous anxieties? Even if we tried to meditate for years on end, we could not feel this as keenly as the soul does now. God help me! If I were able to spend many days and years in trying to realize how great a sin it is to offend God, and in reflecting that those who are damned are His children, and my brothers and sisters, and in meditating upon the dangers in which we live, and in thinking how good it would be for us to depart from this miserable life, would all that suffice? No, daughters; the grief I am referring to is not like that caused by these kinds of meditation.

That grief we could easily achieve, with the Lord's help, by thinking a great deal about those things; but it does not reach to the depths of our being, as does this grief, which, without any effort on the soul's part, and sometimes against its will, seems to tear it to pieces and grind it to powder. What, then, is this grief? Whence does it come? I will tell you.

Have you not heard concerning the Bride (I said this a little while back,[134] though not with reference to the same matter) that God put her in the cellar of wine and ordained charity in her? Well, that is the position here. That soul has now delivered itself into His hands and His great love has so completely subdued it that it neither knows nor desires anything save that God shall do with it what He wills. Never, I think, will God grant this favour save to the soul which He takes for His very own. His will is that, without understanding how, the soul shall go thence sealed with His seal. In reality, the soul in that state does no more than the wax when a seal is impressed upon it — the wax does not impress itself; it is only prepared for the impress: that is, it is soft — and it does not even soften itself so as to be prepared; it merely remains quiet and consenting. Oh, goodness of God, that all this should be done at Thy cost! Thou dost require only our wills and dost ask that Thy wax may offer no impediment.

Here, then, sisters, you see what our God does to the soul in this state so that it may know itself to be His. He gives it something of His own, which is what His Son had in this life: He can grant us no favour greater than that. Who could have wanted to depart from this life more than His Son did? As, indeed, His Majesty said at the Last Supper: "With desire have I desired."[135] "Did not the painful death that Thou wert to die present itself to Thee, O Lord, as something grievous and terrible?" "No, because My great love and My desire that souls shall be saved transcend these pains beyond all comparison and the very terrible things that I have suffered since I lived in the world, and still suffer, are such that by comparison with them these are nothing."

I have often thought about this: I know that the torment which a certain person of my acquaintance[136] has suffered, and suffers still, at seeing the Lord offended, is so intolerable that she would far sooner die than suffer it. And, I reflected, if a soul which has so very little charity by comparison with Christ's that it might be said to be almost nothing beside His felt this torment to be so intolerable, what must the feelings of Our Lord Jesus Christ have been, and what a life must He have lived, if He saw everything and was continually witnessing the great offenses which were being committed against His Father? I think this must certainly have caused Him much greater grief than the pains of His most sacred Passion; for there He could see the end of His trials; and that sight, together with the satisfaction of seeing our redemption achieved through His death, and of proving what love He had for His Father by suffering so much for Him, would alleviate His pains, just as, when those who have great strength of love perform great penances, they hardly feel them, and would like to do more and more, and everything that they do seems very small to them. What, then, would His Majesty feel when He found Himself able to prove so amply to His Father how completely He was fulfilling the obligation of obedience to Him and showing His love for His neighbour? Oh, the great delight of suffering in doing the will of God! But the constant sight of so many offences committed against His Majesty and so many souls going to hell must, I think, have been so painful to Him that, had He not been more than man, one day of that grief would have sufficed to put an end to any number of lives that He might have had, let alone to one.

Chapter III

Continues the same matter. Describes another kind of union which, with the help of God, the soul can attain, and the important part played in it by the love of our neighbour. This chapter is of great profit.

Let us now return to our little dove, and see something of what God gives her in this state. It must always be understood that she will try to advance in the service of Our Lord and in self-knowledge. If she does no more than receive this favour, and, as though she enjoyed complete security, begins to lead a careless life and stray from the road to Heaven — that is, from the Commandments — there will happen to her what happens to the creature that comes out of the silkworm, which leaves seed for the production of more silkworms and then dies for ever. I say it leaves seed because for my own part I believe it is God's will that so great a favour should not be given in vain, and that if the soul that receives it does not profit by it others will do so. For, as the soul possesses these aforementioned desires and virtues, it will always profit other souls so long as it leads a good life, and from its own heat new heat will be transmitted to them. Even after losing this, it may still desire others to profit, and take pleasure in describing the favours given by God to those who love and serve Him.

I knew a person to whom this happened,[137] and who, though having herself gone far astray was glad that others should profit by the favours God had shown her, she would describe the way of prayer to those who did not understand it, and she brought them very, very great profit.[138] Later, the Lord gave her new light. It is true that she had not yet experienced the effects which have been mentioned. But how many are called by the Lord to apostleship, as Judas was, and enjoy communion with Him, or are called to be made kings, as Saul was, and afterwards, through their own fault, are lost! From this, sisters, we may deduce that, if we are to acquire increasing merit, and not, like Saul and Judas, to be lost, our only possible safety consists in obedience and in never swerving from the law of God; I am referring to those to whom He grants these favours, and in fact to all.

Despite all I have said, this Mansion seems to me a little obscure. There is a great deal to be gained by entering it, and those from whom the Lord withholds such supernatural gifts will do well to feel that they are not without hope; for true union can quite well be achieved, with the favour of Our Lord, if we endeavour to attain it by not following our own will but submitting it to whatever is the will of God. Oh, how many of us there are who say we do this and think we want nothing else, and would die for this truth, as I believe I have said! For I tell you, and I shall often repeat this, that when you have obtained this favour from the Lord, you need not strive for that other delectable union which has been described, for the most valuable thing about it is that it proceeds from this union which I am now describing; and we cannot attain to the heights I have spoken of if we are not sure that we have the union in which we resign our wills to the will of God.

Oh, how much to be desired is this union! Happy the soul that has attained to it, for it will live peacefully both in this life and in the next as well. Nothing that happens on earth will afflict it unless it finds itself in peril of losing God, or sees that He is offended — neither sickness nor poverty nor death, except when someone dies who was needed by the Church of God. For this soul sees clearly that He knows what He does better than it knows itself what it desires.

You must observe that there are many kinds of grief. Some of them come upon us suddenly, in natural ways, just as pleasures do; they may even arise from charity, which makes us pity our neighbours, as Our Lord did when He raised Lazarus;[139] and these do not prevent union with the will of God, nor do they cause a restless, unquiet passion which disturbs the soul and lasts for a long time. They are griefs which pass quickly; for, as I said of joys in prayer, they seem not to penetrate to the depth of the soul but only reach these senses and faculties. They characterize all the Mansions so far described but do not enter that which will be dealt with last of all, from which the suspension of the faculties already referred to is inseparable. The Lord can enrich souls in many ways and bring them to these Mansions by many other paths than the short cut which has been described.

But note very carefully, daughters, that the silkworm has of necessity to die; and it is this which will cost you most; for death comes more easily[140] when one can see oneself living a new life, whereas our duty now is to continue living this present life, and yet to die of our own free will.[141] I confess to you that we shall find this much harder, but it is of the greatest value and the reward will be greater too if you gain the victory. But you must not doubt the possibility of this true union with the will of God. This is the union which I have desired all my life; it is for this that I continually beseech Our Lord; it is this which is the most genuine and the safest.

But alas that so few of us are destined to attain it! A person who takes care not to offend the Lord and has entered the religious life may think he has done everything. But oh, there are always a few little worms which do not reveal themselves until, like the worm which gnawed through Jonas's ivy,[142] they have gnawed through our virtues. Such are self-love, self-esteem, censoriousness (even if only in small things) concerning our neighbours, lack of charity towards them, and failure to love them as we love ourselves. For, although late in the day we may fulfil our obligations and so commit no sin, we are far from attaining a point necessary to complete union with the will of God.

What do you suppose His will is, daughters? That we should be altogether perfect, and be one with Him and with the Father,[143] as in His Majesty's prayer. Consider what a long way we are from attaining this. I assure you that it causes me real distress to write in this way because I know how far I am from it myself, and entirely through my own fault. For we do not require great favours from the Lord before we can achieve this; He has given us all we need in giving us His Son to show us the way. Do not think that if, for example, my father or my brother dies, I ought to be in such close conformity with the will of God that I shall not grieve at his loss, or that, if I have trials or illnesses, I must enjoy bearing them. It is good if we can do this and some times it is a matter of common sense: being unable to help ourselves, we make a virtue of necessity. How often philosophers used to act thus in matters of this kind, or in similar matters — and they were very wise men! But here the Lord asks only two things of us: love for His Majesty and love for our neighbour. It is for these two virtues that we must strive, and if we attain them perfectly we are doing His will and so shall be united with Him. But, as I have said, how far we are from doing these two things in the way we ought for a God Who is so great! May His Majesty be pleased to give us grace so that we may deserve to reach this state, as it is in our power to do if we wish.

The surest sign that we are keeping these two commandments is, I think, that we should really be loving our neighbour; for we cannot be sure if we are loving God, although we may have good reasons for believing that we are, but we can know quite well if we are loving our neighbour. And be certain that, the farther advanced you find you are in this, the greater the love you will have for God; for so dearly does His Majesty love us that He will reward our love for our neighbour by increasing the love which we bear to Himself, and that in a thousand ways: this I cannot doubt.

It is most important that we should proceed in this matter very carefully, for, if we have attained great perfection here, we have done everything. Our nature being so evil, I do not believe we could ever attain perfect love for our neighbour unless it had its roots in the love of God. Since this is so important, sisters, let us strive to get to know ourselves better and better, even in the very smallest matters, and take no notice of all the fine plans which come crowding into our minds when we are at prayer, and which we think we will put into practice and carry out for the good of our neighbours in the hope of saving just one soul. If our later actions are not in harmony with those plans, we can have no reason for believing that we should ever have put them into practice. I say the same of humility and of all the virtues; the wiles of the devil are terrible, he will run a thousand times round hell if by so doing he can make us believe that we have a single virtue which we have not. And he is right, for such ideas are very harmful, and such imaginary virtues, when they come from this source, are never unaccompanied by vainglory; just as those which God gives are free both from this and from pride.

I like the way in which some souls, when they are at prayer, think that, for God's sake, they would be glad if they could be humbled and put to open shame — and then try to conceal quite a slight failure. Oh, and if they should be accused of anything that they have not done —— ! God save us from having to listen to them then! Let anyone who cannot bear trials like that be very careful to pay no heed to the resolutions he may have made when he was alone. For they could not in fact have been resolutions made by the will (a genuine act of the will is quite another matter); they must have been due to some freak of the imagination. The devil makes good use of the imagination in practising his surprises and deceptions, and there are many such which he can practise on women, or on unlettered persons, because we do not understand the difference between the faculties and the imagination, and thousands of other things belonging to the interior life. Oh, sisters, how clearly it can be seen what love of your neighbour really means to some of you, and what an imperfect stage it has reached in others! If you understood the importance of this virtue to us all you would strive after nothing but gaining it.

When I see people very diligently trying to discover what kind of prayer they are experiencing and so completely wrapt up[144] in their prayers that they seem afraid to stir, or to indulge in a moment's thought, lest they should lose the slightest degree of the tenderness and devotion which they have been feeling, I realize how little they understand of the road to the attainment of union. They think that the whole thing consists in this. But no, sisters, no; what the Lord desires is works. If you see a sick woman to whom you can give some help, never be affected by the fear that your devotion will suffer, but take pity on her: if she is in pain, you should feel pain too; if necessary, fast so that she may have your food, not so much for her sake as because you know it to be your Lord's will. That is true union with His will. Again, if you hear someone being highly praised, be much more pleased than if they were praising you; this is really easy if you have humility, for in that case you will be sorry to hear yourself praised. To be glad when your sisters' virtues are praised is a great thing, and, when we see a fault in someone, we should be as sorry about it as if it were our own and try to conceal it from others.

I have said a great deal about this elsewhere,[145] sisters, because I know that, if we were to fail here, we should be lost. May the Lord grant us never to fail, and, if that is to be so, I tell you that you must not cease to beg His Majesty for the union which I have described. It may be that you have experienced devotion and consolations, so that you think you have reached this stage, and even enjoyed some brief period of suspension in the Prayer of Quiet, which some people always take to mean that everything is accomplished. But, believe me, if you find you are lacking in this virtue, you have not yet attained union. So ask Our Lord to grant you this perfect love for your neighbour, and allow His Majesty to work, and, if you use your best endeavours and strive after this in every way that you can, He will give you more even than you can desire. You must do violence to your own will, so that your sister's will is done in everything, even though this may cause you to forgo your own rights and forget your own good in your concern for theirs, and however much your physical powers may rebel. If the opportunity presents itself, too, try to shoulder some trial in order to relieve your neighbour of it. Do not suppose that it will cost you nothing or that you will find it all done for you. Think what the love which our Spouse had for us cost Him, when, in order to redeem us from death, He died such a grievous death as the death of the Cross.

Chapter IV

Continues the same subject and gives a further explanation of this kind of prayer. Describes the great importance of proceeding carefully, since the devil is most careful to do all he can to turn souls back from the road they have begun to tread.

I think you will be anxious now to learn what this little dove is doing, and where it is going to settle, for of course it cannot rest in spiritual consolations or in earthly pleasures. It is destined to fly higher than this and I cannot fully satisfy your anxiety until we come to the last Mansion. God grant I may remember it then and find an opportunity to write about it, for almost five months have passed since I began this book, and, as my head is not in a fit state for me to read it through again, it must all be very confused and I may possibly say a few things twice over. As it is for my sisters, however, that matters little.

I want to explain to you still further what I think this Prayer of Union is; and I will make a comparison as well as my wit will allow. Afterwards we will say more about this little butterfly, which never rests — though it is always fruitful in doing good to itself and to other souls — because it has not yet found true reposed.[146] You will often have heard that God betrothes Himself to souls spiritually. Blessed be His mercy, which is pleased so to humble itself! I am only making a rough comparison, but I can find no other which will better explain what I am trying to say than the Sacrament of Matrimony. The two things work differently, for in this matter which we are treating there is nothing that is not spiritual: corporeal union is quite another thing and the spiritual joys and consolations given by the Lord are a thousand leagues removed from those experienced in marriage. It is all a union of love with love, and its operations are entirely pure, and so delicate and gentle that there is no way of describing them; but the Lord can make the soul very deeply conscious of them.

It seems to me that this union has not yet reached the point of spiritual betrothal, but is rather like what happens in our earthly life when two people are about to be betrothed. There is a discussion as to whether or no they are suited to each other and are both in love; and then they meet again so that they may learn to appreciate each other better. So it is here. The contract is already drawn up and the soul has been clearly given to understand the happiness of her lot and is determined to do all the will of her Spouse in every way in which she sees that she can give Him pleasure. His Majesty, Who will know quite well if this is the case, is pleased with the soul, so He grants her this mercy, desiring that she shall get to know Him better, and that, as we may say, they shall meet together,[147] and He shall unite her with Himself. We can compare this kind of union to a short meeting of that nature because it is over in the very shortest time. All giving and taking have now come to an end and in a secret way the soul sees Who this Spouse is that she is to take.[148] By means of the senses and faculties she could not understand in a thousand years what she understands in this way in the briefest space of time. But the Spouse, being Who He is, leaves her, after that one visit, worthier to join hands (as people say) with Him; and the soul becomes so fired with love that for her part she does her utmost not to thwart this Divine betrothal. If she is neglectful, however, and sets her affection on anything other than Himself, she loses everything, and that is a loss every bit as great as are the favours He has been granting her, which are far greater than it is possible to convey.

So, Christian souls, whom the Lord has brought to this point on your journey, I beseech you, for His sake, not to be negligent, but to withdraw from occasions of sin — for even in this state the soul is not strong enough to be able to run into them safely, as it is after the betrothal has been made — that is to say, in the Mansion which we shall describe after this one. For this communication has been no more than (as we might say) one single short meeting,[149] and the devil will take great pains about combating it and will try to hinder the betrothal. Afterwards, when he sees that the soul is completely surrendered to the Spouse, he dare not do this, for he is afraid of such a soul as that, and he knows by experience that if he attempts anything of the kind he will come out very much the loser and the soul will achieve a corresponding gain.

I tell you, daughters, I have known people of a very high degree of spirituality who have reached this state, and whom, notwithstanding, the devil, with great subtlety and craft, has won back to himself. For this purpose he will marshal all the powers of hell, for, as I have often said, if he wins a single soul in this way he will win a whole multitude. The devil has much experience in this matter. If we consider what a large number of people God can draw to Himself through the agency of a single soul, the thought of the thousands converted by the martyrs gives us great cause for praising God. Think of a maiden like Saint Ursula. And of the souls whom the devil must have lost through Saint Dominic and Saint Francis and other founders of Orders, and is losing now through Father Ignatius, who founded the Company[150] — all of whom, of course, as we read, received such favours from God! What did they do but endeavour that this Divine betrothal should not be frustrated through their fault? Oh, my daughters, how ready this Lord still is to grant us favours, just as He was then! In some ways it is even more necessary that we should wish to receive them, for there are fewer than there used to be who think of the Lord's honour! We are so very fond of ourselves and so very careful not to lose any of our rights! Oh, what a great mistake we make! May the Lord in His mercy give us light lest we fall into such darkness.

There are two things about which you may ask me, or be in doubt. The first is this: If the soul is so completely at one with the will of God, as has been said, how can it be deceived, since it never desires to follow its own will? The second: By what avenues can the devil enter and lead you into such peril that your soul may be lost, when you are so completely withdrawn from the world and so often approach the Sacraments? For you are enjoying the companionship, as we might say, of angels, since, by the goodness of the Lord, you have none of you any other desires than to serve and please Him in everything. It would not be surprising, you might add, if this should happen to those who are immersed in the cares of the world. I agree that you are justified in asking this — God has been abundantly merciful to us. But when I read, as I have said, that Judas enjoyed the companionship of the Apostles, had continual intercourse with God Himself, and could listen to His own words, I realize that even this does not guarantee our safety.

To the first question, my reply would be that, if this soul invariably followed the will of God, it is clear that it would not be lost. But the devil comes with his artful wiles, and, under colour of doing good, sets about undermining it in trivial ways, and involving it in practices which, so he gives it to understand, are not wrong; little by little he darkens its understanding, and weakens its will, and causes its self-love to increase, until in one way and another he begins to withdraw it from the love of God and to persuade it to indulge its own wishes. And this is also an answer to the second question, for there is no enclosure so strictly guarded that he cannot enter it, and no desert so solitary that he cannot visit it. And I would make one further remark — namely, that the reason the Lord permits this may possibly be so that He may observe the behaviour of the soul which He wishes to set up as a light to others; for, if it is going to be a failure, it is better that it should be so at the outset than when it can do many souls harm.

What we should be most diligent about, I think, is this. First, we must continually ask God in our prayers to keep us in His hand, and bear constantly in mind that, if He leaves us, we shall at once be down in the depths, as indeed we shall. So we must never have any confidence in ourselves — that would simply be folly. But most of all we must walk with special care and attention, and watch what progress we make in the virtues, and discover if, in any way, we are either improving or going back, especially in our love for each other and in our desire to be thought least of, and in ordinary things; for if we look to this, and beg the Lord to give us light, we shall at once discern whether we have gained or lost. Do not suppose, then, that when God brings a soul to such a point He lets it go so quickly out of His hand that the devil can recapture it without much labour. His Majesty is so anxious for it not to be lost that He gives it a thousand interior warnings of many kinds, and thus it cannot fail to perceive the danger.

Let the conclusion of the whole matter be this. We must strive all the time to advance, and, if we are not advancing, we must cherish serious misgivings, as the devil is undoubtedly anxious to exercise his wiles upon us. For it is unthinkable that a soul which has arrived so far should cease to grow: love is never idle, so failure to advance would be a very bad sign. A soul which has once set out to be the bride of God Himself, and has already had converse with His Majesty and reached the point which has been described, must not lie down and go to sleep again. And so that you may see, daughters, how Our Lord treats those whom He makes His brides, let us begin to discuss the sixth Mansions, and you will see how slight is all the service we can render Him, all the suffering we can undergo for Him, and all the preparation we can make for such great favours. It may have been by Our Lord's ordinance that I was commanded to write this so that we shall forget our trivial earthly pleasures when we fix our eyes on the reward and see how boundless is the mercy which makes Him pleased to communicate and reveal Himself in this way to us worms. So, fired by love of Him, we shall run our race, with our eyes fixed upon His greatness.

May He be pleased to enable me to explain something of these difficult things, which I know will be impossible unless His Majesty and the Holy Spirit[151] guide my pen. Were it not to be for your profit I should beseech Him to prevent me from explaining any of it, for His Majesty knows that, so far as I myself can judge, my sole desire is that His name should be praised, and that we should make every effort to serve a Lord Who gives us such a reward here below, and thus conveys to us some idea of what He will give us in Heaven, without the delays and trials and perils incident to this sea of tempests. For, were it not that we might lose Him and offend Him, it would be a comfort if our life did not end until the end of the world, so that we could work for so great a God and Lord and Spouse. May it please His Majesty that we be worthy to do Him some service, unmarred by the many faults that we always commit, even in doing our good works! Amen.

Sixth Mansions:
In which there are Eleven Chapters

Chapter 1

Shows how, when the Lord begins to grant the soul greater favours, it has also to endure greater trials. Enumerates some of these and describes how those who are in this Mansion must conduct themselves. This is a good chapter for any who suffer interior trials.

Let us now, with the help of the Holy Spirit, come to speak of the sixth Mansions, in which the soul has been wounded with love for the Spouse and seeks more opportunity of being alone, trying, so far as is possible to one in its state, to renounce everything which can disturb it in this its solitude. That sight of Him which it has had is so deeply impressed upon it that its whole desire is to enjoy it once more. Nothing, I must repeat, is seen in this state of prayer which can be said to be really seen, even by the imagination; I use the word "sight" because of the comparison I made.

The soul is now completely determined to take no other spouse; but the Spouse disregards its yearnings for the conclusion of the Betrothal, desiring that they should become still deeper and that this greatest of all blessings should be won by the soul at some cost to itself. And although everything is of but slight importance by comparison with the greatness of this gain, I assure you, daughters, that, if the soul is to bear its trials, it has no less need of the sign and token of this gain which it now holds. Oh, my God, how great are these trials, which the soul will suffer, both within and without, before it enters the seventh Mansion![152] Really, when I think of them, I am sometimes afraid that, if we realized their intensity beforehand, it would be most difficult for us, naturally weak as we are, to muster determination enough to enable us to suffer them or resolution enough for enduring them, however attractively the advantage of so doing might be presented to us, until we reached the seventh Mansion, where there is nothing more to be feared, and the soul will plunge deep into suffering for God's sake. The reason for this is that the soul is almost continuously near His Majesty and its nearness brings it fortitude. I think it will be well if I tell you about some of the things which I know are certain to happen here. Not all souls, perhaps, will be led along this path, though I doubt very much if souls which from time to time really taste the things of Heaven can live in freedom from earthly trials, in one way or in another.

Although I had not intended to treat of this, it has occurred to me that some soul finding itself in this state might be very much comforted if it knew what happens to those whom God grants such favours, at a time when everything really seems to be lost. I shall not take these experiences in the order in which they happen, but as each one presents itself to my memory. I will begin with the least of them. An outcry is made by people with whom such a person is acquainted, and even by those with whom she is not acquainted and who she never in her life supposed would think about her at all. "How holy she's getting!" they exclaim, or "She's only going to these extremes to deceive the world and to make other people look sinful, when really they are better Christians than she is without any of these goings-on!" (Notice, by the way, that she is not really indulging in any "goings-on" at all: she is only trying to live up to her profession.) Then people whom she had thought her friends abandon her and it is they who say the worst things of all and express the deepest regret that (as they put it) she is "going to perdition" and "obviously being deluded", that "this is the devil's work", that "she's going the way of So-and-so and So-and-so, who ruined their own lives and dragged good people down with them", and that "she takes in all her confessors". And they actually go to her confessors and tell them so, illustrating what they say by stories of some who ruined their lives in this way: and they scoff at the poor creature and talk about her like this times without number.

I know of a person[153] to whom these things were happening and who was terribly afraid that there would be nobody willing to hear her confession; but there is so much I could say about that that I will not stop to tell it here. The worst of it is, these things are not soon over — they last all one's life long. People warn each other to be careful not to have anything to do with persons like oneself. You will tell me that there are also those who speak well of one. But oh, daughters, how few there are who believe the good things they say by comparison with the many who dislike us! In any case, to be well spoken of is only one trial more and a worse one than those already mentioned. For the soul sees quite clearly that if there is any good in it this is a gift of God, and not in the least due to itself, for only a short time previously it saw itself in dire poverty and plunged deep into sin. So this praise is an intolerable torment to it, at least at the beginning: afterwards it is less so, and this for various reasons. The first of these is that experience shows it clearly how people will speak well of others as readily as ill, and so it takes no more notice of the former class than of the latter. The second, that the Lord has given it greater light and shown it that anything good it may have does not come from itself, but is His Majesty's gift; so it breaks into praises of God, but as though He were being gracious to a third person, and forgetting that it is itself concerned at all. The third reason is that, having seen others helped by observing the favours which God is granting it, the soul thinks that His Majesty has been pleased for them to think of it as good, though in fact it is not, so that they may be profited. The fourth is that, as the soul now prizes the honour and glory of God more than its own honour and glory, it no longer suffers from a temptation which beset it at first — namely, to think that these praises will do it harm, as it has seen them do to others. It cares little about being dishonoured itself, provided that it can be the cause of God's being even once praised — come afterwards what may.

These and other considerations mitigate the great distress caused by such praises, although some distress is nearly always felt, except when a soul takes no notice of such things whatsoever. But to find itself publicly and unmeritedly described as good is an incomparably greater trial than any of those already mentioned. Once the soul has learned to care little about this, it cares very much less about the other, which, indeed, makes it rejoice and sounds to it like sweetest music. This is absolutely true. The soul is fortified rather than daunted by censure, for experience has shown how great are the benefits it can bring, and it seems to the soul that its persecutors are not offending God, but that His Majesty is permitting this for its great advantage. Being quite clear about this, it conceives a special and most tender love for them and thinks of them as truer friends and greater benefactors than those who speak well of it.

The Lord is also in the habit of sending the most grievous infirmities. This is a much greater trial, especially if the pains are severe; in some ways, when they are very acute, I think they are the greatest earthly trial that exists — the greatest of exterior trials, I mean — however many a soul may suffer: I repeat that it is only to very acute pains that I am referring. For they affect the soul both outwardly and inwardly, till it becomes so much oppressed as not to know what to do with itself, and would much rather suffer any martyrdom than these pains. Still, at the very worst, they do not last so long — no longer, as a rule, than other bad illnesses do. For, after all, God gives us no more than we can bear, and He gives patience first.

I know a person of whom, since the Lord began to grant her this favour aforementioned, forty years ago,[154] it cannot be truly said that she has been a day without pains and other kinds of suffering; I mean because of her poor physical health, to say nothing of other great trials. It is true that she had been very wicked and it was all very slight by comparison with the hell that she had merited. Others, who have not so greatly offended Our Lord, will be led by Him along another way, but I should always choose the way of suffering, if only to imitate Our Lord Jesus Christ, and even were there no other special benefit to be obtained from it — and there are always a great many. But oh, when we come to interior sufferings! If these could be described they would make all physical sufferings seem very slight, but it is impossible to describe interior sufferings and how they happen.

Let us begin with the torture which it costs us to have to do with a confessor so scrupulous and inexperienced that he thinks nothing safe: he is afraid of everything, and doubtful about everything, as soon as he sees that he is dealing with anything out of the ordinary. This is particularly so if he sees any imperfection in the soul that is undergoing these experiences. He thinks that people to whom God grants these favours must be angels; and, as this is impossible while they are in the body, he attributes the whole thing to melancholy or to the devil. The world is so full of melancholy that this certainly does not surprise me; for there is so much abroad just now, and the devil makes so much use of it to work harm, that confessors have very good cause to be afraid of it and to watch for it very carefully. But, when the poor soul, harassed by the same fear, goes to the confessor as to a judge, and he condemns her, she cannot fail to be upset and tortured by what he says — and only a person who has passed through such a trial will know how great it is. For this is another of the great trials suffered by these souls, especially if they have been wicked — namely, to think that because of their sins God will permit them to be deceived — and although, when His Majesty grants them this favour, they feel secure and cannot believe that it comes from any other spirit than a spirit of God, yet, as it is a state which passes quickly, and the soul is ever mindful of its sins, and it sees faults in itself — for these are never lacking — it then begins to suffer this torture. When the confessor reassures the soul, it becomes calm, though in due course it gets troubled again; but when all he can do is to make it still more fearful the thing grows almost intolerable, especially when on top of everything else come periods of aridity, during which the soul feels as if it has never known God and never will know Him, and as if to hear His Majesty spoken of is like hearing of a person from a great distance away.

All this would be nothing to the person concerned were it not followed immediately by the thought that she cannot be describing her case properly to her confessor and has been deceiving him; and, although when she thinks about it she feels sure she has not kept back even the first movement of her mind, it is of no use. For her understanding is so dim that it is incapable of seeing the truth, but believes what the imagination (now mistress of the understanding) presents to it and the nonsense which the devil attempts to present to it, when Our Lord gives him leave to test her soul, and even to make her think herself cast off by God. For there are many things which assault her soul with an interior oppression so keenly felt and so intolerable that I do not know to what it can be compared, save to the torment of those who suffer in hell, for in this spiritual tempest no consolation is possible.

If she decides to take up the matter with her confessor, it would look as if the devils have come to his aid so that he may torture her soul the more. A certain confessor, dealing with a person who had been in this state of torment, after it had passed away, thought that the oppression must have been of a dangerous type, since it had involved her in so many trials; so he told her, whenever she was in this state, to report to him; but this made her so much worse that he came to realize that he could no longer do anything with her. For, although she was quite able to read, she found that, if she took up a book written in the vernacular, she could understand no more of it than if she had not known her alphabet; her understanding was not capable of taking it in.

Briefly, in this tempest, there is no help for it but to wait upon the mercy of God, Who suddenly, at the most unlooked-for hour, with a single word, or on some chance occasion, lifts the whole of this burden from the soul, so that it seems as if it has never been clouded over, but is full of sunshine and far happier than it was before. Then, like one who has escaped from a perilous battle and gained the victory, the soul keeps praising Our Lord, for it is He Who has fought and enabled it to conquer. It knows very well that it did not itself do the fighting. For it saw that all the weapons with which it could defend itself were in the hands of its enemy, and was thus clearly aware of its misery and realized how little we can do of ourselves if the Lord should forsake us.

We have no need of reflection to enable us to understand this, for the soul's experience of enduring it, and of having found itself completely powerless, has made it realize that it is utterly helpless and that we are but miserable creatures. For, though it cannot be devoid of grace, since despite all this torment it does not offend God, and would not do so for anything upon earth, yet this grace is buried so deeply that the soul seems not to feel the smallest spark of any love for God, nor has it ever done so. If it has done anything good, or His Majesty has granted it any favour, the whole thing seems to it like a dream or a fancy: all it knows for certain is that it has sinned.

Oh, Jesus! How sad it is to see a soul thus forsaken, and how little, as I have said, can it gain from any earthly consolation! So do not suppose, sisters, if you ever find yourselves in this condition, that people who are wealthy, or free to do as they like, have any better remedy for such times. No, no; to offer them earthly consolations would be like telling criminals condemned to death about all the joys that there are in the world; not only would this fail to comfort them — it would but increase their torment; comfort must come to them from above, for earthly things are of no value to them any more. This great God desires us to know that He is a

King and we are miserable creatures — a point of great importance for what follows.

Now what will a poor creature like that do if such a thing goes on for a very long time?[155] If she prays, she might as well not be doing so at all — I mean for all the comfort it will bring her, for interiorly she is incapable of receiving any comfort, nor, even when her prayer is vocal, can she understand what she is saying; while mental prayer at such a time is certainly impossible — her faculties are not capable of it. Solitude is still worse for her, though it is also torture for her to be in anyone's company or to be spoken to; and so, despite all her efforts to conceal the fact, she becomes outwardly upset and despondent, to a very noticeable extent. Is it credible that she will be able to say what is the matter with her? The thing is inexpressible, for this distress and oppression are spiritual troubles and cannot be given a name. The best medicine — I do not say for removing the trouble, for I know of none for that, but for enabling the soul to endure it — is to occupy oneself with external affairs and works of charity and to hope in God's mercy, which never fails those who hope in Him. May He be blessed for ever. Amen.[156]

Other trials caused by devils, which are of an exterior kind, will not occur so commonly and thus there is no reason to speak of them nor are they anything like so grievous. For, whatever these devils do, they cannot, in my opinion, go so far as to inhibit the working of the faculties or to disturb the soul, in the way already described. After all, it thinks (and rightly), they cannot do more than the Lord permits, and, so long as it is not lost, nothing matters much by comparison with what has been described above.

We shall next deal with other interior troubles which occur in these Mansions, treating of the different kinds of prayer and favours of the Lord; for, although a few are still harder to bear than those referred to, as will be seen by the effects which they leave upon the body, they do not merit the name of trial, nor is it right that we should give them that name, since they are such great favours of the Lord and the soul understands them to be so, and far beyond its deservings. This severe distress comes just before the soul's entrance into the seventh Mansion, together with many more, only a few of which I shall describe, as it would be impossible to speak of them all, or even to explain their nature. For they are of another type than those already mentioned, and a much higher one; and if, in dealing with those of a lower kind, I have not been able to explain myself in greater detail, still less shall I be able to explain these others. The Lord give me His help in everything I do, through the merits of His Son. Amen.

Chapter 11

Treats of several ways in which Our Lord awakens the soul; there appears to be nothing in these to be feared, although the experience is most sublime and the favours are great ones.

We seem to have left the little dove a long way behind, but we have not done so in reality, for these very trials enable it to make a higher flight. So let us now begin to treat of the way in which the Spouse deals with it, and see how, before it is wholly one with Him, He fills it with fervent desire, by means so delicate that the soul itself does not understand them, nor do I think I shall succeed in describing them in such a way as to be understood, except by those who have experienced it; for these are influences so delicate and subtle that they proceed from the very depth of the heart and I know no comparison that I can make which will fit the case.

All this is very different from what one can achieve in earthly maters, and even from the consolations which have been described. For often when a person is quite unprepared for such a thing, and is not even thinking of God, he is awakened by His Majesty, as though by a rushing comet or a thunderclap. Although no sound is heard,[157] the soul is very well aware that it has been called by God, so much so that sometimes, especially at first, it begins to tremble and complain, though it feels nothing that causes it affliction. It is conscious of having been most delectably wounded, but cannot say how or by whom; but it is certain that this is a precious experience and it would be glad if it were never to be healed of that wound. It complains to its Spouse with words of love, and even cries aloud, being unable to help itself, for it realizes that He is present but will not manifest Himself in such a way as to allow it to enjoy Him, and this is a great grief, though a sweet and delectable one; even if it should desire not to suffer it, it would have no choice — but in any case it never would so desire. It is much more satisfying to a soul than is the delectable absorption, devoid of distress, which occurs in the Prayer of Quiet.

I am straining every nerve,[158] sisters, to explain to you this operation of love, yet I do not know any way of doing so. For it seems a contradiction to say that the Beloved is making it very clear that He is with the soul and seems to be giving it such a clear sign that He is calling it that it cannot doubt the fact, and that the call is so penetrating that it cannot fail to hear Him. For the Spouse, Who is in the seventh Mansion, seems to be calling the soul in a way which involves no clear utterance of speech, and none of the inhabitants of the other Mansions — the senses, the imagination or the faculties — dares to stir. Oh, my powerful God, how great are Thy secrets, and how different are spiritual things from any that can be seen or understood here below. There is no way of describing this favour, small though it is by comparison with the signal favours which souls are granted by Thee.

So powerful is the effect of this upon the soul that it becomes consumed with desire, yet cannot think what to ask, so clearly conscious is it of the presence of its God. Now, if this is so, you will ask me what it desires or what causes it distress.

What greater blessing can it wish for? I cannot say; I know that this distress seems to penetrate to its very bowels; and that, when He that has wounded it draws out the arrow, the bowels seem to come with it, so deeply does it feel this love. I have just been wondering if my God could be described as the fire in a lighted brazier, from which some spark will fly out and touch the soul, in such a way that it will be able to feel the burning heat of the fire; but, as the fire is not hot enough to burn it up, and the experience is very delectable, the soul continues to feel that pain and the mere touch suffices to produce that effect in it. This seems the best comparison that I have been able to find, for this delectable pain, which is not really pain, is not continuous: sometimes it lasts for a long time, while sometimes it comes suddenly to an end, according to the way in which the Lord is pleased to bestow it, for it is a thing which no human means can procure. Although occasionally the experience lasts for a certain length of time, it goes and comes again; it is, in short, never permanent, and for that reason it never completely enkindles the soul; for, just as the soul is about to become enkindled, the spark dies, and leaves the soul yearning once again to suffer that loving pain of which it is the cause.

It cannot for a moment be supposed that this is a phenomenon which has its source in the physical nature, or that it is caused by melancholy, or that it is a deception of the devil, or a mere fancy. It is perfectly clear that it is a movement of which the source is the Lord, Who is unchangeable; and its effects are not like those of other devotions whose genuineness we doubt because of the intense absorption of the joy which we experience. Here all the senses and faculties are active, and there is no absorption; they are on the alert to discover what can be happening, and, so far as I can see, they cause no disturbance, and can neither increase this delectable pain nor remove it. Anyone to whom Our Lord has granted this favour will recognize the fact on reading this; he must give Him most heartfelt thanks and must not fear that it may be deception; let his chief fear be rather lest he show ingratitude for so great a favour, and let him endeavour to serve God and to grow better all his life long and he will see the result of this and find himself receiving more and more. One person who was granted this favour spent several years in the enjoyment of it and so completely did it satisfy her that, if she had served the Lord for very many years by suffering great trials, she would have felt well rewarded. May He be blessed for ever and ever. Amen.

It may be that you wonder why greater security can be felt about this than about other things. For the following reasons, I think. First, because so delectable a pain can never be bestowed upon the soul by the devil: he can give pleasures and delights which seem to be spiritual, but it is beyond his power to unite pain — and such a great pain! — with tranquillity and joy in the soul; for all his powers are in the external sphere, and, when he causes pain, it is never, to my mind, delectable or peaceful, but restless and combative. Secondly, this delectable tempest comes from another region than those over which he has authority. Thirdly, great advantages accrue to the soul, which, as a general rule, becomes filled with a determination to suffer for God's sake and to desire to have many trials to endure, and to be very much more resolute in withdrawing from the pleasures and intercourse of this world, and other things like them.

That this is no fancy is very evident; on other occasions the devil may create fancies of the kind, but he will never be able to counterfeit this. It is so wonderful a thing that it cannot possibly be created by the fancy (I mean, one cannot think it is there when it is not) nor can the soul doubt that it is there; if any doubt about it remains — I mean, if the soul doubts whether or no it has experienced it — it can be sure that the impulses are not genuine, for we perceive it as clearly as we hear a loud voice with our ears. Nor is there any possible way in which it can be due to melancholy, for the fancies created by melancholy exist only in the imagination, whereas this proceeds from the interior of the soul. I may conceivably be mistaken; but, until I hear arguments to the contrary from someone who understands the matter, I shall always be of this opinion; I know, for example, of a person who was terribly afraid of being deceived in this way, and yet who never had any fears about this kind of prayer.

Our Lord, too, has other methods of awakening the soul. Quite unexpectedly, when engaged in vocal prayer and not thinking of interior things, it seems, in some wonderful way, to catch fire. It is just as though there suddenly assailed it a fragrance so powerful that it diffused itself through all the senses or something of that kind (I do not say it is a fragrance; I merely make the comparison) in order to convey to it the consciousness that the Spouse is there. The soul is moved by a delectable desire to enjoy Him and this disposes it to make many acts and to sing praises to Our Lord. The source of this favour is that already referred to; but there is nothing here that causes pain, nor are the soul's desires to enjoy God in any way painful. This is what is most usually felt by the soul. For several of the reasons already alleged I do not think there is much reason here for fear; one must endeavour to receive this favour and give thanks for it.

Chapter III

Treats of the same subject and describes the way in which, when He is pleased to do so, God speaks to the soul. Gives instructions as to how we should behave in such a case: we must not be guided by our own opinions. Sets down a few signs by which we may know when this favour is, and when it is not, a deception. This chapter is very profitable.

There is another way in which God awakens the soul, and which, although in some respects it seems a greater favour than the others, may also be more perilous. For this reason I will spend a short time in describing it. This awakening of the soul is effected by means of locutions, which are of many kinds.[159] Some of them seem to come from without; others from the innermost depths of the soul; others from its higher part; while others, again, are so completely outside the soul that they can be heard with the ears, and seem to be uttered by a human voice. Sometimes — often, indeed — this may be a fancy, especially in persons who are melancholy — I mean, are affected by real melancholy — or have feeble imaginations.

Of persons of these two kinds no notice should be taken, in my view, even if they say they see or hear or are given to understand things, nor should one upset them by telling them that their experiences come from the devil. One should listen to them as one would to sick persons; and the prioress, or the confessor, or whatever person they confide in, should advise them to pay no heed to the matter, because the service of God does not consist in things like these, over which many have been deceived by the devil, although this may not be so with them. One should humour such people so as not to distress them further. If one tells them they are suffering from melancholy, there will be no end to it. They will simply swear they see and hear things, and really believe that they do.

The real solution is to see that such people have less time for prayer, and also that, as far as is possible, they attach no importance to these fancies. For the devil is apt to take advantage of the infirmity of these souls, to the injury of others, if not to their own as well. Both with infirm and with healthy souls there is invariably cause for misgivings about these things until it becomes clear what kind of spirit is responsible. I believe, too, that it is always better for them to dispense with such things at first, for, if they are of God, dispensing with them will help us all the more to advance, since, when put to the proof in this way, they will tend to increase. Yet the soul should not be allowed to become depressed or disquieted, for it really cannot help itself.

Returning now to what I was saying about locutions, these may come from God, in any of the ways I have mentioned, or they may equally well come from the devil or from one's own imagination. I will describe, if I can, with the Lord's help, the signs by which these locutions differ from one another and when they are dangerous. For there are many people given to prayer who experience them, and I would not have you think you are doing wrong, sisters, whether or no you give them credence, when they are only for your own benefit, to comfort you or to warn you of your faults. In such cases it matters little from whom they proceed or if they are only fancies. But of one thing I will warn you: do not think that, even if your locutions come from God, you will for that reason be any the better. After all, He talked a great deal with the Pharisees: any good you may gain will depend upon how you profit by what you hear. Unless it agrees strictly with the Scriptures, take no more notice of it than you would if it came from the devil himself. The words may, in fact, come only from your weak imagination, but they must be taken as a temptation against things pertaining to the Faith and must therefore invariably be resisted so that they may gradually cease; and cease they will, because they will have little power of their own.

To return, then, to our first point: whether they come from within, from above or from without, has nothing to do with their coming from God. The surest signs that one can have of their doing this are, in my opinion, as follows. The first and truest is the sense of power and authority which they bear with them, both in themselves and in the actions which follow them. I will explain myself further. A soul is experiencing all the interior disturbances and tribulations which have been described, and all the aridity and darkness of the understanding. A single word of this kind — just a "Be not troubled" — is sufficient to calm it. No other word need be spoken; a great light comes to it; and all its trouble is lifted from it, although it had been thinking that, if the whole world, and all the learned men in the world, were to combine to give it reasons for not being troubled, they could not relieve it from its distress, however hard they might strive to do so. Or a soul is distressed because its confessor, and others, have told it that what it has is a spirit sent by the devil, and it is full of fear. Yet that single word which it hears: "It is I, fear not,"[160] takes all its fear from it, and it is most marvellously comforted, and believes that no one will ever be able to make it feel otherwise. Or it is greatly exercised because of some important piece of business and it has no idea how this will turn out. It is then given to understand that it must be, and all will turn out well; and it acquires a new confidence and is no longer troubled. And so with many other things.

The second sign is that a great tranquillity dwells in the soul, which becomes peacefully and devoutly recollected, and ready to sing praises to God. Oh, Lord, if there is such power in a word sent by one of Thy messengers (for they say that, in this Mansion, at least, such words are uttered, not by the Lord Himself, but by some angel), what power wilt Thou not leave in the soul that is bound to Thee, as art Thou to it, by love.

The third sign is that these words do not vanish from the memory for a very long time: some, indeed, never vanish at all. Words which we hear on earth — I mean, from men, however weighty and learned they may be — we do not bear so deeply engraven upon our memory, nor, if they refer to the future, do we give credence to them as we do to these locutions. For these last impress us by their complete certainty, in such a way that, although sometimes they seem quite impossible of fulfilment, and we cannot help wondering if they will come true or not, and although our understanding may hesitate about it, yet within the soul itself there is a certainty which cannot be overcome. It may seem to the soul that everything is moving in the contrary direction to what it had been led to expect, and yet, even if many years go by, it never loses its belief that, though God may use other means incomprehensible to men, in the end what He has said will come true; as in fact it does. None the less, as I say, the soul is distressed when it sees things going badly astray. It may be some time since it heard the words; and both their working within it and the certainty which it had at the time that they came from God have passed away. So these doubts arise, and the soul wonders if the whole thing came from the devil, or can have been the work of the imagination. Yet at the time it had no such doubts and it would have died in defence of their veracity. But, as I say, all these imaginings must be put into our minds by the devil in order to distress us and make us fearful, especially if the matter is one in which obeying the locutions will bring others many blessings, or produce good works tending greatly to the honour and service of God but presenting considerable difficulties. What will the devil not do in this case by encouraging such misgivings? At the very least he will weaken the soul's faith, for it is most harmful not to believe that God is powerful and can do works which are incomprehensible to our understanding.

Despite all these conflicts, despite the assertions of some (I refer to confessors) that these locutions are pure nonsense; and despite all the unfortunate happenings which may persuade the soul that they cannot come true, there still remains within it such a living spark of conviction that they will come true (whence this arises I cannot tell) that, though all other hopes may be dead, this spark of certainty could not fail to remain alive, even if the soul wished it to die. And in the end, as I have said, the Lord's word is fulfilled, and the soul is so happy and glad that it would like to do nothing but praise His Majesty everlastingly — much more, however, because it has seen His assurances come true than because of the occurrence itself, even though this may be of very great consequence to it.

I do not know why it is, but the soul is so anxious for these assurances to be proved true that it would not, I think, feel it so much if it were itself caught in the act of lying — as though it could do anything more in the matter than repeat what is said to it! In this connection a certain person used continually to recall what happened to the prophet Jonas, when he feared that Ninive was not to be destroyed.[161] Of course, as the locutions come from the Spirit of God, it is right that we should have this trust in Him, and desire that He should never be thought false, since He is Supreme Truth. Great, therefore, is the joy of one who, after a thousand vicissitudes and in the most difficult circumstances, sees His word come true; such a person may himself have to suffer great trials on that account, but he would rather do this than that what he holds the Lord most certainly told him should not come to pass. Not everybody, perhaps, will have this weakness — if weakness it is, for I cannot myself condemn it as wrong.

If the locutions come from the imagination, none of these signs occur, nor is there any certainty or peace or interior consolation. It might, however, happen (and I even know of a few people to whom it has happened) that, when a person is deeply absorbed in the Prayer of Quiet and in spiritual sleep (for some, because of the weakness of their constitution, or of their imagination, or for some other reason, are so entirely carried out of themselves in this act of deep recollection, that they are unconscious of everything external, and all their senses are in such a state of slumber that they are like a person asleep — at times, indeed, they may even be asleep), he thinks that the locutions come to him in a kind of dream, and sees things and believes that these things are of God, and the effects of these locutions resemble those of a dream. It may also happen that, when such a person asks something of Our Lord with a great love, he thinks that the voices are telling him what he wants to be told; this does in fact sometimes happen. But anyone who has much experience of locutions coming from God will not, I think, be deceived in this way by the imagination.

The devil's locutions are more to be feared than those which come from the imagination; but, if the locutions are accompanied by the signs already described, one may be very confident that they are of God, although not to such an extent that, if what is said is of great importance and involves some action on the part of the hearer, or matters affecting a third person, one should do anything about it, or consider doing anything, without taking the advice of a learned confessor, a man of clear insight and a servant of God, even though one may understand the locutions better and better and it may become evident that they are of God. For this is His Majesty's will, so by carrying it out we are not failing to do what He commands: He has told us that we are to put our confessor in His place, even when it cannot be doubted that the words are His. If the matter is a difficult one, these words will help to give us courage and Our Lord will speak to the confessor and if such is His pleasure will make him recognize the work of His spirit; if He does not, we have no further obligations. I consider it very dangerous for a person to do anything but what he has been told to do and to follow his own opinion in this matter; so I admonish you, sisters, in Our Lord's name, never to act thus.

There is another way in which the Lord speaks to the soul, which for my own part I hold to be very certainly genuine, and that is by a kind of intellectual vision, the nature of which I will explain later. So far down in the depths of the soul does this contact take place, so clearly do the words spoken by the Lord seem to be heard with the soul's own faculty of hearing, and so secretly are they uttered, that the very way in which the soul understands them, together with the effects produced by the vision itself, convinces it and makes it certain that no part in the matter is being played by the devil. The wonderful effects it produces are sufficient to make us believe this; at least one is sure that the locutions do not proceed from the imagination, and, if one reflects upon it, one can always be certain of this, for the following reasons.

The first reason is that some locutions are very much clearer than others. The genuine locution is so clear that, even if it consists of a long exhortation, the hearer notices the omission of a single syllable, as well as the phraseology which is used; but in locutions which are created fancifully by the imagination the voice will be less clear and the words less distinct, they will be like something heard in a half-dream.

The second reason is that often the soul has not been thinking of what it hears — I mean that the voice comes unexpectedly, sometimes even during a conversation, although it frequently has reference to something that was passing quickly through the mind or to what one was previously thinking of. But often it refers to things which one never thought would or could happen, so that the imagination cannot possibly have invented them, and the soul cannot be deceived about things it has not desired or wished for or that have never been brought to its notice.

The third reason is that in genuine locutions the soul seems to be hearing something, whereas in locutions invented by the imagination someone seems to be composing bit by bit what the soul wishes to hear.

The fourth reason is that there is a great difference in the words themselves: in a genuine locution one single word may contain a world of meaning such as the understanding alone could never put rapidly into human language.

The fifth reason is that frequently, not only can words be heard, but, in a way which I shall never be able to explain, much more can be understood than the words themselves convey and this without any further utterance. Of this way of understanding I shall say more elsewhere; it is a very subtle thing, for which Our Lord should be praised. Some people (especially one person with experience of these things, and no doubt others also) have been very dubious about this way of understanding locutions and about the differences between them, and have been quite unable to get the matter straight. I know that this person has thought it all over very carefully, because the Lord has granted her this favour very frequently indeed; her most serious doubt, which used to occur when she first experienced it, was whether she was not imagining the whole thing. When locutions come from the devil their source can be more quickly recognized, though his wiles are so numerous that he can readily counterfeit the spirit of light. He will do this, in my view, by pronouncing his words very clearly, so that there will be no more doubt about their being understood than if they were being spoken by the spirit of truth. But he will not be able to counterfeit the effects which have been described, or to leave in the soul this peace or light, but only restlessness and turmoil. He can do little or no harm if the soul is humble and does what I have said — that is, if it refrains from action, whatever the locutions may say.

If gifts and favours come to it from the Lord, the soul should consider carefully and see if they make it think any the better of itself; and if, as the words grow more and more precious, it does not suffer increasing confusion, it can be sure that the spirit is not of God; for it is quite certain that, when it is so, the greater the favour the soul receives, the less by far it esteems itself, the more keenly it remembers its sins, the more forgetful it is of its own interest, the more fervent are the efforts of its will and memory in seeking nothing but the honour of God rather than being mindful of its own profit, and the greater is its fear of departing in the least from the will of God and its certainty that it has never deserved these favours, but only hell. When these are the results of all the experiences and favours that come to the soul in prayer, it need not be afraid, but may rest confidently in the mercy of the Lord, Who is faithful, and will not allow the devil to deceive it, though it always does well to retain its misgivings.

It may be that those whom the Lord does not lead by this road think that such souls need not listen to these words which are addressed to them; that, if they are interior words, they should turn their attention elsewhere so as not to hear them; and that in this way they will run no risk of incurring these perils. My answer is that that is impossible — and I am not referring now to locutions invented by the fancy, a remedy for which is to be less anxious about certain things and to try to take no notice of one's own imaginings. When the locutions come from God there is no such remedy, for the Spirit Himself, as He speaks, inhibits all other thought and compels attention to what He says. So I really think (and I believe this to be true) that it would be easier for someone with excellent hearing not to hear a person who spoke in a very loud voice, because he might simply pay no heed and occupy his thought and understanding with something else. In the case of which we are speaking, however, that is impossible. We have no ears which we can stop nor have we the power to refrain from thought; we can only think of what is being said; for He who was able, at the request of Josue (I think it was), to make the sun stand still,[162] can still the faculties and all the interior part of the soul in such a way that the soul becomes fully aware that another Lord, greater than itself, is governing that Castle and renders Him the greatest devotion and humility. So it cannot do other than listen: it has no other choice. May His Divine Majesty grant us to fix our eyes only on pleasing Him and to forget ourselves, as I have said: Amen. May He grant that I have succeeded in explaining what I have attempted to explain and that I may have given some help to any who have experience of these locutions.

Chapter IV

Treats of occasions when God suspends the soul in prayer by means of rapture, or ecstasy, or trance (for I think these are all the same), and of how great courage is necessary if we are to receive great favours from His Majesty.

How much rest can this poor little butterfly have amid all these trials and other things that I have described? Its whole will is set on desiring to have ever-increasing fruition of its Spouse; and His Majesty, knowing our weakness, continues to grant it the things it wants, and many more, so that it may have the courage to achieve union with so great a Lord and to take Him for its Spouse.

You will laugh at my saying this and call it ridiculous, for you will all think courage is quite unnecessary and suppose there is no woman, however lowly, who would not be brave enough to betroth herself to the King. This would be so, I think, with an earthly king, but for betrothal with the King of Heaven I must warn you that there is more need of courage than you imagine, because our nature is very timid and lowly for so great an undertaking, and I am certain that, unless God granted us strength,[163] it would be impossible. And now you are going to see what His Majesty does to confirm this betrothal, for this, as I understand it, is what happens when He bestows raptures, which carry the soul out of its senses; for if, while still in possession of its senses, the soul saw that it was so near to such great majesty, it might perhaps be unable to remain alive. It must be understood that I am referring to genuine raptures, and not to women's weaknesses, which we all have in this life, so that we are apt to think everything is rapture and ecstasy. And, as I believe I have said, there are some people who have such poor constitutions that one experience of the Prayer of Quiet kills them. I want to enumerate here some different kinds of rapture which I have got to know about through conversations with spiritual people. I am not sure if I shall succeed in doing so, any more than when I wrote of this before.[164] For various reasons it has been thought immaterial if I should repeat myself in discussing this and other matters connected with it, if for no other object than that of setting down in one place all that there is to be said about each Mansion.

One kind of rapture is this. The soul, though not actually engaged in prayer, is struck by some word, which it either remembers or hears spoken by God. His Majesty is moved with compassion at having seen the soul suffering so long through its yearning for Him, and seems to be causing the spark of which we have already spoken to grow within it, so that, like the phoenix, it catches fire and springs into new life. One may piously believe that the sins of such a soul are pardoned, assuming that it is in the proper disposition and has used the means of grace, as the Church teaches.[165] When it is thus cleansed, God unites it with Himself, in a way which none can understand save it and He, and even the soul itself does not understand this in such a way as to be able to speak of it afterwards, though it is not deprived of its interior senses; for it is not like one who suffers a swoon or a paroxysm so that it can understand nothing either within itself or without.

The position, in this case, as I understand it, is that the soul has never before been so fully awake to the things of God or had such light or such knowledge of His Majesty. This may seem impossible; because, if the faculties are so completely absorbed that we might describe them as dead, and the senses are so as well, how can the soul be said to understand this secret? I cannot say, nor perhaps can any creature, but only the Creator Himself, nor can I speak of many other things that happen in this state — I mean in these two Mansions, for this and the last might be fused in one: there is no closed door to separate the one from the other. As, however, there are things in the latter Mansion which are not shown to those who have not yet reached it, I have thought it best to separate them.

When the soul is in this state of suspension and the Lord sees fit to reveal to it certain mysteries, such as heavenly things and imaginary visions, it is able subsequently to describe these, for they are so deeply impressed upon the memory that they can never again be forgotten. But when they are intellectual visions they cannot be so described; for at these times come visions of so sublime a kind that it is not fitting for those who live on earth to understand them in such a way that they can describe them; although after regaining possession of their senses they can often describe many of these intellectual visions.

It may be that some of you do not understand what is meant by a vision, especially by an intellectual vision. I shall explain this in due course, as I have been commanded to do so by him who has authority over me; and although it may seem irrelevant there may possibly be souls who will find it helpful. "But," you will say to me, "if the soul is not going to remember these sublime favours which the Lord grants it in this state, how can they bring it any profit?" Oh, daughters, the profit is so great that it cannot be exaggerated, for, although one cannot describe these favours, they are clearly imprinted in the very depths of the soul and they are never forgotten. "But," you will say next, "if the soul retains no image of them and the faculties are unable to understand them, how can they be remembered?" This, too, is more than I can understand; but I know that certain truths concerning the greatness of God remains so firmly in the soul that even had it not faith which will tell it Who He is and that it is bound to believe Him to be God, the soul would adore Him as such from that very moment, just as Jacob adored Him when he saw the ladder.[166] He must, of course, have learned other secrets which he could not describe; for, if he had not had more interior light, he would not have understood such great mysteries merely from seeing a ladder on which angels were descending and ascending.

I do not know if I am right in what I am saying, for, although I have heard of the incident, I am not sure if I remember it correctly. Moses, again, could not describe all that he saw in the bush, but only as much as God willed him to;[167] yet, if God had not revealed secret things to his soul in such a way as to make him sure of their truth, so that he should know and believe Him to be God, he would not have taken upon himself so many and such arduous labours. Amid the thorns of that bush he must have learned marvellous things, for it was these things which gave him courage to do what he did for the people of Israel. Therefore, sisters, we must not seek out reasons for understanding the hidden things of God; rather, believing, as we do, in His great power, we must clearly realize that it is impossible for worms like ourselves, with our limited powers, to understand His greatness. Let us give Him hearty praise for being pleased to allow us to understand some part of it.

I am wishing I could find a suitable comparison which would give some sort of explanation of what I am saying. But I can think of none that will answer my purpose. Let us put it like this, however. You enter a private apartment in the palace of a king or a great lord (I think they call it a camarín), where they have an infinite variety of glassware, and earthenware, and all kinds of things, set out in such a way that you can see almost all of them as you enter. I was once taken into a room of this kind in the house of the Duchess of Alba, where I was commanded by obedience to stay,[168] in the course of a journey, at her pressing invitation. When I went in I was astounded and began to wonder what all this mass of things could be used for, and then I realized that the sight of so many different things might lead one to glorify the Lord. It occurs to me now how useful an experience it was for my present purpose. Although I was there for some time, there was so much to be seen that I could not remember it all, so that I could no more recall what was in those rooms than if I had never seen them, nor could I say what the things were made of; I can only remember having seen them as a whole.[169] It is just like that here. The soul becomes one with God. It is brought into this mansion of the empyrean Heaven which we must have in the depths of our souls; for it is clear that, since God dwells in them, He must have one[170] of these mansions. And although while the soul is in ecstasy the Lord will not always wish it to see these secrets (for it is so much absorbed in its fruition of Him that that great blessing suffices it), He is sometimes pleased that it should emerge from its absorption, and then it will at once see what there is in this room; in which case, after coming to itself, it will remember that revelation of the great things it has seen. It will not, however, be able to describe any of them, nor will its nature be able to apprehend more of the supernatural than God has been pleased to reveal to it.

Is this tantamount to an admission on my part that it has really seen something and that this is an imaginary vision? I do not mean that at all, for it is not of imaginary, but of intellectual visions that I am treating; only I have no learning and am too stupid to explain anything; and I am quite clear that, if what I have said so far about this kind of prayer is put correctly, it is not I who have said it. My own belief is that, if the soul to whom God has given these secrets in its raptures never understands any of them, they proceed, not from raptures at all, but from some natural weakness, which is apt to affect people of feeble constitution, such as women. In such cases the spirit, by making a certain effort, can overcome nature and remain in a state of absorption, as I believe I said when dealing with the Prayer of Quiet. Such experiences as these have nothing to do with raptures; for when a person is enraptured you can be sure that God is taking her entire soul to Himself, and that, as she is His own property and has now become His bride, He is showing her some little part of the kingdom which she has gained by becoming so. This part may be only a small one, but everything that is in this great God is very great. He will not allow her to be disturbed either by the faculties or by the senses; so He at once commands that all the doors of these Mansions shall be shut, and only the door of the Mansion in which He dwells remains open so that we may enter. Blessed be such great mercy! Rightly shall those who will not profit by it, and who thus forgo the presence of their Lord, be called accursed.

Oh, my sisters, what nothingness is all that we have given up, and all that we are doing, or can ever do, for a God Who is pleased to communicate Himself in this way to a worm! If we have the hope of enjoying this blessing while we are still in this life, what are we doing about it and why are we waiting? What sufficient reason is there for delaying even a short time instead of seeking this Lord, as the Bride did, through streets and squares?[171] Oh, what a mockery is everything in the world if it does not lead us and help us on the way towards this end, — and would be even though all the worldly delights and riches and joys that we can imagine were to last for ever! For everything is cloying and degrading by comparison with these treasures, which we shall enjoy eternally. And even these are nothing by comparison with having for our own the Lord of all treasures and of Heaven and earth.

Oh, human blindness! How long, how long shall it be before this dust is removed from our eyes? For although, as far as we ourselves are concerned, it seems not to be bad enough to blind us altogether, I can see some motes and particles which, if we allow them to become more numerous, will be sufficient to do us great harm. For the love of God, then, sisters, let us profit by these faults and learn from them what wretched creatures we are, and may they give us clearer sight, as did the clay to the blind man who was healed by our Spouse;[172] and thus, realizing our own imperfections, we shall beseech Him more and more earnestly to bring good out of our wretchedness, so that we may please His Majesty in everything.

Without realizing it, I have strayed far from my theme. Forgive me, sisters; and believe me, now that I have come to these great things of God (come to write about them, I mean), I cannot help feeling the pity of it when I see how much we are losing, and all through our own fault. For, true though it is that these are things which the Lord gives to whom He will, He would give them to us all if we loved Him as He loves us. For He desires nothing else but to have those to whom He may give them, and His riches are not diminished by His readiness to give.

Returning now to what I was saying, the Spouse orders the doors of the Mansions to be shut, and even those of the Castle and its enclosure. For when He means to enrapture this soul, it loses its power of breathing, with the result that, although its other senses sometimes remain active a little longer, it cannot possibly speak. At other times it loses all its powers at once, and the hands and the body grow so cold that the body seems no longer to have a soul — sometimes it even seems doubtful if there is any breath in the body. This lasts only for a short time (I mean, only for a short period at any one time) because, when this profound suspension lifts a little, the body seems to come partly to itself again, and draws breath, though only to die once more, and, in doing so, to give fuller life to the soul. Complete ecstasy, therefore, does not last long.

But, although relief comes, the ecstasy has the effect of leaving the will so completely absorbed and the understanding so completely transported — for as long as a day, or even for several days — that the soul seems incapable of grasping anything that does not awaken the will to love; to this it is fully awake, while asleep as regards all that concerns attachment to any creature.

Oh, what confusion the soul feels when it comes to itself again and what ardent desires it has to be used for God in any and every way in which He may be pleased to employ it! If such effects as have been described result from the former kinds of prayer, what can be said of a favour as great as this? Such a soul would gladly have a thousand lives so as to use them all for God, and it would like everything on earth to be tongue so that it might praise Him. It has tremendous desires to do penance; and whatever penance it does it counts as very little, for its love is so strong that it feels everything it does to be of very small account and realizes clearly that it was not such a great matter for the martyrs to suffer all their tortures, for with the aid of Our Lord such a thing becomes easy. And thus these souls make complaint to Our Lord when He offers them no means of suffering.

When this favour is granted them secretly they esteem it very highly; for so great are the shame and the confusion caused them by having to suffer before others that to some extent they lessen the soul's absorption in what it was enjoying, because of the distress and the anxiety which arise from its thoughts of what others who have seen it will think. For, knowing the malice of the world, they realize that their suffering may perhaps not be attributed to its proper cause but may be made an occasion for criticism instead of for glorifying the Lord. This distress and shame are no longer within the soul's own power of control, yet they seem to me to denote a lack of humility; for if such a person really desires to be despitefully treated, how can she mind if she is? One who was distressed in this way heard Our Lord say: "Be not afflicted, for either they will praise Me or murmur at thee, and in either case thou wilt be the gainer."[173] I learned afterwards that that person had been greatly cheered and consoled by those words; and I set them down here for the sake of any who find themselves in this affliction. It seems that Our Lord wants everyone to realize that such a person's soul is now His and that no one must touch it. People are welcome to attack her body, her honour, and her possessions, for any of these attacks will be to His Majesty's honour. But her soul they may not attack, for unless, with most blameworthy presumption, it tears itself away from its Spouse, He will protect it from the whole world, and indeed from all hell.

I do not know if I have conveyed any impression of the nature of rapture: to give a full idea of it, as I have said, is impossible. Still, I think there has been no harm in my saying this, so that its nature may be understood, since the effects of feigned raptures are so different. (I do not use the word "feigned" because those who experience them wish to deceive, but because they are deceived themselves.)[174]

As the signs and effects of these last do not harmonize with the reception of this great favour, the favour itself becomes discredited, so that those to whom the Lord grants it later on are not believed. May He be for ever blessed and praised. Amen. Amen.

Chapter V

Continues the same subject and gives an example of how God exalts the soul through flights of the spirit in a way different from that described. Gives some reasons why courage is necessary here. Says something of this favour which God grants in a way so delectable. This chapter is highly profitable.

There is another kind of rapture, or flight of the spirit, as I call it, which, though substantially the same, is felt within the soul[175] in a very different way. Sometimes the soul becomes conscious of such rapid motion that the spirit seems to be transported with a speed which, especially at first, fills it with fear, for which reason I told you that great courage is necessary for anyone in whom God is to work these favours, together with faith and confidence and great resignation, so that Our Lord may do with the soul as He wills. Do you suppose it causes but little perturbation to a person in complete possession of his senses when he experiences these transports of the soul? We have even read in some authors that the body is transported as well as the soul, without knowing whither it is going, or who is bearing it away, or how, for when this sudden motion begins the soul has no certainty that it is caused by God.

Can any means of resisting this be found? None whatever: on the contrary, resistance only makes matters worse. This I know from a certain person who said that God's will seems to be to show the soul that, since it has so often and so unconditionally placed itself in His hands, and has offered itself to Him with such complete willingness, it must realize that it is no longer its own mistress, and so the violence with which it is transported becomes markedly greater. This person, therefore, decided to offer no more resistance than a straw does when it is lifted up by amber (if you have ever observed this) and to commit herself into the hands of Him Who is so powerful, seeing that it is but to make a virtue of necessity. And, speaking of straw, it is a fact that a powerful man cannot bear away a straw more easily than this great and powerful Giant of ours can bear away the spirit.

I think that basin of water, of which we spoke in (I believe) the fourth Mansion (but I do not remember exactly where),[176] was being filled at that stage gently and quietly — I mean without any movement. But now this great God, Who controls the sources of the waters and forbids the sea to move beyond its bounds, has loosed the sources whence water has been coming into this basin; and with tremendous force there rises up so powerful a wave that this little ship — our soul — is lifted up on high. And if a ship can do nothing, and neither the pilot nor any of the crew has any power over it, when the waves make a furious assault upon it and toss it about at their will, even less able is the interior part of the soul to stop where it likes, while its senses and faculties can do no more than has been commanded them: the exterior senses, however, are quite unaffected by this.

Really, sisters, the mere writing of this makes me astounded when I reflect how the great power of this great King and Emperor manifests itself here. What, then, must be the feelings of anyone who experiences it? For my own part I believe that, if His Majesty were to reveal Himself to those who journey through the world to their perdition as He does to these souls, they would not dare — out of very fear, though not perhaps out of love — to offend Him. Oh, how great, then, are the obligations attending souls who have been warned in so sublime a way to strive with all their might so as not to offend this Lord! For His sake, sisters, I beseech you, to whom His Majesty has granted these favours or others like them, not merely to receive them and then grow careless, but to remember that anyone who owes much has much to pay.[177]

This is another reason why the soul needs great courage, for the thought is one which makes it very fearful, and, did Our Lord not give it courage, it would continually be in great affliction. When it reflects what His Majesty is doing with it, and then turns to reflect upon itself, it realizes what a little it is doing towards the fulfilment of its obligations and how feeble is that little which it does do and how full of faults and failures. If it does any good action, rather than remember how imperfect this action is, it thinks best to try to forget it, to keep nothing in mind but its sins, and to throw itself upon the mercy of God; and, since it has nothing with which to pay, it craves the compassion and mercy which He has always shown to sinners.

He may perhaps answer it as He answered someone who was very much distressed about this, and was looking at a crucifix and thinking that she had never had anything to offer God or to give up for His sake. The Crucified Himself comforted her by saying that He was giving her all the pains and trials which He had suffered in His Passion, so that she should have them for her own to offer to His Father.[178] That soul, as I have understood from her, was so much comforted and enriched by this experience that she cannot forget it, and, whenever she feels miserable, she remembers it and it comforts and encourages her. There are several other remarks on this subject which I might add; for, as I have had to do with many saintly and prayerful people, I know of a number of such cases, but I do not want you to think that it is to myself that I am referring, so I pass them over. This incident which I have described seems to me a very apt one for helping you to understand how glad Our Lord is when we get to know ourselves and keep trying all the time to realize our poverty and wretchedness, and to reflect that we possess nothing that we have not been given. Therefore, my sisters, courage is necessary for this and for many other things that happen to a soul which the Lord has brought to this state; and, to my thinking, if the soul is humble, more courage is necessary for this last state than for any other. May the Lord, of His own bounty, grant us humility.

Turning now to this sudden transport of the spirit, it may be said to be of such a kind that the soul really seems to have left the body; on the other hand, it is clear that the person is not dead, though for a few moments he cannot even himself be sure if the soul is in the body or no. He feels as if he has been in another world, very different from this in which we live, and has been shown a fresh light there, so much unlike any to be found in this life that, if he had been imagining it, and similar things, all his life long, it would have been impossible for him to obtain any idea of them. In a single instant he is taught so many things all at once that if he were to labour for years on end in trying to fit them all into his imagination and thought, he could not succeed with a thousandth part of them. This is not an intellectual, but an imaginary vision, which is seen with the eyes of the soul very much more clearly than we can ordinarily see things with the eyes of the body; and some of the revelations are communicated to it without words. If, for examples he sees any of the saints, he knows them as well as if he had spent a long time in their company.

Sometimes, in addition to the things which he sees with the eyes of the soul, in intellectual vision, others are revealed to him — in particular, a host of angels, with their Lord; and, though he sees nothing with the eyes of the body or with the eyes of the soul, he is shown the things I am describing and many others which are indescribable, by means of an admirable kind of knowledge. Anyone who has experience of this, and possesses more ability than I, will perhaps know how to express it; to me it seems extremely difficult. If the soul is in the body or not while all this is happening I cannot say; I would not myself swear that the soul is in the body, nor that the body is bereft of the soul.

I have often thought that if the sun can remain in the heavens and yet its rays are so strong that without its moving thence they can none the less reach us here, it must be possible for the soul and the spirit, which are as much the same thing as are the sun and its rays, to remain where they are, and yet, through the power of the heat that comes to them from the true Sun of Justice, for some higher part of them to rise above itself. Really, I hardly know what I am saying; but it is a fact that, as quickly as a bullet leaves a gun when the trigger is pulled, there begins within the soul a flight (I know no other name to give it) which, though no sound is made, is so clearly a movement that it cannot possibly be due to fancy. When the soul, as far as it can understand, is right outside itself, great things are revealed to it; and, when it returns to itself, it finds that it has reaped very great advantages and it has such contempt for earthly things that, in comparison with those it has seen, they seem like dirt to it. Thenceforward to live on earth is a great affliction to it, and, if it sees any of the things which used to give it pleasure, it no longer cares for them. Just as tokens of the nature of the Promised Land were brought back by those whom the Israelites sent on there,[179] so in this case the Lord's wish seems to have been to show the soul something of the country to which it is to travel, so that it may suffer the trials of this trying road,[180] knowing whither it must travel in order to obtain its rest. Although you may think that a thing which passes so quickly cannot be of great profit, the help which it gives the soul is so great that only the person familiar with it can understand its worth.

Clearly, then, this is no work of the devil; such an experience could not possibly proceed from the imagination, and the devil could never reveal things which produce such results in the soul and leave it with such peace and tranquillity and with so many benefits. There are three things in particular which it enjoys to a very high degree. The first is knowledge of the greatness of God: the more we see of this, the more deeply we are conscious of it. The second is self-knowledge and humility at realizing how a thing like the soul, so base by comparison with One Who is the Creator of such greatness, has dared to offend Him and dares to raise its eyes to Him. The third is a supreme contempt for earthly things, save those which can be employed in the service of so great a God.

These are the jewels which the Spouse is beginning to give to His bride, and so precious are they that she will not fail to keep them with the greatest care. These meetings[181] with the Spouse remain so deeply engraven in the memory that I think it is impossible for the soul to forget them until it is enjoying them for ever; if it did so, it would suffer the greatest harm. But the Spouse Who gives them to the soul has power also to give it grace not to lose them.

Returning now to the soul's need of courage, I ask you: Does it seem to you such a trifling thing after all? For the soul really feels that it is leaving the body when it sees the senses leaving it and has no idea why they are going. So He Who gives everything else must needs give courage too. You will say that this fear of the soul's is well rewarded; so too say I. May He Who can give so much be for ever praised. And may it please His Majesty to grant us to be worthy to serve Him. Amen.

Chapter VI

Describes one effect of the prayer referred to in the last chapter, by which it will be known that it is genuine and no deception. Treats of another favour which the Lord grants to the soul so that He may use it to sing His praises.

Having won such great favours, the soul is so anxious to have complete fruition of their Giver that its life becomes sheer, though delectable, torture. It has the keenest longings for death, and so it frequently and tearfully begs God to take it out of this exile. Everything in this life that it sees wearies it; when it finds itself alone it experiences great relief, but immediately this distress returns till it hardly knows itself when it is without it. In short, this little butterfly can find no lasting repose; indeed, her love is so full of tenderness that any occasion whatever which serves to increase the strength of this fire causes the soul to take flight; and thus in this Mansion raptures occur continually and there is no way of avoiding them, even in public. Further, although the soul would fain be free from tears, these persecutions and murmurings never leave her; for these all kinds of persons are responsible, especially confessors.

Although on the one hand she seems to be feeling great interior security, especially when alone with God, on the other hand she is in great distress, for she is afraid that the devil may be going to deceive her so that she shall offend Him for Whom she has such love. She is not hurt by what people say about her except when her own confessor blames her, as though she could prevent these raptures. She does nothing but beg everyone to pray for her and beseech His Majesty to lead her by another road, as she is advised to do, since the road she is on is very dangerous. But she has gained so much from following it (for she cannot help seeing, and she reads and hears and learns from the commandments of God that it leads to Heaven) that, try as she may, she feels unable to desire any other; all she wants to do is to leave herself in His hands. And even this impotence of will distresses her, because she thinks she is not obeying her confessor, for she believes that her only remedy against deception consists in obeying and not offending Our Lord. So she feels that she would not intentionally commit so much as a venial sin, even were she to be cut in pieces; and thus she is greatly distressed to find that, without being aware of the fact, she cannot avoid committing a great many.

God gives these souls the keenest desire not to displease Him in any respect whatsoever, however trivial, or to commit so much as an imperfection if they can avoid doing so. For this reason alone, if for no other, the soul would like to flee from other people, and greatly envies those who lived, or have lived, in deserts. On the other hand it would like to plunge right into the heart of the world, to see if by doing this it could help one soul to praise God more; a woman in this state will be distressed at being prevented from doing this by the obstacle of sex and very envious of those who are free to cry aloud and proclaim abroad Who is this great God of Hosts.

Oh, poor little butterfly, bound by so many fetters, which prevent you from flying whithersoever you will! Have pity on her, my God; and dispose things so that she may be able to do something towards fulfilling her desires to Thy honour

and glory. Remember not the slightness of her merits and the baseness of her
nature. Mighty art Thou, Lord, for Thou didst make the great sea to draw back,
and the great Jordan, and didst allow the Children of Israel to pass over them.[182]
And yet Thou needest not have pity on her, for, with the aid of Thy strength, she
is capable of enduring many trials. And this she is determined to do: to suffer
them is her desire. Stretch out Thy mighty arm, O Lord, and let not her life be
spent in things so base. Let Thy greatness appear in this creature, womanish and
base though she is, so that men may realize that nothing she does comes from
herself and may give Thee praise. Cost what it may, it is this that she desires, and
she would give a thousand lives, if she had them, so that on her account one soul
might praise Thee a little more. She would consider them all well spent, for she
knows that in actual fact she deserves not to suffer the very smallest trial for Thy
sake, still less to die for Thee.

I do not know why I have said this, sisters, nor to what purpose, for I have not
understood it all myself. It should be realized that such, without any kind of doubt,
are the effects which remain after these suspensions or ecstasies; the desires they
inspire are not fleeting but permanent; and when any opportunity occurs of
demonstrating the fact, it becomes evident that the experience was not feigned.
You may ask why I use the word "permanent", since sometimes and in the most
trifling matters the soul feels cowardly, and is so fearful and devoid of courage that
it seems impossible it can be courageous enough to do anything whatsoever. But
this, I take it, occurs at a time when the Lord leaves it to its own nature — an
experience which is extremely good for it, making it realize that any usefulness it
may have had has been a gift bestowed upon it by His Majesty. And this it realizes
with a clearness which annihilates any self-interest in it and imbues it with a
greater knowledge of the mercy of God and of His greatness, which He has been
pleased to demonstrate to it in so small a matter. But more usually it is as we
have already said.

Note one thing, sisters, concerning these great desires of the soul to see Our
Lord: that they will sometimes oppress you so much that you must not encourage
them but put them from you — if you can, I mean; because there are other
desires, of which I shall write later, which cannot possibly be so treated, as you
will see. These of which I am now speaking it is sometimes possible to put from
you, since the reason is free to resign itself to the will of God, and you can echo the
words of Saint Martin[183]; in such a case, where the desires are very oppressive, the
thoughts may be deflected from them. For, as such desires are apparently found
in souls which are very proficient, the devil might encourage them in us, so as to
make us think ourselves proficient too; and it is always well to proceed with
caution. But I do not myself believe he could ever fill the soul with the quietness
and peace caused it by this distress; the feelings he arouses are apt to be
passionate ones, like those which we experience when we are troubled about
things of the world. Anyone without experience of each kind of distress will not
understand that, and, thinking it a great thing to feel like this, will stimulate the
feeling as much as possible. To do this, however, may be to injure the health, for
the distress is continuous, or, at the least, occurs with great frequency.

Note also that distress of this kind is apt to be caused by weak health,
especially in emotional people, who weep for the slightest thing; again and again
they will think they are weeping for reasons which have to do with God but this
will not be so in reality. It may even be the case (I mean when they shed floods of
tears — and for some time they cannot refrain from doing so whenever they think

of God or hear Him spoken of) that some humour has been oppressing the heart, and that it is this, rather than their love of God, which has excited their tears. It seems as if they will never make an end of weeping, having come to believe that tears are good, they make no attempt to control them. In fact, they would not do otherwise than weep even if they could, and they make every effort they can to induce tears. The devil does his best, in such cases, to weaken them, so that they may be unable either to practise prayer or to keep their Rule.

I seem to hear you asking whatever you are to do, as I am telling you there is danger in everything. If I think deception possible in anything as beneficial as shedding tears may I not be deceived myself? Yes, of course I may; but, believe me, I am not talking without having observed this in certain persons. I have never been like it myself, however, for I am not in the least emotional; on the contrary, my hardness of heart sometimes worries me; though, when the fire within my soul is strong, however hard my heart may be, it distils as if in an alembic. You will easily recognize when tears arise from this source, because they are comforting and tranquillizing rather than disturbing, and seldom do any harm. The great thing about this deception, when such it is, will be that, although it may harm the body, it cannot (if the soul is humble, I mean) hurt the soul. If it is not humble, it will do it no harm to keep its suspicions.

Do not let us suppose that if we weep a great deal we have done everything that matters; let us also set to and work hard, and practise the virtues, for these are what we most need. Let the tears come when God is pleased to send them: we ourselves should make no efforts to induce them. They will leave this dry ground of ours well watered and will be of great help in producing fruit; but the less notice we take of them, the more they will do, because they are the water which comes from Heaven.[184] When we ourselves draw water, we tire ourselves by digging for it, and the water we get is not the same; often we dig till we wear ourselves out without having discovered so much as a pool of water, still less a wellspring. For this reason, sisters, I think our best plan is to place ourselves in the Lord's presence, meditate upon His mercy and grace and upon our own lowliness, and leave Him to give us what He wills, whether it be water or aridity. He knows best what is good for us, and in this way we shall walk in tranquillity and the devil will have less opportunity to fool us.

Together with these things, which are at once distressing and delectable, Our Lord sometimes bestows upon the soul a jubilation and a strange kind of prayer, the nature of which it cannot ascertain. I set this down here, so that, if He grants you this favour, you may give Him hearty praise and know that such a thing really happens. I think the position is that the faculties are in close union, but that Our Lord leaves both faculties and senses free to enjoy this happiness, without understanding what it is that they are enjoying and how they are enjoying it. That sounds nonsense but it is certainly what happens. The joy of the soul is so exceedingly great that it would like, not to rejoice in God in solitude, but to tell its joy to all, so that they may help it to praise Our Lord, to which end it directs its whole activity. Oh, what high festival such a one would make to this end and how she would show forth her joy, if she could, so that all should understand it! For she seems to have found herself, and, like the father of the Prodigal Son,[185] she would like to invite everybody and have great festivities because she sees her soul in a place which she cannot doubt is a place of safety, at least for a time. And, for my own part, I believe she is right; for such interior joy in the depths of the soul's being, such peace and such happiness that it calls upon all to praise God cannot possibly have come from the devil.

Impelled as it is by this great joy, the soul cannot be expected to keep silence and dissemble: it would find this no light distress. That must have been the state of mind of Saint Francis, when robbers met him as he was going about the countryside crying aloud and he told them that he was the herald of the great King. Other saints retire to desert places, where they proclaim the same thing as Saint Francis — namely, the praises of their God. I knew one of these, called Fray Peter of Alcántara. Judging from the life he led, I think he is certainly a saint, yet those who heard him from time to time called him mad. Oh, what a blessed madness, sisters! If only God would give it to us all! And how good He has been to you in placing you where, if the Lord should grant you this grace and you show others that He has done so, you will not be spoken against as you would be in the world (where there are so few to proclaim God's praise that it is not surprising if they are spoken against,) but will be encouraged to praise Him the more.

Oh, unhappy are the times and miserable is the life which we now live, and happy are those who have had the good fortune to escape from it! Sometimes it makes me specially glad when we are together and I see these sisters of mine so full of inward joy that each vies with the rest in praising Our Lord for bringing her to the convent; it is very evident that those praises come from the inmost depths of the soul. I should like you to praise Him often, sisters, for, when one of you begins to do so, she arouses the rest. How can your tongues be better employed, when you are together, than in the praises of God, which we have so many reasons for rendering Him?

May it please His Majesty often to bestow this prayer upon us since it brings us such security and such benefit. For, as it is an entirely supernatural thing, we cannot acquire it. It may last for a whole day, and the soul will then be like one who has drunk a great deal, but not like a person so far inebriated as to be deprived of his senses; nor will it be like a melancholiac, who, without being entirely out of his mind, cannot forget a thing that has been impressed upon his imagination, from which no one else can free him either. These are very unskilful comparisons to represent so precious a thing, but I am not clever enough to think out any more: the real truth is that this joy makes the soul so forgetful of itself, and of everything, that it is conscious of nothing, and able to speak of nothing, save of that which proceeds from its joy — namely, the praises of God. Let us join with this soul, my daughters all. Why should we want to be more sensible than she? What can give us greater pleasure than to do as she does? And may all the creatures join with us for ever and ever. Amen, amen, amen.

Chapter VII

Treats of the kind of grief felt for their sins by the souls to Whom God grants the favours aforementioned. Says that, however spiritual people may be, it is a great mistake for them not to practise keeping in mind the Humanity of Our Lord and Saviour Jesus Christ, His most sacred Passion and life, and His glorious Mother and the Saints. This chapter is of great profit.

You will think, sisters, that these souls to whom the Lord communicates Himself in so special a way (I am speaking now particularly to those who have not attained these favours, for if they have been granted the enjoyment of such favours by God, they will know what I am about to say) will by now be so sure that they are to enjoy Him for ever that they will have no reason to fear or to weep for their sins. This will be a very great mistake, for, the more they receive from our God, the greater grows their sorrow for sin; I believe myself that this will never leave us until we reach that place where nothing can cause us affliction.

It is true that this sorrow can be more oppressive at one time than at another, and also that it is of different kinds, for the soul does not now think of the pain which it is bound to suffer on account of its sins, but only of how ungrateful it has been to Him Whom it owes so much, and Who so greatly merits our service. For through these manifestations of His greatness which He communicates to it the soul gains a much deeper knowledge of the greatness of God. It is aghast at having been so bold; it weeps for its lack of reverence; its foolish mistakes in the past seem to it to have been so gross that it cannot stop grieving, when it remembers that it forsook so great a Majesty for things so base. It thinks of this much more than of the favours it receives, great as they are like those which we have described and like those which remain to be described later. It is as if a mighty river were running through the soul and from time to time bringing these favours with it. But its sins are like the river's slimy bed; they are always fresh in its memory, and this is a heavy cross to it.

I know of a person who had ceased wishing she might die so as to see God, but was desiring death in order that she might not suffer such constant distress at the thought of her ingratitude to One to Whom her debts were so great. She thought nobody's evil deeds could equal hers, for she believed there was no one with whom God had borne for so long and to whom He had shown so many favours.

With regard to fear of hell, these souls have none; they are sometimes sorely oppressed by the thought that they may lose God, but this happens seldom. Their sole fear is that God may let them out of His hand and that they may then offend Him, and thus find themselves in as miserable a state as before. They have no anxiety about their own pain or glory. If they desire not to stay long in Purgatory, it is less for the pain which they will have to suffer than because while they are there they will not be with God.

However favoured by God a soul may be, I should not think it secure were it to forget the miserable state it was once in, for, distressing though the reflection is, it is often profitable. Perhaps it is because I myself have been so wicked that I feel like this and for that reason always keep it in mind; those who have been good will have nothing to grieve for, although for as long as we live in this mortal body we shall always have failures. It affords us no relief from this distress to reflect that Our Lord has forgiven and forgotten our sins; in fact the thought of so much goodness and of favours granted to one who has merited only hell makes the distress greater. I think these reflections must have been a regular martyrdom for Saint Peter and for the Magdalen; because, as their love was so great and they had received so many favours and had learned to understand the greatness and majesty of God, they would find them terribly hard to bear, and must have been moved with the deepest emotion.

You will also think that anyone who enjoys such sublime favours will not engage in meditation on the most sacred Humanity of Our Lord Jesus Christ, because by that time he will be wholly proficient in love. This is a thing of which I have written at length elsewhere,[186] and, although I have been contradicted about it and told that I do not understand it, because these are paths along which Our Lord leads us, and that, when we have got over the first stages, we shall do better to occupy ourselves with matters concerning the Godhead and to flee from corporeal things, they will certainly not make me admit that this is a good way. I may be wrong and we may all be meaning the same thing; but it was clear to me that the devil was trying to deceive me in this way, and I have had to learn my lesson. So, although I have often spoken about this,[187] I propose to speak to you about it again, so that you may walk very warily. And observe that I am going so far as to advise you not to believe anyone who tells you otherwise. I will try to explain myself better than I did before. If by any chance a certain person has written about it, as he said he would, it is to be hoped that he has explained it more fully; to write about it in a general way to those of us who are not very intelligent may do a great deal of harm.

Some souls also imagine that they cannot dwell upon the Passion, in which case they will be able still less to meditate upon the most sacred Virgin and the lives of the saints, the remembrance of whom brings us such great profit and encouragement. I cannot conceive what they are thinking of; for, though angelic spirits, freed from everything corporeal, may remain permanently enkindled in love, this is not possible for those of us who live in this mortal body. We need to cultivate, and think upon, and seek the companionship of those who, though living on earth like ourselves, have accomplished such great deeds for God; the last thing we should do is to withdraw of set purpose from our greatest help and blessing, which is the most sacred Humanity of Our Lord Jesus Christ. I cannot believe that people can really do this; it must be that they do not understand themselves and thus do harm to themselves and to others. At any rate, I can assure them that they will not enter these last two Mansions; for, if they lose their Guide, the good Jesus, they will be unable to find their way; they will do well if they are able to remain securely in the other Mansions. For the Lord Himself says that He is the Way;[188] the Lord also says that He is light[189] and that no one can come to the Father save by Him;[190] and "he that seeth Me seeth my Father."[191] It may be said that these words have another meaning. I do not know of any such meaning myself; I have got on very well with the meaning which my soul always feels to be the true one.

There are some people (and a great many of them have spoken to me about this) on whom Our Lord bestows perfect contemplation and who would like to remain in possession of it for ever. That is impossible; but they retain something of this Divine favour, with the result that they can no longer meditate upon the mysteries of the Passion and the life of Christ, as they could before. I do not know the reason for this, but it is quite a common experience in such cases for the understanding to be less apt for meditation. I think the reason must be that the whole aim of meditation is to seek God, and once He is found, and the soul grows accustomed to seeking Him again by means of the will, it has no desire to fatigue itself with intellectual labour. It also seems to me that, as the will is now enkindled, this generous faculty would have no desire to make use of that other faculty,[192] even if it could. There would be nothing wrong in its setting it aside, but it is impossible for it to do so, especially before the soul has reached these last Mansions, and it will only lose time by attempting it, for the aid of the understanding is often needed for the enkindling of the will.

Note this point, sisters, for it is important, so I will explain it further. The soul is desirous of employing itself wholly in love and it would be glad if it could meditate on nothing else. But this it cannot do even if it so desires; for, though the will is not dead, the fire which habitually kindles it is going out, and, if it is to give off heat of itself, it needs someone to fan it into flame. Would it be a good thing for the soul to remain in that state of aridity, hoping for fire to come down from Heaven to burn up this sacrifice of itself which it is making to God as did our father Elias?[193] No, certainly not; nor is it a good thing to expect miracles: the Lord will perform them for this soul when He sees fit to do so, as has been said and as will be said again later. But His Majesty wants us to realize our wickedness, which makes us unworthy of their being wrought, and to do everything we possibly can to come to our own aid. And I believe myself that, however sublime our prayer may be, we shall have to do this until we die.

It is true that anyone whom Our Lord brings to the seventh Mansion very rarely, or never, needs to engage in this activity, for the reason that I shall set down, if I remember to do so, when I come to deal with that Mansion, where in a wonderful way the soul never ceases to walk with Christ our Lord but is ever in the company of both His Divine and His human nature. When, therefore, the aforementioned fire is not kindled in the will, and the presence of God is not felt, we must needs seek it, since this is His Majesty's desire, as the Bride sought it in the Songs.194 Let us ask the creatures who made them, as Saint Augustine says that he did (in his Meditations or Confessions,195 I think) and let us not be so foolish as to lose time by waiting to receive what has been given us once already. At first it may be that the Lord will not give it us, for as long as a year, or even for many years: His Majesty knows why; it is not our business to want to know, nor is there any reason why we should. Since we know the way we have to take to please God — namely, that of keeping His commandments and counsels — let us be very diligent in doing this, and in meditating upon His life and death, and upon all that we owe Him; and let the rest come when the Lord wills.

Such people will reply that they cannot stop to meditate upon these things, and here they may to some extent be right, for the reason already given. You know, of course, that it is one thing to reason with the understanding and quite another for the memory to represent truths to the understanding. You will say, perhaps, that you do not understand me, and it may very well be that I do not understand the matter myself sufficiently to be able to explain it; but I will deal with it as well as I can. By meditation I mean prolonged reasoning with the understanding, in this way. We begin by thinking of the favour which God bestowed upon us by giving us His only Son; and we do not stop there but proceed to consider the mysteries of His whole glorious life. Or we begin with the prayer in the Garden and go on rehearsing the events that follow until we come to the Crucifixion. Or we take one episode of the Passion — Christ's arrest, let us say — and go over this mystery in our mind, meditating in detail upon the points in it which we need to think over and to try to realize, such as the treason of Judas, the flight of the Apostles, and so on. This is an admirable and a most meritorious kind of prayer.

This is the kind of prayer I was referring to which those whom God has raised to supernatural things and to perfect contemplation are right in saying they cannot practise. As I have said, I do not know why this should be the case; but as a rule they are in fact unable to do so. A man will not be right, however, to say that he cannot dwell upon these mysteries, for he often has them in his mind, especially when they are being celebrated by the Catholic Church; nor is it possible that a soul which has received so much from God should forget all these precious signs of His love, for they are living sparks which will enkindle the soul more and more in its love for Our Lord. But these mysteries will not be apprehended by the understanding: the soul will understand them in a more perfect way. First, the understanding will picture them to itself, and then they will be impressed upon the memory, so that the mere sight of the Lord on His knees, in the Garden, covered with that terrible sweat, will suffice us, not merely for an hour, but for many days. We consider, with a simple regard, Who He is and how ungrateful we have been to One Who has borne such pain for us. Then the will is aroused, not perhaps with deep emotion but with a desire to make some kind of return for this great favour, and to suffer something for One Who has suffered so much Himself. And so it is with other subjects, in which both memory and understanding will have a place. This, I think, is why the soul cannot reason properly about the Passion, and it is because of this that it believes itself unable to meditate upon it at all.

But if it does not already meditate in this way, it will be well advised to attempt to do so; for I know that the most sublime kind of prayer will be no obstacle to it and I believe omission to practise it often would be a great mistake. If while the soul is meditating the Lord should suspend it, well and good; for in that case He will make it cease meditation even against its own will. I consider it quite certain that this method of procedure is no hindrance to the soul but a great help to it in everything that is good; whereas, if it laboured hard at meditation in the way I have already described, this would indeed be a hindrance — in fact, I believe such labour is impossible for a person who has attained greater heights. This may not be so with everyone, since God leads souls by many ways, but those who are unable to take this road should not be condemned or judged incapable of enjoying the great blessings contained in the mysteries of Jesus Christ our Good. No one, however spiritual, will persuade me that to neglect these mysteries can be profitable for him.

Some souls, at the beginning of the spiritual life, or even when well advanced in it, get as far as the Prayer of Quiet, and are about to enjoy the favours and consolations given by the Lord in that state, and then think it would be a very great thing to be enjoying these gifts all the time. Let them take my advice, and become less absorbed in them, as I have said elsewhere.[196] For life is long and there are many trials in it and we have need to look at Christ our Pattern, and also at His Apostles and Saints, and to reflect how they bore these trials, so that we, too, may bear them perfectly. The good Jesus is too good company for us to forsake Him and His most sacred Mother. He is very glad when we grieve for His afflictions although sometimes we may be forsaking our own pleasures and consolations in order to do so — though for that matter, daughters, consolations in prayer are not so frequent that there is not time for everything. If anyone told me that she experienced them continuously (I mean so continuously that she could never meditate in the way I have described) I should consider it suspicious. Keep on with your meditation, then, and endeavour to be free from this error, and make every effort to avoid this absorption. If your efforts are not sufficient, tell the prioress, in order that she may give you some work which will keep you so busy that this danger will no longer exist. Any continuous exposure to it would be very bad for the brain and the head, if nothing worse.

I think I have explained what it is well for you to know — namely that, however spiritual you are, you must not flee so completely from corporeal things as to think that meditation on the most sacred Humanity can actually harm you. We are sometimes reminded that the Lord said to His disciples that it was expedient for them that He should go away:[197] I cannot, however, allow that as an argument. He did not say this to His most sacred Mother, because she was firm in the faith and knew that He was God and Man; and, although she loved Him more than they, her love was so perfect that His being on earth was actually a help to her. The Apostles could not at that time have been as firm in the faith as they were later and as we have reason to be now. I assure you, daughters, that I consider this a perilous road and that if we took it the devil might end by causing us to lose our devotion to the Most Holy Sacrament.

The mistake, I think, which I used to make myself did not go as far as this; it was only that I would take less pleasure than previously in thinking of Our Lord Jesus Christ and would go about in that state of absorption, expecting to receive spiritual consolation. Then I saw clearly that I was going wrong; for, as it was impossible always to be having consolations, my thoughts would keep passing from one subject to another, until my soul, I think, got like a bird flying round and round in search of a resting-place and losing a great deal of time, without advancing in the virtues or making progress in prayer. I could not understand the cause — nor, I believe, should I ever have understood it, because I thought I was on the proper road, until one day, when I was telling a person who was a servant of God about my method of prayer, he gave me some counsel. This showed me clearly how far I had gone astray and I have never ceased regretting that there was once a time when I failed to realize that so great a loss could not possibly result in gain. Even if I could obtain it, I want no blessing save that which I acquire through Him by Whom all blessings come to us. May He be praised for ever. Amen.

Chapter VIII

Treats of the way in which God communicates Himself to the soul through intellectual vision.[198] Describes the effects which this produces when genuine. Charges that these favours be kept secret.

In order, sisters, that you may the better appreciate the accuracy of what I have been saying to you and see that the farther a soul progresses the closer becomes its companionship with this good Jesus, it will be well for us to consider how, when His Majesty so wills, we cannot do otherwise than walk with Him all the times as is clear from the ways and methods whereby His Majesty communicates Himself to us, and reveals His love for us by means of such wonderful appearances and visions. Should the Lord grant you any of the favours which I shall describe (I mean, if He grants me ability to describe any of them), you must not be dismayed. Even though it be not to us that He grants them, we must give Him hearty praise that He should be pleased to commune with a creature — He Who is of such great majesty and power.

It may happen that, while the soul is not in the least expecting Him to be about to grant it this favour, which it has never thought it can possibly deserve, it is conscious that Jesus Christ Our Lord is near to it, though it cannot see Him either with the eyes of the body or with those of the soul. This (I do not know why) is called an intellectual vision. I saw a person to whom God had granted this favour, together with other favours which I shall describe later. At first that person was greatly perturbed, for she could not understand what the vision was, not having seen anything. She realized with such certainty that it was Jesus Christ Our Lord Who had revealed Himself to her in that way that she could not doubt it — I mean, could not doubt that that vision was there. But as to its being from God or no she had great misgivings, although the effects which it produced were so remarkable that they suggested it came from Him. She had never heard of an intellectual vision, or realized that there was any such thing, but she understood quite clearly that it was this Lord Who often spoke to her in the way I have described: until He granted her this favour to which I am referring she never knew Who was speaking to her, although she understood the words.

Being frightened about this vision (for it is not like an imaginary vision, which is quickly gone, but lasts for many days — sometimes for more than a year), she went off to her confessor in a state of great perturbation.[199] "If you see nothing," he asked her, "how do you know it is Our Lord?" Then he told her to tell him what His face was like. She replied that she did not know, that she had seen no face, and that she could not tell him more than she had done already: what she did know was that it was He Who was speaking to her and that it was no fancy. And, although people aroused grievous misgivings in her about it, she felt again and again that she could not doubt its genuineness, especially when He said to her: "Be not afraid: it is I." These words had such power that when she heard them she could not doubt, and she was greatly strengthened and gladdened by such good companionship. For she saw plainly that it was a great help to her to be habitually thinking of God wherever she went and to be taking such care to do nothing which would displease Him because she felt that He was always looking at her. Whenever she wanted to draw near to His Majesty in prayer, and at other times as well, she felt He was so near that He could not fail to hear her, although she was unable to hear Him speaking to her whenever she wished, but did so at quite unexpected times, when it became necessary. She was conscious that He was walking at her right hand, but this consciousness arose, not from those senses which tell us that another person is near us, but in another and a subtler way which is indescribable. It is quite as unmistakable, however, and produces a feeling of equal certainty, or even greater. Other things of the kind might be attributable to fancy, but this thing is not, for it brings such great benefits and produces such effects upon the interior life as could not occur if it were the result of melancholy. The devil again, could not do so much good: were it his work, the soul would not have such peace and such constant desires to please God and such scorn for everything that does not lead it to Him. Later, this person attained a clear realization that it was not the work of the devil and came to understand it better and better.

None the less, I know she sometimes felt the gravest misgivings, and at other times the greatest confusion,[200] because she had no idea whence such a great blessing had come to her. She and I were so intimate that nothing happened in her soul of which I was ignorant and thus I can be a good witness and you may be sure that everything I say about it is true. This favour of the Lord brings with it the greatest confusion and humility. If it came from the devil, it would be just the reverse. As it is a thing which can be clearly recognized as the gift of God and such feelings could not possibly be produced by human effort, anyone who has it must know it does not in reality come from him, but is a gift from the hand of God. And although, as I believe, some of the other experiences that have been described are greater favours than this, yet this brings a special knowledge of God, and from this constant companionship is born a most tender love toward His Majesty, and yearnings, even deeper than those already described, to give oneself wholly up to His service, and a great purity of conscience; for the Presence Which the soul has at its side makes it sensitive to everything. For though we know quite well that God is present in all that we do, our nature is such that it makes us lose sight of the fact; but when this favour is granted it can no longer do so, for the Lord, Who is near at hand, awakens it. And even the favours aforementioned occur much more commonly, as the soul experiences a vivid and almost constant love for Him Whom it sees or knows to be at its side.

In short, the greatness and the precious quality of this favour are best seen in what the soul gains from it. It thanks the Lord, Who bestows it on one that has not deserved it, and would exchange it for no earthly treasure or joy. When the Lord is pleased to withdraw it, the soul is left in great loneliness; yet all the possible efforts that it might make to regain His companionship are of little avail, for the Lord gives this when He wills and it cannot be acquired. Sometimes, again, the companionship is that of a saint and this is also a great help to us.

You will ask how, if this Presence cannot be seen, the soul knows that it is that of Christ, or when it is a saint, or His most glorious Mother. This is a question which the soul cannot answer, nor can it understand how it knows what it does; it is perfectly certain, however, that it is right. When it is the Lord, and He speaks, it is natural that He should be easily recognized; but even when it is a saint, and no words are spoken, the soul is able to feel that the Lord is sending him to be a help and a companion to it; and this is more remarkable. There are also other spiritual experiences which cannot be described, but they all help to show us how impotent our nature is, when it comes to understanding the great wonders of God, for we are not capable of understanding these but can only marvel and praise His Majesty for giving them to us. So let us give Him special thanks for them; for, as this is not a favour which is granted to all, it is one which should be highly esteemed and we must try to render the greatest services to God Who has so many ways of helping us. For this reason no one thus favoured has any better opinion of himself on that account. On the contrary, he feels that he is serving God less than anyone else on the earth, and yet that no one else has so great an obligation to serve Him. Any fault which he commits, therefore, pierces his very vitals and has every reason to do so.

These above-described effects which such visions cause in the soul may be observed by any one of you whom the Lord leads by this way, and you will then see that they are due neither to deception nor to fancy. For, as I have said, if they are of the devil, I do not think they can possibly last so long or do the soul such a great deal of good, or bring it such inward peace. It is not usual for one who is so evil to do so much good; he could not, in fact, even if he would. The soul would soon become clouded over by the mist of self-esteem and would begin to think itself better than others. But its continual occupation with God and its fixing of the thought on Him would make the devil so furious that, though he might attempt such a thing once, he would not do so often. God is so faithful that He will not allow the devil to have all this power over a soul whose one aim is to please Him and to devote its whole life to His honour and glory; He will see to it that the devil is speedily disillusioned.

My point is, and will continue to be, that, if the soul walks in the manner described above, and these favours of God are withdrawn from it, His Majesty will see that it is the gainer, and if He sometimes allows the devil to attack it, his efforts will be brought to confusion. Therefore, daughters, if any of you travel along this road, as I have said, do not be alarmed. It is well for us to have misgivings and walk the more warily; and you must not presume upon having received these favours and become careless, for if you do not find them producing in you the result already described it will be a sign that they are not of God. It will be well at first for you to communicate this, in confession, to some very learned man (for it is from such men that we must seek illumination) or to any highly spiritual person if you know one. Should your confessor not be a very spiritual man, someone with learning is better; or, if you know such a person, it is best to consult one both spiritual and learned. If he tells you that it is fancy, do not let that trouble you, for fancy can have little effect on your soul, either for good or for evil: commend yourself to the Divine Majesty and pray Him not to allow you to be deceived. If he tells you that it is the devil, this will be a greater trial to you, though no learned man would say such a thing if you have experienced the effects described; but, if he says it, I know that the Lord Himself, Who is walking at your side, will console you and reassure you, and will continue to give him light, so that he in his turn may give it to you.

If your director, though a man of prayer, has not been led in this way by the Lord, he will at once become alarmed and condemn it; that is why I advise you to go to a man who has both spirituality and great learning if such a one can be found. Your prioress should give you leave to do this; for although, seeing you are leading a good life, she may think your soul is safe, she will be bound to allow you to consult someone for your own safety and for hers as well. When you have finished these consultations, calm yourself and do not go on talking about the matter, for sometimes, when there is no reason for fear, the devil implants such excessive misgivings that they prevent the soul from being content with a single consultation, especially if the confessor has had little experience and treats the matter timorously and enjoins you to go and consult others. In such a case what should by rights be a close secret gets noised abroad and the penitent is persecuted and tormented; for she finds that what she thought was secret has become public, and this leads to many sore trials, which, as things are at present, might affect the Order. Great caution, then, is necessary here and such caution I strongly recommend to prioresses.

And let none of you imagine that, because a sister has had such experiences, she is any better than the rest; the Lord leads each of us as He sees we have need. Such experiences, if we use them aright, prepare us to be better servants of God; but sometimes it is the weakest whom God leads by this road; and so there is no ground here either for approval or for condemnation. We must base our judgments on the virtues. The saintliest will be she who serves Our Lord with the greatest mortification and humility and purity of conscience. Little, however, can be known with any certainty about this on earth, nor until the true Judge gives each his deserts. Then we shall be amazed to see how different His judgment is from the ideas which we have formed on earth. May He be for ever praised. Amen.

Chapter IX

Treats of the way in which the Lord communicates Himself to the soul through imaginary visions and gives an emphatic warning that we should be careful not to desire to walk in this way. Gives reasons for the warning. This chapter is of great profit.

Let us now come to imaginary visions, in which the devil is said to interfere more frequently than in those already described. This may well be the case; but when they come from Our Lord they seem to me in some ways more profitable because they are in closer conformity with our nature, except for those which the Lord bestows in the final Mansion, and with which no others can compare.

Let us now imagine, as I said in the last chapter, that this Lord is here. It is as if in a gold reliquary there were hidden a precious stone of the highest value and the choicest virtues: although we have never seen the stone, we know for certain that it is there and if we carry it about with us we can have the benefit of its virtues. We do not prize it any the less for not having seen it, because we have found by experience that it has cured us of certain illnesses for which it is a sovereign remedy. But we dare not look at it, or open the reliquary in which it is contained, nor are we able to do so; for only the owner of the jewel knows how to open it, and though he has lent it to us so that we may benefit by it, he has kept the key and so it is still his own. He will open it when he wants to show it to us and he will take it back when he sees fit to do so. And that is what God does, too.

And now let us suppose that on some occasion the owner of the reliquary suddenly wants to open it, for the benefit of the person to whom he has lent it. Obviously this person will get much greater pleasure from it if he can recall the wonderful brilliance of the stone, and it will remain the more deeply engraven upon his memory. This is what happens here. When Our Lord is pleased to bestow greater consolations upon this soul, He grants it, in whatever way He thinks best, a clear revelation of His sacred Humanity, either as He was when He lived in the world, or as He was after His resurrection; and although He does this so quickly that we might liken the action to a flash of lightning, this most glorious image is so deeply engraven upon the imagination that I do not believe it can possibly disappear until it is where it can be enjoyed to all eternity.

I speak of an "image", but it must not be supposed that one looks at it as at a painting; it is really alive, and sometimes even speaks to the soul and shows it things both great and secret. But you must realize that, although the soul sees this for a certain length of time, it can no more be gazing at it all the time than it could keep gazing at the sun. So the vision passes very quickly, though this is not because its brilliance hurts the interior sight — that is, the medium by which all such things are seen — as the brilliance of the sun hurts the eyes. When it is a question of exterior sight, I can say nothing about it, for the person I have mentioned, and of whom I can best speak, had not experienced this; and reason can testify only inadequately to things of which it has no experience. The brilliance of this vision is like that of infused light or of a sun covered with some material of the transparency of a diamond, if such a thing could be woven. This raiment looks like the finest cambric. Almost invariably the soul on which God bestows this favour remains in rapture, because its unworthiness cannot endure so terrible a sight.

I say "terrible", because, though the sight is the loveliest and most delightful imaginable, even by a person who lived and strove to imagine it for a thousand years, because it so far exceeds all that our imagination and understanding can compass, its presence is of such exceeding majesty that it fills the soul with a great terror. It is unnecessary to ask here how, without being told, the soul knows Who it is, for He reveals Himself quite clearly as the Lord of Heaven and earth. This the kings of the earth never do: indeed, they would be thought very little of for what they are, but that they are accompanied by their suites, or heralds proclaim them.

O, Lord, how little do we Christians know Thee! What will that day be like when Thou comest to judge us? If when Thou comest here in such a friendly way to hold converse with Thy bride the sight of Thee causes us such fear, what will it be, O daughters, when with that stern voice He says: "Depart, accursed of My Father"![201]

Let us keep that in mind when we remember this favour which God grants to the soul, and we shall find it of no small advantage to us. Even Saint Jerome, holy man though he was, did not banish it from his memory. If we do that we shall care nothing for all we have suffered through keeping strictly to the observances of our Order, for, however long this may take us, the time will be but short by comparison with eternity. I can tell you truly that, wicked as I am, I have never feared the torments of hell, for they seem nothing by comparison with the thought of the wrath which the damned will see in the Lord's eyes — those eyes so lovely and tender and benign. I do not think my heart could bear to see that; and I have felt like this all my life. How much more will anyone fear this to whom He has thus revealed Himself, and given such a consciousness of His presence as will produce unconsciousness![202] It must be for this reason that the soul remains in suspension; the Lord helps it in its weakness so that this may be united with His greatness in this sublime communion with God.

When the soul is able to remain for a long time looking upon the Lord, I do not think it can be a vision at all. It must rather be that some striking idea creates a picture in the imagination: but this will be a dead image by comparison with the other.

Some persons — and I know this is the truth, for they have discussed it with me; and not just three or four of them, but a great many — find that their imagination is so weak, or their understanding is so nimble, or for some other reason their imagination becomes so absorbed, that they think they can actually see everything that is in their mind. If they had ever seen a true vision they would realize their error beyond the possibility of doubt. Little by little they build up the picture which they see with their imagination, but this produces no effect upon them and they remain cold — much more so than they are after seeing a sacred image. No attention, of course, should be paid to such a thing, which will be forgotten much more quickly than a dream.

The experience we are discussing here is quite different. The soul is very far from expecting to see anything and the thought of such a thing has never even passed through its mind. All of a sudden the whole vision is revealed to it and all its faculties and senses are thrown into the direst fear and confusion, and then sink into that blessed state of peace. It is just as when Saint Paul was thrown to the ground and there came that storm and tumult in the sky, just so, in this interior world, there is a great commotion; and then all at once, as I have said, everything grows calm, and the soul, completely instructed in such great truths, has no need of another master. True wisdom, without any effort on its own part, has overcome its stupidity and for a certain space of time it enjoys the complete certainty that this favour comes from God. However often it may be told that this is not so it cannot be induced to fear that it may have been mistaken. Later, when the confessor insinuates this fear, God allows the soul to begin to hesitate as to whether He could possibly grant this favour to such a sinner. But that is all; for, as I have said in these other cases, in speaking of temptations in matters of faith, the devil can disturb the soul, but he cannot shake the firmness of its belief. On the contrary, the more fiercely he attacks it, the more certain it becomes that he could never endow it with so many blessings — which is actually true, for over the interior of the soul he wields less power. He may be able to reveal something to it, but not with the same truth and majesty, nor can he produce the same results.

As confessors cannot see all this for themselves, and a soul to whom God has granted such a favour may be unable to describe it, they have misgivings about it, and quite justifiably. So they have to proceed cautiously, and even to wait for some time to see what results these apparitions produce, and to observe gradually how much humility they leave in the soul and to what extent it is strengthened in virtue; if they come from the devil there will soon be signs of the fact, for he will be caught out in a thousand lies. If the confessor is experienced, and has himself been granted such visions, it will not be long before he is able to form a judgment, for the account which the soul gives will at once show him whether they proceed from God or from the imagination or from the devil, especially if His Majesty has granted him the gift of discerning spirits. If he has this and is a learned man, he will be able to form an opinion perfectly well, even though he may be without experience.

The really essential thing, sisters, is that you should speak to your confessor very plainly and candidly — I do not mean here in confessing your sins, for of course you will do so then, but in describing your experiences in prayer. For unless you do this, I cannot assure you that you are proceeding as you should or that it is God Who is teaching you. God is very anxious for us to speak candidly and clearly to those who are in His place, and to desire them to be acquainted with all our thoughts, and still more with our actions, however trivial these may be. If you do this, you need not be disturbed, or worried, for, even if these things be not of God, they will do you no harm if you are humble and have a good conscience. His Majesty is able to bring good out of evil and you will gain by following the road by which the devil hoped to bring you to destruction. For, as you will suppose that it is God Who is granting you these great favours, you will strive to please Him better and keep His image ever in your mind. A very learned man used to say that the devil is a skilful painter, and that, if he were to show him an absolutely lifelike image of the Lord, it would not worry him, because it would quicken his devotion, and so he would be using the devil's own wicked weapons to make war on him. However evil the painter be, one cannot fail to reverence the picture that he paints, if it is of Him Who is our only Good.

This learned man thought that the counsel, given by some people, to treat any vision of this kind with scorn,[203] was very wrong: we must reverence a painting of our King, he said, wherever we see it. I think he is right; even on a worldly plane we should feel that. If a person who had a great friend knew that insulting things were being said about his portrait he would not be pleased. How much more incumbent upon us is it, then, always to be respectful when we see a crucifix or any kind of portrait of our Emperor!

Although I have written this elsewhere, I have been glad to set it down here, for I knew someone who was in great distress because she had been ordered to adopt this derisive remedy. I do not know who can have invented such advice, for, if it came from her confessor, it would have been a torture to her: she would be bound to obey him, and would have thought herself a lost soul unless she had done so. My own advice is that, if you are given such counsel, you should not accept it and should with all humility put forward this argument that I have given you. I was extremely struck by the good reasons against the practice alleged by the person who advised me in this case.

The soul derives great profit from this favour bestowed by the Lord, for thinking upon Him or upon His life and Passion recalls His most meek and lovely face, which is the greatest comfort, just as in the earthly sphere we get much more comfort from seeing a person who is a great help to us than if we had never known him. I assure you that such a delectable remembrance gives the greatest help and comfort. It also brings many other blessings with it, but as so much has been said about the effects caused by these things, and there is more still to come, I will not fatigue myself or you by adding more just now. I will only warn you that, when you learn or hear that God is granting souls these graces, you must never beseech or desire Him to lead you along this road. Even if you think it a very good one, and to be greatly prized and reverenced, there are certain reasons why such a course is not wise.

The first reason is that it shows a lack of humility to ask to be given what you have never deserved, so I think anyone who asks for this cannot be very humble. A peasant of lowly birth would never dream of wishing to be a king; such a thing seems to him impossible because he does not merit it. Anyone who is humble feels just the same about these other things. I think they will never be bestowed on a person devoid of humility, because before the Lord grants a soul these favours He always gives it a high degree of self-knowledge. And how could one who has such ambitions realize that He is doing him a great favour in not casting him into hell?

The second reason is that such a person is quite certain to be deceived, or to be in great peril, because the devil has only to see a door left slightly ajar to enter and play a thousand tricks on us.

The third reason is to be found in the imagination. When a person has a great desire for something, he persuades himself that he is seeing or hearing what he desires, just as those who go about desiring something all day think so much about it that after a time they begin to dream of it.

The fourth reason is that it is very presumptuous in me to wish to choose my path, because I cannot tell which path is best for me. I must leave it to the Lord, Who knows me, to lead me by the path which is best for me, so that in all things His will may be done.

In the fifth place, do you suppose that the trials suffered by those to whom the Lord grants these favours are light ones? No, they are very heavy, and of many kinds. How do you know if you would be able to bear them?

In the sixth place, you may well find that the very thing from which you had expected gain will bring you loss, just as Saul only lost by becoming a king.

And besides these reasons, sisters, there are others. Believe me, the safest thing is to will only what God wills, for He knows us better than we know ourselves, and

He loves us. Let us place ourselves in His hands so that His will may be done in us; if we cling firmly to this maxim and our wills are resolute we cannot possibly go astray. And you must note that you will merit no more glory for having received many of these favours; on the contrary, the fact that you are receiving more imposes on you greater obligations to serve. The Lord does not deprive us of anything which adds to our merit, for this remains in our own power. There are many saintly people who have never known what it is to receive a favour of this kind, and there are others who receive a favour of this kind, and there are others who received such favours, although they are not saintly. Do not suppose, again, that they occur continually. Each occasion on which the Lord grants them brings with it a great many trials; and thus the soul does not think about receiving more, but only about how to put those it receives to a good use.

It is true that to have these favours must be the greatest help towards attaining a high degree of perfection in the virtues; but anyone who has attained the virtues at the cost of his own toil has earned much more merit. I know of a person to whom the Lord had granted some of these favours — of two indeed; one was a man. Both were desirous of serving His Majesty, at their own cost, and without being given any of these great consolations; and they were so anxious to suffer that they complained to Our Lord because He bestowed favours on them, which, had it been possible, they would have excused themselves from receiving. I am speaking here, not of these visions, which bring us great gain, and are very much to be prized, but of consolations which the Lord gives in contemplation.

It is true that, in my opinion, these desires are supernatural, and come from souls fired with love, who would like the Lord to see that they are not serving Him for pay; for which reason, as I have said, they never spur themselves to greater efforts in God's service by thinking of the glory which they will receive for anything they do; rather do they serve Him for the satisfaction of their love, for the nature of love invariably finds expression in work of a thousand kinds. If it were able, the soul would invent methods by which to be come consumed in Him, and if, for the greater honour of God, it were necessary that it should remain annihilated for ever, it would agree to this very willingly. May He be for ever praised Who is pleased to show forth His greatness by stooping to commune with such miserable creatures. Amen.

Chapter X

Speaks of other favours which God grants to the soul in a different way from those already mentioned, and of the great profit that they bring.

There are many ways in which the Lord communicates Himself to the soul by means of these apparitions. Some of them come when the soul is afflicted; others, when it is about to be visited by some heavy trial; others, so that His Majesty may take His delight in it and at the same time may comfort it. There is no need to particularize about each of these; my intention is only to explain in turn the different experiences which occur on this road, as far as I understand them, so that you, sisters, may understand their nature and the effects which they cause. And I am doing this so that you may not suppose everything you imagine to be a vision, and so that, when you do see a vision, you will know that such a thing is possible and will not be disturbed or distressed. For, when you are, it is a great gain for the devil; he is delighted to see a soul distressed and uneasy, because he knows that this will hinder it from employing itself in loving and praising God. His Majesty also communicates Himself in other ways, which are much more sublime, and are also less dangerous, because, I think, the devil cannot counterfeit them. But, being very secret things, they are difficult to describe, whereas imaginary visions can be explained more readily.

When the Lord so wills, it may happen that the soul will be at prayer, and in possession of all its senses, and that then there will suddenly come to it a suspension in which the Lord communicates most secret things to it, which it seems to see within God Himself. These are not visions of the most sacred Humanity; although I say that the soul "sees" Him, it really sees nothing, for this is not an imaginary, but a notably intellectual, vision, in which is revealed to the soul how all things are seen in God, and how within Himself He contains them all. Such a vision is highly profitable because, although it passes in a moment, it remains engraven upon the soul. It causes us the greatest confusion, by showing us clearly how wrongly we are acting when we offend God, since it is within God Himself — because we dwell within Him, I mean — that we are committing these great sins. I want, if I can, to draw a comparison to explain this, for, although it is a fact and we hear it stated frequently, we either pay no heed to it or refuse to understand it; if we really understood it, I do not think we could possibly be so presumptuous.

Let us imagine that God is like a very large and beautiful mansion or palace. This palace, then, as I say, is God Himself. Now can the sinner go away from it in order to commit his misdeeds? Certainly not, these abominations and dishonourable actions and evil deeds which we sinners commit are done within the palace itself — that is, within God. Oh, fearful thought, worthy of deep consideration and very profitable for us who are ignorant and unable to understand these truths — for if we could understand them we could not possibly be guilty of such foolish presumption! Let us consider, sisters, the great mercy and long-suffering of God in not casting us straight into the depths, and let us render Him the heartiest thanks and be ashamed of worrying over anything that is done or said against us. It is the most dreadful thing in the world that God our Creator should suffer so many misdeeds to be committed by His creatures within Himself, while we ourselves are sometimes worried about a single word uttered in our absence and perhaps not even with a wrong intention.

Oh, human misery! How long will it be, daughters, before we imitate this great God in any way? Oh, let us not deceive ourselves into thinking that we are doing anything whatever by merely putting up with insults! Let us endure everything, and be very glad to do so, and love those who do us wrong; for, greatly as we have offended this great God, He has not ceased loving us, and so He has very good reason for desiring us all to forgive those who have wronged us. I assure you, daughters, that, although this vision passes quickly, it is a great favour for the Lord to bestow it upon those to whom He grants it if they will try to profit by having it habitually present in their minds.

It may also happen that, very suddenly and in a way which cannot be described, God will reveal a truth that is in Himself and that makes any truth to be found in the creatures seem like thick darkness; He will also manifest very clearly that He alone is truth and cannot lie. This is a very good explanation of David's meaning in that Psalm where he says that every man is a liar.[204] One would never take those words in that sense of one's own accord, however many times one heard them, but they express a truth which is infallible. I remember that story about Pilate, who asked Our Lord so many questions, and at the time of His Passion said to Him: "What is truth?"[205] And then I reflect how little we understand of this Sovereign Truth here on earth.

I should like to be able to say more about this matter, but it is impossible. Let us learn from this, sisters, that if we are in any way to grow like our God and Spouse, we shall do well always to study earnestly to walk in this truth. I do not mean simply that we must not tell falsehoods, for as far as that is concerned — glory be to God! — I know that in these convents of ours you take very great care never to lie about anything for any reason whatsoever. I mean that we must walk in truth, in the presence of God and man, in every way possible to us. In particular we must not desire to be reputed better than we are and in all we do we must attribute to God what is His, and to ourselves what is ours, and try to seek after truth in everything. If we do that, we shall make small account of this world, for it is all lying and falsehood and for that reason cannot endure.

I was wondering once why Our Lord so dearly loved this virtue of humility; and all of a sudden — without, I believe, my having previously thought of it — the following reason came into my mind: that it is because God is Sovereign Truth and to be humble is to walk in truth, for it is absolutely true to say that we have no good thing in ourselves, but only misery and nothingness; and anyone who fails to understand this is walking in falsehood. He who best understands it is most pleasing to Sovereign Truth because he is walking in truth. May it please God, sisters, to grant us grace never to fail to have this knowledge of ourselves. Amen.

Our Lord grants the soul favours like these because He is pleased to treat her like a true bride, who is determined to do His will in all things, and to give her some knowledge of the way in which she can do His will and of His greatness. I need say no more; I have said these two things because they seem to me so helpful; for there is no reason to be afraid of these favours, but only to praise the Lord, because He gives them. In my opinion, there is little scope here either for the devil or for the soul's own imagination, and when it knows this the soul experiences a great and lasting happiness.

Chapter XI

Treats of the desires to enjoy God which He gives the soul and which are so great and impetuous that they endanger its life. Treats also of the profit which comes from this favour granted by the Lord.

Have all these favours which the Spouse has granted the soul been sufficient to satisfy this little dove or butterfly (do not suppose that I have forgotten her) and to make her settle down in the place where she is to die? Certainly not; she is in a much worse state than before; for, although she may have been receiving these favours for many years, she is still sighing and weeping, and each of them causes her fresh pain. The reason for this is that, the more she learns about the greatness of her God, while finding herself so far from Him and unable to enjoy Him, the more her desire increases. For the more is revealed to her of how much this great God and Lord deserves to be loved, the more does her love for Him grow. And gradually, during these years, her desire increases, so that she comes to experience great distress, as I will now explain. I have spoken of years, because I am writing about the experiences of the particular person about whom I have been speaking here. But it must be clearly understood that no limitations can be set to God's acts, and that He can raise a soul to the highest point here mentioned in a single moment. His Majesty has the power to do all that He wishes and He is desirous of doing a great deal for us.

The soul, then, has these yearnings and tears and sighs, together with the strong impulses which have already been described. They all seem to arise from our love, and are accompanied by great emotion, but they are all as nothing by comparison with this other, for they are like a smouldering fire, the heat of which is quite bearable, though it causes pain. While the soul is in this condition, and interiorly burning, it often happens that a mere fleeting thought of some kind (there is no way of telling whence it comes, or how) or some remark which the soul hears about death's long tarrying, deals it, as it were, a blow, or, as one might say, wounds it with an arrow of fire. I do not mean that there actually is such an arrow, but, whatever it is, it obviously could not have come from our own nature. Nor is it actually a blow, though I have spoken of it as such; but it makes a deep wound, not, I think, in any region where physical pain can be felt, but in the soul's most intimate depths. It passes as quickly as a flash of lightning and leaves everything in our nature that is earthly reduced to powder. During the time that it lasts we cannot think of anything that has to do with our own existence: it instantaneously enchains the faculties in such a way that they have no freedom to do anything, except what will increase this pain.

I should not like this to sound exaggerated: in reality I am beginning to see, as I go on, that all I say falls short of the truth, which is indescribable. It is an enrapturing of the senses and faculties, except, as I have said, in ways which enhance this feeling of distress. The understanding is keenly on the alert to discover why this soul feels absent from God, and His Majesty now aids it with so lively a knowledge of Himself that it causes the distress to grow until the sufferer cries out aloud. However patient a sufferer she may be, and however accustomed to enduring great pain, she cannot help doing this, because this pain, as I have said, is not in the body, but deep within the soul. It was in this way that the person I have mentioned discovered how much more sensitive the soul is than the body, and it was revealed to her that this suffering resembles that of souls in purgatory; despite their being no longer in the body they suffer much more than do those who are still in the body and on earth.

I once saw a person in this state who I really believed was dying; and this was not at all surprising, because it does in fact involve great peril of death. Although it lasts only for a short time, it leaves the limbs quite disjointed, and, for as long as it continues, the pulse is as feeble as though the soul were about to render itself up to God. It really is quite as bad as this. For, while the natural heat of the body fails, the soul burns so fiercely within that, if the flame were only a little stronger, God would have fulfilled its desires. It is not that it feels any bodily pain whatsoever, notwithstanding such a dislocation of the limbs that for two or three days afterwards it is in great pain and has not the strength even to write; in fact the body seems to me never to be as strong as it was previously. The reason it feels no pain must be that it is suffering so keenly within that it takes no notice of the body. It is as when we have a very acute pain in one spot; we may have many other pains but we feel them less; this I have conclusively proved. In the present case, the soul feels nothing at all, and I do not believe it would feel anything if it were cut into little pieces.

You will tell me that this is imperfection and ask why such a person does not resign herself to the will of God, since she has surrendered herself to Him so completely. Down to this time she had been able to do so, and indeed had spent her life doing so; but now she no longer can because her reason is in such a state that she is not her own mistress, and can think of nothing but the cause of her suffering. Since she is absent from her Good, why should she wish to live? She is conscious of a strange solitude, since there is not a creature on the whole earth who can be a companion to her — in fact, I do not believe she would find any in Heaven, save Him Whom she loves: on the contrary, all earthly companionship is torment to her. She thinks of herself as of a person suspended aloft, unable either to come down and rest anywhere on earth or to ascend into Heaven. She is parched with thirst, yet cannot reach the water; and the thirst is not a tolerable one but of a kind that nothing can quench, nor does she desire it to be quenched, except with that water of which Our Lord spoke to the Samaritan woman,[206] and that is not given to her.

Ah, God help me! Lord, how Thou dost afflict Thy lovers! Yet all this is very little by comparison with what Thou bestowest upon them later. It is well that great things should cost a great deal, especially if the soul can be purified by suffering and enabled to enter the seventh Mansion, just as those who are to enter Heaven are cleansed in purgatory. If this is possible, its suffering is no more than a drop of water in the sea. So true is this that, despite all its torment and distress, which cannot, I believe, be surpassed by any such things on earth (many of which this person had endured, both bodily and spiritual, and they all seemed to her nothing by comparison), the soul feels this affliction to be so precious that it fully realizes it could never deserve it. But the anguish is of such a kind that nothing can relieve it; none the less the soul suffers it very gladly, and, if God so willed, would suffer it all its life long, although this would be not to die once, but to be always dying, for it is really quite as bad as that.

And now, sisters, let us consider the condition of those who are in hell. They are not resigned, as this soul is, nor have they this contentment and delight which God gives it. They cannot see that their suffering is doing them any good, yet they keep suffering more and more — I mean more and more in respect of accidental pains[207] — for the torment suffered by the soul is much more acute than that suffered by the body and the pains which such souls have to endure are beyond comparison greater than what we have here been describing. These unhappy souls know that they will have to suffer in this way for ever and ever: what, then, will become of them? And what is there that we can do — or even suffer — in so short a life as this which will matter in the slightest if it will free us from these terrible and eternal torments? I assure you it is impossible to explain to anyone who has not experienced it what a grievous thing is the soul's suffering and how different it is from the suffering of the body. The Lord will have us understand this so that we may be more conscious of how much we owe Him for bringing us to a state in which by His mercy we may hope that He will set us free and forgive us our sins.

Let us now return to what we were discussing when we left this soul in such affliction. It remains in this state only for a short time (three or four hours at most, I should say); for, if the pain lasted long, it would be impossible, save by a miracle, for natural weakness to suffer it. On one occasion it lasted only for a quarter of an hour and yet produced complete prostration. On that occasion, as a matter of fact, the sufferer entirely lost consciousness. The violent attack came on through her hearing some words about 'life not ending".[208] She was engaged in conversation at the time — it was the last day of Eastertide, and all that Easter she had been affected with such aridity that she hardly knew it was Easter at all. So just imagine anyone thinking that these attacks can be resisted! It is no more possible to resist them than for a person thrown into a fire to make the flames lose their heat and not burn her. She cannot hide her anguish, so all who are present realize the great peril in which she lies, even though they cannot witness what is going on within her. It is true that they can bear her company, but they only seem to her like shadows — as all other earthly things do too.

And now I want you to see that, if at any time you should find yourselves in this condition, it is possible for your human nature, weak as it is, to be of help to you. So let me tell you this. It sometimes happens that, when a person is in this state that you have been considering, and has such yearnings to die,[209] because the pain is more than she can bear, that her soul seems to be on the very point of leaving the body, she is really afraid and would like her distress to be alleviated lest she should in fact die. It is quite evident that this fear comes from natural weakness, and yet, on the other hand, the desire does not leave her, nor can she possibly find any means of dispelling the distress until the Lord Himself dispels it for her. This He does, as a general rule, by granting her a deep rapture or some kind of vision, in which the true Comforter comforts and strengthens her so that she can wish to live for as long as He wills.

This is a distressing thing, but it produces the most wonderful effects and the soul at once loses its fear of any trials which may befall it; for by comparison with the feelings of deep anguish which its spirit has experienced these seem nothing. Having gained so much, the soul would be glad to suffer them all again and again; but it has no means of doing so nor is there any method by which it can reach that state again until the Lord wills, just as there is no way of resisting or escaping it when it comes. The soul has far more contempt for the world than it had previously, for it sees that no worldly thing was of any avail to it in its torment; and it is very much more detached from the creatures, because it sees that it can be comforted and satisfied only by the Creator, and it has the greatest fear and anxiety not to offend Him, because it sees that He can torment as well as comfort.

There are two deadly perils, it seems to me, on this spiritual road. This is one of them — and it is indeed a peril and no light one. The other is the peril of excessive rejoicing and delight, which can be carried to such an extreme that it really seems as if the soul is swooning, and as if the very slightest thing would be enough to drive it out of the body: this would really bring it no little happiness.

Now, sisters, you will see if I was not right in saying that courage is necessary for us here and that if you ask the Lord for these things He will be justified in answering you as He answered the sons of Zebedee: "Can you drink the chalice?"[210] I believe, sisters, that we should all reply: "We can"; and we should be quite right to do so, for His Majesty gives the strength to those who, He sees, have need of it, and He defends these souls in every way and stands up for them if they are persecuted and spoken ill of, as He did for the Magdalen[211] — by His actions if not in words. And in the end — ah, in the end, before they die, He repays them for everything at once, as you are now going to see. May He be for ever blessed and may all creatures praise Him. Amen.

Seventh Mansions:
In which there are Four Chapters

Chapter 1

Treats of great favours which God bestows on the souls that have attained entrance to the Seventh Mansions. Describes how in the author's opinion there is some difference between the soul and the spirit although both are one. There are notable things in this chapter.

You will think, sisters, that so much has been said about this spiritual road that there cannot possibly be any more to say. It would be a great mistake to think that; just as the greatness of God is without limit, even so are His works. Who will ever come to an end of recounting His mercies and wonders? It is impossible that any should do so; do not be surprised, therefore, at what has been said and at what will be said now, for it is only a fraction of the things that still remain to be related about God. Great is the mercy that He shows us in communicating these things in such a way that we may come to learn of them; for the more we know of His communion with creatures, the more we shall praise His greatness, and we shall strive not to despise a soul in which the Lord takes such delight. Each of us possesses a soul, but we do not prize our souls as creatures made in God's image deserve and so we do not understand the great secrets which they contain. If it be His Majesty's will, may it please Him to guide my pen, and give me to understand how I may tell you some of the many things which there are to be said and which God reveals to every soul that He brings into this Mansion. Earnestly have I besought His Majesty, since He knows my intention is that His mercies be not hidden, to the greater praise and glory of His name.

I am hopeful, sisters, that, not for my sake but for your sakes, He will grant me this favour, so that you may understand how important it is that no fault of yours should hinder the celebration of His Spiritual Marriage with your souls, which, as you will see, brings with it so many blessings. O great God! Surely a creature as miserable as I must tremble to treat of anything so far beyond what I deserve to understand. And indeed I have been in a state of great confusion and have wondered if it will not be better for me in a few words to bring my account of this Mansion to an end. I am so much afraid it will be thought that my knowledge of it comes from experience, and this makes me very much ashamed; for, knowing myself as I do for what I am, such a thought is terrible. On the other hand, whatever your judgment about it may be, it has seemed to me that this shame is due to temptation and weakness. Let the whole world cry out upon me, so long as God is praised and understood a little better. At all events I may perhaps be dead when this comes to be seen. Blessed be He Who lives and shall live for ever. Amen.

When Our Lord is pleased to have pity upon this soul, which suffers and has suffered so much out of desire for Him, and which He has now taken spiritually to be His bride, He brings her into this Mansion of His, which is the seventh, before consummating the Spiritual Marriage. For He must needs have an abiding-place in the soul, just as He has one in Heaven, where His Majesty alone dwells: so let us call this a second Heaven. It is very important, sisters, that we should not think of the soul as of something dark. It must seem dark to most of us, as we cannot see it, for we forget that there is not only a light which we can see, but also an interior light, and so we think that within our soul there is some kind of darkness. Of the soul that is not in grace, I grant you, that is true — not, however, from any defect in the Sun of Justice, Who is within it and is giving it being, but because, as I think I said in describing the first Mansion, this soul is not capable[212] of receiving the light. A certain person came to see that these unhappy souls are, as it were, in a dark prison, with their feet and hands bound so that they can do no good thing which will help them to win merit;[213] they are both blind and dumb. We do well to take pity on them, realizing that there was a time when we were ourselves like them and that the Lord may have mercy on them also.

Let us take especial care, sisters, to pray to Him for them, and not be negligent. To pray for those who are in mortal sin is the best kind of almsgiving — a much better thing than it would be to loose a Christian whom we saw with his hands tied behind him, bound with a stout chain, made fast to a post and dying of hunger, not for lack of food, since he has beside him the most delicious things to eat, but because he cannot take them and put them into his mouth although he is weary to death and actually knows that he is on the point of dying, and not merely a death of the body, but one which is eternal. Would it not be extremely cruel to stand looking at such a man and not give him this food to eat? And supposing you could loose his chains by means of your prayers? You see now what I mean. For the love of God, I beg you always to remember such souls when you pray.[214]

However, it is not of these that we are now speaking, but of those who, by God's mercy, have done penance for their sins and are in grace. We must not think of souls like theirs as mean and insignificant; for each is an interior world, wherein are the many and beauteous Mansions that you have seen; it is reasonable that this should be so, since within each soul there is a mansion for God. Now, when His Majesty is pleased to grant the soul the aforementioned favour of this Divine Marriage, He first of all brings it into His own Mansion. And His Majesty is pleased that it should not be as on other occasions, when He has granted it raptures, in which I certainly think it is united with Him, as it is in the above-mentioned Prayer of Union, although the soul does not feel called to enter into its own centre, as here in this Mansion, but is affected only in its higher part. Actually it matters little what happens: whatever it does, the Lord unites it with Himself, but He makes it blind and dumb, as He made Saint Paul at his conversion,[215] and so prevents it from having any sense of how or in what way that favour comes which it is enjoying; the great delight of which the soul is then conscious is the realization of its nearness to God. But when He unites it with Him, it understands nothing; the faculties are all lost.

But in this Mansion everything is different. Our good God now desires to remove the scales from the eyes of the soul,[216] so that it may see and understand something of the favour which He is granting it, although He is doing this in a strange manner. It is brought into this Mansion by means of an intellectual vision,[217] in which, by a representation of the truth in a particular way, the Most Holy Trinity reveals Itself, in all three Persons.[218] First of all the spirit becomes enkindled and is illumined, as it were, by a cloud of the greatest brightness. It sees these three Persons, individually, and yet, by a wonderful kind of knowledge which is given to it, the soul realizes that most certainly and truly all these three Persons are one Substance and one Power and one Knowledge and one God alone; so that what we hold by faith the soul may be said here to grasp[219] by sight, although nothing is seen by the eyes, either of the body or of the soul,[220] for it is no imaginary vision. Here all three Persons communicate Themselves to the soul and speak to the soul and explain to it those words which the Gospel attributes to the Lord — namely, that He and the Father and the Holy Spirit will come to dwell with the soul which loves Him and keeps His commandments.[221]

Oh, God help me! What a difference there is between hearing and believing these words[222] and being led in this way to realize how true they are! Each day this soul wonders more, for she feels that they have never left her, and perceives quite clearly, in the way I have described, that They are in the interior of her heart — in the most interior place of all and in its greatest depths. So although, not being a learned person, she cannot say how this is, she feels within herself this Divine companionship.

This may lead you to think that such a person will not remain in possession of her senses but will be so completely absorbed that she will be able to fix her mind upon nothing. But no: in all that belongs to the service of God she is more alert than before; and, when not otherwise occupied, she rests in that happy companionship. Unless her soul fails God, He will never fail, I believe, to give her the most certain assurance of His Presence. She has great confidence that God will not leave her, and that, having granted her this favour, He will not allow her to lose it. For this belief the soul has good reason, though all the time she is walking more carefully than ever, so that she may displease Him in nothing.

This Presence is not of course always realized so fully — I mean so clearly — as it is when it first comes, or on certain other occasions when God grants the soul this consolation; if it were, it would be impossible for the soul to think of anything else, or even to live among men. But although the light which accompanies it may not be so clear, the soul is always aware that it is experiencing this companionship. We might compare the soul to a person who is with others in a very bright room; and then suppose that the shutters are closed so that the people are all in darkness. The light by which they can be seen has been taken away, and, until it comes back, we shall be unable to see them, yet we are none the less aware that they are there. It may be asked if, when the light returns, and this person looks for them again, she will be able to see them. To do this is not in her power; it depends on when Our Lord is pleased that the shutters of the understanding shall be opened. Great is the mercy which He grants the soul in never going away from her and in willing that she shall understand this so clearly.

It seems that the Divine Majesty, by means of this wonderful companionship, is desirous of preparing the soul for yet more. For clearly she will be greatly assisted to go onward in perfection and to lose the fear which previously she sometimes had of the other favours that were granted to her, as has been said above. The person already referred to found herself better in every way, however numerous were her trials and business worries, the essential part of her soul seemed never to move from that dwelling-place. So in a sense she felt that her soul was divided; and when she was going through great trials, shortly after God had granted her this favour, she complained of her soul, just as Martha complained of Mary.[223] Sometimes she would say that it was doing nothing but enjoy itself in that quietness, while she herself was left with all her trials and occupations so that she could not keep it company.

You will think this absurd, daughters, but it is what actually happens. Although of course the soul is not really divided, what I have said is not fancy, but a very common experience. As I was saying, it is possible to make observations concerning interior matters and in this way we know that there is some kind of difference, and a very definite one, between the soul and the spirit, although they are both one. So subtle is the division perceptible between them that sometimes the operation of the one seems as different from that of the other as are the respective joys that the Lord is pleased to give them. It seems to me, too, that the soul is a different thing from the faculties and that they are not all one and the same. There are so many and such subtle things in the interior life that it would be presumptuous for me to begin to expound them. But we shall see everything in the life to come if the Lord, of His mercy, grants us the favour of bringing us to the place where we shall understand these secrets.

Chapter 11

Continues the same subject. Describes the difference between spiritual union and spiritual marriage. Explains this by subtle comparisons.

Let us now come to treat of the Divine and Spiritual Marriage, although this great Favour cannot be fulfilled perfectly in us during our lifetime, for if we were to withdraw ourselves from God this great blessing would be lost. When granting this favour for the first time, His Majesty is pleased to reveal Himself to the soul through an imaginary vision of His most sacred Humanity, so that it may clearly understand what is taking place and not be ignorant of the fact that it is receiving so sovereign a gift. To other people the experience will come in a different way. To the person of whom we have been speaking the Lord revealed Himself one day, when she had just received Communion, in great splendour and beauty and majesty, as He did after His resurrection, and told her that it was time she took upon her His affairs as if they were her own and that He would take her affairs upon Himself; and He added other words which are easier to understand than to repeat.[224]

This, you will think, was nothing new, since on other occasions the Lord had revealed Himself to that soul in this way. But it was so different that it left her quite confused and dismayed: for one reason, because this vision came with great force; for another, because of the words which He spoke to her, and also because, in the interior of her soul, where He revealed Himself to her, she had never seen any visions but this. For you must understand that there is the greatest difference between all the other visions we have mentioned and those belonging to this Mansion, and there is the same difference between the Spiritual Betrothal and the Spiritual Marriage as there is between two betrothed persons and two who are united so that they cannot be separated any more.

As I have already said, one makes these comparisons because there are no other appropriate ones, yet it must be realized that the Betrothal has no more to do with the body than if the soul were not in the body, and were nothing but spirit. Between the Spiritual Marriage and the body there is even less connection, for this secret union takes place in the deepest centre of the soul, which must be where God Himself dwells, and I do not think there is any need of a door by which to enter it. I say there is no need of a door because all that has so far been described seems to have come through the medium of the senses and faculties and this appearance of the Humanity of the Lord must do so too. But what passes in the union of the Spiritual Marriage is very different. The Lord appears in the centre of the soul, not through an imaginary, but through an intellectual vision (although this is a subtler one than that already mentioned),[225] just as He appeared to the Apostles, without entering through the door, when He said to them: "Pax vobis".[226] This instantaneous communication of God to the soul is so great a secret and so sublime a favour, and such delight is felt by the soul, that I do not know with what to compare it, beyond saying that the Lord is pleased to manifest to the soul at that moment the glory that is in Heaven, in a sublimer manner than is possible through any vision or spiritual consolation. It is impossible to say more than that, as far as one can understand, the soul (I mean the spirit of this soul) is made one with God, Who, being likewise a Spirit, has been pleased to reveal the love that He has for us by showing to certain persons the extent of that love, so that we may praise His greatness. For He has been pleased to unite Himself with His creature in such a way that they have become like two who cannot be separated from one another: even so He will not separate Himself from her.

The Spiritual Betrothal is different: here the two persons are frequently separated, as is the case with union, for, although by union is meant the joining of two things into one, each of the two, as is a matter of common observation, can be separated and remain a thing by itself. This favour of the Lord passes quickly and afterwards the soul is deprived of that companionship — I mean so far as it can understand. In this other favour of the Lord it is not so: the soul remains all the time in that centre with its God. We might say that union is as if the ends of two wax candles were joined so that the light they give is one: the wicks and the wax and the light are all one, yet afterwards the one candle can be perfectly well separated from the other and the candles become two again, or the wick may be withdrawn from the wax. But here it is like rain falling from the heavens into a river or a spring; there is nothing but water there and it is impossible to divide or separate the water belonging to the river from that which fell from the heavens. Or it is as if a tiny streamlet enters the sea, from which it will find no way of separating itself, or as if in a room there were two large windows through which the light streamed in: it enters in different places but it all becomes one.

Perhaps when St. Paul says: "He who is joined to God becomes one spirit with Him,"[227] he is referring to this sovereign Marriage, which presupposes the entrance of His Majesty into the soul by union. And he also says: Mihi vivere Christus est, mori lucrum.[228] This, I think, the soul may say here, for it is here that the little butterfly to which we have referred dies, and with the greatest joy, because Christ is now its life.

This, with the passage of time, becomes more evident through its effects; for the soul clearly understands, by certain secret aspirations, that it is endowed with life by God. Very often these aspirations are so vehement that what they teach cannot[229] possibly be doubted: though they cannot be described, the soul experiences them very forcibly. One can only say that this feeling is produced at times by certain delectable words which, it seems, the soul cannot help uttering, such as: "O life of my life, and sustenance that sustaineth me!" and things of that kind. For from those Divine breasts, where it seems that God is ever sustaining the soul, flow streams of milk, which solace all who dwell in the Castle; it seems that it is the Lord's will for them to enjoy all that the soul enjoys, so that, from time to time, there should flow from this mighty river, in which this tiny little spring is swallowed up, a stream of this water, to sustain those who in bodily matters have to serve the Bridegroom and the bride. And just as a person suddenly plunged into such water would become aware of it, and, however unobservant he might be, could not fail to become so, the same thing may be said, with even greater confidence, of these operations to which I refer. For just as a great stream of water could never fall on us without having an origin somewhere, as I have said, just so it becomes evident that there is someone in the interior of the soul who sends forth these arrows and thus gives life to this life, and that there is a sun whence this great light proceeds, which is transmitted to the faculties in the interior part of the soul. The soul, as I have said, neither moves from that centre nor loses its peace, for He Who gave His peace to the Apostles when they were all together[230] can give peace to the soul.

It has occurred to me that this salutation of the Lord must mean much more than the mere words suggest, as must also His telling the glorious Magdalen to go in peace;[231] for the words of the Lord are like acts wrought in us, and so they must have produced some effect in those who were already prepared to put away from them everything corporeal and to leave the soul in a state of pure spirituality, so that it might be joined with Uncreated Spirit in this celestial union. For it is quite certain that, when we empty ourselves of all that is creature and rid ourselves of it for the love of God, that same Lord will fill our souls with Himself. Thus, one day, when Jesus Christ was praying for His Apostles (I do not know where this occurs),[232] He asked that they might become one with the Father and with Him, even as Jesus Christ our Lord is in the Father and the Father is in Him. I do not know what greater love there can be than this. And we shall none of us fail to be included here, for His Majesty went on to say: "Not for them alone do I pray, but also for all who believe in Me"[233]; and again: "I am in them."[234]

Oh, God help me! How true are these words and how well the soul understands them, for in this state it can actually see their truth for itself. And how well we should all understand them were it not for our own fault! The words of Jesus Christ our King and Lord cannot fail; but, because we ourselves fail by not preparing ourselves and departing from all that can shut out this light, we do not see ourselves in this mirror into which we are gazing and in which our image is engraved.[235]

Let us now return to what we were saying. When Our Lord brings the soul into this Mansion of His, which is the centre of the soul itself (for they say that the empyrean heaven, where Our Lord is, does not move like the other heavens), it seems, on entering, to be subject to none of the usual movements of the faculties and the imagination, which injure it and take away its peace. I may seem to be giving the impression that, when the soul reaches the state in which God grants it this favour, it is sure of its salvation and free from the risk of backsliding. But that is not my meaning, and whenever I treat of this matter and say that the soul seems to be in safety I should be understood as meaning for so long as the Divine Majesty holds it thus by the hand and it does not offend Him. At all events, I know for certain that, even when it finds itself in this state, and even if the state has lasted for years, it does not consider itself safe, but goes on its way with much greater misgiving than before and refrains more carefully from committing the smallest offence against God. It is also strongly desirous of serving Him, as will be explained later on, and is habitually afflicted and confused when it sees how little it is able to do and how great is the extent of its obligations, which is no small cross to it and a very grievous penance; for the harder the penance which this soul performs, the greater is its delight. Its real penance comes when God takes away its health and strength so that it can no longer perform any. I have described elsewhere the great distress which this brings, but it is much greater here. This must be due to the nature of the ground in which the soul is planted, for a tree planted by the streams of water is fresher and gives more fruit,[236] so how can we marvel at the desires of this soul, since its spirit is verily made one with the celestial water of which we have been speaking?

Returning to what I was saying, it must not be thought that the faculties and senses and passions are always in this state of peace, though the soul itself is. In the other Mansions there are always times of conflict and trial and weariness, but they are not of such a kind as to rob the soul of its peace and stability — at least, not as a rule. This "centre" of our soul, or "spirit," is something so difficult to describe, and indeed to believe, that I think, sisters, as I am so bad at explaining myself, I will not subject you to the temptation of disbelieving what I say, for it is difficult to understand how the soul can have trials and afflictions and yet be in peace. I want to put before you one or two comparisons: God grant they may be of some value, but, if they are not, I know that what I have said is the truth.

A king is living in His palace: many wars are waged in his kingdom and many other distressing things happen there, but he remains where he is despite them all. So it is here: although in the other Mansions there are many disturbances and poisonous creatures, and the noise of all this can be heard, nobody enters this Mansion and forces the soul to leave it; and, although the things which the soul hears cause it some distress, they are not of a kind to disturb it or to take away its peace, for the passions are already vanquished, and thus are afraid to enter there because to do so would only exhaust them further. Our whole body may be in pain, yet if our head is sound the fact that the body is in pain will not cause it to ache as well. These comparisons make me smile and I do not like them at all, but I know no others. Think what you will; what I have said is the truth.

Chapter III

Treats of the striking effects produced by this prayer aforementioned. It is necessary to observe and remember the effects it produces, for the difference between them and those already described is remarkable.

As we are saying, then, this little butterfly has now died, full of joy at having found rest, and within her lives Christ. Let us see what her new life is like, and how different it is from her earlier one, for it is by the effects which result from this prayer that we shall know if what has been said is true. As far as I can understand, the effects are these.

First, there is a self-forgetfulness which is so complete that it really seems as though the soul no longer existed, because it is such that she has neither knowledge nor remembrance that there is either heaven or life or honour for her, so entirely is she employed in seeking the honour of God. It appears that the words which His Majesty addressed to her have produced their effect — namely, that she must take care of His business and He will take care of hers.[237] And thus, happen what may, she does not mind in the least, but lives in so strange a state of forgetfulness that, as I say, she seems no longer to exist, and has no desire to exist — no, absolutely none — save when she realizes that she can do something to advance the glory and honour of God, for which she would gladly lay down her life.

Do not understand by this, daughters, that she neglects to eat and sleep (though having to do this is no little torment to her), or to do anything which is made incumbent upon her by her profession. We are talking of interior matters: as regards exterior ones there is little to be said. Her great grief is to see that all she can do of her own strength is as nothing. Anything that she is capable of doing and knows to be of service to Our Lord she would not fail to do for any reason upon earth.

The second effect produced is a great desire to suffer, but this is not of such a kind as to disturb the soul, as it did previously. So extreme is her longing for the will of God to be done in her that whatever His Majesty does she considers to be for the best: if He wills that she should suffer, well and good; if not, she does not worry herself to death as she did before.

When these souls are persecuted again, they have a great interior joy, and much more peace than in the state described above. They bear no enmity to those who ill-treat them, or desire to do so. Indeed they conceive a special love for them, so that, if they see them in some trouble, they are deeply grieved and would do anything possible to relieve them; they love to commend them to God, and they would rejoice at not being given some of the honours which His Majesty bestows upon them if their enemies might have them instead and thus be prevented from offending Our Lord.

What surprises me most is this. You have already seen what trials and afflictions these souls have suffered because of their desire to die and thus to enjoy Our Lord. They have now an equally strong desire to serve Him, and to sing His praise, and to help some soul if they can. So what they desire now is not merely not to die but to live for a great many years and to suffer the severest trials, if by so doing they can become the means whereby the Lord is praised, even in the smallest thing. If they knew for certain that, on leaving the body, they would have fruition of God, their attitude would not be affected, nor is it altered when they think of the glory which belongs to the saints, for they do not desire as yet to attain this. Their conception of glory is of being able in some way to help the Crucified, especially when they see how often people offend Him and how few there are who really care about His honour and are detached from everything else.

True, they sometimes forget this, turn with tender longing to the thought of enjoying God and desire to escape from this exile, especially when they see how little they are doing to serve Him. But then they turn back and look within themselves and remember that they have Him with them continually; and they are content with this and offer His Majesty their will to live as the most costly oblation they can give Him. They are no more afraid of death than they would be of gentle rapture. The explanation of this is that it is He Who gave the soul those earlier desires, accompanied by such excessive torment, that now gives it these others. May He be blessed and praised for ever.

In short, the desires of these souls are no longer for consolations or favours, for they have with them the Lord Himself and it is His Majesty Who now lives in them. His life, of course, was nothing but a continual torment and so He is making our life the same, at least as far as our desires go. In other respects, He treats us as weaklings, though He has ample fortitude to give us when He sees that we need it. These souls have a marked detachment from everything and a desire to be always either alone or busy with something that is to some soul's advantage. They have no aridities or interior trials but a remembrance of Our Lord and a tender love for Him, so that they would like never to be doing anything but giving Him praise. When the soul is negligent, the Lord Himself awakens it in the way that has been described, so that it sees quite clearly that this impulse, or whatever it is called, proceeds from the interior of the soul, as we said when discussing these impulses. It is now felt very gently, but it proceeds neither from the thought nor from the memory, nor can it be supposed that the soul has had any part in it. This is so usual and occurs so frequently that it has been observed with special care: just as the flames of a fire, however great, never travel downwards, but always upwards, so here it is evident that this interior movement proceeds from the centre of the soul and awakens the faculties.

Really, were there nothing else to be gained from this way of prayer but our realization of God's special care for us in His communing with us and of the way He keeps begging us to dwell with Him (for He seems to be doing nothing less), I believe that all trials would be well endured if they led to the enjoyment of these gentle yet penetrating touches of His love. This, sisters, you will have experienced, for I think that, when the soul reaches the Prayer of Union, the Lord begins to exercise this care over us if we do not neglect the keeping of His commandments. When this experience comes to you, remember that it belongs to this innermost Mansion, where God dwells in our souls, and give Him fervent praise, for it is He who sends it to you, like a message, or a letter, written very lovingly and in such a way that He would have you alone be able to understand what He has written and what He is asking of you in it.[238] On no account must you fail to answer His Majesty, even if you are busy with exterior affairs and engaged in conversation. It may often happen that Our Lord will be pleased to bestow this secret favour upon you in public, as your reply must needs be an interior one, it will be very easy for you to do what I say and make an act of love or exclaim with Saint Paul: "Lord, what wilt Thou have me to do?"[239] Then He will show you many ways of pleasing Him. For now is the accepted time: He seems indeed to be listening to us and this delicate touch almost always prepares the soul to be able to do, with a resolute will, what He has commanded it.

The difference between this Mansion and the rest has already been explained. There are hardly any of the periods of aridity or interior disturbance in it which at one time or another have occurred in all the rest, but the soul is almost always in tranquility. It is not afraid that this sublime favour may be counterfeited by the devil but retains the unwavering certainty that it comes from God. For, as has been said, the senses and faculties have no part in this: His Majesty has revealed Himself to the soul and taken it with Him into a place where, as I believe, the devil will not enter, because the Lord will not allow him to do so; and all the favours which the Lord grants the soul here, as I have said, come quite independently of the acts of the soul itself, apart from that of its having committed itself wholly to God.

So tranquilly and noiselessly does the Lord teach the soul in this state and do it good that I am reminded of the building of Solomon's temple, during which no noise could be heard; just so, in this temple of God, in this Mansion of His, He and the soul alone have fruition of each other in the deepest silence. There is no reason now for the understanding to stir, or to seek out anything, for the Lord Who created the soul is now pleased to calm it and would have it look, as it were, through a little chink, at what is passing. Now and then it loses sight of it and is unable to see anything; but this is only for a very brief time. The faculties, I think, are not lost here; it is merely that they do not work but seem to be dazed.

And I am quite dazed myself when I observe that, on reaching this state, the soul has no more raptures (accompanied, that is to say, by the suspension of the senses),[240] save very occasionally, and even then it has not the same transports and flights of the spirit. These raptures, too, happen only rarely, and hardly ever in public as they very often did before.[241] Nor have they any connection, as they had before, with great occasions of devotion; if we see a devotional image or hear a sermon, it is almost as if we had heard nothing, and it is the same with music. Previously, the poor little butterfly was always so worried that everything frightened her and made her fly away. But it is not so now, whether because she has found her rest, or because the soul has seen so much in this Mansion that it can be frightened at nothing, or because it no longer has that solitude which it was wont to have, now that it is enjoying such companionship. Well, sisters, I do not know what the reason may be, but, when the Lord begins to reveal the contents of this Mansion and brings souls into it, they lose the great weakness which was such a trial to them and of which previously they could not rid themselves. Perhaps the reason is that the Lord has so greatly strengthened and dilated and equipped the soul, or it may be that, for reasons which His Majesty alone knows, He was anxious to make a public revelation of His secret dealings with such souls, for His judgments surpass all that we can imagine here on earth.

These effects God bestows, together with all those other good effects already described in the above-mentioned degrees of prayer, when the soul approaches Him, and He also gives the soul that kiss for which the Bride besought Him; for I understand it to be in this Mansion that that petition is fulfilled. Here to this wounded hart are given waters in abundance. Here the soul delights in the tabernacle of God.[242] Here the dove sent out by Noe to see if the storm is over finds the olive-branch[243] — the sign that it has discovered firm ground amidst the waters and storms of this world.

Oh, Jesus! If only one knew how many things there are in Scripture which describe this peace of the soul! My God, since Thou seest how needful it is for us, do Thou inspire Christians to desire to seek it; take it not, by Thy mercy, from those to whom Thou hast given it, and who, until Thou give them true peace and take them where peace will never end, must always live in fear. I say "true" peace, not because I think this peace is not true, but because in this life war might always begin again if we were to withdraw from God.

And what will be the feeling of these souls when they realize that they might lack so great a blessing? The thought makes them walk the more warily and endeavour to bring strength out of their weakness, so as not to be responsible for losing any opportunity which might offer itself to them of pleasing God better. The more they are favoured by God, the more timorous and fearful do they become concerning themselves, and as they have learned more about their own wretchedness by comparing it with His greatness and their sins are now so much more serious to them, they often go about, like the Publican, without daring to lift up their eyes.[244] At other times, they long to reach the end of their lives so as to be in safety, though they are soon anxious again to live longer so that they may serve Him because of the love which they bear Him, as has been said, and they trust all that concerns themselves to His mercy. Sometimes the many favours they receive leave them overwhelmed, and afraid lest they be like an overladen ship sinking to the bottom of the sea.

I assure you, sisters, that they have no lack of crosses, but these do not unsettle them or deprive them of their peace. The few storms pass quickly, like waves of the sea, and fair weather returns, and then the Presence of the Lord which they have within them makes them forget everything. May He be for ever blessed and praised by all His creatures. Amen.

Chapter IV

Concludes by describing what appears to be Our Lord's aim in granting the soul such great favours and says how necessary it is for Martha and Mary to walk in each other's company. This chapter is very profitable.

You must not take it, sisters, that the effects which I have described as occurring in these souls are invariably present all the time; it is for this reason that, whenever I have remembered to do so, I have referred to them as being present "habitually". Sometimes Our Lord leaves such souls to their own nature, and when that happens, all the poisonous things in the environs and mansions of this castle seem to come together to avenge themselves on them for the time during which they have not been able to have them in their power.

It is true that this lasts only for a short time — for a single day, or a little longer, at the most — and in the course of the ensuing turmoil, which as a rule is the result of some chance happening, it becomes clear what the soul is gaining from the good Companion Who is with it. For the Lord gives it great determination, so that it will on no account turn aside from His service and from its own good resolutions. On the contrary, these resolutions seem to increase, and so the soul will not make the slightest move which may deflect it from its resolve. This, as I say, happens rarely, but Our Lord's will is for the soul not to forget what it is — for one reason, so that it may always be humble; for another, so that it may the better realize what it owes to His Majesty and what a great favour it is receiving, and may praise Him.

Do not, of course, for one moment imagine that, because these souls have such vehement desires and are so determined not to commit a single imperfection for anything in the world, they do not in fact commit many imperfections, and even sins. Not intentionally, it is true, for the Lord will give such persons very special aid as to this: I am referring to venial sins, for from mortal sins, as far as they know, they are free, though they are not completely proof against them; and the thought that they may commit some without knowing it will cause them no small agony. It also distresses them to see so many souls being lost; and, although on the one hand they have great hopes of not being among them, yet, when they remember some whom the Scriptures describe as having been favoured of the Lord — like Solomon, who enjoyed such converse with His Majesty[245] — they cannot, as I have said, but be afraid. And let whichever of you feels surest of herself fear most, for, says David, "Blessed is the man that feareth God."[246] May His Majesty always protect us; let us beseech Him to do so, that we may not offend Him; this is the greatest security that we can have. May He be for ever praised. Amen.

It will be a good thing, sisters, if I tell you why it is that the Lord grants so many favours in this world. Although you will have learned this from the effects they produce, if you have observed them, I will speak about it further here, so that none of you shall think that He does it simply to give these souls pleasure. That would be to make a great error. For His Majesty can do nothing greater for us than grant us a life which is an imitation of that lived by His Beloved Son. I feel certain, therefore, that these favours are given us to strengthen our weakness, as I have sometimes said here, so that we may be able to imitate Him in His great sufferings.

We always find that those who walked closest to Christ Our Lord were those who had to bear the greatest trials. Consider the trials suffered by His glorious Mother and by the glorious Apostles. How do you suppose Saint Paul could endure such terrible trials? We can see in his life the effects of genuine visions and of contemplation coming from Our Lord and not from human imagination or from the deceit of the devil. Do you imagine that he shut himself up with his visions so as to enjoy those Divine favours and pursue no other occupation? You know very well that, so far as we can learn, he took not a day's rest, nor can he have rested by night, since it was then that he had to earn his living[247] I am very fond of the story of how, when Saint Peter was fleeing from prison, Our Lord appeared to him and told him to go back to Rome and be crucified. We never recite the Office on his festival, in which this story is found, without my deriving a special consolation from it.[248] How did Saint Peter feel after receiving this favour from the Lord? And what did he do? He went straight to his death; and the Lord showed him no small mercy in providing someone to kill him.

Oh, my sisters, how little one should think about resting, and how little one should care about honours, and how far one ought to be from wishing to be esteemed in the very least if the Lord makes His special abode in the soul. For if the soul is much with Him, as it is right it should be, it will very seldom think of itself; its whole thought will be concentrated upon finding ways to please Him and upon showing Him how it loves Him. This, my daughters, is the aim of prayer: this is the purpose of the Spiritual Marriage, of which are born good works and good works alone.

Such works, as I have told you, are the sign of every genuine favour and of everything else that comes from God. It will profit me a little if I am alone and deeply recollected, and make acts of love to Our Lord and plan and promise to work wonders in His service, and then, as soon as I leave my retreat and some occasion presents itself, I do just the opposite. I was wrong when I said it will profit me little, for anyone who is with God must profit greatly, and, although after making these resolutions we may be too weak to carry them out, His Majesty will sometimes grant us grace to do so, even at great cost to ourselves, as often happens. For, when He sees a very timorous soul, He sends it, much against its own will, some very sore trial the bearing of which does it a great deal of good; and later, when the soul becomes aware of this, it loses its fear and offers itself to Him the more readily. What I meant was that the profit is small by comparison with the far greater profit which comes from conformity between our deeds on the one hand and our resolutions and the words we use on the other. Anyone who cannot achieve everything at once must progress little by little. If she wishes to find help in prayer, she must learn to subdue her own will and in these little nooks of ours there will be very many occasions when you can do this.

Reflect carefully on this, for it is so important that I can hardly lay too much stress on it. Fix your eyes on the Crucified and nothing else will be of much importance to you. If His Majesty revealed His love to us by doing and suffering such amazing things, how can you expect to please Him by words alone? Do you know when people really become spiritual? It is when they become the slaves of God and are branded with His sign, which is the sign of the Cross, in token that they have given Him their freedom. Then He can sell them as slaves to the whole world, as He Himself was sold, and if He does this He will be doing them no wrong but showing them no slight favour. Unless they resolve to do this, they need not expect to make great progress. For the foundation of this whole edifice, as I have said, is humility, and, if you have not true humility, the Lord will not wish it to reach any great height: in fact, it is for your own good that it should not; if it did, it would fall to the ground. Therefore, sisters, if you wish to lay good foundations, each of you must try to be the least of all, and the slave of God, and must seek a way and means to please and serve all your companions. If you do that, it will be of more value to you than to them and your foundation will be so firmly laid that your Castle will not fall.

I repeat that if you have this in view you must not build upon foundations of prayer and contemplation alone, for, unless you strive after the virtues and practise them, you will never grow to be more than dwarfs. God grant that nothing worse than this may happen — for, as you know, anyone who fails to go forward begins to go back, and love, I believe, can never be content to stay for long where it is.

You may think that I am speaking about beginners, and that later on one may rest: but, as I have already told you, the only repose that these souls enjoy is of an interior kind; of outward repose they get less and less, and they have no wish to get more. What is the purpose, do you suppose, of these inspirations — or, more correctly, of these aspirations — which I have described, and of these messages which are sent by the soul from its innermost centre to the folk outside the Castle and to the Mansions which are outside that in which it is itself dwelling? Is it to send them to sleep? No, no, no. The soul, where it now is, is fighting harder to keep the faculties and senses and every thing to do with the body from being idle than it did when it suffered with them. For it did not then understand what great gain can be derived from trials, which may indeed have been means whereby God has brought it to this state, nor did it realize how the companionship which it now enjoys would give it much greater strength than it ever had before. For if, as David says, with the holy we shall be holy,[249] it cannot be doubted that, if we are made one with the Strong, we shall gain strength through the most sovereign union of spirit with Spirit, and we shall appreciate the strength of the saints which enabled them to suffer and die.

It is quite certain that, with the strength it has gained, the soul comes to the help of all who are in the Castle, and, indeed, succours the body itself. Often the body appears to feel nothing, but the strength derived from the vigour gained by the soul after it has drunk of the wine from this cellar, where its Spouse has brought it and which He will not allow it to leave, overflows into the weak body, just as on the earthly plane the food which is introduced into the stomach gives strength to the head and to the whole body. In this life, then, the soul has a very bad time, for, however much it accomplishes, it is strong enough inwardly to attempt much more and this causes such strife within it that nothing it can do seems to it of any importance. This must be the reason for the great penances done by many saints, especially by the glorious Magdalen, who had been brought up in such luxury all her life long; there was also that hunger for the honour of his God suffered by our father Elias;[250] and the zeal of Saint Dominic and Saint Francis for bringing souls to God, so that He might be praised. I assure you that, forgetful as they were of themselves, they must have endured no little suffering.

This, my sisters, I should like us to strive to attain: we should desire and engage in prayer, not for our enjoyment, but for the sake of acquiring this strength which fits us for service. Let us not try to walk along an untrodden path, or at the best we shall waste our time: it would certainly be a novel idea to think of receiving these favours from God through any other means than those used by Him and by all His saints. Let us not even consider such a thing: believe me, Martha and Mary must work together when they offer the Lord lodging, and must have Him ever with them, and they must not entertain Him badly and give Him nothing to eat. And how can Mary give Him anything, seated as she is at His feet, unless her sister helps her? His food consists in our bringing Him souls, in every possible way, so that they may be saved and may praise Him for ever.

You will reply to me by making two observations. The first, that Mary was said to have chosen the better part[251] — and she had already done the work of Martha and shown her love for the Lord by washing His feet and wiping them with her hair.[252] And do you think it would be a trifling mortification to a woman in her position to go through those streets — perhaps alone, for her fervour was such that she cared nothing how she went — to enter a house that she had never entered before and then to have to put up with uncharitable talk from the Pharisee[253] and from very many other people, all of which she was forced to endure? What a sight it must have been in the town to see such a woman as she had been making this change in her life! Such wicked people as we know the Jews to have been would only need to see that she was friendly with the Lord, Whom they so bitterly hated, to call to mind the life which she had lived and to realize that she now wanted to become holy, for she would of course at once have changed her style of dress and everything else. Think how we gossip about people far less notorious than she and then imagine what she must have suffered. I assure you, sisters, that that better part came to her only after sore trials and great mortification — even to see her Master so much hated must have been an intolerable trial to her. And how many such trials did she not endure later, after the Lord's death! I think myself that the reason she was not granted martyrdom was that she had already undergone it through witnessing the Lord's death.[254] The later years of her life, too, during which she was absent from Him, would have been years of terrible torment; so she was not always enjoying the delights of contemplation at the Lord's feet.

The other thing you may say is that you are unable to lead souls to God, and have no means of doing so; that you would gladly do this, but, being unable to teach and preach like the Apostles, you do not know how. That is an objection which I have often answered in writing, though I am not sure if I have done so in discussing this Castle. But, as it is a thing which I think must occur to you, in view of the desires which the Lord implants in you, I will not omit to speak of it here. I told you elsewhere that the devil sometimes puts ambitious desires into our hearts, so that, instead of setting our hand to the work which lies nearest to us, and thus serving Our Lord in ways within our power, we may rest content with having desired the impossible. Apart from praying for people, by which you can do a great deal for them, do not try to help everybody, but limit yourselves to your own companions; your work will then be all the more effective because you have the greater obligation to do it. Do you imagine it is a small advantage that you should have so much humility and mortification, and should be the servants of all and show such great charity towards all, and such fervent love for the Lord that it resembles a fire kindling all their souls, while you constantly awaken their zeal by your other virtues? This would indeed be a great service to the Lord and one very pleasing to Him. By your doing things which you really can do, His Majesty will know that you would like to do many more, and thus He will reward you exactly as if you had won many souls for Him.

"But we shall not be converting anyone," you will say, "for all our sisters are good already." What has that to do with it? If they become still better, their praises will be more pleasing to the Lord, and their prayers of greater value to their neighbours. In a word, my sisters, I will end by saying that we must not build towers without foundations, and that the Lord does not look so much at the magnitude of anything we do as at the love with which we do it. If we accomplish what we can, His Majesty will see to it that we become able to do more each day. We must not begin by growing weary; but during the whole of this short life, which for any one of you may be shorter than you think, we must offer the Lord whatever interior and exterior sacrifice we are able to give Him, and His Majesty will unite it with that which He offered to the Father for us upon the Cross, so that it may have the value won for it by our will, even though our actions in themselves may be trivial.

May it please His Majesty, my sisters and daughters, to bring us all to meet where we may praise Him and to give me grace to do some of the things of which I have told you, through the merits of His Son, Who liveth and reigneth for ever, Amen. As I say this to you I am full of shame and by the same Lord I beg you not to forget this poor miserable creature in your prayers.

JHS.

Although when I began to write what I have set down here it was with great reluctance, as I said at the beginning, I am very glad I did so now that it is finished, and I think my labour has been well spent, though I confess it has cost me very little. And considering how strictly you are cloistered, my sisters, how few opportunities you have of recreation and how insufficient in number are your houses, I think it will be a great consolation for you, in some of your convents, to take your delight in this Interior Castle, for you can enter it and walk about in it at any time without asking leave from your superiors.

It is true that, however strong you may think yourselves, you cannot enter all the Mansions by your own efforts: the Lord of the Castle Himself must admit you to them. So, if you meet with any resistance, I advise you not to make any effort to get in, for if you do you will displease Him so much that He will never admit you. He is a great Lover of humility. If you consider yourselves unworthy of entering even the third Mansions, He will more quickly give you the will to reach the fifth, and thenceforward you may serve Him by going to these Mansions again and again, till He brings you into the Mansion which He reserves as His own and which you will never leave, except when you are called away by the prioress, whose wishes this great Lord is pleased that you should observe as if they were His own. And even if, at her command, you are often outside these Mansions, He will always keep the door open against your return. Once you have been shown how to enjoy this Castle, you will find rest in everything, even in the things which most try you, and you will cherish a hope of returning to it which nobody can take from you.

Although I have spoken here only of seven Mansions, yet in each there are comprised many more, both above and below and around, with lovely gardens and fountains[255] and things so delectable that you will want to lose yourselves in praise of the great God Who created it in His image and likeness. If you find anything good in this book which helps you to learn to know Him better, you can be quite sure that it is His Majesty Who has said it, and if you find anything bad, that it has been said by me.

By the earnest desire that I have to be of some use in helping you to serve this my God and Lord, I beg you, in my own name, whenever you read this, to give great praise to His Majesty and beg Him to multiply His Church and to give light to the Lutherans and to pardon my sins and set me free from Purgatory, where perhaps, by the mercy of God,[256] I shall be when this is given you to read, if, after being revised by learned men, it is ever published. And if there is any error in it, that is due to my lack of understanding, for in all things I submit to what is held by the Holy Roman Catholic Church, in which I live, and protest and promise that I will both live and die. Praised and blessed for ever be God our Lord. Amen, Amen.

The writing of this was finished in the convent of Saint Joséph of Avila, in the year one thousand five hundred and seventy seven, on the vigil of Saint Andrew, to the glory of God, Who liveth and reigneth for ever and ever. Amen

Footnotes

[1][As has been said above, it is as Las Moradas ("The Mansions") that this book is known in Spain.]

[2]The letter [printed, in Spanish, by P. Silverio, II, 490-505] is dated September 4, 1588. The anecdote is told more briefly in Yepes' biography of St. Teresa, Bk. II, Chap. XX.

[3]Cf. The Life of Teresa of Jesus, translated and edited by E. Allison Peers; Image Books Edition, p. 62.

[4]Cf. Relations, VI (Vol. I, The Complete Works of St. Teresa, translated and edited by E. Allison Peers; Sheed and Ward, p. 334).

[5]Dilucidario del verdadero espíritu, Chap. V.

[6][A fuller exposition, in English, will be found in S.S.M., I, 162-91.]

[7]The titles are here given in the form in which they appear in the editio princeps, which is practically identical with that of the Toledo copy.

[8]See p. 23, n. 1, below.

[9]Cf. p. 264, below. Some critics write as if there were an interruption of five months during the composition of the book, but that is not what the passage says. Were it so, it would mean that the book was written in about four weeks.

[10][Cit. P. Silverio, IV, xxxvi.]

[11]Op. cit., IV, xxxvii.

[12]Op. Cit., IV, xxxviii.

[13]As a kind of sub-title St. Teresa wrote on the back of the first page of the autograph: "This treatise, called 'Interior Castle', was written by Teresa of Jesus, nun of Our Lady of Carmel to her sisters and daughters the Discalced Carmelite nuns." Below this is a note by P. Ribera (formerly attributed to Fray Luis de León) which asserts [somewhat verbosely, for which reason the full text is not here translated] that the marginal emendations in the autograph are often inconsistent with other parts of the text and in any case are inferior to the author's own words, and begs readers to respect "the words and letters written by that most holy hand". [It is noteworthy that the word "mansions (moradas: n. 18, below), by which the book is generally known in Spain, does not appear in the title or sub-title of the autograph, though it occurs in the title of each of the seven sections of the book.]

[14]Lit.: "literally."

[15]June 2, 1577.

[16]The words "Roman Catholic" are inserted by the author interlineally.

[17][Aposentos — a rather more pretentious word than the English "room": dwellingplace, abode, apartment.]

[18][Moradas: derived from morar, to dwell, and not, therefore, absolute identical in sense with "mansions". The reference, however, is to St. John xiv, 2.]

[19]Proverbs viii, 31.

[20]Genesis i, 26.

[21]Here the Saint erased several words and inserted others, leaving the phrase as it is in the text.

[22][Moradas (see n. 18, above).]

[23]St. John ix, 2.

[24]Genesis xix, 26.

[25][Lit., "into such bestiality".] P. Gracián deletes "bestiality" and substitutes "abomination." [I think the translation in the text, however, is a more successful way of expressing what was in St. Teresa's mind: cf. St. John of the Cross's observations on "animal penances" — penitencias de bestias — in his Dark Night, I, vi (Complete Works, I, 365-6.)]

[26]P. Gracián corrects this to "thirty-eight years." St. John v, 5.

[27]St. Matthew vi, 21.

28Psalm i, 3.

29Lit.: "fruit", for which P. Gracián substitutes "merit."

[30]St. Teresa herself. See Relation XXIV (Vol. I, The Complete Works of St. Teresa, translated and edited by E. Allison Peers, p. 345).

[31]Psalm cxxvi, 2 [AV., cxxvii, 1].

[32]The palmito is a shrub, common in the south and east of Spain, with thick layers of leaves enclosing a succulent edible kernel.

[33][The autograph has, after the word "room", "Oh, but if it is (Uh, que si es) in (the room of) self-knowledge!" Previous editors have altered this difficult Spanish phrase to aunque sea, "not even if it is." St. Teresa's meaning however, seems to me quite clearly the opposite of this, though it is impossible to translate her exclamation literally.]

[34][Lit.: "excess is as bad as defect."]

[35][Ratero: creeping, flying low, content with a low standard.]

[36]Lit., "a million."

[37]Lit: "and had earth on his eyes."

[38]See Life, Chapter XIII and Method for the visitation of convents.

[39]Below this line St. Teresa wrote "Chapter," to which Luis de León prefixed the word "Only."

[40]Life, Chaps. XI-XIII; Way of perfection, The Complete Works of St. Teresa, Chaps. XX-XXIX.

[41][The word (guisar: "season", "dress") is a homely one: "dished up" would hardly be too colloquial a translation.]

[42][St. Luke xv, 15-16].

[43]Judges vii, 5. "With Gedeon in the Judges," adds P. Gracián in the margin, crossing out the words "I forget with whom".

[44]Life, Chap. XI.

[45][Probably a conscious reference to St. Matthew vii, 26-7.]

[46]St. Matthew xx, 22.

[47]The autograph has, not casas ("homes") but cosas ("things"). Luis de León, however, read casas and succeeding editors have followed him.

[48]St. John xx, 21.

[49]Life, Chaps. XI, XIX.

[50]Ecclesiasticus iii, 27.

[51]St. John xiv, 6.

[52]P. Gracián crossed through the bracketed words and wrote in the margin: "Both are said by St. John, Chapter xiv." [Actually the words are: "No man cometh. . . ."]

[53]St. John xiv, 9.

[54]St. Matthew x, 24.

[55]St. Matthew xxiv, 41.

[56]Psalm cxi, 1 (A.V. cxii, 1).

[57]St. John xi, 16. The last four words are a marginal addition of the author's.

[58]Gracián adds "in Heaven"; the addition is deleted by Ribera.

[59]Gracián alters this to: "some who, although they are saints [a more exact translation would be "are saintly"], yet fell," but Ribera restores St. Teresa's reading.

[60]Gracián alters this to: "we have no certainty of abandoning them and of doing, etc."

[61]The bracketed words, which St. Teresa wrote in the margin of the autograph, are crossed out with two strokes. But Ribera has written underneath them: "This is not to be deleted."

[62][A striking example of St. Teresa's untranslatably concise language. The original is: Recia obediencia ha sido! Lit.: "Rigorous obedience (it) has been!"]

[63]Gracián altered this word to "Absalom" but Ribera wrote in the margin: "This should read 'Solomon', as the holy Mother said."

[64]Psalm cxi, 1 (A.V., cxii, 1).

[65]The autograph makes this sentence negative, but partially deletes the negative particle. Luis de León, followed by later editors, omits it.

[66]St. Matthew xix, 16-22.

[67]The phrase "like . . . Gospel" was written by St. Teresa in the margin. [No doubt she recalled the reference to St. Matthew xix, 16-22, which she had made just above.]

[68][Or this clause might mean: "yet a person who gives all that he has thinks that he gives in fullest measure." But the interpretation in the text seems preferable.]

[69][St. Luke xvii, 10.] Gracián, in a note, gives the correct authorship.

[70]"For what He has suffered for us" was substituted for the phrase by Gracián but the original text was restored by Ribera.

[71]Gracián deleted the words "I write . . . truth" but Ribera wrote in the margin: "Nothing is to be deleted, for what the Saint says is well said."

[72][Lit.: "drove me silly" — "me traían tonta": a typically homely and forcible expression. Cf. n. 91, below.]

[73]"Very easily," added Gracián, interlinearly, but the addition is crossed out.

[74]St. Luke xxii, 42.

[75][Lit.: "the Surgeon".]

[76][The Spanish phrase means, literally, "anyone of their humour", but there is no such "saying" as this in English.]

[77]Cf. St. Teresa's definition of supernatural prayer in Relation V (Vol. I, p. 327).

[78]From the outline of St. Teresa's life, Image Books Edition, (Vol. 1, pp. 27-37), it will be seen that this computation is approximately correct. The reference is to Life, Chaps. XI-XXVII.

[79][The word is the same as is used above for "sweetness" — i.e., contentos, but in the singular. Such word-play, as we have seen, is common in St. Teresa: in the title of this very chapter we have an identical play on contentos ("sweetness") and contento ("happiness").]

[80][contentos.]

[81][contento.]

[82][contentos.]

[83][Psalm cxviii, 32: "(I have run the way of thy commandments,) when thou didst enlarge my heart". A.V. cxix, 32.]

[84][contento.]

[85]The remainder of this paragraph was scored through in the autograph by Gracián and are omitted from the Córdoba copy. They are, however, quite legible.

[86][Lit.: "from how the disposition is."]

[87]Life, Chap. XII.

[88]The words in brackets were written in the margin by St. Teresa and lightly scored out. Ribera, however, adds: "Nothing to be deleted." Gracián has added, interlineally, after "imagination": "for so we women generally call it."

[89][tan tortolito, an expressive phrase: "so like a little tórtola (turtle-dove)" — i.e. not only timid, but irresolute and apparently stupid, like an inexperienced fledgling.]

[90][Here there is a play on words difficult to render in English: the word translated both "restrain" and "uniting" is atar — "tie", "bind."]

[91][Traíame tonta. Cf. n. 72, above.]

[92]Gracián scores out this sentence in the autograph.

[93]Canticles viii, 1. Gracián has copied in the margin of the autograph the Spanish text of Canticles viii, 1-4.

[94][The original is quite colloquial: "in the mess I have got into" or "in what I have let myself in for" would be nearer its spirit.]

[95] Psalm cxviii, 32 (A.V., cxix, 32). Cf. n. 83, above.

[96]Again, as above (n. 78), the Saint's computation is exactly correct.

[97][A very strong word, estrujarse. In its non-reflexive form, the verb means to squeeze, crush or press hard, or to extract something by so doing. The sense is, therefore, that with all our efforts we cannot squeeze out a drop of this water.]

[98]Life, Chap. XVI; Way of perfection, Chaps. XXVIII, XXIX; Relations, V.

[99]There is little doubt that St. Teresa is here using Bk. IX, Chap. VII of Francisco de Osuna's Third Spiritual Alphabet.

[100]Confessions, Bk. X, Chap. XXVII [or Soliloquies, Chap. XXXI: cf. St. John of the Cross: II, 33, 196, n. 9.]

[101][Lit.: "conscious of a gentle interior shrinking": encogimiento, the noun used, means "shrinkage", "contraction"; it should be distinguished from recogimiento, a word often used by St. Teresa and translated "recollection".]

[102]Osuna (op. cit., Bk. VI, Chap. IV) uses this simile of the hedgehog in much the same way.

[103]The reference is presumably to the famous "Eighth Counsel" of the Treatise of Prayer and Meditation [Cf. S.S.M., II, 113-14].

[104]"With his human skill", adds Gracián, interlinearly.

[105]Way of perfection, Chap. XXXI.

[106]St. Teresa had written "to discuss the effects of" but deleted the last three words.

[107][The two Spanish words, on which St. Teresa plays so trenchantly, are added to their English equivalents so as to make the phrase intelligible.]

[108]Gracián has scored through part of this sentence in the autograph.

[109]St. Matthew xx, 16.

[110]Gracián substitutes for "are": "follow the rule of being."

[111]Gracián inserts the word "perhaps".

[112]Luis de León modifies this passage [which has been slightly paraphrased in translation, the construction in the Spanish being rather obscure], reading, after "delight": "for, although it [the soul] is in Him, according to the truth, it appears

to have withdrawn so far from the body, in order to come closer to God, that I do not know, etc."

113 "Of the soul alone", inserts Gracián, interlineally.

[114]Gracián deletes "the essence of".

[115]Gracián substitutes "understanding" for "thoughts" and adds a marginal note: "This is (to be) understood of acts of the understanding and the will, for the thoughts of the imagination are clearly seen by the devil unless God blinds him in that respect." Luis de León included the marginal note in the text of his edition but Gracián did not reproduce it in either the text or the margin of the Córdoba copy though he altered "thoughts" to "understanding".

[116]Gracián inserts the word "nature" here, interlineally.

[117][P. Silverio refers here to Way of perfection, Chap. XXXI, but I hardly think this can be meant. Perhaps the author's allusion is to the first chapter of the Fourth Mansions or possibly to something she once said viva voce.]

[118][Lit.: "a something": the Spanish is un no sé qué, an expression corresponding to the French un je ne sais quoi.]

[119]Gracián alters "as" to "as being, I think".

[120]Gracián inserts: "it thinks."

[121]Gracián amends the following phrase to read: "but that there has since remained with it, as it thinks, a certainty, etc."

[122]Gracián alters this phrase to: "which made her understand this in such a way."

[123]St. Teresa refers to this experience of hers in Life, Chap. XVIII (Image Books Edition, p. 180). Later, a favour which she received (Relations, LIV: Vol. I, p. 361.) enlightened her further on this point. According to Yepes (II, xx) she asked him for theological guidance about it just before she began the Interior Castle.

[124]The rest of this paragraph was omitted by Luis de León.

[125]Canticles i, 3; ii, 4. Gracián deletes the bracketed phrase but writes "put" above "brought".

[126]Canticles iii, 2.

[127]Here and just below Gracián has crossed out the word "centre".

[128]St. John xx, 19.

[129]"Mustard-seeds," writes Gracián, interlineally, deleting the bracketed sentence which follows and adding the words: "It is so, for I have seen it."

[130]Colossians iii, 3. Gracián deletes "for that . . . my purpose" and supplies text and source in the margin.

[131][Lit.: "Whether this be so or not." But the meaning is clear from the context.]

[132]The words "I meant . . . at all" are omitted from the editio princeps.

[133]A characteristically emphatic phrase — en fin, fin.

[134][Cf. Ch. 1, above. The reference here is clearly to Canticles ii, 4.]

[135]St. Luke xxii, 15.

[136]St. Teresa herself.

[137]St. Teresa herself. Cf. Life, Chap. VII (Image Books Edition, p. 105).

[138][The phrase is very emphatic: Harto provecho, harto — "exceedingly great profit, exceedingly."]

[139]St. John xi, 35.

[140]St. Teresa added here the word acullá, "yonder", which Luis de León altered to en lo susodicho, "in what is (said) above". [This affects the sense: Luis de León's alteration suggests that the silkworm is referred to, which seems to me unlikely. I take acullá to refer to the end of one's life and acá to mean "here and now".]

[141][Lit.: "to kill it ourselves." By "it", which in the Spanish can only stand for "life", is presumably meant the Pauline "old man".]

[142]Jonas iv, 6-7 [The "gourd" of A.V.]

[143]St. John xvii, 22.

[144][Encapotadas: lit., covering their faces with a cloak, muffled up. Metaphorically, the word can mean "frowning", "sullen". Here a less reprehensible meaning seems indicated.]

[145]Cf. Way of perfection, Chap. VII.

[146]The words "in . . . souls" were written by St. Teresa interlineally and "because . . . repose" were added by her in the margin.

[147][Vengan a vistas: lit., "have sight of each other", "have an interview with each other"; and, in that sense, "come together" or "meet".]

[148][This sounds contradictory, but the word "take" (tomar each time in the Spanish) is of course used in two different senses.]

[149]No fué más de una vista. [Cf. n. 147, above.]

[150]Luis de León omitted the reference to St. Ignatius of Loyola and the Society of Jesus from his edition, reading: "and other founders of Orders, all of whom, as we read, etc."

[151]Gracián deletes, and León omits, the words "and the Holy Spirit".

[152][St. Teresa is not always consistent in her use of singular and plural in referring to each stage of the Mystic Way. The translation, throughout, follows her here exactly.]

[153]St. Teresa herself: cf. Life, Chap. XXVIII.

[154]The person referred to is no doubt the author. [It was almost exactly forty years since she had professed at the Incarnation.]

[155][Lit.: "for many days"; but, as we have already seen, St. Teresa often uses that phrase vaguely.]

[156]At this point in the autograph, St. Teresa wrote the word "Chapter", evidently intending to end the first chapter of the Sixth Mansions here, but deleted it again. Luis de León treated the insertion as valid and began the new chapter with the following paragraph: he was followed by other editors until the mid-nineteenth century. The autograph, however, does not support this procedure.

[157]The author had first written: "or a lightning-flash. Although no light is seen"; but she deleted this and substituted the phrase in the text.

[158][The verb used is deshacerse, "to undo oneself", implying here the utmost effort.]

[159]A. Francisco de Santo Tomás, O.C.D., in his Médula mystica (Trat. VI, Cap. i), has a succinct description of the three types of locution referred to by St. Teresa, a classification applicable to visions also: "Some are corporeal, some imaginary and some spiritual or intellectual. Corporeal locutions are those actually heard by the physical powers of hearing. . . . Imaginary locutions are not heard in that way but the impression apprehended and received by the imaginative faculty is the same as though they had been. . . . In spiritual or intellectual locutions God imprints what He is about to say in the depth of the spirit: there is no sound, or voice, or either corporeal or imaginary representation of such, but an expression of (certain) concepts in the depth of the spirit and in the faculty of the understanding, and as this is not corporeal, but spiritual, the species, or similitudes, under which it is apprehended are not corporeal, but spiritual." Intellectual locutions, as explained

by St. John of the Cross (Ascent of Mount Carmel, Book II, Chaps. XXVI-XXX), are of three kinds: successive, formal and substantial.

[160][St. Luke xxiv, 36.]

161Jonas iv.

[162]Josue x, 12-13.

[163][The original here interpolates two clauses, con cuanto veis, u que nos está bien, which, translated literally as "with all that you see or that it is acceptable to us", make no sense. I suspect that, if St. Teresa had re-read her work, the phrase would have been omitted or clarified. Freely it might be rendered: "wonderful as you see it to be and much as we appreciate it", or, "however many visions you see or however much we desire them", but I am not convinced that either of these translations represents the author's meaning and other paraphrases are admissible.]

[164]Life, Chap. XX; Relations, V.

[165]The phrase "assuming . . . teaches" was added by St. Teresa, in the autograph, as a marginal note.

[166]Genesis xxviii, 12.

[167]Exodus iii, 2.

[168]"Two days" adds the editio princeps. The visit was made at the beginning of 1574: see "Outline, etc.", Vol. I, p. xxxi, above.

[169]The sentence "I can . . . whole" was written by St. Teresa in the margin of the autograph.

[170][Or "some": the Spanish word, alguna, can have either a singular or a plural sense.]

[171][The "streets and the broad ways" of Canticles iii, 2.]

[172]St. John ix, 6-7.

[173]Cf. Life, Chap. XXXI [Image Books Edition, 292].

[174]This is Luis de León's emendation of the sentence in the autograph, which reads: "I do not use the word 'feigned', because those who experience them do not wish to deceive, but because [sic] they are deceived themselves." Gracián, in the Córdoba copy, emends similarly, though not identically. Both evidently express what St. Teresa meant but failed to put clearly.

[175]The mystics concur with St. Thomas in holding that ecstasy, rapture, transport, flight of the spirit, etc., are in substance one and the same, though there are accidental differences between them, as St. Teresa explains here, in Life, Chap. XX, and in Relations, V.

[176]IV, chapter ii.

[177]St. Luke xii, 28.

[178]St. Teresa received this favour at Seville about 1575-6. Cf. Relations, LI (Vol. I, The Complete Works of St. Teresa, p. 360.)

[179]Numbers xiii, 18-24.

[180][Los trabajos de este camino tan trabajoso: the word-play is intentional.]

[181][Vistas. Cf. n. 147, above.]

[182]Exodus xiv, 21-2; Josue iii, 13.

[183]In the office of this Saint the Church recalls these words of his: "Lord, if I am still necessary to Thy people, I do not refuse toil: Thy will be done."

[184][Cf. Life, Chap. XVIII: Image Books Edition, p. 168].

[185]St. Luke xv, 11-32.

[186]Life, Chap. XXII.

[187]Life, Chaps. XXII-XXIV.

[188]St. John xiv, 6.

[189]The words "the Lord . . . light" [which clearly interrupt the thought of the passage] are in the author's hand, but are marginal.

[190]St. John xiv, 6.

[191]St. John xiv, 9.

[192][I.e., the understanding.]

[193]3 Kings [A.V., 1 Kings] xviii, 30-9.

[194]Canticles iii, 3.

[195] "Or Confessions" is a marginal addition in St. Teresa's hand. The passage alluded to comes from Chapter XXXI of the Soliloquies, a work first published in Spanish at Venice in 1512 and often reprinted in Spain during the sixteenth century. A passage very similar to this will be found in the Confessions, Bk. X, Chap. VI.

[196]Foundations, Chap. VI.

[197]St. John xvi, 7.

[198]For St. Teresa's treatment of intellectual vision, see Life, Chaps. XXVII, XXVIII.

[199][Cf. Life, Chap. XXVII.]

[200]Ibid.

[201]St. Matthew xxv, 41. [The abrupt change of pronoun is reproduced exactly from the Spanish.]

[202][This characteristic example of St. Teresa's word-play is allowed to stand in translation, though to English ears it may sound artificial. See Introduction, Life; Image Books Edition, pp. 20-21].

[203][Dar higas. Cf. note on this phrase, The Life of Teresa of Avila, trans. and edited, by E. Allison Peers; Image Books Edition, p. 243, n: 9. The theologian referred to was P. Báñez: cf. Life, Chap. XXIX, Foundations, Chap. VIII.]

[204]Psalm cxv, 11 [: "I said in my excess: 'Every man as a liar,'" Cf. A.V., Psalm cxvi. 11.]

[205]St. John xvii, 38.

[206]St. John iv, 7-13.

[207]The words of the parenthesis were inserted by St. Teresa in the margin of the autograph.

[208]Cf. Relations XV. [The Complete Works of St. Teresa Vol. I., p. 340. This incident took place at Salamanca in 1571. The singer was M. Isabel de Jesús. The song begins:

Let mine eyes behold Thee, Sweetest Jesu, nigh; Let mine eyes behold Thee, And at once I'll die.

[It has no verbal reference, as our text suggests, to "life not ending", but this is its general theme, as it is also that of several poems by St. Teresa herself.]

[209][Lit.: "and is dying in order to die" — a reference, no doubt, to the poem to be found in Vol. III, The Complete Works of St. Teresa, pp. 277-9].

[210]St. Matthew xx, 22: "'Can you drink the chalice that I shall drink?' They say to Him: 'We can.'"

[211]St. Luke vii, 44.

[212]Gracián altered "capable" to "prepared".

[213]"To win merit" is the Saint's marginal addition.

[214]This paragraph was considerably altered in the editio princeps.

[215]Acts ix, 8.

[216][Acts ix, 18.]

[217]Gracián reads: "vision or knowledge, born of faith."

[218]Luis de León added the following note here: "Though man in this life, if so raised by God, may lose the use of his senses and have a fleeting glimpse of the Divine Essence, as was probably the case with St. Paul and Moses and certain others, the Mother is not speaking here of this kind of vision, which, though fleeting, is intuitive and clear, but of a knowledge of this mystery which God gives to certain souls, through a most powerful light which He infuses into them, not without created species. But as this species is not corporeal, nor figured in the imagination, the Mother says that this vision is intellectual and not imaginary.

[219]Gracián reads: "grasp better, it seems."

[220]Gracián reads: "either of the body (for God is Spirit) or of the imagination.

[221]St. John xiv, 23.

[222]Gracián adds: "as they are commonly believed and heard."

[223]St. Luke x, 40.

[224]Cf. Relations, XXXV (Vol. I, The Complete Works of St. Teresa, pp. 351-2.)

[225]The words "but through an intellectual" and "although . . . mentioned" are substituted by St. Teresa for others which she has deleted.

[226]St. John xx, 19, 21.

[227]1 Corinthians vi, 17. [The Spanish has two verbs, arrimarse and allegarse, corresponding to "joined", and linked by the word "and". The Scriptural text reads: "He who is joined to the Lord is one spirit."] The whole of the passage "He who . . . by union" is St. Teresa's interlinear substitution for something deleted.

[228]Philippians i, 21: "For to me, to live is Christ; and to die is gain."

[229][Lit.: "that they cannot."] The words "that what . . . doubted" are scored through in the original — we suspect by Gracián.

[230]St. John xx, 19, 21 [Cf. p. 214, n. 226, above.]

[231]St. Luke vi, 50.

[232]Gracián deletes the bracketed words and substitutes the Scriptural test, giving its source (St. John xvii, 21) in the margin.

[233]St. John xvii, 20.

[234]St. John xvii, 23.

[235][Cf. St. Teresa's poem on this theme, Vol. III, The Complete Words of St. Teresa, pp. 287-8.]

[236]Psalm i, 3.

[237][Cf. VII, n. 224, above;] Relations, XXXV (Vol. I, The Complete Works of St. Teresa, p. 352).

[238]In the margin of the autograph St. Teresa wrote at this point: "Cuando dice aquí: os pide, léase luego este papel." ["When you get to the words asking of you in it, go straight on to this paper."] "This paper" is no longer extant, but Luis de León evidently had it, as the rest of this paragraph, though not in the autograph, figures in his edition. It is also found, with slight modifications, in early copies.

[239]Acts ix, 6.

[240]The bracketed phrase is St. Teresa's marginal addition.

[241]Luis de León modifies this paragraph thus. After "save very occasionally" he adds, in parenthesis: "that is, as I say here, with respect to these exterior epoch of the suspension of the senses and loss of heat; but they tell me that only the accidents disappear and that interiorly there is rather an increase." He then continues: "So the raptures, in the way I describe, cease, and it [the soul] has not these raptures and Bights of the spirit; or, if it has them, only rarely, and hardly ever in public as it very often had before."

[242]Apocalypse xxi, 3.

[243]Genesis viii, 8, 9.

[244]St. Luke xviii, 13.

[245]3 Kings [A.V. 1 Kings] xi.

[246]Psalm cxi [A.V., cxii], 1.

[247]1 Thessalonians ii, 9.

[248]In the old Carmelite Breviary, which St. Teresa would have used, the Antiphon of the Magnificat at First Vespers on June 29 runs: "The Blessed Apostle Peter saw Christ coming to meet him. Adoring Him, he said: 'Lord, whither goest Thou?' 'I am going to Rome to be crucified afresh.'" The story has it that St. Peter returned to Rome and was crucified.

[249]Psalm xvii (A.V. xviii), 26.

[250]3 Kings [A.V. 1 Kings] xix, 10.

[251]St. Luke x, 42.

[252]St. Luke vii, 37-8.

[253]St. Luke vii, 39.

[254]This sentence is authentic but marginal.

[255]"And mazes", adds Luis de León. The words also occur in several copies of the autograph, including that of Toledo, but not in the autograph itself. There is reason to suppose, however, that there may have been two autographs of this epilogue.

[256]"By the mercy of God" is the Saint's marginal addition.

Dark Night of the Soul
by St. John of the Cross
Translated by E. Allison Peers

"He soars on the wings of Divine love . . ."

"It is perhaps not an exaggeration to say that the verse and prose works combined of St. John of the Cross form at once the most grandiose and the most melodious spiritual canticle to which any one man has ever given utterance.

The most sublime of all the Spanish mystics, he soars aloft on the wings of Divine love to heights known to hardly any of them. . . . True to the character of his thought, his style is always forceful and energetic, even to a fault.

When we study his treatises— principally that great composite work known as the Ascent of Mount Carmel and the Dark Night— we have the impression of a mastermind that has scaled the heights of mystical science; and from their summit looks down upon and dominates the plain below and the paths leading upward. . . . Nowhere else, again, is he quite so appealingly human; for, though he is human even in his loftiest and sublimest passages, his intermingling of philosophy with mystical theology; makes him seem particularly so. These treatises are a wonderful illustration of the theological truth that graced far from destroying nature, ennobles and dignifies it, and of the agreement always found between the natural and the supernatural— between the principles of sound reason and the sublimest manifestations of Divine grace."

E. Allison Peers

Principal Abbreviations

A.V.—Authorized Version of the Bible (1611).

D.V.—Douai Version of the Bible (1609).

C.W.S.T.J.—The Complete Works of Saint Teresa of Jesus, translated and edited by E. Allison Peers from the critical edition of P. Silverio de Santa Teresa, C.D. London, Sheed and Ward, 1946. 3 vols.

H.—E. Allison Peers: Handbook to the Life and Times of St. Teresa and St. John of the Cross. London, Burns Oates and Washbourne, 1953.

LL.—The Letters of Saint Teresa of Jesus, translated and edited by E. Allison Peers from the critical edition of P. Silverio de Santa Teresa, C.D. London, Burns Oates and Washbourne, 1951. 2 vols.

N.L.M.—National Library of Spain (Biblioteca Nacional), Madrid.

Obras (P. Silv.)—Obras de San Juan de la Cruz, Doctor de la Iglesia, editadas y anotadas por el P. Silverio de Santa Teresa, C.D. Burgos, 1929-31. 5 vols.

S.S.M.—E. Allison Peers: Studies of the Spanish Mystics. Vol. I, London, Sheldon Press, 1927; 2nd ed., London, S.P.C.K., 1951. Vol. II, London, Sheldon Press, 1930.

Sobrino.—Jose Antonio de Sobrino, S.J.: Estudios sobre San Juan de la Cruz y nuevos textos de su obra. Madrid, 1950.

Introduction

Somewhat reluctantly, out of respect for a venerable tradition, we publish the Dark Night as a separate treatise, though in reality it is a continuation of the Ascent of Mount Carmel and fulfils the undertakings given in it:

The first night or purgation is of the sensual part of the soul, which is treated in the present stanza, and will be treated in the first part of this book. And the second is of the spiritual part; of this speaks the second stanza, which follows; and of this we shall treat likewise, in the second and the third part, with respect to the activity of the soul; and in the fourth part, with respect to its passivity.[1]

This 'fourth part' is the Dark Night. Of it the Saint writes in a passage which follows that just quoted:

And the second night, or purification, pertains to those who are already proficient, occurring at the time when God desires to bring them to the state of union with God. And this latter night is a more obscure and dark and terrible purgation, as we shall say afterwards.[2]

In his three earlier books he has written of the Active Night, of Sense and of Spirit; he now proposes to deal with the Passive Night, in the same order. He has already taught us how we are to deny and purify ourselves with the ordinary help of grace, in order to prepare our senses and faculties for union with God through love. He now proceeds to explain, with an arresting freshness, how these same senses and faculties are purged and purified by God with a view to the same end—that of union. The combined description of the two nights completes the presentation of active and passive purgation, to which the Saint limits himself in these treatises, although the subject of the stanzas which he is glossing is a much wider one, comprising the whole of the mystical life and ending only with the Divine embraces of the soul transformed in God through love.

The stanzas expounded by the Saint are taken from the same poem in the two treatises. The commentary upon the second, however, is very different from that upon the first, for it assumes a much more advanced state of development. The Active Night has left the senses and faculties well prepared, though not completely prepared, for the reception of Divine influences and illuminations in greater abundance than before. The Saint here postulates a principle of dogmatic theology—that by himself, and with the ordinary aid of grace, man cannot attain to that degree of purgation which is essential to his transformation in God. He needs Divine aid more abundantly. 'However greatly the soul itself labours,' writes the Saint, 'it cannot actively purify itself so as to be in the least degree prepared for the Divine union of perfection of love, if God takes not its hand and purges it not in that dark fire.'[3]

The Passive Nights, in which it is God Who accomplishes the purgation, are based upon this incapacity. Souls 'begin to enter' this dark night

when God draws them forth from the state of beginners—which is the state of those that meditate on the spiritual road—and begins to set them in the state of progressives—which is that of those who are already contemplatives—to the end that, after passing through it, they may arrive at the state of the perfect, which is that of the Divine union of the soul with God.[4]

Before explaining the nature and effects of this Passive Night, the Saint touches, in passing, upon certain imperfections found in those who are about to enter it and which it removes by the process of purgation. Such travellers are still untried proficients, who have not yet acquired mature habits of spirituality and who therefore still conduct themselves as children. The imperfections are examined one by one, following the order of the seven deadly sins, in chapters (ii-viii) which once more reveal the author's skill as a director of souls. They are easy chapters to understand, and of great practical utility, comparable to those in the first book of the Ascent which deal with the active purgation of the desires of sense.

In Chapter viii, St. John of the Cross begins to describe the Passive Night of the senses, the principal aim of which is the purgation or stripping of the soul of its imperfections and the preparation of it for fruitive union. The Passive Night of Sense, we are told, is 'common' and 'comes to many,' whereas that of Spirit 'is the portion of very few.'[5] The one is 'bitter and terrible' but 'the second bears no comparison with it,' for it is 'horrible and awful to the spirit.'[6] A good deal of literature on the former Night existed in the time of St. John of the Cross and he therefore promises to be brief in his treatment of it. Of the latter, on the other hand, he will 'treat more fully . . . since very little has been said of this, either in speech or in writing, and very little is known of it, even by experience.'[7]

Having described this Passive Night of Sense in Chapter viii, he explains with great insight and discernment how it may be recognized whether any given aridity is a result of this Night or whether it comes from sins or imperfections, or from frailty or lukewarmness of spirit, or even from indisposition or 'humours' of the body. The Saint is particularly effective here, and we may once more compare this chapter with a similar one in the Ascent (II, xiii)—that in which he fixes the point where the soul may abandon discursive meditation and enter the contemplation which belongs to loving and simple faith.

Both these chapters have contributed to the reputation of St. John of the Cross as a consummate spiritual master. And this not only for the objective value of his observations, but because, even in spite of himself, he betrays the sublimity of his own mystical experiences. Once more, too, we may admire the crystalline transparency of his teaching and the precision of the phrases in which he clothes it. To judge by his language alone, one might suppose at times that he is speaking of mathematical, rather than of spiritual operations.

In Chapter x, the Saint describes the discipline which the soul in this Dark Night must impose upon itself; this, as might be logically deduced from the Ascent, consists in 'allowing the soul to remain in peace and quietness,' content 'with a peaceful and loving attentiveness toward God.'[8] Before long it will experience enkindlings of love (Chapter xi), which will serve to purify its sins and imperfections and draw it gradually nearer to God; we have here, as it were, so many stages of the ascent of the Mount on whose summit the soul attains to transforming union. Chapters xii and xiii detail with great exactness the benefits that the soul receives from this aridity, while Chapter xiv briefly expounds the last line of the first stanza and brings to an end what the Saint desires to say with respect to the first Passive Night.

At only slightly greater length St. John of the Cross describes the Passive Night of the Spirit, which is at once more afflictive and more painful than those which have preceded it. This, nevertheless, is the Dark Night par excellence, of which the Saint speaks in these words: 'The night which we have called that of sense may and should be called a kind of correction and restraint of the desire rather than purgation. The reason is that all the imperfections and disorders of the sensual part have their strength and root in the spirit, where all habits, both good and bad, are brought into subjection, and thus, until these are purged, the rebellions and depravities of sense cannot be purged thoroughly.'[9]

Spiritual persons, we are told, do not enter the second night immediately after leaving the first; on the contrary, they generally pass a long time, even years, before doing so,[10] for they still have many imperfections, both habitual and actual (Chapter ii). After a brief introduction (Chapter iii), the Saint describes with some fullness the nature of this spiritual purgation or dark contemplation referred to in the first stanza of his poem and the varieties of pain and affliction caused by it, whether in the soul or in its faculties (Chapters iv-viii). These chapters are brilliant beyond all description; in them we seem to reach the culminating point of their author's mystical experience; any excerpt from them would do them an injustice. It must suffice to say that St. John of the Cross seldom again touches those same heights of sublimity.

Chapter ix describes how, although these purgations seem to blind the spirit, they do so only to enlighten it again with a brighter and intenser light, which it is preparing itself to receive with greater abundance. The following chapter makes the comparison between spiritual purgation and the log of wood which gradually becomes transformed through being immersed in fire and at last takes on the fire's own properties. The force with which the familiar similitude is driven home impresses indelibly upon the mind the fundamental concept of this most sublime of all purgations. Marvellous, indeed, are its effects, from the first enkindlings and burnings of Divine love, which are greater beyond comparison than those produced by the Night of Sense, the one being as different from the other as is the body from the soul. 'For this (latter) is an enkindling of spiritual love in the soul, which, in the midst of these dark confines, feels itself to be keenly and sharply wounded in strong Divine love, and to have a certain realization and foretaste of God.'[11] No less wonderful are the effects of the powerful Divine illumination which from time to time enfolds the soul in the splendours of glory. When the effects of the light that wounds and yet illumines are combined with those of the enkindlement that melts the soul with its heat, the delights experienced are so great as to be ineffable.

The second line of the first stanza of the poem is expounded in three admirable chapters (xi-xiii), while one short chapter (xiv) suffices for the three lines remaining. We then embark upon the second stanza, which describes the soul's security in the Dark Night—due, among other reasons, to its being freed 'not only from itself, but likewise from its other enemies, which are the world and the devil.'[12]

This contemplation is not only dark, but also secret (Chapter xvii), and in Chapter xviii is compared to the 'staircase' of the poem. This comparison suggests to the Saint an exposition (Chapters xviii, xix) of the ten steps or degrees of love which comprise St. Bernard's mystical ladder. Chapter xxi describes the soul's 'disguise,' from which the book passes on (Chapters xxii, xxiii) to extol the 'happy chance' which led it to journey 'in darkness and concealment' from its enemies, both without and within.

Chapter xxiv glosses the last line of the second stanza—'my house being now at rest.' Both the higher and the lower 'portions of the soul' are now tranquillized and prepared for the desired union with the Spouse, a union which is the subject that the Saint proposed to treat in his commentary on the five remaining stanzas. As far as we know, this commentary was never written. We have only the briefest outline of what was to have been covered in the third, in which, following the same effective metaphor of night, the Saint describes the excellent properties of the spiritual night of infused contemplation, through which the soul journeys with no other guide or support, either outward or inward, than the Divine love 'which burned in my heart.'

It is difficult to express adequately the sense of loss that one feels at the premature truncation of this eloquent treatise.[13] We have already given our opinion[14] upon the commentaries thought to have been written on the final stanzas of the 'Dark Night.' Did we possess them, they would explain the birth of the light—'dawn's first breathings in the heav'ns above'—which breaks through the black darkness of the Active and the Passive Nights; they would tell us, too, of the soul's further progress towards the Sun's full brightness. It is true, of course, that some part of this great gap is filled by St. John of the Cross himself in his other treatises, but it is small compensation for the incomplete state in which he left this edifice of such gigantic proportions that he should have given us other and smaller buildings of a somewhat similar kind. Admirable as are the Spiritual Canticle and the Living Flame of Love, they are not so completely knit into one whole as is this great double treatise. They lose both in flexibility and in substance through the closeness with which they follow the stanzas of which they are the exposition. In the Ascent and the Dark Night, on the other hand, we catch only the echoes of the poem, which are all but lost in the resonance of the philosopher's voice and the eloquent tones of the preacher. Nor have the other treatises the learning and the authority of these. Nowhere else does the genius of St. John of the Cross for infusing philosophy into his mystical dissertations find such an outlet as here. Nowhere else, again, is he quite so appealingly human; for, though he is human even in his loftiest and sublimest passages, this intermingling of philosophy with mystical theology makes him seem particularly so. These treatises are a wonderful illustration of the theological truth that grace, far from destroying nature, ennobles and dignifies it, and of the agreement always found between the natural and the supernatural—between the principles of sound reason and the sublimest manifestations of Divine grace.

Manuscripts of the Dark Night
The autograph of the Dark Night, like that of the Ascent of Mount Carmel, is unknown to us: the second seems to have disappeared in the same period as the first. There are extant, however, as many as twelve early copies of the Dark Night, some of which, though none of them is as palaeographically accurate as the best copy of the Ascent, are very reliable; there is no trace in them of conscious adulteration of the original or of any kind of modification to fit the sense of any passage into a preconceived theory. We definitely prefer one of these copies to the others but we nowhere follow it so literally as to incorporate in our text its evident discrepancies from its original.

MS. 3,446. An early MS. in the clear masculine hand of an Andalusian: MS. 3,446 in the National Library, Madrid. Like many others, this MS. was transferred to the library from the Convento de San Hermenegildo at the time of the religious persecutions in the early nineteenth century; it had been presented to the Archives of the Reform by the Fathers of Los Remedios, Seville—a Carmelite house founded by P. Grecián in 1574. It has no title and a fragment from the Living Flame of Love is bound up with it.

This MS. has only two omissions of any length; these form part respectively of Book II, Chapters xix and xxiii, dealing with the Passive Night of the Spirit. It has many copyist's errors. At the same time, its antiquity and origin, and the good faith of which it shows continual signs, give it, in our view, primacy over the other copies now to come under consideration. It must be made clear, nevertheless, that there is no extant copy of the Dark Night as trustworthy and as skilfully made as the Alcaudete MS. of the Ascent.

MS. of the Carmelite Nuns of Toledo. Written in three hands, all early. Save for a few slips of the copyist, it agrees with the foregoing; a few of its errors have been corrected. It bears no title, but has a long sub-title which is in effect a partial summary of the argument.

MS. of the Carmelite Nuns of Valladolid. This famous convent, which was one of St. Teresa's foundations, is very rich in Teresan autographs, and has also a number of important documents relating to St. John of the Cross, together with some copies of his works. That here described is written in a large, clear hand and probably dates from the end of the sixteenth century. It has a title similar to that of the last-named copy. With few exceptions it follows the other most important MSS.

MS. Alba de Tormes. What has been said of this in the introduction to the Ascent (Image Books edition, pp. 6-7) applies also to the Dark Night. It is complete, save for small omissions on the part of the amanuensis, the 'Argument' at the beginning of the poem, the verses themselves and a few lines from Book II, Chapter vii.

MS. 6,624. This copy is almost identical with the foregoing. It omits the 'Argument' and the poem itself but not the lines from Book II, Chapter vii.

MS. 8,795. This contains the Dark Night, Spiritual Canticle, Living Flame of Love, a number of poems by St. John of the Cross and the Spiritual Colloquies between Christ and the soul His Bride. It is written in various hands, all very early and some feminine. A note by P. Andrés de la Encarnación, on the reverse of the first folio, records that the copy was presented to the Archives of the Reform by the Discalced Carmelite nuns of Baeza. This convent was founded in 1589, two years before the Saint's death, and the copy may well date from about this period. On the second folio comes the poem 'I entered in—I knew not where.' On the reverse of the third folio begins a kind of preface to the Dark Night, opening with the words: 'Begin the stanzas by means of which a soul may occupy itself and become fervent in the love of God. It deals with the Dark Night and is divided into two books. The first treats of the purgation of sense, and the second of the spiritual purgation of man. It was written by P. Fr. Juan de la Cruz, Discalced Carmelite.' On the next folio, a so-called 'Preface: To the Reader' begins: 'As a beginning and an explanation of these two purgations of the Dark Night which are to be expounded hereafter, this chapter will show how narrow is the path that leads to eternal life and how completely detached and disencumbered must be those that are to enter thereby.' This fundamental idea is developed for the space of two folios. There follows a sonnet on the Dark Night,[15] and immediately afterwards comes the text of the treatise.

The copy contains many errors, but its only omission is that of the last chapter. There is no trace in it of any attempt to modify its original; indeed, the very nature and number of the copyist's errors are a testimony to his good faith.

MS. 12,658. A note by P. Andrés states that he acquired it in Madrid but has no more detailed recollection of its provenance. 'The Dark Night,' it adds, 'begins on folio 43; our holy father is described simply as "the second friar of the new Reformation,"[16] which is clear evidence of its antiquity.'

The Codex contains a number of opuscules, transcribed no doubt with a devotional aim by the copyist. Its epoch is probably the end of the sixteenth century; it is certainly earlier than the editions. There is no serious omission except that of six lines of the 'Argument.' The authors of the other works copied include St. Augustine, B. Juan de Ávila, P. Baltasar Álvarez and P. Tomás de Jesús.

The copies which remain to be described are all mutilated or abbreviated and can be disposed of briefly:

MS. 13,498. This copy omits less of the Dark Night than of the Ascent but few pages are without their omissions. In one place a meticulous pair of scissors has removed the lower half of a folio on which the Saint deals with spiritual luxury.

MS. of the Carmelite Friars of Toledo. Dates from early in the seventeenth century and has numerous omissions, especially in the chapters on the Passive Night of the Spirit. The date is given (in the same hand as that which copies the title) as 1618. This MS. also contains an opuscule by Suso and another entitled 'Brief compendium of the most eminent Christian perfection of P. Fr. Juan de la Cruz.'

MS. 18,160. The copyist has treated the Dark Night little better than the Ascent; except from the first ten and the last three chapters, he omits freely.

MS. 12,411. Entitled by its copyist 'Spiritual Compendium,' this MS. contains several short works of devotion, including one by Ruysbroeck. Of St. John of the Cross's works it copies the Spiritual Canticle as well as the Dark Night; the latter is headed: 'Song of one soul alone.' It also contains a number of poems, some of them by the Saint, and many passages from St. Teresa. It is in several hands, all of the seventeenth century. The copy of the Dark Night is most unsatisfactory; there are omissions and abbreviations everywhere.

M.S. of the Carmelite Nuns of Pamplona. This MS. also omits and abbreviates continually, especially in the chapters on the Passive Night of Sense, which are reduced to a mere skeleton.

Editio princeps. This is much more faithful to its original in the Dark Night than in the Ascent. Both the passages suppressed[17] and the interpolations[18] are relatively few and unimportant. Modifications of phraseology are more frequent and alterations are also made with the aim of correcting hyperbaton. In the first book about thirty lines are suppressed; in the second, about ninety. All changes which are of any importance have been shown in the notes.

The present edition. We have given preference, as a general rule, to MS. 3,446, subjecting it, however, to a rigorous comparison with the other copies. Mention has already been made in the introduction to the Ascent (Image Books edition, pp. lxiii-lxvi) of certain apparent anomalies and a certain lack of uniformity in the Saint's method of dividing his commentaries. This is nowhere more noticeable than in the Dark Night. Instead of dividing his treatise into books, each with its proper title, the Saint abandons this method and uses titles only occasionally. As this makes comprehension of his argument the more difficult, we have adopted the divisions which were introduced by P. Salablanca and have been copied by successive editors.

M. Baruzi (Bulletin Hispanique, 1922, Vol. xxiv, pp. 18-40) complains that this division weighs down the spiritual rhythm of the treatise and interrupts its movement. We do not agree. In any case, we greatly prefer the gain of clarity, even if the rhythm occasionally halts, to the other alternative—the constant halting of the understanding. We have, of course, indicated every place where the title is taken from the editio princeps and was not the work of the author.

The following abbreviations are adopted in the footnotes:

A = MS. of the Discalced Carmelite Friars of Alba.
B = MS. 6,624 (National Library, Madrid).
Bz. = MS. 8,795 (N.L.M.).
C = MS. 13,498 (N.L.M.).
G = MS. 18,160 (N.L.M.).
H = MS. 3,446 (N.L.M.).
M = MS. of the Discalced Carmelite Nuns of Toledo.
Mtr. = MS. 12,658.
P = MS. of the Discalced Carmelite Friars of Toledo.
V = MS. of the Discalced Carmelite Nuns of Valladolid.
E.p. = Editio princeps (1618).

MS. 12,411 and the MS. of the Discalced Carmelite nuns of Pamplona are cited without abbreviations.

Exposition of the stanzas describing the method followed by the soul in its journey upon the spiritual road to the attainment of the perfect union of love with God, to the extent that is possible in this life. Likewise are described the properties belonging to the soul that has attained to the said perfection, according as they are contained in the same stanzas.

Prologue

In this book are first set down all the stanzas which are to be expounded; afterwards, each of the stanzas is expounded separately, being set down before its exposition; and then each line is expounded separately and in turn, the line itself also being set down before the exposition. In the first two stanzas are expounded the effects of the two spiritual purgations: of the sensual part of man and of the spiritual part. In the other six are expounded various and wondrous effects of the spiritual illumination and union of love with God.

Stanzas of the Soul

On a dark night,
Kindled in love with yearnings
—oh, happy chance!
I went forth without being observed,
My house being now at rest.

In darkness and secure,
By the secret ladder, disguised
—oh, happy chance!
In darkness and in concealment,
My house being now at rest.

In the happy night,
In secret, when none saw me,
Nor I beheld aught,
Without light or guide,
Save that which burned in my heart.

This light guided me
More surely than the light of noonday
To the place where he (well I knew who!) was awaiting me
— A place where none appeared.

Oh, night that guided me,
Oh, night more lovely than the dawn,
Oh, night that joined Beloved with lover,
Lover transformed in the Beloved!

Upon my flowery breast,
Kept wholly for himself alone,
There he stayed sleeping, and I caressed him,
And the fanning of the cedars made a breeze.

The breeze blew from the turret
As I parted his locks;
With his gentle hand he wounded my neck
And caused all my senses to be suspended.

I remained, lost in oblivion;
My face I reclined on the Beloved.
All ceased and I abandoned myself,
Leaving my cares forgotten among the lilies.

Begins the exposition of the stanzas which treat of the way and manner which the soul follows upon the road of the union of love with God.

Before we enter upon the exposition of these stanzas, it is well to understand here that the soul that utters them is now in the state of perfection, which is the union of love with God, having already passed through severe trials and straits, by means of spiritual exercise in the narrow way of eternal life whereof Our Saviour speaks in the Gospel, along which way the soul ordinarily passes in order to reach this high and happy union with God. Since this road (as the Lord Himself says likewise) is so strait, and since there are so few that enter by it,[19] the soul considers it a great happiness and good chance to have passed along it to the said perfection of love, as it sings in this first stanza, calling this strait road with full propriety 'dark night,' as will be explained hereafter in the lines of the said stanza. The soul, then, rejoicing at having passed along this narrow road whence so many blessings have come to it, speaks after this manner.

BOOK THE FIRST

Which treats of the Night of Sense.

Stanza the First

On a dark night, Kindled in love with yearnings—oh, happy chance!— I went forth without being observed, My house being now at rest.

Exposition

In this first stanza the soul relates the way and manner which it followed in going forth, as to its affection, from itself and from all things, and in dying to them all and to itself, by means of true mortification, in order to attain to living the sweet and delectable life of love with God; and it says that this going forth from itself and from all things was a 'dark night,' by which, as will be explained hereafter, is here understood purgative contemplation, which causes passively in the soul the negation of itself and of all things referred to above.

And this going forth it says here that it was able to accomplish in the strength and ardour which love for its Spouse gave to it for that purpose in the dark contemplation aforementioned. Herein it extols the great happiness which it found in journeying to God through this night with such signal success that none of the three enemies, which are world, devil and flesh (who are they that ever impede this road), could hinder it; inasmuch as the aforementioned night of purgative[20] contemplation lulled to sleep and mortified, in the house of its sensuality, all the passions and desires with respect to their mischievous desires and motions. The line, then, says: On a dark night

Chapter 1

Sets down the first line and begins to treat of the imperfections of beginners.

Into this dark night souls begin to enter when God draws them forth from the state of beginners—which is the state of those that meditate on the spiritual road—and begins to set them in the state of progressives—which is that of those who are already contemplatives—to the end that, after passing through it, they may arrive at the state of the perfect, which is that of the Divine union of the soul with God. Wherefore, to the end that we may the better understand and explain what night is this through which the soul passes, and for what cause God sets it therein, it will be well here to touch first of all upon certain characteristics of beginners (which, although we treat them with all possible brevity, will not fail to be of service likewise to the beginners themselves), in order that, realizing the weakness of the state wherein they are, they may take courage, and may desire that God will bring them into this night, wherein the soul is strengthened and confirmed in the virtues, and made ready for the inestimable delights of the love of God. And, although we may tarry here for a time, it will not be for longer than is necessary, so that we may go on to speak at once of this dark night.

It must be known, then, that the soul, after it has been definitely converted to the service of God, is, as a rule, spiritually nurtured and caressed by God, even as is the tender child by its loving mother, who warms it with the heat of her bosom and nurtures it with sweet milk and soft and pleasant food, and carries it and caresses it in her arms; but, as the child grows bigger, the mother gradually ceases caressing it, and, hiding her tender love, puts bitter aloes upon her sweet breast, sets down the child from her arms and makes it walk upon its feet, so that it may lose the habits of a child and betake itself to more important and substantial occupations. The loving mother is like the grace of God, for, as soon as the soul is regenerated by its new warmth and fervour for the service of God, He treats it in the same way; He makes it to find spiritual milk, sweet and delectable, in all the things of God, without any labour of its own, and also great pleasure in spiritual exercises, for here God is giving to it the breast of His tender love, even as to a tender child.

Therefore, such a soul finds its delight in spending long periods—perchance whole nights—in prayer; penances are its pleasures; fasts its joys; and its consolations are to make use of the sacraments and to occupy itself in Divine things. In the which things spiritual persons (though taking part in them with great efficacy and persistence and using and treating them with great care) often find themselves, spiritually speaking, very weak and imperfect. For since they are moved to these things and to these spiritual exercises by the consolation and pleasure that they find in them, and since, too, they have not been prepared for them by the practice of earnest striving in the virtues, they have many faults and imperfections with respect to these spiritual actions of theirs; for, after all, any man's actions correspond to the habit of perfection attained by him. And, as these persons have not had the opportunity of acquiring the said habits of strength, they have necessarily to work like feebler children, feebly. In order that this may be seen more clearly, and likewise how much these beginners in the virtues lacks with respect to the works in which they so readily engage with the pleasure aforementioned, we shall describe it by reference to the seven capital sins, each in its turn, indicating some of the many imperfections which they have under each heading; wherein it will be clearly seen how like to children are these persons in all they do. And it will also be seen how many blessings the dark night of which we shall afterwards treat brings with it, since it cleanses the soul and purifies it from all these imperfections.

Chapter 11

Of certain spiritual imperfections which beginners have with respect to the habit of pride.

As these beginners feel themselves to be very fervent and diligent in spiritual things and devout exercises, from this prosperity (although it is true that holy things of their own nature cause humility) there often comes to them, through their imperfections, a certain kind of secret pride, whence they come to have some degree of satisfaction with their works and with themselves. And hence there comes to them likewise a certain desire, which is somewhat vain, and at times very vain, to speak of spiritual things in the presence of others, and sometimes even to teach such things rather than to learn them. They condemn others in their heart when they see that they have not the kind of devotion which they themselves desire; and sometimes they even say this in words, herein resembling the Pharisee, who boasted of himself, praising God for his own good works and despising the publican.[21]

In these persons the devil often increases the fervour that they have and the desire to perform these and other works more frequently, so that their pride and presumption may grow greater. For the devil knows quite well that all these works and virtues which they perform are not only valueless to them, but even become vices in them. And such a degree of evil are some of these persons wont to reach that they would have none appear good save themselves; and thus, in deed and word, whenever the opportunity occurs, they condemn them and slander them, beholding the mote in their brother's eye and not considering the beam which is in their own;[22] they strain at another's gnat and themselves swallow a camel.[23]

Sometimes, too, when their spiritual masters, such as confessors and superiors, do not approve of their spirit and behavior (for they are anxious that all they do shall be esteemed and praised), they consider that they do not understand them, or that, because they do not approve of this and comply with that, their confessors are themselves not spiritual. And so they immediately desire and contrive to find some one else who will fit in with their tastes; for as a rule they desire to speak of spiritual matters with those who they think will praise and esteem what they do, and they flee, as they would from death, from those who disabuse them in order to lead them into a safe road—sometimes they even harbour ill-will against them. Presuming thus,[24] they are wont to resolve much and accomplish very little. Sometimes they are anxious that others shall realize how spiritual and devout they are, to which end they occasionally give outward evidence thereof in movements, sighs and other ceremonies; and at times they are apt to fall into certain ecstasies, in public rather than in secret, wherein the devil aids them, and they are pleased that this should be noticed, and are often eager that it should be noticed more.[25]

Many such persons desire to be the favourites of their confessors and to become intimate with them, as a result of which there beset them continual occasions of envy and disquiet.[26] They are too much embarrassed to confess their sins nakedly, lest their confessors should think less of them, so they palliate them and make them appear less evil, and thus it is to excuse themselves rather than to accuse themselves that they go to confession. And sometimes they seek another confessor to tell the wrongs that they have done, so that their own confessor shall think they have done nothing wrong at all, but only good; and thus they always take pleasure in telling him what is good, and sometimes in such terms as make it appear to be greater than it is rather than less, desiring that he may think them to be good, when it would be greater humility in them, as we shall say, to depreciate it, and to desire that neither he nor anyone else should consider them of account.

Some of these beginners, too, make little of their faults, and at other times become over-sad when they see themselves fall into them, thinking themselves to have been saints already; and thus they become angry and impatient with themselves, which is another imperfection. Often they beseech God, with great yearnings, that He will take from them their imperfections and faults, but they do this that they may find themselves at peace, and may not be troubled by them, rather than for God's sake; not realizing that, if He should take their imperfections from them, they would probably become prouder and more presumptuous still. They dislike praising others and love to be praised themselves; sometimes they seek out such praise. Herein they are like the foolish virgins, who, when their lamps could not be lit, sought oil from others.[27]

From these imperfections some souls go on to develop[28] many very grave ones, which do them great harm. But some have fewer and some more, and some, only the first motions thereof or little beyond these; and there are hardly any such beginners who, at the time of these signs of fervour,[29] fall not into some of these errors.[30] But those who at this time are going on to perfection proceed very differently and with quite another temper of spirit; for they progress by means of humility and are greatly edified, not only thinking naught of their own affairs, but having very little satisfaction with themselves; they consider all others as far better, and usually have a holy envy of them, and an eagerness to serve God as they do. For the greater is their fervour, and the more numerous are the works that they perform, and the greater is the pleasure that they take in them, as they progress in humility, the more do they realize how much God deserves of them, and how little is all that they do for His sake; and thus, the more they do, the less are they satisfied. So much would they gladly do from charity and love for Him, that all they do seems to them naught; and so greatly are they importuned, occupied and absorbed by this loving anxiety that they never notice what others do or do not; or if they do notice it, they always believe, as I say, that all others are far better than they themselves. Wherefore, holding themselves as of little worth, they are anxious that others too should thus hold them, and should despise and depreciate that which they do. And further, if men should praise and esteem them, they can in no wise believe what they say; it seems to them strange that anyone should say these good things of them.

Together with great tranquillity and humbleness, these souls have a deep desire to be taught by anyone who can bring them profit; they are the complete opposite of those of whom we have spoken above, who would fain be always teaching, and who, when others seem to be teaching them, take the words from their mouths as if they knew them already. These souls, on the other hand, being far from desiring to be the masters of any, are very ready to travel and set out on another road than that which they are actually following, if they be so commanded, because they never think that they are right in anything whatsoever. They rejoice when others are praised; they grieve only because they serve not God like them. They have no desire to speak of the things that they do, because they think so little of them that they are ashamed to speak of them even to their spiritual masters, since they seem to them to be things that merit not being spoken of. They are more anxious to speak of their faults and sins, or that these should be recognized rather than their virtues; and thus they incline to talk of their souls with those who account their actions and their spirituality of little value. This is a characteristic of the spirit which is simple, pure, genuine and very pleasing to God. For as the wise Spirit of God dwells in these humble souls, He moves them and inclines them to keep His treasures secretly within and likewise to cast out from themselves all evil. God gives this grace to the humble, together with the other virtues, even as He denies it to the proud.

These souls will give their heart's blood to anyone that serves God, and will help others to serve Him as much as in them lies. The imperfections into which they see themselves fall they bear with humility, meekness of spirit and a loving fear of God, hoping in Him. But souls who in the beginning journey with this kind of perfection are, as I understand, and as has been said, a minority, and very few are those who we can be glad do not fall into the opposite errors. For this reason, as we shall afterwards say, God leads into the dark night those whom He desires to purify from all these imperfections so that He may bring them farther onward.

Chapter III

Of some imperfections which some of these souls are apt to have, with respect to the second capital sin, which is avarice, in the spiritual sense.

Many of these beginners have also at times great spiritual avarice. They will be found to be discontented with the spirituality which God gives them; and they are very disconsolate and querulous because they find not in spiritual things the consolation that they would desire. Many can never have enough of listening to counsels and learning spiritual precepts, and of possessing and reading many books which treat of this matter, and they spend their time on all these things rather than on works of mortification and the perfecting of the inward poverty of spirit which should be theirs. Furthermore, they burden themselves with images and rosaries which are very curious; now they put down one, now take up another; now they change about, now change back again; now they want this kind of thing, now that, preferring one kind of cross to another, because it is more curious. And others you will see adorned with agnusdeis[31] and relics and tokens,[32] like children with trinkets. Here I condemn the attachment of the heart, and the affection which they have for the nature, multitude and curiosity of these things, inasmuch as it is quite contrary to poverty of spirit which considers only the substance of devotion, makes use only of what suffices for that end and grows weary of this other kind of multiplicity and curiosity. For true devotion must issue from the heart, and consist in the truth and substances alone of what is represented by spiritual things; all the rest is affection and attachment proceeding from imperfection; and in order that one may pass to any kind of perfection it is necessary for such desires to be killed.

I knew a person who for more than ten years made use of a cross roughly formed from a branch[33] that had been blessed, fastened with a pin twisted round it; he had never ceased using it, and he always carried it about with him until I took it from him; and this was a person of no small sense and understanding. And I saw another who said his prayers using beads that were made of bones from the spine of a fish; his devotion was certainly no less precious on that account in the sight of God, for it is clear that these things carried no devotion in their workmanship or value. Those, then, who start from these beginnings and make good progress attach themselves to no visible instruments, nor do they burden themselves with such, nor desire to know more than is necessary in order that they may act well; for they set their eyes only on being right with God and on pleasing Him, and therein consists their covetousness. And thus with great generosity they give away all that they have, and delight to know that they have it not, for God's sake and for charity to their neighbour, no matter whether these be spiritual things or temporal. For, as I say, they set their eyes only upon the reality of interior perfection, which is to give pleasure to God and in naught to give pleasure to themselves.

But neither from these imperfections nor from those others can the soul be perfectly purified until God brings it into the passive purgation of that dark night whereof we shall speak presently. It befits the soul, however, to contrive to labour, in so far as it can, on its own account, to the end that it may purge and perfect itself, and thus may merit being taken by God into that Divine care wherein it becomes healed of all things that it was unable of itself to cure. Because, however greatly the soul itself labours, it cannot actively purify itself so as to be in the least degree prepared for the Divine union of perfection of love, if God takes not its hand and purges it not in that dark fire, in the way and manner that we have to describe.

Chapter IV

Of other imperfections which these beginners are apt to have with respect to the third sin, which is luxury.

Many of these beginners have many other imperfections than those which I am describing with respect to each of the deadly sins, but these I set aside, in order to avoid prolixity, touching upon a few of the most important, which are, as it were, the origin and cause of the rest. And thus, with respect to this sin of luxury (leaving apart the falling of spiritual persons into this sin, since my intent is to treat of the imperfections which have to be purged by the dark night), they have many imperfections which might be described as spiritual luxury, not because they are so, but because the imperfections proceed from spiritual things. For it often comes to pass that, in their very spiritual exercises, when they are powerless to prevent it, there arise and assert themselves in the sensual part of the soul impure acts and motions, and sometimes this happens even when the spirit is deep in prayer, or engaged in the Sacrament of Penance or in the Eucharist. These things are not, as I say, in their power; they proceed from one of three causes.

The first cause from which they often proceed is the pleasure which human nature takes in spiritual things. For when the spirit and the sense are pleased, every part of a man is moved by that pleasure[34] to delight according to its proportion and nature. For then the spirit, which is the higher part, is moved to pleasure[35] and delight in God; and the sensual nature, which is the lower part, is moved to pleasure and delight of the senses, because it cannot possess and lay hold upon aught else, and it therefore lays hold upon that which comes nearest to itself, which is the impure and sensual. Thus it comes to pass that the soul is in deep prayer with God according to the spirit, and, on the other hand, according to sense it is passively conscious, not without great displeasure, of rebellions and motions and acts of the senses, which often happens in Communion, for when the soul receives joy and comfort in this act of love, because this Lord bestows it (since it is to that end that He gives Himself), the sensual nature takes that which is its own likewise, as we have said, after its manner. Now as, after all, these two parts are combined in one individual, they ordinarily both participate in that which one of them receives, each after its manner; for, as the philosopher says, everything that is received is in the recipient after the manner of the same recipient. And thus, in these beginnings, and even when the soul has made some progress, its sensual part, being imperfect, oftentimes receives the Spirit of God with the same imperfection. Now when this sensual part is renewed by the purgation of the dark night which we shall describe, it no longer has these weaknesses; for it is no longer this part that receives aught, but rather it is itself received into the Spirit. And thus it then has everything after the manner of the Spirit.

The second cause whence these rebellions sometimes proceed is the devil, who, in order to disquiet and disturb the soul, at times when it is at prayer or is striving to pray, contrives to stir up these motions of impurity in its nature; and if the soul gives heed to any of these, they cause it great harm. For through fear of these not only do persons become lax in prayer—which is the aim of the devil when he begins to strive with them—but some give up prayer altogether, because they think that these things attack them more during that exercise than apart from it, which is true, since the devil attacks them then more than at other times, so that they may give up spiritual exercises. And not only so, but he succeeds in portraying to them very vividly things that are most foul and impure, and at times are very closely related to certain spiritual things and persons that are of profit to their souls, in order to terrify them and make them fearful; so that those who are affected by this dare not even look at anything or meditate upon anything, because they immediately encounter this temptation. And upon those who are inclined to melancholy this acts with such effect that they become greatly to be pitied since they are suffering so sadly; for this trial reaches such a point in certain persons, when they have this evil humour, that they believe it to be clear that the devil is ever present with them and that they have no power to prevent this, although some of these persons can prevent his attack by dint of great effort and labour. When these impurities attack such souls through the medium of melancholy, they are not as a rule freed from them until they have been cured of that kind of humour, unless the dark night has entered the soul, and rids them of all impurities, one after another.[36]

The third source whence these impure motions are apt to proceed in order to make war upon the soul is often the fear which such persons have conceived for these impure representations and motions. Something that they see or say or think brings them to their mind, and this makes them afraid, so that they suffer from them through no fault of their own.

There are also certain souls of so tender and frail a nature that, when there comes to them some spiritual consolation or some grace in prayer, the spirit of luxury is with them immediately, inebriating and delighting their sensual nature in such manner that it is as if they were plunged into the enjoyment and pleasure of this sin; and the enjoyment remains, together with the consolation, passively, and sometimes they are able to see that certain impure and unruly acts have taken place. The reason for this is that, since these natures are, as I say, frail and tender, their humours are stirred up and their blood is excited at the least disturbance. And hence come these motions; and the same thing happens to such souls when they are enkindled with anger or suffer any disturbance or grief.[37]

Sometimes, again, there arises within these spiritual persons, whether they be speaking or performing spiritual actions, a certain vigour and bravado, through their having regard to persons who are present, and before these persons they display a certain kind of vain gratification. This also arises from luxury of spirit, after the manner wherein we here understand it, which is accompanied as a rule by complacency in the will.

Some of these persons make friendships of a spiritual kind with others, which oftentimes arise from luxury and not from spirituality; this may be known to be the case when the remembrance of that friendship causes not the remembrance and love of God to grow, but occasions remorse of conscience. For, when the friendship is purely spiritual, the love of God grows with it; and the more the soul remembers it, the more it remembers the love of God, and the greater the desire it has for God; so that, as the one grows, the other grows also. For the spirit of God has this property, that it increases good by adding to it more good, inasmuch as there is likeness and conformity between them. But, when this love arises from the vice of sensuality aforementioned, it produces the contrary effects; for the more the one grows, the more the other decreases, and the remembrance of it likewise. If that sensual love grows, it will at once be observed that the soul's love of God is becoming colder, and that it is forgetting Him as it remembers that love; there comes to it, too, a certain remorse of conscience. And, on the other hand, if the love of God grows in the soul, that other love becomes cold and is forgotten; for, as the two are contrary to one another, not only does the one not aid the other, but the one which predominates quenches and confounds the other, and becomes strengthened in itself, as the philosophers say. Wherefore Our Saviour said in the Gospel: 'That which is born of the flesh is flesh, and that which is born of the Spirit is spirit.'[38] That is to say, the love which is born of sensuality ends in sensuality, and that which is of the spirit ends in the spirit of God and causes it to grow. This is the difference that exists between these two kinds of love, whereby we may know them.

When the soul enters the dark night, it brings these kinds of love under control. It strengthens and purifies the one, namely that which is according to God; and the other it removes and brings to an end; and in the beginning it causes both to be lost sight of, as we shall say hereafter.

Chapter V

Of the imperfections into which beginners fall with respect to the sin of wrath.

By reason of the concupiscence which many beginners have for spiritual consolations, their experience of these consolations is very commonly accompanied by many imperfections proceeding from the sin of wrath; for, when their delight and pleasure in spiritual things come to an end, they naturally become embittered, and bear that lack of sweetness which they have to suffer with a bad grace, which affects all that they do; and they very easily become irritated over the smallest matter—sometimes, indeed, none can tolerate them. This frequently happens after they have been very pleasantly recollected in prayer according to sense; when their pleasure and delight therein come to an end, their nature is naturally vexed and disappointed, just as is the child when they take it from the breast of which it was enjoying the sweetness. There is no sin in this natural vexation, when it is not permitted to indulge itself, but only imperfection, which must be purged by the aridity and severity of the dark night.

There are other of these spiritual persons, again, who fall into another kind of spiritual wrath: this happens when they become irritated at the sins of others, and keep watch on those others with a sort of uneasy zeal. At times the impulse comes to them to reprove them angrily, and occasionally they go so far as to indulge it[39] and set themselves up as masters of virtue. All this is contrary to spiritual meekness.

There are others who are vexed with themselves when they observe their own imperfectness, and display an impatience that is not humility; so impatient are they about this that they would fain be saints in a day. Many of these persons purpose to accomplish a great deal and make grand resolutions; yet, as they are not humble and have no misgivings about themselves, the more resolutions they make, the greater is their fall and the greater their annoyance, since they have not the patience to wait for that which God will give them when it pleases Him; this likewise is contrary to the spiritual meekness aforementioned, which cannot be wholly remedied save by the purgation of the dark night. Some souls, on the other hand, are so patient as regards the progress which they desire that God would gladly see them less so.

Chapter VI

Of imperfections with respect to spiritual gluttony.

With respect to the fourth sin, which is spiritual gluttony, there is much to be said, for there is scarce one of these beginners who, however satisfactory his progress, falls not into some of the many imperfections which come to these beginners with respect to this sin, on account of the sweetness which they find at first in spiritual exercises. For many of these, lured by the sweetness and pleasure which they find in such exercises, strive more after spiritual sweetness than after spiritual purity and discretion, which is that which God regards and accepts throughout the spiritual journey.[40] Therefore, besides the imperfections into which the seeking for sweetness of this kind makes them fall, the gluttony which they now have makes them continually go to extremes, so that they pass beyond the limits of moderation within which the virtues are acquired and wherein they have their being. For some of these persons, attracted by the pleasure which they find therein, kill themselves with penances, and others weaken themselves with fasts, by performing more than their frailty can bear, without the order or advice of any, but rather endeavouring to avoid those whom they should obey in these matters; some, indeed, dare to do these things even though the contrary has been commanded them.

These persons are most imperfect and unreasonable; for they set bodily penance before subjection and obedience, which is penance according to reason and discretion, and therefore a sacrifice more acceptable and pleasing to God than any other. But such one-sided penance is no more than the penance of beasts, to which they are attracted, exactly like beasts, by the desire and pleasure which they find therein. Inasmuch as all extremes are vicious, and as in behaving thus such persons[41] are working their own will, they grow in vice rather than in virtue; for, to say the least, they are acquiring spiritual gluttony and pride in this way, through not walking in obedience. And many of these the devil assails, stirring up this gluttony in them through the pleasures and desires which he increases within them, to such an extent that, since they can no longer help themselves, they either change or vary or add to that which is commanded them, as any obedience in this respect is so bitter to them. To such an evil pass have some persons come that, simply because it is through obedience that they engage in these exercises, they lose the desire and devotion to perform them, their only desire and pleasure being to do what they themselves are inclined to do, so that it would probably be more profitable for them not to engage in these exercises at all.

You will find that many of these persons are very insistent with their spiritual masters to be granted that which they desire, extracting it from them almost by force; if they be refused it they become as peevish as children and go about in great displeasure, thinking that they are not serving God when they are not allowed to do that which they would. For they go about clinging to their own will and pleasure, which they treat as though it came from God;[42] and immediately their directors[43] take it from them, and try to subject them to the will of God, they become peevish, grow faint-hearted and fall away. These persons think that their own satisfaction and pleasure are the satisfaction and service of God.

There are others, again, who, because of this gluttony, know so little of their own unworthiness and misery and have thrust so far from them the loving fear and reverence which they owe to the greatness of God, that they hesitate not to insist continually that their confessors shall allow them to communicate often. And, what is worse, they frequently dare to communicate without the leave and consent[44] of the minister and steward of Christ, merely acting on their own opinion, and contriving to conceal the truth from him. And for this reason, because they desire to communicate continually, they make their confessions carelessly,[45] being more eager to eat than to eat cleanly and perfectly, although it would be healthier and holier for them had they the contrary inclination and begged their confessors not to command them to approach the altar so frequently: between these two extremes, however, the better way is that of humble resignation. But the boldness referred to is[46] a thing that does great harm, and men may fear to be punished for such temerity.

These persons, in communicating, strive with every nerve to obtain some kind of sensible sweetness and pleasure, instead of humbly doing reverence and giving praise within themselves to God. And in such wise do they devote themselves to this that, when they have received no pleasure or sweetness in the senses, they think that they have accomplished nothing at all. This is to judge God very unworthily; they have not realized that the least of the benefits which come from this Most Holy Sacrament is that which concerns the senses; and that the invisible part of the grace that it bestows is much greater; for, in order that they may look at it with the eyes of faith, God oftentimes withholds from them these other consolations and sweetnesses of sense. And thus they desire to feel and taste God as though He were comprehensible by them and accessible to them, not only in this, but likewise in other spiritual practices. All this is very great imperfection and completely opposed to the nature of God, since it is Impurity in faith.

These persons have the same defect as regards the practice of prayer, for they think that all the business of prayer consists in experiencing sensible pleasure and devotion and they strive to obtain this by great effort,[47] wearying and fatiguing their faculties and their heads; and when they have not found this pleasure they become greatly discouraged, thinking that they have accomplished nothing. Through these efforts they lose true devotion and spirituality, which consist in perseverance, together with patience and humility and mistrust of themselves, that they may please God alone. For this reason, when they have once failed to find pleasure in this or some other exercise, they have great disinclination and repugnance to return to it, and at times they abandon it. They are, in fact, as we have said, like children, who are not influenced by reason, and who act, not from rational motives, but from inclination.[48] Such persons expend all their effort in seeking spiritual pleasure and consolation; they never tire therefore, of reading books; and they begin, now one meditation, now another, in their pursuit of this pleasure which they desire to experience in the things of God. But God, very justly, wisely and lovingly, denies it to them, for otherwise this spiritual gluttony and inordinate appetite would breed innumerable evils. It is, therefore, very fitting that they should enter into the dark night, whereof we shall speak,[49] that they may be purged from this childishness.

These persons who are thus inclined to such pleasures have another very great imperfection, which is that they are very weak and remiss in journeying upon the hard[50] road of the Cross; for the soul that is given to sweetness naturally has its face set against all self-denial, which is devoid of sweetness.[51]

These persons have many other imperfections which arise hence, of which in time the Lord heals them by means of temptations, aridities and other trials, all of which are part of the dark night. All these I will not treat further here, lest I become too lengthy; I will only say that spiritual temperance and sobriety lead to another and a very different temper, which is that of mortification, fear and submission in all things. It thus becomes clear that the perfection and worth of things consist not in the multitude and the pleasantness of one's actions, but in being able to deny oneself in them; this such persons must endeavour to compass, in so far as they may, until God is pleased to purify them indeed, by bringing them[52] into the dark night, to arrive at which I am hastening on with my account of these imperfections.

Chapter VII

Of imperfections with respect to spiritual envy and sloth.

With respect likewise to the other two vices, which are spiritual envy and sloth, these beginners fail not to have many imperfections. For, with respect to envy, many of them are wont to experience movements of displeasure at the spiritual good of others, which cause them a certain sensible grief at being outstripped upon this road, so that they would prefer not to hear others praised; for they become displeased at others' virtues and sometimes they cannot refrain from contradicting what is said in praise of them, depreciating it as far as they can; and their annoyance thereat grows[53] because the same is not said of them, for they would fain be preferred in everything. All this is clean contrary to charity, which, as Saint Paul says, rejoices in goodness.[54] And, if charity has any envy, it is a holy envy, comprising grief at not having the virtues of others, yet also joy because others have them, and delight when others outstrip us in the service of God, wherein we ourselves are so remiss.

With respect also to spiritual sloth, beginners are apt to be irked by the things that are most spiritual, from which they flee because these things are incompatible with sensible pleasure. For, as they are so much accustomed to sweetness in spiritual things, they are wearied by things in which they find no sweetness. If once they failed to find in prayer the satisfaction which their taste required (and after all it is well that God should take it from them to prove them), they would prefer not to return to it: sometimes they leave it; at other times they continue it unwillingly. And thus because of this sloth they abandon the way of perfection (which is the way of the negation of their will and pleasure for God's sake) for the pleasure and sweetness of their own will, which they aim at satisfying in this way rather than the will of God.

And many of these would have God will that which they themselves will, and are fretful at having to will that which He wills, and find it repugnant to accommodate their will to that of God. Hence it happens to them that oftentimes they think that that wherein they find not their own will and pleasure is not the will of God; and that, on the other hand, when they themselves find satisfaction, God is satisfied. Thus they measure God by themselves and not themselves by God, acting quite contrarily to that which He Himself taught in the Gospel, saying: That he who should lose his will for His sake, the same should gain it; and he who should desire to gain it, the same should lose it.[55]

These persons likewise find it irksome when they are commanded to do that wherein they take no pleasure. Because they aim at spiritual sweetness and consolation, they are too weak to have the fortitude and bear the trials of perfection.[56] They resemble those who are softly nurtured and who run fretfully away from everything that is hard, and take offense at the Cross, wherein consist the delights of the spirit. The more spiritual a thing is, the more irksome they find it, for, as they seek to go about spiritual matters with complete freedom and according to the inclination of their will, it causes them great sorrow and repugnance to enter upon the narrow way, which, says Christ, is the way of life.[57]

Let it suffice here to have described these imperfections, among the many to be found in the lives of those that are in this first state of beginners, so that it may be seen how greatly they need God to set them in the state of proficients. This He does by bringing them into the dark night whereof we now speak; wherein He weans them from the breasts of these sweetnesses and pleasures, gives them pure aridities and inward darkness, takes from them all these irrelevances and puerilities, and by very different means causes them to win the virtues. For, however assiduously the beginner practises the mortification in himself of all these actions and passions of his, he can never completely succeed—very far from it—until God shall work it in him passively by means of the purgation of the said night. Of this I would fain speak in some way that may be profitable; may God, then, be pleased to give me His Divine light, because this is very needful in a night that is so dark and a matter that is so difficult to describe and to expound.

The line, then, is: In a dark night.

Chapter VIII

Wherein is expounded the first line of the first stanza, and a beginning is made of the explanation of this dark night.

This night, which, as we say, is contemplation, produces in spiritual persons two kinds of darkness or purgation, corresponding to the two parts of man's nature—namely, the sensual and the spiritual. And thus the one night or purgation will be sensual, wherein the soul is purged according to sense, which is subdued to the spirit; and the other is a night or purgation which is spiritual, wherein the soul is purged and stripped according to the spirit, and subdued and made ready for the union of love with God. The night of sense is common and comes to many: these are the beginners; and of this night we shall speak first. The night of the spirit is the portion of very few, and these are they that are already practised and proficient, of whom we shall treat hereafter.

The first purgation or night is bitter and terrible to sense, as we shall now show.[58] The second bears no comparison with it, for it is horrible and awful to the spirit, as we shall show[59] presently. Since the night of sense is first in order and comes first, we shall first of all say something about it briefly, since more is written of it, as of a thing that is more common; and we shall pass on to treat more fully of the spiritual night, since very little has been said of this, either in speech[60] or in writing, and very little is known of it, even by experience.

Since, then, the conduct of these beginners upon the way of God is ignoble,[61] and has much to do with their love of self and their own inclinations, as has been explained above, God desires to lead them farther. He seeks to bring them out of that ignoble kind of love to a higher degree of love for Him, to free them from the ignoble exercises of sense and meditation (wherewith, as we have said, they go seeking God so unworthily and in so many ways that are unbefitting), and to lead them to a kind of spiritual exercise wherein they can commune with Him more abundantly and are freed more completely from imperfections. For they have now had practice for some time in the way of virtue and have persevered in meditation and prayer, whereby, through the sweetness and pleasure that they have found therein, they have lost their love of the things of the world and have gained some degree of spiritual strength in God; this has enabled them to some extent to refrain from creature desires, so that for God's sake they are now able to suffer a light burden and a little aridity without turning back to a time[62] which they found more pleasant. When they are going about these spiritual exercises with the greatest delight and pleasure, and when they believe that the sun of Divine favour is shining most brightly upon them, God turns all this light of theirs into darkness, and shuts against them the door and the source of the sweet spiritual water which they were tasting in God whensoever and for as long as they desired. (For, as they were weak and tender, there was no door closed to them, as Saint John says in the Apocalypse, iii, 8). And thus He leaves them so completely in the dark that they know not whither to go with their sensible imagination and meditation; for they cannot advance a step in meditation, as they were wont to do afore time, their inward senses being submerged in this night, and left with such dryness that not only do they experience no pleasure and consolation in the spiritual things and good exercises wherein they were wont to find their delights and pleasures, but instead, on the contrary, they find insipidity and bitterness in the said things. For, as I have said, God now sees that they have grown a little, and are becoming strong enough to lay aside their swaddling clothes and be taken from the gentle breast; so He sets them down from His arms and teaches them to walk on their own feet; which they feel to be very strange, for everything seems to be going wrong with them.

To recollected persons this commonly happens sooner after their beginnings than to others, inasmuch as they are freer from occasions of backsliding, and their desires turn more quickly from the things of the world, which is necessary if they are to begin to enter this blessed night of sense. Ordinarily no great time passes after their beginnings before they begin to enter this night of sense; and the great majority of them do in fact enter it, for they will generally be seen to fall into these aridities.

With regard to this way of purgation of the senses, since it is so common, we might here adduce a great number of quotations from Divine Scripture, where many passages relating to it are continually found, particularly in the Psalms and the Prophets. However, I do not wish to spend time upon these, for he who knows not how to look for them there will find the common experience of this purgation to be sufficient.

Chapter IX

Of the signs by which it will be known that the spiritual person is walking along the way of this night and purgation of sense.

But since these aridities might frequently proceed, not from the night and purgation of the sensual desires aforementioned, but from sins and imperfections, or from weakness and lukewarmness, or from some bad humour or indisposition of the body, I shall here set down certain signs by which it may be known if such aridity proceeds from the aforementioned purgation, or if it arises from any of the aforementioned sins. For the making of this distinction I find that there are three principal signs.

The first is whether, when a soul finds no pleasure or consolation in the things of God, it also fails to find it in any thing created; for, as God sets the soul in this dark night to the end that He may quench and purge its sensual desire, He allows it not to find attraction or sweetness in anything whatsoever. In such a case it may be considered very probable[63] that this aridity and insipidity proceed not from recently committed sins or imperfections. For, if this were so, the soul would feel in its nature some inclination or desire to taste other things than those of God; since, whenever the desire is allowed indulgence in any imperfection, it immediately feels inclined thereto, whether little or much, in proportion to the pleasure and the love that it has put into it. Since, however, this lack of enjoyment in things above or below might proceed from some indisposition or melancholy humour, which oftentimes makes it impossible for the soul to take pleasure in anything, it becomes necessary to apply the second sign and condition.

The second sign whereby a man may believe himself to be experiencing the said purgation is that the memory is ordinarily centred upon God, with painful care and solicitude, thinking that it is not serving God, but is backsliding, because it finds itself without sweetness in the things of God. And in such a case it is evident that this lack of sweetness and this aridity come not from weakness and lukewarmness; for it is the nature of lukewarmness not to care greatly or to have any inward solicitude for the things of God. There is thus a great difference between aridity and lukewarmness, for lukewarmness consists in great weakness and remissness in the will and in the spirit, without solicitude as to serving God; whereas purgative aridity is ordinarily accompanied by solicitude, with care and grief as I say, because the soul is not serving God. And, although this may sometimes be increased by melancholy or some other humour (as it frequently is), it fails not for that reason to produce a purgative effect upon the desire, since the desire is deprived of all pleasure and has its care centred upon God alone. For, when mere humour is the cause, it spends itself in displeasure and ruin of the physical nature, and there are none of those desires to sense God which belong to purgative aridity. When the cause is aridity, it is true that the sensual part of the soul has fallen low, and is weak and feeble in its actions, by reason of the little pleasure which it finds in them; but the spirit, on the other hand, is ready and strong.

For the cause of this aridity is that God transfers to the spirit the good things and the strength of the senses, which, since the soul's natural strength and senses are incapable of using them, remain barren, dry and empty. For the sensual part of a man has no capacity for that which is pure spirit, and thus, when it is the spirit that receives the pleasure, the flesh is left without savour and is too weak to perform any action. But the spirit, which all the time is being fed, goes forward in strength, and with more alertness and solicitude than before, in its anxiety not to fail God; and if it is not immediately conscious of spiritual sweetness and delight, but only of aridity and lack of sweetness, the reason for this is the strangeness of the exchange; for its palate has been accustomed to those other sensual pleasures upon which its eyes are still fixed, and, since the spiritual palate is not made ready or purged for such subtle pleasure, until it finds itself becoming prepared for it by means of this arid and dark night, it cannot experience spiritual pleasure and good, but only aridity and lack of sweetness, since it misses the pleasure which aforetime it enjoyed so readily.

These souls whom God is beginning to lead through these solitary places of the wilderness are like to the children of Israel, to whom in the wilderness God began to give food from Heaven, containing within itself all sweetness, and, as is there said, it turned to the savour which each one of them desired. But withal the children of Israel felt the lack of the pleasures and delights of the flesh and the onions which they had eaten aforetime in Egypt, the more so because their palate was accustomed to these and took delight in them, rather than in the delicate sweetness of the angelic manna; and they wept and sighed for the fleshpots even in the midst of the food of Heaven.[64] To such depths does the vileness of our desires descend that it makes us to long for our own wretched food[65] and to be nauseated by the indescribable[66] blessings of Heaven.

But, as I say, when these aridities proceed from the way of the purgation of sensual desire, although at first the spirit feels no sweetness, for the reasons that we have just given, it feels that it is deriving strength and energy to act from the substance which this inward food gives it, the which food is the beginning of a contemplation that is dark and arid to the senses; which contemplation is secret and hidden from the very person that experiences it; and ordinarily, together with the aridity and emptiness which it causes in the senses, it gives the soul an inclination and desire to be alone and in quietness, without being able to think of any particular thing or having the desire to do so. If those souls to whom this comes to pass knew how to be quiet at this time, and troubled not about performing any kind of action, whether inward or outward, neither had any anxiety about doing anything, then they would delicately experience this inward refreshment in that ease and freedom from care. So delicate is this refreshment that ordinarily, if a man have desire or care to experience it, he experiences it not; for, as I say, it does its work when the soul is most at ease and freest from care; it is like the air which, if one would close one's hand upon it, escapes.

In this sense we may understand that which the Spouse said to the Bride in the Songs, namely: 'Withdraw thine eyes from me, for they make me to soar aloft.'[67] For in such a way does God bring the soul into this state, and by so different a path does He lead it that, if it desires to work with its faculties, it hinders the work which God is doing in it rather than aids it; whereas aforetime it was quite the contrary. The reason is that, in this state of contemplation, which the soul enters when it forsakes meditation for the state of the proficient, it is God Who is now working in the soul; He binds its interior faculties, and allows it not to cling to the understanding, nor to have delight in the will, nor to reason with the memory. For anything that the soul can do of its own accord at this time serves only, as we have said, to hinder inward peace and the work which God is accomplishing in the spirit by means of that aridity of sense. And this peace, being spiritual and delicate, performs a work which is quiet and delicate, solitary, productive of peace and satisfaction[68] and far removed from all those earlier pleasures, which were very palpable and sensual. This is the peace which, says David, God speaks in the soul to the end that He may make it spiritual.[69] And this leads us to the third point.

The third sign whereby this purgation of sense may be recognized is that the soul can no longer meditate or reflect in the imaginative sphere of sense as it was wont, however much it may of itself endeavour to do so. For God now begins to communicate Himself to it, no longer through sense, as He did aforetime, by means of reflections which joined and sundered its knowledge, but by pure spirit, into which consecutive reflections enter not; but He communicates Himself to it by an act of simple contemplation, to which neither the exterior nor the interior senses of the lower part of the soul can attain. From this time forward, therefore, imagination and fancy can find no support in any meditation, and can gain no foothold by means thereof.

With regard to this third sign, it is to be understood that this embarrassment and dissatisfaction of the faculties proceed not from indisposition, for, when this is the case, and the indisposition, which never lasts for long,[70] comes to an end, the soul is able once again, by taking some trouble about the matter, to do what it did before, and the faculties find their wonted support. But in the purgation of the desire this is not so: when once the soul begins to enter therein, its inability to reflect with the faculties grows ever greater. For, although it is true that at first, and with some persons, the process is not as continuous as this, so that occasionally they fail to abandon their pleasures and reflections of sense (for perchance by reason of their weakness it was not fitting to wean them from these immediately), yet this inability grows within them more and more and brings the workings of sense to an end, if indeed they are to make progress, for those who walk not in the way of contemplation act very differently. For this night of aridities is not usually continuous in their senses. At times they have these aridities; at others they have them not. At times they cannot meditate; at others they can. For God sets them in this night only to prove them and to humble them, and to reform their desires, so that they go not nurturing in themselves a sinful gluttony in spiritual things. He sets them not there in order to lead them in the way of the spirit, which is this contemplation; for not all those who walk of set purpose in the way of the spirit are brought by God to contemplation, nor even the half of them—why, He best knows. And this is why He never completely weans the senses of such persons from the breasts of meditations and reflections, but only for short periods and at certain seasons, as we have said.

Chapter X

Of the way in which these souls are to conduct themselves in this dark night.

During the time, then, of the aridities of this night of sense (wherein God effects the change of which we have spoken above, drawing forth the soul from the life of sense into that of the spirit—that is, from meditation to contemplation—wherein it no longer has any power to work or to reason with its faculties concerning the things of God, as has been said), spiritual persons suffer great trials, by reason not so much of the aridities which they suffer, as of the fear which they have of being lost on the road, thinking that all spiritual blessing is over for them and that God has abandoned them since they find no help or pleasure in good things. Then they grow weary, and endeavour (as they have been accustomed to do) to concentrate their faculties with some degree of pleasure upon some object of meditation, thinking that, when they are not doing this and yet are conscious of making an effort, they are doing nothing. This effort they make not without great inward repugnance and unwillingness on the part of their soul, which was taking pleasure in being in that quietness and ease, instead of working with its faculties. So they have abandoned the one pursuit,[71] yet draw no profit from the other; for, by seeking what is prompted by their own spirit,[72] they lose the spirit of tranquillity and peace which they had before. And thus they are like to one who abandons what he has done in order to do it over again, or to one who leaves a city only to re-enter it, or to one who is hunting and lets his prey go in order to hunt it once more. This is useless here, for the soul will gain nothing further by conducting itself in this way, as has been said.

These souls turn back at such a time if there is none who understands them; they abandon the road or lose courage; or, at the least, they are hindered from going farther by the great trouble which they take in advancing along the road of meditation and reasoning. Thus they fatigue and overwork their nature, imagining that they are failing through negligence or sin. But this trouble that they are taking is quite useless, for God is now leading them by another road, which is that of contemplation, and is very different from the first; for the one is of meditation and reasoning, and the other belongs neither to imagination nor yet to reasoning.

It is well for those who find themselves in this condition to take comfort, to persevere in patience and to be in no wise afflicted. Let them trust in God, Who abandons not those that seek Him with a simple and right heart, and will not fail to give them what is needful for the road, until He bring them into the clear and pure light of love. This last He will give them by means of that other dark night, that of the spirit, if they merit His bringing them thereto.

The way in which they are to conduct themselves in this night of sense is to devote themselves not at all to reasoning and meditation, since this is not the time for it, but to allow the soul to remain in peace and quietness, although it may seem clear to them that they are doing nothing and are wasting their time, and although it may appear to them that it is because of their weakness that they have no desire in that state to think of anything. The truth is that they will be doing quite sufficient if they have patience and persevere in prayer without making any effort.[73] What they must do is merely to leave the soul free and disencumbered and at rest from all knowledge and thought, troubling not themselves, in that state, about what they shall think or meditate upon, but contenting themselves with merely a peaceful and loving attentiveness toward God, and in being without anxiety, without the ability and without desired to have experience of Him or to perceive Him. For all these yearnings disquiet and distract the soul from the peaceful quiet and sweet ease of contemplation which is here granted to it.

And although further scruples may come to them—that they are wasting their time, and that it would be well for them to do something else, because they can neither do nor think anything in prayer—let them suffer these scruples and remain in peace, as there is no question save of their being at ease and having freedom of spirit. For if such a soul should desire to make any effort of its own with its interior faculties, this means that it will hinder and lose the blessings which, by means of that peace and ease of the soul, God is instilling into it and impressing upon it. It is just as if some painter were painting or dyeing a face; if the sitter were to move because he desired to do something, he would prevent the painter from accomplishing anything and would disturb him in what he was doing. And thus, when the soul desires to remain in inward ease and peace, any operation and affection or attentions wherein it may then seek to indulge[74] will distract it and disquiet it and make it conscious of aridity and emptiness of sense. For the more a soul endeavours to find support in affection and knowledge, the more will it feel the lack of these, which cannot now be supplied to it upon that road.

Wherefore it behoves such a soul to pay no heed if the operations of its faculties become lost to it; it is rather to desire that this should happen quickly. For, by not hindering the operation of infused contemplation that God is bestowing upon it, it can receive this with more peaceful abundance, and cause its spirit to be enkindled and to burn with the love which this dark and secret contemplation brings with it and sets firmly in the soul. For contemplation is naught else than a secret, peaceful and loving infusion from God, which, if it be permitted, enkindles the soul with the spirit of love, according as the soul declares in the next lines, namely:

Kindled in love with yearnings.

Chapter XI

Wherein are expounded the three lines of the stanza.

This enkindling of love is not as a rule felt at the first, because it has not begun to take hold upon the soul, by reason of the impurity of human nature, or because the soul has not understood its own state, as we have said, and has therefore given it no peaceful abiding-place within itself. Yet sometimes, nevertheless, there soon begins to make itself felt a certain yearning toward God; and the more this increases, the more is the soul affectioned and enkindled in love toward God, without knowing or understanding how and whence this love and affection come to it, but from time to time seeing this flame and this enkindling grow so greatly within it that it desires God with yearning of love; even as David, when he was in this dark night, said of himself in these words,[75] namely: 'Because my heart was enkindled (that is to say, in love of contemplation), my reins also were changed': that is, my desires for sensual affections were changed, namely from the way of sense to the way of the spirit, which is the aridity and cessation from all these things whereof we are speaking. And I, he says, was dissolved in nothing and annihilated, and I knew not; for, as we have said, without knowing the way whereby it goes, the soul finds itself annihilated with respect to all things above and below which were accustomed to please it; and it finds itself enamoured, without knowing how. And because at times the enkindling of love in the spirit grows greater, the yearnings for God become so great in the soul that the very bones seem to be dried up by this thirst, and the natural powers to be fading away, and their warmth and strength to be perishing through the intensity[76] of the thirst of love, for the soul feels that this thirst of love is a living thirst. This thirst David had and felt, when he said: 'My soul thirsted for the living God.'[77] Which is as much as to say: A living thirst was that of my soul. Of this thirst, since it is living, we may say that it kills. But it is to be noted that the vehemence of this thirst is not continuous, but occasional although as a rule the soul is accustomed to feel it to a certain degree.

But it must be noted that, as I began to say just now, this love is not as a rule felt at first, but only the dryness and emptiness are felt whereof we are speaking. Then in place of this love which afterwards becomes gradually enkindled, what the soul experiences in the midst of these aridities and emptinesses of the faculties is an habitual care and solicitude with respect to God, together with grief and fear that it is not serving Him. But it is a sacrifice which is not a little pleasing to God that the soul should go about afflicted and solicitous for His love. This solicitude and care leads the soul into that secret contemplation, until, the senses (that is, the sensual part) having in course of time been in some degree purged of the natural affections and powers by means of the aridities which it causes within them, this Divine love begins to be enkindled in the spirit. Meanwhile, however, like one who has begun a cure, the soul knows only suffering in this dark and arid purgation of the desire; by this means it becomes healed of many imperfections,

and exercises itself in many virtues in order to make itself meet for the said love, as we shall now say with respect to the line following:
Oh, happy chance!

When God leads the soul into this night of sense in order to purge the sense of its lower part and to subdue it, unite it and bring it into conformity with the spirit, by setting it in darkness and causing it to cease from meditation (as He afterwards does in order to purify the spirit to unite it with God, as we shall afterwards say), He brings it into the night of the spirit, and (although it appears not so to it) the soul gains so many benefits that it holds it to be a happy chance to have escaped from the bonds and restrictions of the senses of or its lower self, by means of this night aforesaid; and utters the present line, namely: Oh, happy chance! With respect to this, it behoves us here to note the benefits which the soul finds in this night, and because of which it considers it a happy chance to have passed through it; all of which benefits the soul includes in the next line, namely:
I went forth without being observed.

This going forth is understood of the subjection to its sensual part which the soul suffered when it sought God through operations so weak, so limited and so defective as are those of this lower part; for at every step it stumbled into numerous imperfections and ignorances, as we have noted above in writing of the seven capital sins. From all these it is freed when this night quenches within it all pleasures, whether from above or from below, and makes all meditation darkness to it, and grants it other innumerable blessings in the acquirement of the virtues, as we shall now show. For it will be a matter of great pleasure and great consolation, to one that journeys on this road, to see how that which seems to the soul so severe and adverse, and so contrary to spiritual pleasure, works in it so many blessings. These, as we say, are gained when the soul goes forth, as regards its affection and operation, by means of this night, from all created things, and when it journeys to eternal things, which is great happiness and good fortune:[78] first, because of the great blessing which is in the quenching of the desire and affection with respect to all things; secondly, because they are very few that endure and persevere in entering by this strait gate and by the narrow way which leads to life, as says Our Saviour.[79] The strait gate is this night of sense, and the soul detaches itself from sense and strips itself thereof that it may enter by this gate, and establishes itself in faith, which is a stranger to all sense, so that afterwards it may journey by the narrow way, which is the other night—that of the spirit—and this the soul afterwards enters in order in journey to God in pure faith, which is the means whereby the soul is united to God. By this road, since it is so narrow, dark and terrible (though there is no comparison between this night of sense and that other, in its darkness and trials, as we shall say later), they are far fewer that journey, but its benefits are far greater without comparison than those of this present night. Of these benefits we shall now begin to say something, with such brevity as is possible, in order that we may pass to the other night.

Chapter XII

Of the benefits which this night causes in the soul.

This night and purgation of the desire, a happy one for the soul, works in it so many blessings and benefits (although to the soul, as we have said, it rather seems that blessings are being taken away from it) that, even as Abraham made a great feast when he weaned his son Isaac,[80] even so is there joy in Heaven because God is now taking this soul from its swaddling clothes, setting it down from His arms, making it to walk upon its feet, and likewise taking from it the milk of the breast and the soft and sweet food proper to children, and making it to eat bread with crust, and to begin to enjoy the food of robust persons. This food, in these aridities and this darkness of sense, is now given to the spirit, which is dry and emptied of all the sweetness of sense. And this food is the infused contemplation whereof we have spoken.

This is the first and principal benefit caused by this arid and dark night of contemplation: the knowledge of oneself and of one's misery. For, besides the fact that all the favours which God grants to the soul are habitually granted to them enwrapped in this knowledge, these aridities and this emptiness of the faculties, compared with the abundance which the soul experienced aforetime and the difficulty which it finds in good works, make it recognize its own lowliness and misery, which in the time of its prosperity it was unable to see. Of this there is a good illustration in the Book of Exodus, where God, wishing to humble the children of Israel and desiring that they should know themselves, commanded them to take away and strip off the festal garments and adornments wherewith they were accustomed to adorn themselves in the Wilderness, saying: 'Now from henceforth strip yourselves of festal ornaments and put on everyday working dress, that ye may know what treatment ye deserve.'[81] This is as though He had said: Inasmuch as the attire that ye wear, being proper to festival and rejoicing, causes you to feel less humble concerning yourselves than ye should, put off from you this attire, in order that henceforth, seeing yourselves clothed with vileness, ye may know that ye merit no more, and may know who ye are. Wherefore the soul knows the truth that it knew not at first, concerning its own misery; for, at the time when it was clad as for a festival and found in God much pleasure, consolation and support, it was somewhat more satisfied and contented, since it thought itself to some extent to be serving God. It is true that such souls may not have this idea explicitly in their minds; but some suggestion of it at least is implanted in them by the satisfaction which they find in their pleasant experiences. But, now that the soul has put on its other and working attire—that of aridity and abandonment—and now that its first lights have turned into darkness, it possesses these lights more truly in this virtue of self-knowledge, which is so excellent and so necessary, considering itself now as nothing and experiencing no satisfaction in itself; for it sees that it does nothing of itself neither can do anything. And the smallness of this self-satisfaction, together with the soul's affliction at not serving God, is considered and esteemed by God as greater than all the consolations which the soul formerly experienced and the works which it wrought, however great they were, inasmuch as they were the occasion of many imperfections and ignorances. And from this attire of aridity proceed, as from their fount and source of self-knowledge, not only the things which we have described already, but also the benefits which we shall now describe and many more which will have to be omitted.

In the first place, the soul learns to commune with God with more respect and more courtesy, such as a soul must ever observe in converse with the Most High. These it knew not in its prosperous times of comfort and consolation, for that comforting favour which it experienced made its craving for God somewhat bolder than was fitting, and discourteous and ill-considered. Even so did it happen to Moses, when he perceived that God was speaking to him; blinded by that pleasure and desire, without further consideration, he would have made bold to go to Him if God had not commanded him to stay and put off his shoes. By this incident we are shown the respect and discretion in detachment of desire wherewith a man is to commune with God. When Moses had obeyed in this matter, he became so discreet and so attentive that the Scripture says that not only did he not make bold to draw near to God, but that he dared not even look at Him. For, having taken off the shoes of his desires and pleasures, he became very conscious of his wretchedness in the sight of God, as befitted one about to hear the word of God. Even so likewise the preparation which God granted to Job in order that he might speak with Him consisted not in those delights and glories which Job himself reports that he was wont to have in his God, but in leaving him naked upon a dung-hill,[82] abandoned and even persecuted by his friends, filled with anguish and bitterness, and the earth covered with worms. And then the Most High God, He that lifts up the poor man from the dunghill, was pleased to come down and speak with him there face to face, revealing to him the depths and heights[83] of His wisdom, in a way that He had never done in the time of his prosperity.

And here we must note another excellent benefit which there is in this night and aridity of the desire of sense, since we have had occasion to speak of it. It is that, in this dark night of the desire (to the end that the words of the Prophet may be fulfilled, namely: 'Thy light shall shine in the darkness'[84]), God will enlighten the soul, giving it knowledge, not only of its lowliness and wretchedness, as we have said, but likewise of the greatness and excellence of God. For, as well as quenching the desires and pleasures and attachments of sense, He cleanses and frees the understanding that it may understand the truth; for pleasure of sense and desire, even though it be for spiritual things, darkens and obstructs the spirit, and furthermore that straitness and aridity of sense enlightens and quickens the understanding, as says Isaias.[85] Vexation makes us to understand how the soul that is empty and disencumbered, as is necessary for His Divine influence, is instructed supernaturally by God in His Divine wisdom, through this dark and arid night of contemplation,[86] as we have said; and this instruction God gave not in those first sweetnesses and joys.

This is very well explained by the same prophet Isaias, where he says: 'Whom shall God teach His knowledge, and whom shall He make to understand the hearing?' To those, He says, that are weaned from the milk and drawn away from the breasts.[87] Here it is shown that the first milk of spiritual sweetness is no preparation for this Divine influence, neither is there preparation in attachment to the breast of delectable meditations, belonging to the faculties of sense, which gave the soul pleasure; such preparation consists rather in the lack of the one and withdrawal from the other. Inasmuch as, in order to listen to God, the soul needs to stand upright and to be detached, with regard to affection and sense, even as the Prophet says concerning himself, in these words: I will stand upon my watch (this is that detachment of desire) and I will make firm my step (that is, I will not meditate with sense), in order to contemplate (that is, in order to understand that which may come to me from God).[88] So we have now arrived at this, that from this arid night there first of all comes self-knowledge, whence, as from a foundation, rises this other knowledge of God. For which cause Saint Augustine said to God: 'Let me know myself, Lord, and I shall know Thee.'[89] For, as the philosophers say, one extreme can be well known by another.

And in order to prove more completely how efficacious is this night of sense, with its aridity and its desolation, in bringing the soul that light which, as we say, it receives there from God, we shall quote that passage of David, wherein he clearly describes the great power which is in this night for bringing the soul this lofty knowledge of God. He says, then, thus: 'In the desert land, waterless, dry and pathless, I appeared before Thee, that I might see Thy virtue and Thy glory.'[90] It is a wondrous thing that David should say here that the means and the preparation for his knowledge of the glory of God were not the spiritual delights and the many pleasures which he had experienced, but the aridities and detachments of his sensual nature, which is here to be understood by the dry and desert land. No less wondrous is it that he should describe as the road to his perception and vision of the virtue of God, not the Divine meditations and conceptions of which he had often made use, but his being unable to form any conception of God or to walk by meditation produced by imaginary consideration, which is here to be understood by the pathless land. So that the means to a knowledge of God and of oneself is this dark night with its aridities and voids, although it leads not to a knowledge of Him of the same plenitude and abundance that comes from the other night of the spirit, since this is only, as it were, the beginning of that other.

Likewise, from the aridities and voids of this night of the desire, the soul draws spiritual humility, which is the contrary virtue to the first capital sin, which, as we said, is spiritual pride. Through this humility, which is acquired by the said knowledge of self, the soul is purged from all those imperfections whereinto it fell with respect to that sin of pride, in the time of its prosperity. For it sees itself so dry and miserable that the idea never even occurs to it that it is making better progress than others, or outstripping them, as it believed itself to be doing before. On the contrary, it recognizes that others are making better progress than itself.

And hence arises the love of its neighbours, for it esteems them, and judges them not as it was wont to do aforetime, when it saw that itself had great fervour and others not so. It is aware only of its own wretchedness, which it keeps before its eyes to such an extent that it never forgets it, nor takes occasion to set its eyes on anyone else. This was described wonderfully by David, when he was in this night, in these words: 'I was dumb and was humbled and kept silence from good things and my sorrow was renewed.'[91] This he says because it seemed to him that the good that was in his soul had so completely departed that not only did he neither speak nor find any language concerning it, but with respect to the good of others he was likewise dumb because of his grief at the knowledge of his misery.

In this condition, again, souls become submissive and obedient upon the spiritual road, for, when they see their own misery, not only do they hear what is taught them, but they even desire that anyone soever may set them on the way and tell them what they ought to do. The affective presumption which they sometimes had in their prosperity is taken from them; and finally, there are swept away from them on this road all the other imperfections which we noted above with respect to this first sin, which is spiritual pride.

Chapter XIII

Of other benefits which this night of sense causes in the soul.

With respect to the soul's imperfections of spiritual avarice, because of which it coveted this and that spiritual thing and found no satisfaction in this and that exercise by reason of its covetousness for the desire and pleasure which it found therein, this arid and dark night has now greatly reformed it. For, as it finds not the pleasure and sweetness which it was wont to find, but rather finds affliction and lack of sweetness, it has such moderate recourse to them that it might possibly now lose, through defective use, what aforetime it lost through excess; although as a rule God gives to those whom He leads into this night humility and readiness, albeit with lack of sweetness, so that what is commanded them they may do for God's sake alone; and thus they no longer seek profit in many things because they find no pleasure in them.

With respect to spiritual luxury, it is likewise clearly seen that, through this aridity and lack of sensible sweetness which the soul finds in spiritual things, it is freed from those impurities which we there noted; for we said that, as a rule, they proceeded from the pleasure which overflowed from spirit into sense.

But with regard to the imperfections from which the soul frees itself in this dark night with respect to the fourth sin, which is spiritual gluttony, they may be found above, though they have not all been described there, because they are innumerable; and thus I will not detail them here, for I would fain make an end of this night in order to pass to the next, concerning which we shall have to pronounce grave words and instructions. Let it suffice for the understanding of the innumerable benefits which, over and above those mentioned, the soul gains in this night with respect to this sin of spiritual gluttony, to say that it frees itself from all those imperfections which have there been described, and from many other and greater evils, and vile abominations which are not written above, into which fell many of whom we have had experience, because they had not reformed their desire as concerning this inordinate love of spiritual sweetness. For in this arid and dark night wherein He sets the soul, God has restrained its concupiscence and curbed its desire so that the soul cannot feed upon any pleasure or sweetness of sense, whether from above or from below; and this He continues to do after such manner that the soul is subjected, reformed and repressed with respect to concupiscence and desire. It loses the strength of its passions and concupiscence and it becomes sterile, because it no longer consults its likings. Just as, when none is accustomed to take milk from the breast, the courses of the milk are dried up, so the desires of the soul are dried up. And besides these things there follow admirable benefits from this spiritual sobriety, for, when desire and concupiscence are quenched, the soul lives in spiritual tranquillity and peace; for, where desire and concupiscence reign not, there is no disturbance, but peace and consolation of God.

From this there arises another and a second benefit, which is that the soul habitually has remembrance of God, with fear and dread of backsliding upon the spiritual road, as has been said. This is a great benefit, and not one of the least that results from this aridity and purgation of the desire, for the soul is purified and cleansed of the imperfections that were clinging to it because of the desires and affections, which of their own accord deaden and darken the soul.

There is another very great benefit for the soul in this night, which is that it practices several virtues together, as, for example, patience and longsuffering, which are often called upon in these times of emptiness and aridity, when the soul endures and perseveres in its spiritual exercises without consolation and without pleasure. It practises the charity of God, since it is not now moved by the pleasure of attraction and sweetness which it finds in its work, but only by God. It likewise practises here the virtue of fortitude, because, in these difficulties and insipidities which it finds in its work, it brings strength out of weakness and thus becomes strong. All the virtues, in short—the theological and also the cardinal and moral—both in body and in spirit, are practised by the soul in these times of aridity.

And that in this night the soul obtains these four benefits which we have here described (namely, delight of peace, habitual remembrance and thought of God, cleanness and purity of soul and the practice of the virtues which we have just described), David tells us, having experienced it himself when he was in this night, in these words: 'My soul refused consolations, I had remembrance of God, I found consolation and was exercised and my spirit failed.'[92] And he then says: 'And I meditated by night with my heart and was exercised, and I swept and purified my spirit'—that is to say, from all the affections.[93]

With respect to the imperfections of the other three spiritual sins which we have described above, which are wrath, envy and sloth, the soul is purged hereof likewise in this aridity of the desire and acquires the virtues opposed to them; for, softened and humbled by these aridities and hardships and other temptations and trials wherein God exercises it during this night, it becomes meek with respect to God, and to itself, and likewise with respect to its neighbour. So that it is no longer disturbed and angry with itself because of its own faults, nor with its neighbour because of his, neither is it displeased with God, nor does it utter unseemly complaints because He does not quickly make it holy.

Then, as to envy, the soul has charity toward others in this respect also; for, if it has any envy, this is no longer a vice as it was before, when it was grieved because others were preferred to it and given greater advantage. Its grief now comes from seeing how great is its own misery, and its envy (if it has any) is a virtuous envy, since it desires to imitate others, which is great virtue.

Neither are the sloth and the irksomeness which it now experiences concerning spiritual things vicious as they were before. For in the past these sins proceeded from the spiritual pleasures which the soul sometimes experienced and sought after when it found them not. But this new weariness proceeds not from this insuffficiency of pleasure, because God has taken from the soul pleasure in all things in this purgation of the desire.

Besides these benefits which have been mentioned, the soul attains innumerable others by means of this arid contemplation. For often, in the midst of these times of aridity and hardship, God communicates to the soul, when it is least expecting it, the purest spiritual sweetness and love, together with a spiritual knowledge which is sometimes very delicate, each manifestation of which is of greater benefit and worth than those which the soul enjoyed aforetime; although in its beginnings the soul thinks that this is not so, for the spiritual influence now granted to it is very delicate and cannot be perceived by sense.

Finally, inasmuch as the soul is now purged from the affections and desires of sense, it obtains liberty of spirit, whereby in ever greater degree it gains the twelve fruits of the Holy Spirit. Here, too, it is wondrously delivered from the hands of its three enemies—devil, world and flesh; for, its pleasure and delight of sense being quenched with respect to all things, neither the devil nor the world nor sensuality has any arms or any strength wherewith to make war upon the spirit.

These times of aridity, then, cause the soul to journey in all purity in the love of God, since it is no longer influenced in its actions by the pleasure and sweetness of the actions themselves, as perchance it was when it experienced sweetness, but only by a desire to please God. It becomes neither presumptuous nor self-satisfied, as perchance it was wont to become in the time of its prosperity, but fearful and timid with regard to itself, finding in itself no satisfaction whatsoever; and herein consists that holy fear which preserves and increases the virtues. This aridity, too, quenches natural energy and concupiscence, as has also been said. Save for the pleasure, indeed, which at certain times God Himself infuses into it, it is a wonder if it finds pleasure and consolation of sense, through its own diligence, in any spiritual exercise or action, as has already been said.

There grows within souls that experience this arid night concern for God and yearnings to serve Him, for in proportion as the breasts of sensuality, wherewith it sustained and nourished the desires that it pursued, are drying up, there remains nothing in that aridity and detachment save the yearning to serve God, which is a thing very pleasing to God. For, as David says, an afflicted spirit is a sacrifice to God.[94]

When the soul, then, knows that, in this arid purgation through which it has passed, it has derived and attained so many and such precious benefits as those which have here been described, it tarries not in crying, as in the stanza of which we are expounding the lines, 'Oh, happy chance!—I went forth without being observed.' That is, 'I went forth' from the bonds and subjection of the desires of sense and the affections, 'without being observed'—that is to say, without the three enemies aforementioned being able to keep me from it. These enemies, as we have said, bind the soul as with bonds, in its desires and pleasures, and prevent it from going forth from itself to the liberty of the love of God; and without these desires and pleasures they cannot give battle to the soul, as has been said.

When, therefore, the four passions of the soul—which are joy, grief, hope and fear—are calmed through continual mortification; when the natural desires have been lulled to sleep, in the sensual nature of the soul, by means of habitual times of aridity; and when the harmony of the senses and the interior faculties causes a suspension of labour and a cessation from the work of meditation, as we have said (which is the dwelling and the household of the lower part of the soul), these enemies cannot obstruct this spiritual liberty, and the house remains at rest and quiet, as says the following line:

My house being now at rest.

Chapter XIV

Expounds this last line of the first stanza.

When this house of sensuality was now at rest—that is, was mortified—its passions being quenched and its desires put to rest and lulled to sleep by means of this blessed night of the purgation of sense, the soul went forth, to set out upon the road and way of the spirit, which is that of progressives and proficients, and which, by another name, is called the way of illumination or of infused contemplation, wherein God Himself feeds and refreshes the soul, without meditation, or the soul's active help. Such, as we have said, is the night and purgation of sense in the soul. In those who have afterwards to enter the other and more formidable night of the spirit, in order to pass to the Divine union of love of God (for not all pass habitually thereto, but only the smallest number), it is wont to be accompanied by formidable trials and temptations of sense, which last for a long time, albeit longer in some than in others. For to some the angel of Satan presents himself—namely, the spirit of fornication—that he may buffet their senses with abominable and violent temptations, and trouble their spirits with vile considerations and representations which are most visible to the imagination, which things at times are a greater affliction to them than death.

At other times in this night there is added to these things the spirit of blasphemy, which roams abroad, setting in the path of all the conceptions and thoughts of the soul intolerable blasphemies. These it sometimes suggests to the imagination with such violence that the soul almost utters them, which is a grave torment to it.

At other times another abominable spirit, which Isaias calls Spiritus vertiginis,[95] is allowed to molest them, not in order that they may fall, but that it may try them. This spirit darkens their senses in such a way that it fills them with numerous scruples and perplexities, so confusing that, as they judge, they can never, by any means, be satisfied concerning them, neither can they find any help for their judgment in counsel or thought. This is one of the severest goads and horrors of this night, very closely akin to that which passes in the night of the spirit.

As a rule these storms and trials are sent by God in this night and purgation of sense to those whom afterwards He purposes to lead into the other night (though not all reach it), to the end that, when they have been chastened and buffeted, they may in this way continually exercise and prepare themselves, and continually accustom their senses and faculties to the union of wisdom which is to be bestowed upon them in that other night. For, if the soul be not tempted, exercised and proved with trials and temptations, it cannot quicken its sense of Wisdom. For this reason it is said in Ecclesiasticus: 'He that has not been tempted, what does he know? And he that has not been proved, what are the things that he recognizes?'[96] To this truth Jeremias bears good witness, saying: 'Thou didst chastise me, Lord, and I was instructed.'[97] And the most proper form of this chastisement, for one who will enter into Wisdom, is that of the interior trials which we are here describing, inasmuch as it is these which most effectively purge sense of all favours and consolations to which it was affected, with natural weakness, and by which the soul is truly humiliated in preparation for the exaltation which it is to experience.

For how long a time the soul will be held in this fasting and penance of sense, cannot be said with any certainty; for all do not experience it after one manner, neither do all encounter the same temptations. For this is meted out by the will of God, in conformity with the greater or the smaller degree of imperfection which each soul has to purge away. In conformity, likewise, with the degree of love of union to which God is pleased to raise it, He will humble it with greater or less intensity or in greater or less time. Those who have the disposition and greater strength to suffer, He purges with greater intensity and more quickly. But those who are very weak are kept for a long time in this night, and these He purges very gently and with slight temptations. Habitually, too, He gives them refreshments of sense so that they may not fall away, and only after a long time do they attain to purity of perfection in this life, some of them never attaining to it at all. Such are neither properly in the night nor properly out of it; for, although they make no progress, yet, in order that they may continue in humility and self-knowledge, God exercises them for certain periods and at certain times[98] in those temptations and aridities; and at other times and seasons He assists them with consolations, lest they should grow faint and return to seek the consolations of the world. Other souls, which are weaker, God Himself accompanies, now appearing to them, now moving farther away, that He may exercise them in His love; for without such turnings away they would not learn to reach God.

But the souls which are to pass on to that happy and high estate, the union of love, are wont as a rule to remain for a long time in these aridities and temptations, however quickly God may lead them, as has been seen by experience. It is time, then, to begin to treat of the second night.

BOOK THE SECOND

Of the Dark Night of the Spirit.

Chapter 1

Which begins to treat of the dark nights of the spirit and says at what time it begins.

The soul which God is about to lead onward is not led by His Majesty into this night of the spirit as soon as it goes forth from the aridities and trials of the first purgation and night of sense; rather it is wont to pass a long time, even years, after leaving the state of beginners, in exercising itself in that of proficients. In this latter state it is like to one that has come forth from a rigorous imprisonment;[99] it goes about the things of God with much greater freedom and satisfaction of the soul, and with more abundant and inward delight than it did at the beginning before it entered the said night. For its imagination and faculties are no longer bound, as they were before, by meditation and anxiety of spirit, since it now very readily finds in its spirit the most serene and loving contemplation and spiritual sweetness without the labour of meditation; although, as the purgation of the soul is not complete (for the principal part thereof, which is that of the spirit, is wanting, without which, owing to the communication that exists between the one part and the other,[100] since the subject is one only, the purgation of sense, however violent it may have been, is not yet complete and perfect), it is never without certain occasional necessities, aridities, darknesses and perils which are sometimes much more intense than those of the past, for they are as tokens and heralds of the coming night of the spirit, and are not of as long duration as will be the night which is to come. For, having passed through a period, or periods, or days of this night and tempest, the soul soon returns to its wonted serenity; and after this manner God purges certain souls which are not to rise to so high a degree of love as are others, bringing them at times, and for short periods, into this night of contemplation and purgation of the spirit, causing night to come upon them and then dawn, and this frequently, so that the words of David may be fulfilled, that He sends His crystal—that is, His contemplation—like morsels,[101] although these morsels of dark contemplation are never as intense as is that terrible night of contemplation which we are to describe, into which, of set purpose, God brings the soul that He may lead it to Divine union.

This sweetness, then, and this interior pleasure which we are describing, and which these progressives find and experience in their spirits so easily and so abundantly, is communicated to them in much greater abundance than aforetime, overflowing into their senses more than was usual previously to this purgation of sense; for, inasmuch as the sense is now purer, it can more easily feel the pleasures of the spirit after its manner. As, however, this sensual part of the soul is weak and incapable of experiencing the strong things of the spirit, it follows that these proficients, by reason of this spiritual communication which is made to their sensual part endure therein many frailties and sufferings and weaknesses of the stomach, and in consequence are fatigued in spirit. For, as the Wise Man says: 'The corruptible body presseth down the soul.'[102] Hence comes it that the communications that are granted to these souls cannot be very strong or very intense or very spiritual, as is required for Divine union with God, by reason of the weakness and corruption of the sensual nature which has a part in them. Hence arise the raptures and trances and dislocations of the bones which always happen when the communications are not purely spiritual—that is, are not given to the spirit alone, as are those of the perfect who are purified by the second night of the spirit, and in whom these raptures and torments of the body no longer exist, since they are enjoying liberty of spirit, and their senses are now neither clouded nor transported.

And in order that the necessity for such souls to enter this night of the spirit may be understood, we will here note certain imperfections and perils which belong to these proficients.

Chapter 11

Describes other imperfections[103] which belong to these proficients.

These proficients have two kinds of imperfection: the one kind is habitual; the other actual. The habitual imperfections are the imperfect habits and affections which have remained all the time in the spirit, and are like roots, to which the purgation of sense has been unable to penetrate. The difference between the purgation of these and that of this other kind is the difference between the root and the branch, or between the removing of a stain which is fresh and one which is old and of long standing. For, as we said, the purgation of sense is only the entrance and beginning of contemplation leading to the purgation of the spirit, which, as we have likewise said, serves rather to accommodate sense to spirit than to unite spirit with God. But there still remain in the spirit the stains of the old man, although the spirit thinks not that this is so, neither can it perceive them; if these stains be not removed with the soap and strong lye of the purgation of this night, the spirit will be unable to come to the purity of Divine union.

These souls have likewise the hebetudo mentis[104] and the natural roughness which every man contracts through sin, and the distraction and outward clinging of the spirit, which must be enlightened, refined and recollected by the afflictions and perils of that night. These habitual imperfections belong to all those who have not passed beyond this state of the proficient; they cannot coexist, as we say, with the perfect state of union through love.

To actual imperfections all are not liable in the same way. Some, whose spiritual good is so superficial and so readily affected by sense, fall into greater difficulties and dangers, which we described at the beginning of this treatise. For, as they find so many and such abundant spiritual communications and apprehensions, both in sense and in spirit wherein they oftentimes see imaginary and spiritual visions (for all these things, together with other delectable feelings, come to many souls in this state, wherein the devil and their own fancy very commonly practise deceptions on them), and, as the devil is apt to take such pleasure in impressing upon the soul and suggesting to it the said apprehensions and feelings, he fascinates and deludes it with great ease unless it takes the precaution of resigning itself to God, and of protecting itself strongly, by means of faith, from all these visions and feelings. For in this state the devil causes many to believe in vain visions and false prophecies; and strives to make them presume that God and the saints are speaking with them; and they often trust their own fancy. And the devil is also accustomed, in this state, to fill them with presumption and pride, so that they become attracted by vanity and arrogance, and allow themselves to be seen engaging in outward acts which appear holy, such as raptures and other manifestations. Thus they become bold with God, and lose holy fear, which is the key and the custodian of all the virtues; and in some of these souls so many are the falsehoods and deceits which tend to multiply, and so inveterate do they grow, that it is very doubtful if such souls will return to the pure road of virtue and true spirituality. Into these miseries they fall because they are beginning to give themselves over to spiritual feelings and apprehensions with too great security, when they were beginning to make some progress upon the way.

There is much more that I might say of these imperfections and of how they are the more incurable because such souls consider them to be more spiritual than the others, but I will leave this subject. I shall only add, in order to prove how necessary, for him that would go farther, is the night of the spirit, which is purgation, that none of these proficients, however strenuously he may have laboured, is free, at best, from many of those natural affections and imperfect habits, purification from which, we said, is necessary if a soul is to pass to Divine union.

And over and above this (as we have said already), inasmuch as the lower part of the soul still has a share in these spiritual communications, they cannot be as intense, as pure and as strong as is needful for the aforesaid union; wherefore, in order to come to this union, the soul must needs enter into the second night of the spirit, wherein it must strip sense and spirit perfectly from all these apprehensions and from all sweetness, and be made to walk in dark and pure faith, which is the proper and adequate means whereby the soul is united with God, according as Osee says, in these words: 'I will betroth thee—that is, I will unite thee—with Me through faith.'[105]

Chapter III

Annotation for that which follows.

These souls, then, have now become proficients, because of the time which they have spent in feeding the senses with sweet communications, so that their sensual part, being thus attracted and delighted by spiritual pleasure, which came to it from the spirit, may be united with the spirit and made one with it; each part after its own manner eating of one and the same spiritual food and from one and the same dish, as one person and with one sole intent, so that thus they may in a certain way be united and brought into agreement, and, thus united, may be prepared for the endurance of the stern and severe purgation of the spirit which awaits them. In this purgation these two parts of the soul, the spiritual and the sensual, must be completely purged, since the one is never truly purged without the other, the purgation of sense becoming effective when that of the spirit has fairly begun. Wherefore the night which we have called that of sense may and should be called a kind of correction and restraint of the desire rather than purgation. The reason is that all the imperfections and disorders of the sensual part have their strength and root in the spirit, where all habits, both good and bad, are brought into subjection, and thus, until these are purged, the rebellions and depravities of sense cannot be purged thoroughly.

Wherefore, in this night following, both parts of the soul are purged together, and it is for this end that it is well to have passed through the corrections of the first night, and the period of tranquillity which proceeds from it, in order that, sense being united with spirit, both may be purged after a certain manner and may then suffer with greater fortitude. For very great fortitude is needful for so violent and severe a purgation, since, if the weakness of the lower part has not first been corrected and fortitude has not been gained from God through the sweet and delectable communion which the soul has afterwards enjoyed with Him, its nature will not have the strength or the disposition to bear it.

Therefore, since these proficients are still at a very low stage of progress, and follow their own nature closely in the intercourse and dealings which they have with God, because the gold of their spirit is not yet purified and refined, they still think of God as little children, and speak of God as little children, and feel and experience God as little children, even as Saint Paul says,[106] because they have not reached perfection, which is the union of the soul with God. In the state of union, however, they will work great things in the spirit, even as grown men, and their works and faculties will then be Divine rather than human, as will afterwards be said. To this end God is pleased to strip them of this old man and clothe them with the new man, who is created according to God, as the Apostle says,[107] in the newness of sense. He strips their faculties, affections and feelings, both spiritual and sensual, both outward and inward, leaving the understanding dark, the will dry, the memory empty and the affections in the deepest affliction, bitterness and constraint, taking from the soul the pleasure and experience of spiritual blessings which it had aforetime, in order to make of this privation one of the principles which are requisite in the spirit so that there may be introduced into it and united with it the spiritual form of the spirit, which is the union of love. All this the Lord works in the soul by means of a pure and dark contemplation, as the soul explains in the first stanza. This, although we originally interpreted it with reference to the first night of sense, is principally understood by the soul of this second night of the spirit, since this is the principal part of the purification of the soul. And thus we shall set it down and expound it here again in this sense.

Chapter IV

Sets down the first stanza and the exposition thereof.

On a dark night, Kindled in love with yearnings—oh, happy chance!—I went forth without being observed, My house being now at rest.

Exposition

Interpreting this stanza now with reference to purgation, contemplation or detachment or poverty of spirit, which here are almost one and the same thing, we can expound it after this manner and make the soul speak thus: In poverty, and without protection or support in all the apprehensions of my soul—that is, in the darkness of my understanding and the constraint of my will, in affliction and anguish with respect to memory, remaining in the dark in pure faith, which is dark night for the said natural faculties, the will alone being touched by grief and afflictions and yearnings for the love of God—I went forth from myself—that is, from my low manner of understanding, from my weak mode of loving and from my poor and limited manner of experiencing God, without being hindered therein by sensuality or the devil.

This was a great happiness and a good chance for me; for, when the faculties had been perfectly annihilated and calmed, together with the passions, desires and affections of my soul, wherewith I had experienced and tasted God after a lowly manner, I went forth from my own human dealings and operations to the operations and dealings of God. That is to say, my understanding went forth from itself, turning from the human and natural to the Divine; for, when it is united with God by means of this purgation, its understanding no longer comes through its natural light and vigour, but through the Divine Wisdom wherewith it has become united. And my will went forth from itself, becoming Divine; for, being united with Divine love, it no longer loves with its natural strength after a lowly manner, but with strength and purity from the Holy Spirit; and thus the will, which is now near to God, acts not after a human manner, and similarly the memory has become transformed into eternal apprehensions of glory. And finally, by means of this night and purgation of the old man, all the energies and affections of the soul are wholly renewed into a Divine temper and Divine delight.

There follows the line: On a dark night.

Chapter V

Sets down the first line and begins to explain how this dark contemplation is not only night for the soul but is also grief and torment.

This dark night is an inflowing of God into the soul, which purges it from its ignorances and imperfections, habitual natural and spiritual, and which is called by contemplatives infused contemplation, or mystical theology. Herein God secretly teaches the soul and instructs it in perfection of love without its doing anything, or understanding of what manner is this infused contemplation. Inasmuch as it is the loving wisdom of God, God produces striking effects in the soul for, by purging and illumining it, He prepares it for the union of love with God. Wherefore the same loving wisdom that purges the blessed spirits and enlightens them is that which here purges the soul and illumines it.

But the question arises: Why is the Divine light (which as we say, illumines and purges the soul from its ignorances) here called by the soul a dark night? To this the answer is that for two reasons this Divine wisdom is not only night and darkness for the soul, but is likewise affliction and torment. The first is because of the height of Divine Wisdom, which transcends the talent of the soul, and in this way is darkness to it; the second, because of its vileness and impurity, in which respect it is painful and afflictive to it, and is also dark.

In order to prove the first point, we must here assume a certain doctrine of the philosopher, which says that, the clearer and more manifest are Divine things in themselves the darker and more hidden are they to the soul naturally; just as, the clearer is the light, the more it blinds and darkens the pupil of the owl, and, the more directly we look at the sun, the greater is the darkness which it causes in our visual faculty, overcoming and overwhelming it through its own weakness. In the same way, when this Divine light of contemplation assails the soul which is not yet wholly enlightened, it causes spiritual darkness in it; for not only does it overcome it, but likewise it overwhelms it and darkens the act of its natural intelligence. For this reason Saint Dionysius and other mystical theologians call this infused contemplation a ray of darkness—that is to say, for the soul that is not enlightened and purged—for the natural strength of the intellect is transcended and overwhelmed by its great supernatural light. Wherefore David likewise said: That near to God and round about Him are darkness and cloud;[108] not that this is so in fact, but that it is so to our weak understanding, which is blinded and darkened by so vast a light, to which it cannot attain.[109] For this cause the same David then explained himself, saying: 'Through the great splendour of His presence passed clouds'[110]—that is, between God and our understanding. And it is for this cause that, when God sends it out from Himself to the soul that is not yet transformed, this illumining ray of His secret wisdom causes thick darkness in the understanding.

And it is clear that this dark contemplation is in these its beginnings painful likewise to the soul; for, as this Divine infused contemplation has many excellences that are extremely good, and the soul that receives them, not being purged, has many miseries that are likewise extremely bad, hence it follows that, as two contraries cannot coexist in one subject—the soul—it must of necessity have pain and suffering, since it is the subject wherein these two contraries war against each other, working the one against the other, by reason of the purgation of the imperfections of the soul which comes to pass through this contemplation. This we shall prove inductively in the manner following.

In the first place, because the light and wisdom of this contemplation is most bright and pure, and the soul which it assails is dark and impure, it follows that the soul suffers great pain when it receives it in itself, just as, when the eyes are dimmed by humours, and become impure and weak, the assault made upon them by a bright light causes them pain. And when the soul suffers the direct assault of this Divine light, its pain, which results from its impurity, is immense; because, when this pure light assails the soul, in order to expel its impurity, the soul feels itself to be so impure and miserable that it believes God to be against it, and thinks that it has set itself up against God. This causes it sore grief and pain, because it now believes that God has cast it away: this was one of the greatest trials which Job felt when God sent him this experience, and he said: 'Why hast Thou set me contrary to Thee, so that I am grievous and burdensome to myself?'[111] For, by means of this pure light, the soul now sees its impurity clearly (although darkly), and knows clearly that it is unworthy of God or of any creature. And what gives it most pain is that it thinks that it will never be worthy and that its good things are all over for it. This is caused by the profound immersion of its spirit in the knowledge and realization of its evils and miseries; for this Divine and dark light now reveals them all to the eye, that it may see clearly how in its own strength it can never have aught else. In this sense we may understand that passage from David, which says: 'For iniquity Thou hast corrected man and hast made his soul to be undone and consumed: he wastes away as the spider.'[112]

The second way in which the soul suffers pain is by reason of its weakness, natural, moral and spiritual; for, when this Divine contemplation assails the soul with a certain force, in order to strengthen it and subdue it, it suffers such pain in its weakness that it nearly swoons away. This is especially so at certain times when it is assailed with somewhat greater force; for sense and spirit, as if beneath some immense and dark load, are in such great pain and agony that the soul would find advantage and relief in death. This had been experienced by the prophet Job, when he said: 'I desire not that He should have intercourse with me in great strength, lest He oppress me with the weight of His greatness.'[113]

Beneath the power of this oppression and weight the soul feels itself so far from being favoured that it thinks, and correctly so, that even that wherein it was wont to find some help has vanished with everything else, and that there is none who has pity upon it. To this effect Job says likewise: 'Have pity upon me, have pity upon me, at least ye my friends, because the hand of the Lord has touched me.'[114] A thing of great wonder and pity is it that the soul's weakness and impurity should now be so great that, though the hand of God is of itself so light and gentle, the soul should now feel it to be so heavy and so contrary,[115] though it neither weighs it down nor rests upon it, but only touches it, and that mercifully, since He does this in order to grant the soul favours and not to chastise it.

Chapter VI

Of other kinds of pain that the soul suffers in this night.

The third kind of suffering and pain that the soul endures in this state results from the fact that two other extremes meet here in one, namely, the Divine and the human. The Divine is this purgative contemplation, and the human is the subject—that is, the soul. The Divine assails the soul in order to renew it and thus to make it Divine; and, stripping it of the habitual affections and attachments of the old man, to which it is very closely united, knit together and conformed, destroys and consumes its spiritual substance, and absorbs it in deep and profound darkness. As a result of this, the soul feels itself to be perishing and melting away, in the presence and sight of its miseries, in a cruel spiritual death, even as if it had been swallowed by a beast and felt itself being devoured in the darkness of its belly, suffering such anguish as was endured by Jonas in the belly of that beast of the sea.[116] For in this sepulchre of dark death it must needs abide until the spiritual resurrection which it hopes for.

A description of this suffering and pain, although in truth it transcends all description, is given by David, when he says: 'The lamentations of death compassed me about; the pains of hell surrounded me; I cried in my tribulation.'[117] But what the sorrowful soul feels most in this condition is its clear perception, as it thinks, that God has abandoned it, and, in His abhorrence of it, has flung it into darkness; it is a grave and piteous grief for it to believe that God has forsaken it. It is this that David also felt so much in a like case, saying: 'After the manner wherein the wounded are dead in the sepulchres,' being now cast off by Thy hand, so that Thou rememberest them no more, even so have they set me in the deepest and lowest lake, in the dark places and in the shadow of death, and Thy fury is confirmed upon me and all Thy waves Thou hast brought in upon me.'[118] For indeed, when this purgative contemplation is most severe, the soul feels very keenly the shadow of death and the lamentations of death and the pains of hell, which consist in its feeling itself to be without God, and chastised and cast out, and unworthy of Him; and it feels that He is wroth with it. All this is felt by the soul in this condition—yea, and more, for it believes that it is so with it for ever.

It feels, too, that all creatures have forsaken it, and that it is contemned by them, particularly by its friends. Wherefore David presently continues, saying: 'Thou hast put far from me my friends and acquaintances; they have counted me an abomination.'[119] To all this will Jonas testify, as one who likewise experienced it in the belly of the beast, both bodily and spiritually. 'Thou hast cast me forth (he says) into the deep, into the heart of the sea, and the flood hath compassed me; all its billows and waves have passed over me. And I said, "I am cast away out of the sight of Thine eyes, but I shall once again see Thy holy temple" (which he says, because God purifies the soul in this state that it may see His temple); the waters compassed me, even to the soul, the deep hath closed me round about, the ocean hath covered my head, I went down to the lowest parts of the mountains; the bars of the earth have shut me up for ever.'[120] By these bars are here understood, in this sense, imperfections of the soul, which have impeded it from enjoying this delectable contemplation.

The fourth kind of pain is caused in the soul by another excellence of this dark contemplation, which is its majesty and greatness, from which arises in the soul a consciousness of the other extreme which is in itself—namely, that of the deepest poverty and wretchedness: this is one of the chiefest pains that it suffers in this purgation. For it feels within itself a profound emptiness and impoverishment of three kinds of good, which are ordained for the pleasure of the soul which are the temporal, the natural and the spiritual; and finds itself set in the midst of the evils contrary to these, namely, miseries of imperfection, aridity and emptiness of the apprehensions of the faculties and abandonment of the spirit in darkness. Inasmuch as God here purges the soul according to the substance of its sense and spirit, and according to the interior and exterior faculties, the soul must needs be in all its parts reduced to a state of emptiness, poverty and abandonment and must be left dry and empty and in darkness. For the sensual part is purified in aridity, the faculties are purified in the emptiness of their perceptions and the spirit is purified in thick darkness.

All this God brings to pass by means of this dark contemplation; wherein the soul not only suffers this emptiness and the suspension of these natural supports and perceptions, which is a most afflictive suffering (as if a man were suspended or held in the air so that he could not breathe), but likewise He is purging the soul, annihilating it, emptying it or consuming in it (even as fire consumes the mouldiness and the rust of metal) all the affections and imperfect habits which it has contracted in its whole life. Since these are deeply rooted in the substance of the soul, it is wont to suffer great undoings and inward torment, besides the said poverty and emptiness, natural and spiritual, so that there may here be fulfilled that passage from Ezechiel which says: 'Heap together the bones and I will burn them in the fire; the flesh shall be consumed and the whole composition shall be burned and the bones shall be destroyed.'[121] Herein is understood the pain which is suffered in the emptiness and poverty of the substance of the soul both in sense and in spirit. And concerning this he then says: 'Set it also empty upon the coals, that its metal may become hot and molten, and its uncleanness may be destroyed within it, and its rust may be consumed.'[122] Herein is described the grave suffering which the soul here endures in the purgation of the fire of this contemplation, for the Prophet says here that, in order for the rust of the affections which are within the soul to be purified and destroyed, it is needful that, in a certain manner, the soul itself should be annihilated and destroyed, since these passions and imperfections have become natural to it.

Wherefore, because the soul is purified in this furnace like gold in a crucible, as says the Wise Man,[123] it is conscious of this complete undoing of itself in its very substance, together with the direst poverty, wherein it is, as it were, nearing its end, as may be seen by that which David says of himself in this respect, in these words: 'Save me, Lord (he cries to God), for the waters have come in even unto my soul; I am made fast in the mire of the deep and there is no place where I can stand; I am come into the depth of the sea and a tempest hath overwhelmed me; I have laboured crying, my throat has become hoarse, mine eyes have failed whilst I hope in my God.'[124] Here God greatly humbles the soul in order that He may afterwards greatly exalt it; and if He ordained not that, when these feelings arise within the soul, they should speedily be stilled, it would die in a very short space;

but there are only occasional periods when it is conscious of their greatest intensity. At times, however, they are so keen that the soul seems to be seeing hell and perdition opened. Of such are they that in truth go down alive into hell, being purged here on earth in the same manner as there, since this purgation is that which would have to be accomplished there. And thus the soul that passes through this either enters not that place[125] at all, or tarries there but for a very short time; for one hour of purgation here is more profitable than are many there.

Chapter VII

Continues the same matter and considers other afflictions end constraints of the will.

The afflictions and constraints of the will are now very great likewise, and of such a kind that they sometimes transpierce the soul with a sudden remembrance of the evils in the midst of which it finds itself, and with the uncertainty of finding a remedy for them. And to this is added the remembrance of times of prosperity now past; for as a rule souls that enter this night have had many consolations from God, and have rendered Him many services, and it causes them the greater grief to see that they are far removed from that happiness and unable to enter into it. This was also described by Job, who had had experience of it, in these words: 'I, who was wont to be wealthy and rich, am suddenly undone and broken to pieces; He hath taken me by my neck; He hath broken me and set me up for His mark to wound me; He hath compassed me round about with His lances; He hath wounded all my loins; He hath not spared; He hath poured out my bowels on the earth; He hath broken me with wound upon wound; He hath assailed me as a strong giant; I have sewed sackcloth upon my skin and have covered my flesh with ashes; my face is become swollen with weeping and mine eyes are blinded.'[126]

So many and so grievous are the afflictions of this night, and so many passages of Scripture are there which could be cited to this purpose, that time and strength would fail us to write of them, for all that can be said thereof is certainly less than the truth. From the passages already quoted some idea may be gained of them. And, that we may bring the exposition of this line to a close and explain more fully what is worked in the soul by this night, I shall tell what Jeremias felt about it, which, since there is so much of it, he describes and bewails in many words after this manner: 'I am the man that see my poverty in the rod of His indignation; He hath threatened me and brought me into darkness and not into light. So far hath He turned against me and hath converted His hand upon me all the day! My skin and my flesh hath He made old; He hath broken my bones; He hath made a fence around me and compassed me with gall and trial; He hath set me in dark places, as those that are dead for ever. He hath made a fence around me and against me, that I may not go out; He hath made my captivity heavy. Yea, and when I have cried and have entreated, He hath shut out my prayer. He hath enclosed my paths and ways out with square stones; He hath thwarted my steps. He hath set ambushes for me; He hath become to me a lion in a secret place. He hath turned aside my steps and broken me in pieces, He hath made me desolate; He hath bent His bow and set me as a mark for His arrow. He hath shot into my reins the daughters of His quiver. I have become a derision to all the people, and laughter and scorn for them all the day. He hath filled me with bitterness and hath made me drunken with wormwood. He hath broken my teeth by number; He hath fed me with ashes. My soul is cast out from peace; I have forgotten good things. And I said: "Mine end is frustrated and cut short, together with my desire and my hope from the Lord. Remember my poverty and my excess, the wormwood and the gall. I shall be mindful with remembrance and my soul shall be undone within me in pains.'"[127]

All these complaints Jeremias makes about these pains and trials, and by means of them he most vividly depicts the sufferings of the soul in this spiritual night and purgation. Wherefore the soul that God sets in this tempestuous and horrible night is deserving of great compassion. For, although it experiences much happiness by reason of the great blessings that must arise on this account within it, when, as Job says, God raises up profound blessings in the soul out of darkness, and brings up to light the shadow of death,[128] so that, as David says, His light comes to be as was His darkness;[129] yet notwithstanding, by reason of the dreadful pain which the soul is suffering, and of the great uncertainty which it has concerning the remedy for it, since it believes, as this prophet says here, that its evil will never end, and it thinks, as David says likewise, that God set it in dark places like those that are dead,[130] and for this reason brought its spirit within it into anguish and troubled its heart,[131] it suffers great pain and grief, since there is added to all this (because of the solitude and abandonment caused in it by this dark night) the fact that it finds no consolation or support in any instruction nor in a spiritual master. For, although in many ways its director may show it good reason for being comforted because of the blessings which are contained in these afflictions, it cannot believe him. For it is so greatly absorbed and immersed in the realization of those evils wherein it sees its own miseries so clearly, that it thinks that, as its director observes not that which it sees and feels, he is speaking in this manner because he understands it not; and so, instead of comfort, it rather receives fresh affliction, since it believes that its director's advice contains no remedy for its troubles. And, in truth, this is so; for, until the Lord shall have completely purged it after the manner that He wills, no means or remedy is of any service or profit for the relief of its affliction; the more so because the soul is as powerless in this case as one who has been imprisoned in a dark dungeon, and is bound hand and foot, and can neither move nor see, nor feel any favour whether from above or from below, until the spirit is humbled, softened and purified, and grows so keen and delicate and pure that it can become one with the Spirit of God, according to the degree of union of love which His mercy is pleased to grant it; in proportion to this the purgation is of greater or less severity and of greater or less duration.

But, if it is to be really effectual, it will last for some years, however severe it be; since the purgative process allows intervals of relief wherein, by the dispensation of God, this dark contemplation ceases to assail the soul in the form and manner of purgation, and assails it after an illuminative and a loving manner, wherein the soul, like one that has gone forth from this dungeon and imprisonment, and is brought into the recreation of spaciousness and liberty, feels and experiences great sweetness of peace and loving friendship with God, together with a ready abundance of spiritual communication. This is to the soul a sign of the health which is being wrought within it by the said purgation and a foretaste of the abundance for which it hopes. Occasionally this is so great that the soul believes its trials to be at last over. For spiritual things in the soul, when they are most purely spiritual, have this characteristic that, if trials come to it, the soul believes that it will never escape from them, and that all its blessings are now over, as has been seen in the passages quoted; and, if spiritual blessings come, the soul believes in the same way that its troubles are now over, and that blessings will never fail it. This was so with David, when he found himself in the midst of them, as he confesses in these words: 'I said in my abundance: "I shall never be moved."'[132]

This happens because the actual possession by the spirit of one of two contrary things itself makes impossible the actual possession and realization of the other contrary thing; this is not so, however, in the sensual part of the soul, because its apprehension is weak. But, as the spirit is not yet completely purged and cleansed from the affections that it has contracted from its lower part, while changing not in so far as it is spirit, it can be moved to further afflictions in so far as these affections sway it. In this way, as we see, David was afterwards moved, and experienced many ills and afflictions, although in the time of his abundance he had thought and said that he would never be moved. Just so is it with the soul in this condition, when it sees itself moved by that abundance of spiritual blessings, and, being unable to see the root of the imperfection and impurity which still remain within it, thinks that its trials are over.

This thought, however, comes to the soul but seldom, for, until spiritual purification is complete and perfected, the sweet communication is very rarely so abundant as to conceal from the soul the root which remains hidden, in such a way that the soul can cease to feel that there is something that it lacks within itself or that it has still to do. Thus it cannot completely enjoy that relief, but feels as if one of its enemies were within it, and although this enemy is, as it were, hushed and asleep, it fears that he will come to life again and attack it.[133] And this is what indeed happens, for, when the soul is most secure and least alert, it is dragged down and immersed again in another and a worse degree of affliction which is severer and darker and more grievous than that which is past; and this new affliction will continue for a further period of time, perhaps longer than the first. And the soul once more comes to believe that all its blessings are over for ever. Although it had thought during its first trial that there were no more afflictions which it could suffer, and yet, after the trial was over, it enjoyed great blessings, this experience is not sufficient to take away its belief, during this second degree of trial, that all is now over for it and that it will never again be happy as in the past. For, as I say, this belief, of which the soul is so sure, is caused in it by the actual apprehension of the spirit, which annihilates within it all that is contrary to it.

This is the reason why those who lie in purgatory suffer great misgivings as to whether they will ever go forth from it and whether their pains will ever be over. For, although they have the habit of the three theological virtues—faith, hope and charity—the present realization which they have of their afflictions and of their deprivation of God allows them not to enjoy the present blessing and consolation of these virtues. For, although they are able to realize that they have a great love for God, this is no consolation to them, since they cannot think that God loves them or that they are worthy that He should do so; rather, as they see that they are deprived of Him, and left in their own miseries, they think that there is that in themselves which provides a very good reason why they should with perfect justice be abhorred and cast out by God for ever.[134] And thus although the soul in this purgation is conscious that it has a great love for God and would give a thousand lives for Him (which is the truth, for in these trials such souls love their God very earnestly), yet this is no relief to it, but rather brings it greater affliction. For it loves Him so much that it cares about naught beside; when, therefore, it sees itself to be so wretched that it cannot believe that God loves it, nor that there is or will ever be reason why He should do so, but rather that there is reason why it should be abhorred, not only by Him, but by all creatures for ever, it is grieved to see in itself reasons for deserving to be cast out by Him for Whom it has such great love and desire.

Chapter VIII

Of other pains which afflict the soul in this state.

But there is another thing here that afflicts and distresses the soul greatly, which is that, as this dark night has hindered its faculties and affections in this way, it is unable to raise its affection or its mind to God, neither can it pray to Him, thinking, as Jeremias thought concerning himself, that God has set a cloud before it through which its prayer cannot pass.[135] For it is this that is meant by that which is said in the passage referred to, namely: 'He hath shut and enclosed my paths with square stones.'[136] And if it sometimes prays it does so with such lack of strength and of sweetness that it thinks that God neither hears it nor pays heed to it, as this Prophet likewise declares in the same passage, saying: 'When I cry and entreat, He hath shut out my prayer.'[137] In truth this is no time for the soul to speak with God; it should rather put its mouth in the dust, as Jeremias says, so that perchance there may come to it some present hope,[138] and it may endure its purgation with patience. It is God Who is passively working here in the soul; wherefore the soul can do nothing. Hence it can neither pray nor pay attention when it is present at the Divine offices,[139] much less can it attend to other things and affairs which are temporal. Not only so, but it has likewise such distractions and times of such profound forgetfulness of the memory that frequent periods pass by without its knowing what it has been doing or thinking, or what it is that it is doing or is going to do, neither can it pay attention, although it desire to do so, to anything that occupies it.

Inasmuch as not only is the understanding here purged of its light, and the will of its affections, but the memory is also purged of meditation and knowledge, it is well that it be likewise annihilated with respect to all these things, so that that which David says of himself in this purgation may by fulfilled, namely: 'I was annihilated and I knew not.'[140] This unknowing refers to these follies and forgetfulnesses of the memory, which distractions and forgetfulnesses are caused by the interior recollection wherein this contemplation absorbs the soul. For, in order that the soul may be divinely prepared and tempered with its faculties for the Divine union of love, it would be well for it to be first of all absorbed, with all its faculties, in this Divine and dark spiritual light of contemplation, and thus to be withdrawn from all the affections and apprehensions of the creatures, which condition ordinarily continues in proportion to its intensity. And thus, the simpler and the purer is this Divine light in its assault upon the soul, the more does it darken it, void it and annihilate it according to its particular apprehensions and affections, with regard both to things above and to things below; and similarly, the less simple and pure is it in this assault, the less deprivation it causes it and the less dark is it. Now this is a thing that seems incredible, to say that, the brighter and purer is supernatural and Divine light, the more it darkens the soul, and that, the less bright and pure is it, the less dark it is to the soul. Yet this may readily be understood if we consider what has been proved above by the dictum of the philosopher—namely, that the brighter and the more manifest in themselves are supernatural things the darker are they to our understanding.

And, to the end that this may be understood the more clearly, we shall here set down a similitude referring to common and natural light. We observe that a ray of sunlight which enters through the window is the less clearly visible according as it is the purer and freer from specks, and the more of such specks and motes there are in the air, the brighter is the light to the eye. The reason is that it is not the light itself that is seen; the light is but the means whereby the other things that it strikes are seen, and then it is also seen itself, through its reflection in them; were it not for this, neither it nor they would have been seen. Thus if the ray of sunlight entered through the window of one room and passed out through another on the other side, traversing the room, and if it met nothing on the way, or if there were no specks in the air for it to strike, the room would have no more light than before, neither would the ray of light be visible. In fact, if we consider it carefully, there is more darkness where the ray is, since it absorbs and obscures any other light, and yet it is itself invisible, because, as we have said, there are no visible objects which it can strike.

Now this is precisely what this Divine ray of contemplation does in the soul. Assailing it with its Divine light, it transcends the natural power of the soul, and herein it darkens it and deprives it of all natural affections and apprehensions which it apprehended aforetime by means of natural light; and thus it leaves it not only dark, but likewise empty, according to its faculties and desires, both spiritual and natural. And, by thus leaving it empty and in darkness, it purges and illumines it with Divine spiritual light, although the soul thinks not that it has this light, but believes itself to be in darkness, even as we have said of the ray of light, which although it be in the midst of the room, yet, if it be pure and meet nothing on its path, is not visible. With regard, however, to this spiritual light by which the soul is assailed, when it has something to strike—that is, when something spiritual presents itself to be understood, however small a speck it be and whether of perfection or imperfection, or whether it be a judgment of the falsehood or the truth of a thing—it then sees and understands much more clearly than before it was in these dark places. And exactly in the same way it discerns the spiritual light which it has in order that it may readily discern the imperfection which is presented to it; even as, when the ray of which we have spoken, within the room, is dark and not itself visible, if one introduce a hand or any other thing into its path, the hand is then seen and it is realized that that sunlight is present.

Wherefore, since this spiritual light is so simple, pure and general, not appropriated or restricted to any particular thing that can be understood, whether natural or Divine (since with respect to all these apprehensions the faculties of the soul are empty and annihilated), it follows that with great comprehensiveness and readiness the soul discerns and penetrates whatsoever thing presents itself to it, whether it come from above or from below; for which cause the Apostle said: That the spiritual man searches all things, even the deep things of God.[141] For by this general and simple wisdom is understood that which the Holy Spirit says through the Wise Man, namely:

That it reaches wheresoever it wills by reason of its purity;[142] that is to say, because it is not restricted to any particular object of the intellect or affection. And this is the characteristic of the spirit that is purged and annihilated with respect to all particular affections and objects of the understanding, that in this state wherein it has pleasure in nothing and understands nothing in particular, but dwells in its emptiness, darkness and obscurity, it is fully prepared to embrace everything to the end that those words of Saint Paul may be fulfilled in it: Nihil habentes, et omnia possidentes.[143]For such poverty of spirit as this would deserve such happiness.

Chapter IX

How, although this night brings darkness to the spirit, it does so in order to illumine it and give it light.

It now remains to be said that, although this happy night brings darkness to the spirit, it does so only to give it light in everything; and that, although it humbles it and makes it miserable, it does so only to exalt it and to raise it up; and, although it impoverishes it and empties it of all natural affection and attachment, it does so only that it may enable it to stretch forward, divinely, and thus to have fruition and experience of all things, both above and below, yet to preserve its unrestricted liberty of spirit in them all. For just as the elements, in order that they may have a part in all natural entities and compounds, must have no particular colour, odour or taste, so as to be able to combine with all tastes odours and colours, just so must the spirit be simple, pure and detached from all kinds of natural affection, whether actual or habitual, to the end that it may be able freely to share in the breadth of spirit of the Divine Wisdom, wherein, through its purity, it has experience of all the sweetness of all things in a certain pre-eminently excellent way.[144] And without this purgation it will be wholly unable to feel or experience the satisfaction of all this abundance of spiritual sweetness. For one single affection remaining in the spirit, or one particular thing to which, actually or habitually, it clings, suffices to hinder it from feeling or experiencing or communicating the delicacy and intimate sweetness of the spirit of love, which contains within itself all sweetness to a most eminent degree.[145]

For, even as the children of Israel, solely because they retained one single affection and remembrance—namely, with respect to the fleshpots and the meals which they had tasted in Egypt[146]—could not relish the delicate bread of angels, in the desert, which was the manna, which, as the Divine Scripture says, held sweetness for every taste and turned to the taste that each one desired;[147] even so the spirit cannot succeed in enjoying the delights of the spirit of liberty, according to the desire of the will, if it be still affectioned to any desire, whether actual or habitual, or to particular objects of understanding, or to any other apprehension. The reason for this is that the affections, feelings and apprehensions of the perfect spirit, being Divine, are of another kind and of a very different order from those that are natural. They are pre-eminent, so that, in order both actually and habitually to possess the one, it is needful to expel and annihilate the other, as with two contrary things, which cannot exist together in one person. Therefore it is most fitting and necessary, if the soul is to pass to these great things, that this dark night of contemplation should first of all annihilate and undo it in its meannesses, bringing it into darkness, aridity, affliction and emptiness; for the light which is to be given to it is a Divine light of the highest kind, which transcends all natural light, and which by nature can find no place in the understanding.

And thus it is fitting that, if the understanding is to be united with that light and become Divine in the state of perfection, it should first of all be purged and annihilated as to its natural light, and, by means of this dark contemplation, be brought actually into darkness. This darkness should continue for as long as is needful in order to expel and annihilate the habit which the soul has long since formed in its manner of understanding, and the Divine light and illumination will then take its place. And thus, inasmuch as that power of understanding which it had aforetime is natural, it follows that the darkness which it here suffers is profound and horrible and most painful, for this darkness, being felt in the deepest substance of the spirit, seems to be substantial darkness. Similarly, since the affection of love which is to be given to it in the Divine union of love is Divine, and therefore very spiritual, subtle and delicate, and very intimate, transcending every affection and feeling of the will, and every desire thereof, it is fitting that, in order that the will may be able to attain to this Divine affection and most lofty delight, and to feel it and experience it through the union of love, since it is not, in the way of nature, perceptible to the will, it be first of all purged and annihilated in all its affections and feelings, and left in a condition of aridity and constraint, proportionate to the habit of natural affections which it had before, with respect both to Divine things and to human. Thus, being exhausted, withered and thoroughly tried in the fire of this dark contemplation, and having driven away every kind[148] of evil spirit (as with the heart of the fish which Tobias set on the coals[149]), it may have a simple and pure disposition, and its palate may be purged and healthy, so that it may feel the rare and sublime touches of Divine love, wherein it will see itself divinely transformed, and all the contrarieties, whether actual or habitual, which it had aforetime, will be expelled, as we are saying.

Moreover, in order to attain the said union to which this dark night is disposing and leading it, the soul must be filled and endowed with a certain glorious magnificence in its communion with God, which includes within itself innumerable blessings springing from delights which exceed all the abundance that the soul can naturally possess. For by nature the soul is so weak and impure that it cannot receive all this. As Isaias says: 'Eye hath not seen, nor ear heard, neither hath it entered into the heart of man, that which God hath prepared, etc.'[150] It is meet, then, that the soul be first of all brought into emptiness and poverty of spirit and purged from all help, consolation and natural apprehension with respect to all things, both above and below. In this way, being empty, it is able indeed to be poor in spirit and freed from the old man, in order to live that new and blessed life which is attained by means of this night, and which is the state of union with God.

And because the soul is to attain to the possession of a sense, and of a Divine knowledge, which is very generous and full of sweetness, with respect to things Divine and human, which fall not within the common experience and natural knowledge of the soul (because it looks on them with eyes as different from those of the past as spirit is different from sense and the Divine from the human), the spirit must be straitened[151] and inured to hardships as regards its common and natural experience, and be brought by means of this purgative contemplation into great anguish and affliction, and the memory must be borne far from all agreeable and peaceful knowledge, and have an intimated sense and feeling that it is making a pilgrimage and being a stranger to all things, so that it seems to it that all things are strange and of a different kind from that which they were wont to be. For this night is gradually drawing the spirit away from its ordinary and common experience of things and bringing it nearer the Divine sense, which is a stranger and an alien to all human ways. It seems now to the soul that it is going forth from its very self, with much affliction. At other times it wonders if it is under a charm or a spell, and it goes about marvelling at the things that it sees and hears, which seem to it very strange and rare, though they are the same that it was accustomed to experience aforetime. The reason of this is that the soul is now becoming alien and remote from common sense and knowledge of things, in order that, being annihilated in this respect, it may be informed with the Divine—which belongs rather to the next life than to this.

The soul suffers all these afflictive purgations of the spirit to the end that it may be begotten anew in spiritual life by means of this Divine inflowing, and in these pangs may bring forth the spirit of salvation, that the saying of Isaias may be fulfilled: 'In Thy sight, O Lord, we have conceived, and we have been as in the pangs of labour, and we have brought forth the spirit of salvation.'[152] Moreover, since by means of this contemplative night the soul is prepared for the attainment of inward peace and tranquillity, which is of such a kind and so delectable that, as the Scripture says, it passes all understanding,[153] it behoves the soul to abandon all its former peace. This was in reality no peace at all, since it was involved in imperfections; but to the soul aforementioned it appeared to be so, because it was following its own inclinations, which were for peace. It seemed, indeed, to be a twofold peace—that is, the soul believed that it had already acquired the peace of sense and that of spirit, for it found itself to be full of the spiritual abundance of this peace of sense and of spirit—as I say, it is still imperfect. First of all, then, it must be purged of that former peace and disquieted concerning it and withdrawn from it.[154] Even so was Jeremias when, in the passage which we quoted from him, he felt and lamented[155] thus, in order to express the calamities of this night that is past, saying: 'My soul is withdrawn and removed from peace.'[156]

This is a painful disturbance, involving many misgivings, imaginings, and strivings which the soul has within itself, wherein, with the apprehension and realization of the miseries in which it sees itself, it fancies that it is lost and that its blessings have gone for ever. Wherefore the spirit experiences pain and sighing so deep that they cause it vehement spiritual groans and cries, to which at times it gives vocal expression; when it has the necessary strength and power it dissolves into tears, although this relief comes but seldom. David describes this very aptly, in a Psalm, as one who has had experience of it, where he says: 'I was exceedingly afflicted and humbled; I roared with the groaning of my heart.'[157] This roaring implies great pain; for at times, with the sudden and acute remembrance of these miseries wherein the soul sees itself, pain and affliction rise up and surround it, and I know not how the affections of the soul could be described[158] save in the similitude of holy Job, when he was in the same trials, and uttered these words: 'Even as the overflowing of the waters, even so is my roaring.'[159] For just as at times the waters make such inundations that they overwhelm and fill everything, so at times this roaring and this affliction of the soul grow to such an extent that they overwhelm it and penetrate it completely, filling it with spiritual pain and anguish in all its deep affections and energies, to an extent surpassing all possibility of exaggeration.

Such is the work wrought in the soul by this night that hides the hopes of the light of day. With regard to this the prophet Job says likewise: 'In the night my mouth is pierced with sorrows and they that feed upon me sleep not.'[160] Now here by the mouth is understood the will, which is transpierced with these pains that tear the soul to pieces, neither ceasing nor sleeping, for the doubts and misgivings which transpierce the soul in this way never cease.

Deep is this warfare and this striving, for the peace which the soul hopes for will be very deep; and the spiritual pain is intimate and delicate, for the love which it will possess will likewise be very intimate and refined. The more intimate and the more perfect the finished work is to be and to remain, the more intimate, perfect and pure must be the labour; the firmer the edifice, the harder the labour. Wherefore, as Job says, the soul is fading within itself, and its vitals are being consumed without any hope.[161] Similarly, because in the state of perfection toward which it journeys by means of this purgative night the soul will attain to the possession and fruition of innumerable blessings, of gifts and virtues, both according to the substance of the soul and likewise according to its faculties, it must needs see and feel itself withdrawn from them all and deprived of them all and be empty and poor without them; and it must needs believe itself to be so far from them that it cannot persuade itself that it will ever reach them, but rather it must be convinced that all its good things are over. The words of Jeremias have a similar meaning in that passage already quoted, where he says: 'I have forgotten good things.'[162]

But let us now see the reason why this light of contemplation, which is so sweet and blessed to the soul that there is naught more desirable (for, as has been said above, it is the same wherewith the soul must be united and wherein it must find all the good things in the state of perfection that it desires), produces, when it assails the soul, these beginnings which are so painful and these effects which are so disagreeable, as we have here said.

This question is easy for us to answer, by explaining, as we have already done in part, that the cause of this is that, in contemplation and the Divine inflowing, there is naught that of itself can cause affliction, but that they rather cause great sweetness and delight, as we shall say hereafter. The cause is rather the weakness and imperfection from which the soul then suffers, and the dispositions which it has in itself and which make it unfit for the reception of them. Wherefore, when the said Divine light assails the soul, it must needs cause it to suffer after the manner aforesaid.

Chapter X

Explains this purgation fully by a comparison.

For the greater clearness of what has been said, and of what has still to be said, it is well to observe at this point that this purgative and loving knowledge or Divine light whereof we here speak acts upon the soul which it is purging and preparing for perfect union with it in the same way as fire acts upon a log of wood in order to transform it into itself; for material fire, acting upon wood, first of all begins to dry it, by driving out its moisture and causing it to shed the water which it contains within itself. Then it begins to make it black, dark and unsightly, and even to give forth a bad odour, and, as it dries it little by little, it brings out and drives away all the dark and unsightly accidents which are contrary to the nature of fire. And, finally, it begins to kindle it externally and give it heat, and at last transforms it into itself and makes it as beautiful as fire. In this respect, the wood has neither passivity nor activity of its own, save for its weight, which is greater, and its substance, which is denser, than that of fire, for it has in itself the properties and activities of fire. Thus it is dry and it dries; it is hot and heats; it is bright and gives brightness; and it is much less heavy than before. All these properties and effects are caused in it by the fire.

In this same way we have to philosophize with respect to this Divine fire of contemplative love, which, before it unites and transforms the soul in itself, first purges it of all its contrary accidents. It drives out its unsightliness, and makes it black and dark, so that it seems worse than before and more unsightly and abominable than it was wont to be. For this Divine purgation is removing all the evil and vicious humours which the soul has never perceived because they have been so deeply rooted and grounded in it; it has never realized, in fact, that it has had so much evil within itself. But now that they are to be driven forth and annihilated, these humours reveal themselves, and become visible to the soul because it is so brightly illumined by this dark light of Divine contemplation (although it is no worse than before, either in itself or in relation to God); and, as it sees in itself that which it saw not before, it is clear to it that not only is it unfit to be seen by God, but deserves His abhorrence, and that He does indeed abhor it. By this comparison we can now understand many things concerning what we are saying and purpose to say.

First, we can understand how the very light and the loving wisdom which are to be united with the soul and to transform it are the same that at the beginning purge and prepare it: even as the very fire which transforms the log of wood into itself, and makes it part of itself, is that which at the first was preparing it for that same purpose.

Secondly, we shall be able to see how these afflictions are not felt by the soul as coming from the said Wisdom, since, as the Wise Man says, all good things together come to the soul with her.[163] They are felt as coming from the weakness and imperfection which belong to the soul; without such purgation, the soul cannot receive its Divine light, sweetness and delight, even as the log of wood, when the fire acts upon it, cannot immediately be transformed until it be made ready; wherefore the soul is greatly afflicted. This statement is fully supported by the Preacher, where he describes all that he suffered in order that he might attain to union with wisdom and to the fruition of it, saying thus: 'My soul hath wrestled with her and my bowels were moved in acquiring her; therefore it shall possess a good possession.'[164]

Thirdly, we can learn here incidentally in what manner souls are afflicted in purgatory. For the fire would have no power over them, even though they came into contact with it, if they had no imperfections for which to suffers. These are the material upon which the fire of purgatory seizes; when that material is consumed there is naught else that can burn. So here, when the imperfections are consumed, the affliction of the soul ceases and its fruition remains.

The fourth thing that we shall learn here is the manner wherein the soul, as it becomes purged and purified by means of this fire of love, becomes ever more enkindled in love, just as the wood grows hotter in proportion as it becomes the better prepared by the fire. This enkindling of love, however, is not always felt by the soul, but only at times when contemplation assails it less vehemently, for then it has occasion to see, and even to enjoy, the work which is being wrought in it, and which is then revealed to it. For it seems that the worker takes his hand from the work, and draws the iron out of the furnace, in order that something of the work which is being done may be seen; and then there is occasion for the soul to observe in itself the good which it saw not while the work was going on. In the same way, when the flame ceases to attack the wood, it is possible to see how much of it has been enkindled.

Fifthly, we shall also learn from this comparison what has been said above—namely, how true it is that after each of these periods of relief the soul suffers once again, more intensely and keenly than before. For, after that revelation just referred to has been made, and after the more outward imperfections of the soul have been purified, the fire of love once again attacks that which has yet to be consumed and purified more inwardly. The suffering of the soul now becomes more intimate, subtle and spiritual, in proportion as the fire refines away the finer,[165] more intimate and more spiritual imperfections, and those which are most deeply rooted in its inmost parts. And it is here just as with the wood, upon which the fire, when it begins to penetrate it more deeply, acts with more force and vehemence[166] in preparing its most inward part to possess it.

Sixthly, we shall likewise learn here the reason why it seems to the soul that all its good is over, and that it is full of evil, since naught comes to it at this time but bitterness; it is like the burning wood, which is touched by no air nor by aught else than by consuming fire. But, when there occur other periods of relief like the first, the rejoicing of the soul will be more interior because the purification has been more interior also.

Seventhly, we shall learn that, although the soul has the most ample joy at these periods (so much so that, as we said, it sometimes thinks that its trials can never return again, although it is certain that they will return quickly), it cannot fail to realize, if it is aware (and at times it is made aware) of a root of imperfection which remains, that its joy is incomplete, because a new assault seems to be threatening it;[167] when this is so, the trial returns quickly. Finally, that which still remains to be purged and enlightened most inwardly cannot well be concealed from the soul in view of its experience of its former purification;[168] even as also in the wood it is the most inward part that remains longest unkindled,[169] and the difference between it and that which has already been purged is clearly perceptible; and, when this purification once more assails it most inwardly, it is no wonder if it seems to the soul once more that all its good is gone, and that it never expects to experience it again, for, now that it has been plunged into these most inward sufferings, all good coming from without is over.[170]

Keeping this comparison, then, before our eyes, together with what has already been said upon the first line of the first stanza concerning this dark night and its terrible properties, it will be well to leave these sad experiences of the soul and to begin to speak of the fruit of its tears and their blessed properties, whereof the soul begins to sing from this second line:

Kindled in love[171] with yearnings,

Chapter XI

Begins to explain the second line of the first stanza. Describes how, as the fruit of these rigorous constraints, the soul finds itself with the vehement passion of Divine love.

In this line the soul describes the fire of love which, as we have said, like the material fire acting upon the wood, begins to take hold upon the soul in this night of painful contemplation. This enkindling now described, although in a certain way it resembles that which we described above as coming to pass in the sensual part of the soul, is in some ways as different from that other as is the soul from the body, or the spiritual part from the sensual. For this present kind is an enkindling of spiritual love in the soul, which, in the midst of these dark confines, feels itself to be keenly and sharply wounded in strong Divine love, and to have a certain realization and foretaste of God, although it understands nothing definitely, for, as we say, the understanding is in darkness.

The spirit feels itself here to be deeply and passionately in love, for this spiritual enkindling produces the passion of love. And, inasmuch as this love is infused, it is passive rather than active, and thus it begets in the soul a strong passion of love. This love has in it something of union with God, and thus to some degree partakes of its properties, which are actions of God rather than of the soul, these being subdued within it passively. What the soul does here is to give its consent; the warmth and strength and temper and passion of love—or enkindling, as the soul here calls it—belong[172] only to the love of God, which enters increasingly into union with it. This love finds in the soul more occasion and preparation to unite itself with it and to wound it, according as all the soul's desires are the more recollected,[173] and are the more withdrawn from and disabled for the enjoyment of aught either in Heaven or in earth.

This takes place to a great extent, as has already been said, in this dark purgation, for God has so weaned all the inclinations and caused them to be so recollected[174] that they cannot find pleasure in anything they may wish. All this is done by God to the end that, when He withdraws them and recollects them in Himself, the soul may have more strength and fitness to receive this strong union of love of God, which He is now beginning to give it through this purgative way, wherein the soul must love with great strength and with all its desires and powers both of spirit and of sense; which could not be if they were dispersed in the enjoyment of aught else. For this reason David said to God, to the end that he might receive the strength of the love of this union with God: 'I will keep my strength for Thee;'[175] that is, I will keep the entire capacity and all the desires and energies of my faculties, nor will I employ their operation or pleasure in aught else than Thyself.

In this way it can be realized in some measure how great and how strong may be this enkindling of love in the spirit, wherein God keeps in recollection all the energies, faculties and desires of the soul, both of spirit and of sense, so that all this harmony may employ its energies and virtues in this love, and may thus attain to a true fulfilment of the first commandment, which sets aside nothing pertaining to man nor excludes from this love anything that is his, but says: 'Thou shalt love thy God with all thy heart and with all thy mind, with all thy soul and with all thy strength.'[176]

When all the desires and energies of the soul, then, have been recollected in this enkindling of love, and when the soul itself has been touched and wounded in them all, and has been inspired with passion, what shall we understand the movements and digressions of all these energies and desires to be, if they find themselves enkindled and wounded with strong love and without the possession and satisfaction thereof, in darkness and doubt? They will doubtless be suffering hunger, like the dogs of which David speaks as running about the city[177]; finding no satisfaction in this love, they keep howling and groaning. For the touch of this love and Divine fire dries up the spirit and enkindles its desires, in order to satisfy its thirst for this Divine love, so much so that it turns upon itself a thousand times and desires God in a thousand ways and manners, with the eagerness and desire of the appetite. This is very well explained by David in a psalm, where he says: 'My soul thirsted for Thee: in how many manners does my soul long for Thee!'[178]—that is, in desires. And another version reads: 'My soul thirsted for Thee, my soul is lost (or perishes) for Thee.'

It is for this reason that the soul says in this line that it was 'kindled in love with yearnings.'[179] For in all the things and thoughts that it revolves within itself, and in all the affairs and matters that present themselves to it, it loves in many ways, and also desires and suffers in the desire in many ways, at all times and in all places, finding rest in naught, and feeling this yearning in its enkindled wound, even as the prophet Job declares, saying: 'As the hart[180] desireth the shadow, and as the hireling desireth the end of his work, so I also had vain months and numbered to myself wearisome and laborious nights. If I lie down to sleep, I shall say: "When shall I arise?" And then I shall await the evening and shall be full of sorrows even until the darkness of night.'[181] Everything becomes cramping to this soul: it cannot live[182] within itself; it cannot live either in Heaven or on earth; and it is filled with griefs until the darkness comes to which Job here refers, speaking spiritually and in the sense of our interpretation. What the soul here endures is afflictions and suffering without the consolation of a certain hope of any light and spiritual good. Wherefore the yearning and the grief of this soul in this enkindling of love are greater because it is multiplied in two ways: first, by the spiritual darkness wherein it finds itself, which afflicts it with its doubts and misgivings; and then by the love of God, which enkindles and stimulates it, and, with its loving wound, causes it a wondrous fear. These two kinds of suffering at such a season are well described by Isaias, where he says: 'My soul desired Thee in the night'[183]—that is, in misery.

This is one kind of suffering which proceeds from this dark night; but, he goes on to say, with my spirit, in my bowels, until the morning, I will watch for Thee. And this is the second way of grieving in desire and yearning which comes from love in the bowels of the spirit, which are the spiritual affections. But in the midst of these dark and loving afflictions the soul feels within itself a certain companionship and strength, which bears it company and so greatly strengthens it that, if this burden of grievous darkness be taken away, it often feels itself to be alone, empty and weak. The cause of this is that, as the strength and efficacy of the soul were derived and communicated passively from the dark fire of love which assailed it, it follows that, when that fire ceases to assail it, the darkness and power and heat of love cease in the soul.

Chapter XII

Shows how this horrible night is purgatory, and how in it the Divine wisdom illumines men on earth with the same illumination that purges and illumines the angels in Heaven.

From what has been said we shall be able to see how this dark night of loving fire, as it purges in the darkness, so also in the darkness enkindles the soul. We shall likewise be able to see that, even as spirits are purged in the next life with dark material fire, so in this life they are purged and cleansed with the dark spiritual fire of love. The difference is that in the next life they are cleansed with fire, while here below they are cleansed and illumined with love only. It was this love that David entreated, when he said: Cor mundum crea in me, Deus, etc.[184] For cleanness of heart is nothing less than the love and grace of God. For the clean of heart are called by our Saviour 'blessed'; which is as if He had called them 'enkindled with love',[185] since blessedness is given by nothing less than love.

And Jeremias well shows how the soul is purged when it is illumined with this fire of loving wisdom (for God never grants mystical wisdom without love, since love itself infuses it), where he says: 'He hath sent fire into my bones, and hath taught me.'[186] And David says that the wisdom of God is silver tried in fire[187]—that is, in purgative fire of love. For this dark contemplation infuses into the soul love and wisdom jointly, to each one according to his capacity and need, enlightening the soul and purging it, in the words of the Wise Man, from its ignorances, as he said was done to himself.

From this we shall also infer that the very wisdom of God which purges these souls and illumines them purges the angels from their ignorances, giving them knowledge, enlightening them as to that which they knew not, and flowing down from God through the first hierarchies even to the last, and thence to men.[188] All the works, therefore, which are done by the angels, and all their inspirations, are said in the Scriptures, with truth and propriety, to be the work of God and of themselves; for ordinarily these inspirations come through the angels, and they receive them likewise one from another without any delay—as quickly as a ray of sunshine is communicated through many windows arranged in order. For although it is true that the sun's ray itself passes through them all, still each one passes it on and infuses it into the next, in a modified form, according to the nature of the glass, and with rather more or rather less power and brightness, according as it is nearer to the sun or farther from it.

Hence it follows that, the nearer to God are the higher spirits and the lower, the more completely are they purged and enlightened with more general purification; and that the lowest of them will receive this illumination very much less powerfully and more remotely. Hence it follows that man, who is the lowest of all those to whom this loving contemplation flows down continually from God, will, when God desires to give it him, receive it perforce after his own manner in a very limited way and with great pain. For, when the light of God illumines an angel, it enlightens him and enkindles[189] him in love, since, being pure spirit, he is prepared for that infusion. But, when it illumines man, who is impure and weak, it illumines him, as has been said above, according to his nature. It plunges him into darkness and causes him affliction and distress, as does the sun to the eye that is weak;[190] it enkindles him with passionate yet afflictive love, until he be spiritualized and refined by this same fire of love; and it purifies him until he can receive with sweetness the union of this loving infusion after the manner of the angels, being now purged, as by the help of the Lord we shall explain later. But meanwhile he receives this contemplation and loving knowledge in the constraint and yearning of love of which we are here speaking.

This enkindling and yearning of love are not always perceived by the soul. For in the beginning, when this spiritual purgation commences, all this Divine fire is used in drying up and making ready the wood (which is the soul) rather than in giving it heat. But, as time goes on, the fire begins to give heat to the soul, and the soul then very commonly feels this enkindling and heat of love. Further, as the understanding is being more and more purged by means of this darkness, it sometimes comes to pass that this mystical and loving theology, as well as enkindling the will, strikes and illumines the other faculty also—that of the understanding—with a certain Divine light and knowledge, so delectably and delicately that it aids the will to conceive a marvellous fervour, and, without any action of its own, there burns in it this Divine fire of love, in living flames, so that it now appears to the soul a living fire by reason of the living understanding which is given to it. It is of this that David speaks in a Psalm, saying: 'My heart grew hot within me, and, as I meditated, a certain fire was enkindled.'[191]

This enkindling of love, which accompanies the union of these two faculties, the understanding and the will, which are here united, is for the soul a thing of great richness and delight; for it is a certain touch of the Divinity and is already the beginning[192] of the perfection of the union of love for which it hopes. Now the soul attains not to this touch of so sublime a sense and love of God, save when it has passed through many trials and a great part of its purgation. But for other touches which are much lower than these, and which are of ordinary occurrence, so much purgation is not needful.

From what we have said it may here be inferred how in these spiritual blessings, which are passively infused by God into the soul, the will may very well love even though the understanding understand not; and similarly the understanding may understand and the will love not. For, since this dark night of contemplation consists of Divine light and love, just as fire contains light and heat, it is not unbefitting that, when this loving light is communicated, it should strike the will at times more effectively by enkindling it with love and leaving the understanding in darkness instead of striking it with light; and, at other times, by enlightening it with light, and giving it understanding, but leaving the will in aridity (as it is also true that the heat of the fire can be received without the light being seen, and also the light of it can be seen without the reception of heat); and this is wrought by the Lord, Who infuses as He wills.[193]

Chapter XIII

Of other delectable effects which are wrought in the soul by this dark night of contemplation.

This type of enkindling will explain to us certain of the delectable effects which this dark night of contemplation works in the soul. For at certain times, as we have just said, the soul becomes enlightened in the midst of all this darkness, and the light shines in the darkness;[194] this mystical intelligence flows down into the understanding and the will remains in dryness—I mean, without actual union of love, with a serenity and simplicity which are so delicate and delectable to the sense of the soul that no name can be given to them. Thus the presence of God is felt, now after one manner, now after another.

Sometimes, too, as has been said, it wounds the will at the same time, and enkindles love sublimely, tenderly and strongly; for we have already said that at certain times these two faculties, the understanding and the will, are united, when, the more they see, the more perfect and delicate is the purgation of the understanding. But, before this state is reached, it is more usual for the touch of the enkindling of love to be felt in the will than for the touch of intelligence to be felt in the understanding.

But one question arises here, which is this: Why, since these two faculties are being purged together, are the enkindling and the love of purgative contemplation at first more commonly felt in the will than the intelligence thereof is felt in the understanding? To this it may be answered that this passive love does not now directly strike the will, for the will is free, and this enkindling of love is a passion of love rather than the free act of the will; for this heat of love strikes the substance of the soul and thus moves the affections passively. And so this is called passion of love rather than a free act of the will, an act of the will being so called only in so far as it is free. But these passions and affections subdue the will, and therefore it is said that, if the soul conceives passion with a certain affection, the will conceives passion; and this is indeed so, for in this manner the will is taken captive and loses its liberty, according as the impetus and power of its passion carry it away. And therefore we can say that this enkindling of love is in the will—that is, it enkindles the desire of the will; and thus, as we say, this is called passion of love rather than the free work of the will. And, because the receptive passion of the understanding can receive intelligence only in a detached and passive way (and this is impossible without its having been purged), therefore until this happens the soul feels the touch of intelligence less frequently than that of the passion of love. For it is not necessary to this end that the will should be so completely purged with respect to the passions, since these very passions help it to feel impassioned love.

This enkindling and thirst of love, which in this case belongs to the spirit, is very different from that other which we described in writing of the night of sense. For, though the sense has also its part here, since it fails not to participate in the labour of the spirit, yet the source and the keenness of the thirst of love is felt in the superior part of the soul—that is, in the spirit. It feels, and understands what it feels and its lack of what it desires, in such a way that all its affliction of sense, although greater without comparison than in the first night of sense, is as naught to it, because it recognizes within itself the lack of a great good which can in no way be measured.

But here we must note that although, at the beginning, when this spiritual night commences, this enkindling of love is not felt, because this fire of love has not begun to take a hold, God gives the soul, in place of it, an estimative love of Himself so great that, as we have said, the greatest sufferings and trials of which it is conscious in this night are the anguished thoughts that it[195] has lost God and the fears that He has abandoned it. And thus we may always say that from the very beginning of this night the soul is touched with yearnings of love, which is now that of estimation,[196] and now again, that of enkindling. And it is evident that the greatest suffering which it feels in these trials is this misgiving; for, if it could be certified at that time that all is not lost and over, but that what is happening to it is for the best—as it is—and that God is not wroth, it would care naught for all these afflictions, but would rejoice to know that God is making use of them for His good pleasure. For the love of estimation which it has for God is so great, even though it may not realize this and may be in darkness, that it would be glad, not only to suffer in this way, but even to die many times over in order to give Him satisfaction. But when once the flame has enkindled the soul, it is wont to conceive, together with the estimation that it already has for God, such power and energy, and such yearning for Him, when He communicates to it the heat of love, that, with great boldness, it disregards everything and ceases to pay respect to anything, such are the power and the inebriation of love and desire. It regards not what it does, for it would do strange and unusual things in whatever way and manner may present themselves, if thereby its soul might find Him Whom it loves.

It was for this reason that Mary Magdalene, though as greatly concerned for her own appearance as she was aforetime, took no heed of the multitude of men who were at the feast, whether they were of little or of great importance; neither did she consider that it was not seemly, and that it looked ill, to go and weep and shed tears among the guests provided that, without delaying an hour or waiting for another time and season, she could reach Him for love of Whom her soul was already wounded and enkindled. And such is the inebriating power and the boldness of love, that, though she knew her Beloved to be enclosed in the sepulchre by the great sealed stone, and surrounded by soldiers who were guarding Him lest His disciples should steal Him away,[197] she allowed none of these things to impede her, but went before daybreak with the ointments to anoint Him.

And finally, this inebriating power and yearning of love caused her to ask one whom she believed to be a gardener and to have stolen Him away from the sepulchre, to tell her, if he had taken Him, where he had laid Him, that she might take Him away;[198] considering not that such a question, according to independent judgment and reason, was foolish; for it was evident that, if the other had stolen Him, he would not say so, still less would he allow Him to be taken away. It is a characteristic of the power and vehemence of love that all things seem possible to it, and it believes all men to be of the same mind as itself. For it thinks that there is naught wherein one may be employed, or which one may seek, save that which it seeks itself and that which it loves; and it believes that there is naught else to be desired, and naught wherein it may be employed, save that one thing, which is pursued by all. For this reason, when the Bride went out to seek her Beloved, through streets and squares,[199] thinking that all others were doing the same, she begged them that, if they found Him, they would speak to Him and say that she was pining for love of Him.[200] Such was the power of the love of this Mary that she thought that, if the gardener would tell her where he had hidden Him, she would go and take Him away, however difficult it might be made for her.

Of this manner, then, are the yearnings of love whereof this soul becomes conscious when it has made some progress in this spiritual purgation. For it rises up by night (that is, in this purgative darkness) according to the affections of the will. And with the yearnings and vehemence of the lioness or the she-bear going to seek her cubs when they have been taken away from her and she finds them not, does this wounded soul go forth to seek its God. For, being in darkness, it feels itself to be without Him and to be dying of love for Him. And this is that impatient love wherein the soul cannot long subsist without gaining its desire or dying. Such was Rachel's desire for children when she said to Jacob: 'Give me children, else shall I die.'[201]

But we have now to see how it is that the soul which feels itself so miserable and so unworthy of God, here in this purgative darkness, has nevertheless strength, and is sufficiently bold and daring, to journey towards union with God. The reason is that, as love continually gives it strength wherewith it may love indeed, and as the property of love is to desire to be united, joined and made equal and like to the object of its love, that it may perfect itself in love's good things, hence it comes to pass that, when this soul is not perfected in love, through not having as yet attained to union, the hunger and thirst that it has for that which it lacks (which is union) and the strength set by love in the will which has caused it to become impassioned, make it bold and daring by reason of the enkindling of its will, although in its understanding, which is still dark and unenlightened, it feels itself to be unworthy and knows itself to be miserable.

I will not here omit to mention the reason why this Divine light, which is always light to the soul, illumines it not as soon as it strikes it, as it does afterwards, but causes it the darkness and the trials of which we have spoken. Something has already been said concerning this, but the question must now be answered directly. The darkness and the other evils of which the soul is conscious when this Divine light strikes it are not darkness or evils caused by this light, but pertain to the soul itself, and the light illumines it so that it may see them. Wherefore it does indeed receive light from this Divine light; but the soul cannot see at first, by its aid, anything beyond what is nearest to it, or rather, beyond what is within it—namely, its darknesses or its miseries, which it now sees through the mercy of God, and saw not aforetime, because this supernatural light illumined it not. And this is the reason why at first it is conscious of nothing beyond darkness and evil; after it has been purged, however, by means of the knowledge and realization of these, it will have eyes to see, by the guidance of this light, the blessings of the Divine light; and, once all these darknesses and imperfections have been driven out from the soul, it seems that the benefits and the great blessings which the soul is gaining in this blessed night of contemplation become clearer.

From what has been said, it is clear that God grants the soul in this state the favour of purging it and healing it with this strong lye of bitter purgation, according to its spiritual and its sensual part, of all the imperfect habits and affections which it had within itself with respect to temporal things and to natural, sensual and spiritual things, its inward faculties being darkened, and voided of all these, its spiritual and sensual affections being constrained and dried up, and its natural energies being attenuated and weakened with respect to all this (a condition which it could never attain of itself, as we shall shortly say). In this way God makes it to die to all that is not naturally God, so that, once it is stripped and denuded of its former skin, He may begin to clothe it anew. And thus its youth is renewed like the eagle's and it is clothed with the new man, which, as the Apostle says, is created according to God.[202] This is naught else but His illumination of the understanding with supernatural light, so that it is no more a human understanding but becomes Divine through union with the Divine. In the same way the will is informed with Divine love, so that it is a will that is now no less than Divine, nor does it love otherwise than divinely, for it is made and united in one with the Divine will and love. So, too, is it with the memory; and likewise the affections and desires are all changed and converted divinely, according to God. And thus this soul will now be a soul of heaven, heavenly, and more Divine than human. All this, as we have been saying, and because of what we have said, God continues to do and to work in the soul by means of this night, illumining and enkindling it divinely with yearnings for God alone and for naught else whatsoever. For which cause the soul then very justly and reasonably adds the third line to the song, which says:

. . . oh, happy chance!——I went forth without being observed.

Chapter XIV

Wherein are set down and explained the last three lines of the first stanza.

This happy chance was the reason for which the soul speaks, in the next lines, as follows:

I went forth without being observed, My house being now at rest.

It takes the metaphor from one who, in order the better to accomplish something, leaves his house by night and in the dark, when those that are in the house are now at rest, so that none may hinder him. For this soul had to go forth to perform a deed so heroic and so rare—namely to become united with its Divine Beloved—and it had to leave its house, because the Beloved is not found save alone and without, in solitude. It was for this reason that the Bride desired to find Him alone, saying: 'Who would give Thee to me, my brother, that I might find Thee alone, without, and that my love might be communicated to Thee.'[203] It is needful for the enamoured soul, in order to attain to its desired end, to do likewise, going forth at night, when all the domestics in its house are sleeping and at rest—that is, when the low operations, passions and desires of the soul (who are the people of the household) are, because it is night, sleeping and at rest. When these are awake, they invariably hinder the soul from seeking its good, since they are opposed to its going forth in freedom. These are they of whom Our Saviour speaks in the Gospel, saying that they are the enemies of man.[204] And thus it would be meet that their operations and motions should be put to sleep in this night, to the end that they may not hinder the soul from attaining the supernatural blessings of the union of love of God, for, while these are alive and active, this cannot be. For all their work and their natural motions hinder, rather than aid, the soul's reception of the spiritual blessings of the union of love, inasmuch as all natural ability is impotent with respect to the supernatural blessings that God, by means of His own infusion, bestows upon the soul passively, secretly and in silence. And thus it is needful that all the faculties should receive this infusion, and that, in order to receive it, they should remain passive, and not interpose their own base acts and vile inclinations.

It was a happy chance for this soul that on this night God should put to sleep all the domestics in its house—that is, all the faculties, passions, affections and desires which live in the soul, both sensually and spiritually. For thus it went forth 'without being observed'—that is, without being hindered by these affections, etc., for they were put to sleep and mortified in this night, in the darkness of which they were left, that they might not notice or feel anything after their own low and natural manner, and might thus be unable to hinder the soul from going forth from itself and from the house of its sensuality. And thus only could the soul attain to the spiritual union of perfect love of God.

Oh, how happy a chance is this for the soul which can free itself from the house of its sensuality! None can understand it, unless, as it seems to me, it be the soul that has experienced it. For such a soul will see clearly how wretched was the servitude in which it lay and to how many miseries it was subject when it was at the mercy of its faculties and desires, and will know how the life of the spirit is true liberty and wealth, bringing with it inestimable blessings. Some of these we shall point out, as we proceed, in the following stanzas, wherein it will be seen more clearly what good reason the soul has to sing of the happy chance of its passage from this dreadful night which has been described above.

Chapter XV

Sets down the second stanza and its exposition.

In darkness and secure, By the secret ladder, disguised—oh, happy chance! In darkness and concealment, My house being now at rest.

In this stanza the soul still continues to sing of certain properties of the darkness of this night, reiterating how great is the happiness which came to it through them. It speaks of them in replying to a certain tacit objection, saying that it is not to be supposed that, because in this night and darkness it has passed through so many tempests of afflictions, doubts, fears and horrors, as has been said, it has for that reason run any risk of being lost. On the contrary, it says, in the darkness of this night it has gained itself. For in the night it has freed itself and escaped subtly from its enemies, who were continually hindering its progress. For in the darkness of the night it changed its garments and disguised itself with three liveries and colours which we shall describe hereafter; and went forth by a very secret ladder, which none in the house knew, the which ladder, as we shall observe likewise in the proper place, is living faith. By this ladder the soul went forth in such complete hiding and concealment, in order the better to execute its purpose, that it could not fail to be in great security; above all since in this purgative night the desires, affections and passions of the soul are put to sleep, mortified and quenched, which are they that, when they were awake and alive, consented not to this.

The first line, then, runs thus:[205]

In darkness and secure.

Chapter XVI

Explains how, though in darkness, the soul walks securely.

The darkness which the soul here describes relates, as we have said, to the desires and faculties, sensual, interior and spiritual, for all these are darkened in this night as to their natural light, so that, being purged in this respect, they may be illumined with respect to the supernatural. For the spiritual and the sensual desires are put to sleep and mortified, so that they can experience[206] nothing, either Divine or human; the affections of the soul are oppressed and constrained, so that they can neither move nor find support in anything; the imagination is bound and can make no useful reflection; the memory is gone; the understanding is in darkness, unable to understand anything; and hence the will likewise is arid and constrained and all the faculties are void and useless; and in addition to all this a thick and heavy cloud is upon the soul, keeping it in affliction, and, as it were, far away from God.[207] It is in this kind of 'darkness' that the soul says here it travelled 'securely.'

The reason for this has been clearly expounded; for ordinarily the soul never strays save through its desires or its tastes or its reflections or its understanding or its affections; for as a rule it has too much or too little of these, or they vary or go astray, and hence the soul becomes inclined to that which behoves it not. Wherefore, when all these operations and motions are hindered, it is clear that the soul is secure against being led astray by them; for it is free, not only from itself, but likewise from its other enemies, which are the world and the devil. For when the affections and operations of the soul are quenched, these enemies cannot make war upon it by any other means or in any other manner.

It follows from this that, the greater is the darkness wherein the soul journeys and the more completely is it voided of its natural operations, the greater is its security. For, as the Prophet says,[208] perdition comes to the soul from itself alone—that is, from its sensual and interior desires and operations; and good, says God, comes from Me alone. Wherefore, when it is thus hindered from following the things that lead it into evil, there will then come to it forthwith the blessings of union with God in its desires and faculties, which in that union He will make Divine and celestial. Hence, at the time of this darkness, if the soul considers the matter, it will see very clearly how little its desire and its faculties are being diverted to things that are useless and harmful; and how secure it is from vainglory and pride and presumption, vain and false rejoicing and many other things. It follows clearly, then, that, by walking in darkness, not only is the soul not lost, but it has even greatly gained, since it is here gaining the virtues.

But there is a question which at once arises here—namely, since the things of God are of themselves profitable to the soul and bring it gain and security, why does God, in this night, darken the desires and faculties with respect to these good things likewise, in such a way that the soul can no more taste of them or busy itself with them than with these other things, and indeed in some ways can do so less? The answer is that it is well for the soul to perform no operation touching spiritual things at that time and to have no pleasure in such things, because its faculties and desires are base, impure and wholly natural; and thus, although these faculties be given the desire and interest in things supernatural and Divine, they could not receive them save after a base and a natural manner, exactly in their own fashion. For, as the philosopher says, whatsoever is received comes to him that receives it after the manner of the recipient. Wherefore, since these natural faculties have neither purity nor strength nor capacity to receive and taste things that are supernatural after the manner of those things, which manner is Divine, but can do so only after their own manner, which is human and base, as we have said, it is meet that its faculties be in darkness concerning these Divine things likewise. Thus, being weaned and purged and annihilated in this respect first of all, they may lose that base and human way of receiving and acting, and thus all these faculties and desires of the soul may come to be prepared and tempered in such a way as to be able to receive, feel and taste that which is Divine and supernatural after a sublime and lofty manner, which is impossible if the old man die not first of all.

Hence it follows that all spiritual things, if they come not from above and be not communicated by the Father of lights to human desire and free will (howsoever much a man may exercise his taste and faculties for God, and howsoever much it may seem to the faculties that they are experiencing these things), will not be experienced after a Divine and spiritual manner, but after a human and natural manner, just as other things are experienced, for spiritual blessings go not from man to God, but come from God to man. With respect to this (if this were the proper place for it) we might here explain how there are many persons whose many tastes and affections and the operations of whose faculties are fixed upon God or upon spiritual things, and who may perhaps think that this is supernatural and spiritual, when it is perhaps no more than the most human and natural desires and actions. They regard these good things with the same disposition as they have for other things, by means of a certain natural facility which they possess for directing their desires and faculties to anything whatever.

If perchance we find occasion elsewhere in this book, we shall treat of this, describing certain signs which indicate when the interior actions and motions of the soul, with respect to communion with God, are only natural, when they are spiritual, and when they are both natural and spiritual. It suffices for us here to know that, in order that the interior motions and acts of the soul may come to be moved by God divinely, they must first be darkened and put to sleep and hushed to rest naturally as touching all their capacity and operation, until they have no more strength.

Therefore, O spiritual soul, when thou seest thy desire obscured, thy affections arid and constrained, and thy faculties bereft of their capacity for any interior exercise, be not afflicted by this, but rather consider it a great happiness, since God is freeing thee from thyself and taking the matter from thy hands. For with those hands, howsoever well they may serve thee, thou wouldst never labour so effectively, so perfectly and so securely (because of their clumsiness and uncleanness) as now, when God takes thy hand and guides thee in the darkness, as though thou wert blind, to an end and by a way which thou knowest not. Nor couldst thou ever hope to travel with the aid of thine own eyes and feet, howsoever good thou be as a walker.

The reason, again, why the soul not only travels securely, when it travels thus in the darkness, but also achieves even greater gain and progress, is that usually, when the soul is receiving fresh advantage and profit, this comes by a way that it least understands—indeed, it quite commonly believes that it is losing ground. For, as it has never experienced that new feeling which drives it forth and dazzles it and makes it depart recklessly from its former way of life, it thinks itself to be losing ground rather than gaining and progressing, since it sees that it is losing with respect to that which it knew and enjoyed, and is going by a way which it knows not and wherein it finds no enjoyment. It is like the traveller, who, in order to go to new and unknown lands, takes new roads, unknown and untried, and journeys unguided by his past experience, but doubtingly and according to what others say. It is clear that such a man could not reach new countries, or add to his past experience, if he went not along new and unknown roads and abandoned those which were known to him. Exactly so, one who is learning fresh details concerning any office or art always proceeds in darkness, and receives no guidance from his original knowledge, for if he left not that behind he would get no farther nor make any progress; and in the same way, when the soul is making most progress, it is travelling in darkness, knowing naught. Wherefore, since God, as we have said, is the Master and Guide of this blind soul, it may well and truly rejoice, once it has learned to understand this, and say: 'In darkness and secure.'

There is another reason why the soul has walked securely in this darkness, and this is because it has been suffering; for the road of suffering is more secure and even more profitable than that of fruition and action: first, because in suffering the strength of God is added to that of man, while in action and fruition the soul is practising its own weaknesses and imperfections; and second, because in suffering the soul continues to practise and acquire the virtues and become purer, wiser and more cautious.

But there is another and a more important reason why the soul now walks in darkness and securely; this emanates from the dark light or wisdom aforementioned. For in such a way does this dark night of contemplation absorb and immerse the soul in itself, and so near does it bring the soul to God, that it protects and delivers it from all that is not God. For this soul is now, as it were, undergoing a cure, in order that it may regain its health—its health being God Himself. His Majesty restricts it to a diet and abstinence from all things, and takes away its appetite for them all. It is like a sick man, who, if he is respected by those in his house, is carefully tended so that he may be cured; the air is not allowed to touch him, nor may he even enjoy the light, nor must he hear footsteps, nor yet the noise of those in the house; and he is given food that is very delicate, and even that only in great moderation—food that is nourishing rather than delectable.

All these particularities (which are for the security and safekeeping of the soul) are caused by this dark contemplation, because it brings the soul nearer to God. For the nearer the soul approaches Him, the blacker is the darkness which it feels and the deeper is the obscurity which comes through its weakness; just as, the nearer a man approaches the sun, the greater are the darkness and the affliction caused him through the great splendour of the sun and through the weakness and impurity of his eyes. In the same way, so immense is the spiritual light of God, and so greatly does it transcend our natural understanding, that the nearer we approach it, the more it blinds and darkens us. And this is the reason why, in Psalm xvii, David says that God made darkness His hiding-place and covering, and His tabernacle around Him dark water in the clouds of the air.[209] This dark water in the clouds of the air is dark contemplation and Divine wisdom in souls, as we are saying. They continue to feel it is a thing which is near Him, as the tabernacle wherein He dwells, when God brings them ever nearer to Himself. And thus, that which in God is supreme light and refulgence is to man blackest darkness, as Saint Paul says, according as David explains in the same Psalm, saying: 'Because of the brightness which is in His presence, passed clouds and cataracts'[210]—that is to say, over the natural understanding, the light whereof, as Isaias says in chapter V: Obtenebrata est in caligine ejus.[211]

Oh, miserable is the fortune of our life, which is lived in such great peril and wherein it is so difficult to find the truth. For that which is most clear and true is to us most dark and doubtful; wherefore, though it is the thing that is most needful for us, we flee from it. And that which gives the greatest light and satisfaction to our eyes we embrace and pursue, though it be the worst thing for us, and make us fall at every step. In what peril and fear does man live, since the very natural light of his eyes by which he has to guide himself is the first light that dazzles him and leads him astray on his road to God! And if he is to know with certainty by what road he travels, he must perforce keep his eyes closed and walk in darkness, that he may be secure from the enemies who inhabit his own house—that is, his senses and faculties.

Well hidden, then, and well protected is the soul in these dark waters, when it is close to God. For, as these waters serve as a tabernacle and dwelling-place for God Himself, they will serve the soul in the same way and for a perfect protection and security, though it remain in darkness, wherein, as we have said, it is hidden and protected from itself, and from all evils that come from creatures; for to such the words of David refer in another Psalm, where he says: 'Thou shalt hide them in the hiding-place of Thy face from the disturbance of men; Thou shalt protect them in Thy tabernacle from the contradiction of tongues.'[212] Herein we understand all kinds of protection; for to be hidden in the face of God from the disturbance of men is to be fortified with this dark contemplation against all the chances which may come upon the soul from men. And to be protected in His tabernacle from the contradiction of tongues is for the soul to be engulfed in these dark waters, which are the tabernacle of David whereof we have spoken. Wherefore, since the soul has all its desires and affections weaned and its faculties set in darkness, it is free from all imperfections which contradict the spirit, whether they come from its own flesh or from other creatures. Wherefore this soul may well say that it journeys 'in darkness and secure.'

There is likewise another reason, which is no less effectual than the last, by which we may understand how the soul journeys securely in darkness; it is derived from the fortitude by which the soul is at once inspired in these obscure and afflictive dark waters of God. For after all, though the waters be dark, they are none the less waters, and therefore they cannot but refresh and fortify the soul in that which is most needful for it, although in darkness and with affliction. For the soul immediately perceives in itself a genuine determination and an effectual desire to do naught which it understands to be an offence to God, and to omit to do naught that seems to be for His service. For that dark love cleaves to the soul, causing it a most watchful care and an inward solicitude concerning that which it must do, or must not do, for His sake, in order to please Him. It will consider and ask itself a thousand times if it has given Him cause to be offended; and all this it will do with much greater care and solicitude than before, as has already been said with respect to the yearnings of love. For here all the desires and energies and faculties of the soul are recollected from all things else, and its effort and strength are employed in pleasing its God alone. After this manner the soul goes forth from itself and from all created things to the sweet and delectable union of love of God, 'In darkness and secure.'

By the secret ladder, disguised.

Chapter XVII

Explains how this dark contemplation is secret.

Three things have to be expounded with reference to three words contained in this present line. Two (namely, 'secret' and 'ladder') belong to the dark night of contemplation of which we are treating; the third (namely, 'disguised') belongs to the soul by reason of the manner wherein it conducts itself in this night. As to the first, it must be known that in this line the soul describes this dark contemplation, by which it goes forth to the union of love, as a secret ladder, because of the two properties which belong to it—namely, its being secret and its being a ladder. We shall treat of each separately.

First, it describes this dark contemplation as 'secret,' since, as we have indicated above, it is mystical theology, which theologians call secret wisdom, and which, as Saint Thomas says is communicated and infused into the soul through love.[213] This happens secretly and in darkness, so as to be hidden from the work of the understanding and of other faculties. Wherefore, inasmuch as the faculties aforementioned attain not to it, but the Holy Spirit infuses and orders it in the soul, as says the Bride in the Songs, without either its knowledge or its understanding, it is called secret. And, in truth, not only does the soul not understand it, but there is none that does so, not even the devil; inasmuch as the Master Who teaches the soul is within it in its substance, to which the devil may not attain, neither may natural sense nor understanding.

And it is not for this reason alone that it may be called secret, but likewise because of the effects which it produces in the soul. For it is secret not only in the darknesses and afflictions of purgation, when this wisdom of love purges the soul, and the soul is unable to speak of it, but equally so afterwards in illumination, when this wisdom is communicated to it most clearly. Even then it is still so secret that the soul cannot speak of it and give it a name whereby it may be called; for, apart from the fact that the soul has no desire to speak of it, it can find no suitable way or manner or similitude by which it may be able to describe such lofty understanding and such delicate spiritual feeling. And thus, even though the soul might have a great desire to express it and might find many ways in which to describe it, it would still be secret and remain undescribed. For, as that inward wisdom is so simple, so general and so spiritual that it has not entered into the understanding enwrapped or cloaked in any form or image subject to sense, it follows that sense and imagination (as it has not entered through them nor has taken their form and colour) cannot account for it or imagine it, so as to say anything concerning it, although the soul be clearly aware that it is experiencing and partaking of that rare and delectable wisdom. It is like one who sees something never seen before, whereof he has not even seen the like; although he might understand its nature and have experience of it, he would be unable to give it a name, or say what it is, however much he tried to do so, and this in spite of its being a thing which he had perceived with the senses. How much less, then, could

he describe a thing that has not entered through the senses! For the language of
God has this characteristic that, since it is very intimate and spiritual in its
relations with the soul, it transcends every sense and at once makes all harmony
and capacity of the outward and inward senses to cease and be dumb.

For this we have both authorities and examples in the Divine Scripture. For the
incapacity of man to speak of it and describe it in words was shown by Jeremias,[214]
when, after God had spoken with him, he knew not what to say, save 'Ah, ah, ah!'
This interior incapacity—that is, of the interior sense of the imagination—and also
that of the exterior sense corresponding to it was also demonstrated in the case of
Moses, when he stood before God in the bush;[215] not only did he say to God that
after speaking with Him he knew not neither was able to speak, but also that not
even (as is said in the Acts of the Apostles)[216] with the interior imagination did he
dare to meditate, for it seemed to him that his imagination was very far away and
was too dumb, not only to express any part of that which he understood
concerning God, but even to have the capacity to receive aught therefrom.
Wherefore, inasmuch as the wisdom of this contemplation is the language of God
to the soul, addressed by pure spirit to pure spirit, naught that is less than spirit,
such as the senses, can perceive it, and thus to them it is secret, and they know it
not, neither can they say it,[217] nor do they desire to do so, because they see it not.

We may deduce from this the reason why certain persons—good and fearful
souls—who walk along this road and would like to give an account of their
spiritual state to their director,[218] are neither able to do so nor know how. For the
reason we have described, they have a great repugnance in speaking of it,
especially when their contemplation is of the purer sort, so that the soul itself is
hardly conscious of it. Such a person is only able to say that he is satisfied, tranquil
and contented and that he is conscious of the presence of God, and that, as it
seems to him, all is going well with him; but he cannot describe the state of his
soul, nor can he say anything about it save in general terms like these. It is a
different matter when the experiences of the soul are of a particular kind, such as
visions, feelings, etc., which, being ordinarily received under some species
wherein sense participates, can be described under that species, or by some other
similitude. But this capacity for being described is not in the nature of pure
contemplation, which is indescribable, as we have said, for the which reason it is
called secret.

And not only for that reason is it called secret, and is so, but likewise because
this mystical knowledge has the property of hiding the soul within itself. For,
besides performing its ordinary function, it sometimes absorbs the soul and
engulfs it in its secret abyss, in such a way that the soul clearly sees that it has
been carried far away from every creature and; has become most remote
therefrom;[219] so that it considers itself as having been placed in a most profound
and vast retreat, to which no human creature can attain, such as an immense
desert, which nowhere has any boundary, a desert the more delectable, pleasant
and lovely for its secrecy, vastness and solitude, wherein, the more the soul is
raised up above all temporal creatures, the more deeply does it find itself hidden.
And so greatly does this abyss of wisdom raise up and exalt the soul at this time,
making it to penetrate the veins of the science of love, that it not only shows it how
base are all properties of the creatures by comparison with this supreme
knowledge and Divine feeling, but likewise it learns how base and defective, and,
in some measure, how inapt, are all the terms and words which are used in this
life to treat of Divine things, and how impossible it is, in any natural way or

manner, however learnedly and sublimely they may be spoken of, to be able to know and perceive them as they are, save by the illumination of this mystical theology. And thus, when by means of this illumination the soul discerns this truth, namely, that it cannot reach it, still less explain it, by common or human language, it rightly calls it secret.

This property of secrecy and superiority over natural capacity, which belongs to this Divine contemplation, belongs to it, not only because it is supernatural, but also inasmuch as it is a road that guides and leads the soul to the perfections of union with God; which, as they are things unknown after a human manner, must be approached, after a human manner, by unknowing and by Divine ignorance. For, speaking mystically, as we are speaking here, Divine things and perfections are known and understood as they are, not when they are being sought after and practised, but when they have been found and practised. To this purpose speaks the prophet Baruch concerning this Divine wisdom: 'There is none that can know her ways nor that can imagine her paths.'[220] Likewise the royal Prophet speaks in this manner concerning this road of the soul, when he says to God: 'Thy lightnings lighted and illumined the round earth; the earth was moved and trembled. Thy way is in the sea and Thy paths are in many waters; and Thy footsteps shall not be known.'[221]

All this, speaking spiritually, is to be understood in the sense wherein we are speaking. For the illumination of the round earth[222] by the lightnings of God is the enlightenment which is produced by this Divine contemplation in the faculties of the soul; the moving and trembling of the earth is the painful purgation which is caused therein; and to say that the way and the road of God whereby the soul journeys to Him is in the sea, and His footprints are in many waters and for this reason shall not be known, is as much as to say that this road whereby the soul journeys to God is as secret and as hidden from the sense of the soul as the way of one that walks on the sea, whose paths and footprints are not known, is hidden from the sense of the body. The steps and footprints which God is imprinting upon the souls that He desires to bring near to Himself, and to make great in union with His Wisdom, have also this property, that they are not known. Wherefore in the Book of Job mention is made of this matter, in these words: 'Hast thou perchance known the paths of the great clouds or the perfect knowledges?'[223] By this are understood the ways and roads whereby God continually exalts souls and perfects them in His Wisdom, which souls are here understood by the clouds. It follows, then, that this contemplation which is guiding the soul to God is secret wisdom.

Chapter XVIII

Explains how this secret wisdom is likewise a ladder.

It now remains to consider the second point—namely, how this secret wisdom is likewise a ladder. With respect to this it must be known that we can call this secret contemplation a ladder for many reasons. In the first place, because, just as men mount by means of ladders and climb up to possessions and treasures and things that are in strong places, even so also, by means of this secret contemplation, without knowing how, the soul ascends and climbs up to a knowledge and possession of[224] the good things and treasures of Heaven. This is well expressed by the royal prophet David, when he says: 'Blessed is he that hath Thy favour and help, for such a man hath placed in his heart ascensions into the vale of tears in the place which he hath appointed; for after this manner the Lord of the law shall give blessing, and they shall go from virtue to virtue as from step to step, and the God of gods shall be seen in Sion.'[225] This God is the treasure of the strong place of Sion, which is happiness.

We may also call it a ladder because, even as the ladder has those same steps in order that men may mount, it has them also that they may descend; even so is it likewise with this secret contemplation, for those same communications which it causes in the soul raise it up to God, yet humble it with respect to itself. For communications which are indeed of God have this property, that they humble the soul and at the same time exalt it. For, upon this road, to go down is to go up, and to go up, to go down, for he that humbles himself is exalted and he that exalts himself is humbled.[226] And besides the fact that the virtue of humility is greatness, for the exercise of the soul therein, God is wont to make it mount by this ladder so that it may descend, and to make it descend so that it may mount, that the words of the Wise Man may thus be fulfilled, namely: 'Before the soul is exalted, it is humbled; and before it is humbled, it is exalted.'[227]

Speaking now in a natural way, the soul that desires to consider it will be able to see how on this road (we leave apart the spiritual aspect, of which the soul is not conscious) it has to suffer many ups and downs, and how the prosperity which it enjoys is followed immediately by certain storms and trials; so much so, that it appears to have been given that period of calm in order that it might be forewarned and strengthened against the poverty which has followed; just as after misery and torment there come abundance and calm. It seems to the soul as if, before celebrating that festival, it has first been made to keep that vigil. This is the ordinary course and proceeding of the state of contemplation until the soul arrives at the state of quietness; it never remains in the same state for long together, but is ascending and descending continually.

The reason for this is that, as the state of perfection, which consists in the perfect love of God and contempt for self, cannot exist unless it have these two parts, which are the knowledge of God and of oneself, the soul has of necessity to be practised first in the one and then in the other, now being given to taste of the one—that is, exaltation—and now being made to experience the other—that is, humiliation—until it has acquired perfect habits; and then this ascending and descending will cease, since the soul will have attained to God and become united with Him, which comes to pass at the summit of this ladder, for the ladder rests and leans upon Him. For this ladder of contemplation, which, as we have said, comes down from God, is prefigured by that ladder which Jacob saw as he slept, whereon angels were ascending and descending, from God to man, and from man to God, Who Himself was leaning upon the end of the ladder.[228] All this, says Divine Scripture, took place by night, when Jacob slept, in order to express how secret is this road and ascent to God, and how different from that of man's knowledge. This is very evident, since ordinarily that which is of the greatest profit in it—namely, to be ever losing oneself and becoming as nothing[229]—is considered the worst thing possible; and that which is of least worth, which is for a soul to find consolation and sweetness (wherein it ordinarily loses rather than gains), is considered best.

But, speaking now somewhat more substantially and properly of this ladder of secret contemplation, we shall observe that the principal characteristic of contemplation, on account of which it is here called a ladder, is that it is the science of love. This, as we have said, is an infused and loving knowledge of God, which enlightens the soul and at the same time enkindles it with love, until it is raised up step by step, even unto God its Creator. For it is love alone that unites and joins the soul with God. To the end that this may be seen more clearly, we shall here indicate the steps of this Divine ladder one by one, pointing out briefly the marks and effects of each, so that the soul may conjecture hereby on which of them it is standing. We shall therefore distinguish them by their effects, as do Saint Bernard and Saint Thomas,[230] for to know them in themselves is not possible after a natural manner, inasmuch as this ladder of love is, as we have said, so secret that God alone is He that measures and weighs it.

Chapter XIX

Begins to explain the ten steps[231] of the mystic ladder of Divine love, according to Saint Bernard and Saint Thomas. The first five are here treated.

We observe, then, that the steps of this ladder of love by which the soul mounts, one by one, to God, are ten. The first step of love causes the soul to languish, and this to its advantage. The Bride is speaking from this step of love when she says: 'I adjure you, daughters of Jerusalem, that, if ye find my Beloved, ye tell Him that I am sick with love.'[232] This sickness, however, is not unto death, but for the glory of God, for in this sickness the soul swoons as to sin and as to all things that are not God, for the sake of God Himself, even as David testifies, saying: 'My soul hath swooned away'[233]—that is, with respect to all things, for Thy salvation. For just as a sick man first of all loses his appetite and taste for all food, and his colour changes, so likewise in this degree of love the soul loses its taste and desire for all things and changes its colour and the other accidentals of its past life, like one in love. The soul falls not into this sickness if excess of heat be not communicated to it from above, even as is expressed in that verse of David which says: Pluviam voluntariam segregabis, Deus, haereditati tuae, et infirmata est,[234] etc. This sickness and swooning to all things, which is the beginning and the first step on the road to God, we clearly described above, when we were speaking of the annihilation wherein the soul finds itself when it begins to climb[235] this ladder of contemplative purgation, when it can find no pleasure, support, consolation or abiding-place in anything soever. Wherefore from this step it begins at once to climb to the second.

The second step causes the soul to seek God without ceasing. Wherefore, when the Bride says that she sought Him by night upon her bed (when she had swooned away according to the first step of love) and found Him not, she said: 'I will arise and will seek Him Whom my soul loveth.'[236] This, as we say, the soul does without ceasing as David counsels it, saying: 'Seek ye ever the face of God, and seek ye Him in all things, tarrying not until ye find Him;'[237] like the Bride, who, having enquired for Him of the watchmen, passed on at once and left them. Mary Magdalene did not even notice the angels at the sepulchre.[238] On this step the soul now walks so anxiously that it seeks the Beloved in all things. In whatsoever it thinks, it thinks at once of the Beloved. Of whatsoever it speaks, in whatsoever matters present themselves, it is speaking and communing at once with the Beloved. When it eats, when it sleeps, when it watches, when it does aught soever, all its care is about the Beloved, as is said above with respect to the yearnings of love. And now, as love begins to recover its health and find new strength in the love of this second step, it begins at once to mount to the third, by means of a certain degree[239] of new purgation in the night, as we shall afterwards describe, which produces in the soul the following effects.

The third step of the ladder of love is that which causes the soul to work and gives it fervour so that it fails not. Concerning this the royal Prophet says: 'Blessed is the man that feareth the Lord, for in His commandments he is eager to labour greatly.'[240] Wherefore if fear, being the son of love, causes within him this eagerness to labour,[241] what will be done by love itself? On this step the soul considers great works undertaken for the Beloved as small; many things as few; and the long time for which it serves Him as short, by reason of the fire of love wherein it is now burning. Even so to Jacob, though after seven years he had been made to serve seven more, they seemed few because of the greatness of his love.[242] Now if the love of a mere creature could accomplish so much in Jacob, what will love of the Creator be able to do when on this third step it takes possession of the soul? Here, for the great love which the soul bears to God, it suffers great pains and afflictions because of the little that it does for God; and if it were lawful for it to be destroyed a thousand times for Him it would be comforted. Wherefore it considers itself useless in all that it does and thinks itself to be living in vain. Another wondrous effect produced here in the soul is that it considers itself as being, most certainly, worse than all other souls: first, because love is continually teaching it how much is due to God;[243] and second, because, as the works which it here does for God are many and it knows them all to be faulty and imperfect, they all bring it confusion and affliction, for it realizes in how lowly a manner it is working for God, Who is so high. On this third step, the soul is very far from vainglory or presumption, and from condemning others. These anxious effects, with many others like them, are produced in the soul by this third step; wherefore it gains courage and strength from them in order to mount to the fourth step, which is that that follows.

The fourth step of this ladder of love is that whereby there is caused in the soul an habitual suffering because of the Beloved, yet without weariness. For, as Saint Augustine says, love makes all things that are great, grievous and burdensome to be almost naught. From this step the Bride was speaking when, desiring to attain to the last step, she said to the Spouse: 'Set me as a seal upon thy heart, as a seal upon thine arm; for love—that is, the act and work of love—is strong as death, and emulation and importunity last as long as hell.'[244] The spirit here has so much strength that it has subjected the flesh and takes as little account of it as does the tree of one of its leaves. In no way does the soul here seek its own consolation or pleasure, either in God, or in aught else, nor does it desire or seek to pray to God for favours, for it sees clearly that it has already received enough of these, and all its anxiety is set upon the manner wherein it will be able to do something that is pleasing to God and to render Him some service such as He merits and in return for what it has received from Him, although it be greatly to its cost. The soul says in its heart and spirit: Ah, my God and Lord! How many are there that go to seek in Thee their own consolation and pleasure, and desire Thee to grant them favours and gifts; but those who long to do Thee pleasure and to give Thee something at their cost, setting their own interests last, are very few. The failure, my God, is not in Thy unwillingness to grant us new favours, but in our neglect to use those that we have received in Thy service alone, in order to constrain Thee to grant them to us continually. Exceeding lofty is this step of love; for, as the soul goes ever after God with love so true, imbued with the spirit of suffering for His sake, His Majesty oftentimes and quite habitually grants it joy, and visits it sweetly and delectably in the spirit; for the boundless love of Christ, the Word, cannot suffer the afflictions of His lover without succouring him. This He affirmed through Jeremias, saying: 'I have remembered thee, pitying thy youth and tenderness, when thou wentest after Me in the wilderness.'[245] Speaking spiritually, this denotes the detachment which the soul now has interiorly from every creature, so that it rests not and nowhere finds quietness. This fourth step enkindles the soul and makes it to burn in such desire for God that it causes it to mount to the fifth, which is that which follows.

The fifth step of this ladder of love makes the soul to desire and long for God impatiently. On this step the vehemence of the lover to comprehend the Beloved and be united with Him is such that every delay, however brief, becomes very long, wearisome and oppressive to it, and it continually believes itself to be finding the Beloved. And when it sees its desire frustrated (which is at almost every moment), it swoons away with its yearning, as says the Psalmist, speaking from this step, in these words: 'My soul longs and faints for the dwellings of the Lord.'[246] On this step the lover must needs see that which he loves, or die; at this step was Rachel, when, for the great longing that she had for children, she said to Jacob, her spouse: 'Give me children, else shall I die.'[247] Here men suffer hunger like dogs and go about and surround the city of God. On this step, which is one of hunger,[248] the soul is nourished upon love; for, even as is its hunger, so is its abundance; so that it rises hence to the sixth step, producing the effects which follow.

Chapter XX

Wherein are treated the other five steps of love.

On the sixth step the soul runs swiftly to God and touches Him again and again; and it runs without fainting by reason of its hope. For here the love that has made it strong makes it to fly swiftly. Of this step the prophet Isaias speaks thus: 'The saints that hope in God shall renew their strength; they shall take wings as the eagle; they shall fly and shall not faint,'[249] as they did at the fifth step. To this step likewise alludes that verse of the Psalm: 'As the hart desires the waters, my soul desires Thee, O God.'[250] For the hart, in its thirst, runs to the waters with great swiftness. The cause of this swiftness in love which the soul has on this step is that its charity is greatly enlarged within it, since the soul is here almost wholly purified, as is said likewise in the Psalm, namely: Sine iniquitate cucurri.[251]And in another Psalm: 'I ran the way of Thy commandments when Thou didst enlarge my heart';[252] and thus from this sixth step the soul at once mounts to the seventh, which is that which follows.

The seventh step of this ladder makes the soul to become vehement in its boldness. Here love employs not its judgment in order to hope, nor does it take counsel so that it may draw back, neither can any shame restrain it; for the favour which God here grants to the soul causes it to become vehement in its boldness. Hence follows that which the Apostle says, namely: That charity believeth all things, hopeth all things and is capable of all things.[253] Of this step spake Moses, when he entreated God to pardon the people, and if not, to blot out his name from the book of life wherein He had written it.[254] Men like these obtain from God that which they beg of Him with desire. Wherefore David says: 'Delight thou in God and He will give thee the petitions of thy heart.'[255] On this step the Bride grew bold, and said: Osculetur me osculo oris sui.[256]To this step it is not lawful for the soul to aspire boldly, unless it feel the interior favour of the King's sceptre extended to it, lest perchance it fall from the other steps which it has mounted up to this point, and wherein it must ever possess itself in humility. From this daring and power which God grants to the soul on this seventh step, so that it may be bold with God in the vehemence of love, follows the eighth, which is that wherein it takes the Beloved captive and is united with Him, as follows.

The eighth step of love causes the soul to seize Him and hold Him fast without letting Him go, even as the Bride says, after this manner: 'I found Him Whom my heart and soul love; I held Him and I will not let Him go.'[257] On this step of union the soul satisfies her desire, but not continuously. Certain souls climb some way,[258] and then lose their hold; for, if this state were to continue, it would be glory itself in this life; and thus the soul remains therein for very short periods of time. To the prophet Daniel, because he was a man of desires, was sent a command from God to remain on this step, when it was said to him: 'Daniel, stay upon thy step, because thou art a man of desires.'[259] After this step follows the ninth, which is that of souls now perfect, as we shall afterwards say, which is that that follows.

The ninth step of love makes the soul to burn with sweetness. This step is that of the perfect, who now burn sweetly in God. For this sweet and delectable ardour is caused in them by the Holy Spirit by reason of the union which they have with God. For this cause Saint Gregory says, concerning the Apostles, that when the Holy Spirit came upon them visibly they burned inwardly and sweetly through love.[260] Of the good things and riches of God which the soul enjoys on this step, we cannot speak; for if many books were to be written concerning it the greater part would still remain untold. For this cause, and because we shall say something of it hereafter, I say no more here than that after this follows the tenth and last step of this ladder of love, which belongs not to this life.

The tenth and last step of this secret ladder of love causes the soul to become wholly assimilated to God, by reason of the clear and immediate[261] vision of God which it then possesses; when, having ascended in this life to the ninth step, it goes forth from the flesh. These souls, who are few, enter not into purgatory, since they have already been wholly purged by love. Of these Saint Matthew says: Beati mundo corde: quoniam ipsi Deum videbunt.[262] And, as we say, this vision is the cause of the perfect likeness of the soul to God, for, as Saint John says, we know that we shall be like Him.[263] Not because the soul will come to have the capacity of God, for that is impossible; but because all that it is will become like to God, for which cause it will be called, and will be, God by participation.

This is the secret ladder whereof the soul here speaks, although upon these higher steps it is no longer very secret to the soul, since much is revealed to it by love, through the great effects which love produces in it. But, on this last step of clear vision, which is the last step of the ladder whereon God leans, as we have said already, there is naught that is hidden from the soul, by reason of its complete assimilation. Wherefore Our Saviour says: 'In that day ye shall ask Me nothing,' etc.[264] But, until that day, however high a point the soul may reach, there remains something hidden from it—namely, all that it lacks for total assimilation in the Divine Essence. After this manner, by this mystical theology and secret love, the soul continues to rise above all things and above itself, and to mount upward to God. For love is like fire, which ever rises upward with the desire to be absorbed in the centre of its sphere.

Chapter XXI

Which explains the word 'disguised,' and describes the colours of the disguise of the soul in this night.

Now that we have explained the reasons why the soul called this contemplation a 'secret ladder,' it remains for us to explain likewise the word 'disguised,' and the reason why the soul says also that it went forth by this 'secret ladder' in 'disguise.'

For the understanding of this it must be known that to disguise oneself is naught else but to hide and cover oneself beneath another garb and figure than one's own—sometimes in order to show forth, under that garb or figure, the will and purpose which is in the heart to gain the grace and will of one who is greatly loved; sometimes, again, to hide oneself from one's rivals and thus to accomplish one's object better. At such times a man assumes the garments and livery which best represent and indicate the affection of his heart and which best conceal him from his rivals.

The soul, then, touched with the love of Christ the Spouse, and longing to attain to His grace and gain His goodwill, goes forth here disguised with that disguise which most vividly represents the affections of its spirit and which will protect it most securely on its journey from its adversaries and enemies, which are the devil, the world and the flesh. Thus the livery which it wears is of three chief colours—white, green and purple—denoting the three theological virtues, faith, hope and charity. By these the soul will not only gain the grace and goodwill of its Beloved, but it will travel in security and complete protection from its three enemies: for faith is an inward tunic of a whiteness so pure that it completely dazzles the eyes of the understanding.[265] And thus, when the soul journeys in its vestment of faith, the devil can neither see it nor succeed in harming it, since it is well protected by faith—more so than by all the other virtues—against the devil, who is at once the strongest and the most cunning of enemies.

It is clear that Saint Peter could find no better protection than faith to save him from the devil, when he said: Cui resistite fortes in fide.[266] And in order to gain the grace of the Beloved, and union with Him, the soul cannot put on a better vest and tunic,[267] to serve as a foundation and beginning of the other vestments of the virtues, than this white garment[268] of faith, for without it, as the Apostle says, it is impossible to please God, and with it, it is impossible to fail to please Him. For He Himself says through a prophet: Sponsabo te mihi in fide.[269] Which is as much as to say: If thou desirest, O soul, to be united and betrothed to Me, thou must come inwardly clad in faith.

This white garment of faith was worn by the soul on its going forth from this dark night, when, walking in interior constraint and darkness, as we have said before, it received no aid, in the form of light, from its understanding, neither from above, since Heaven seemed to be closed to it and God hidden from it, nor from below, since those that taught it satisfied it not. It suffered with constancy and persevered, passing through those trials without fainting or failing the Beloved,

Who in trials and tribulations proves the faith of His Bride, so that afterwards she may truly repeat this saying of David, namely: 'By the words of Thy lips I kept hard ways.'[270]

Next, over this white tunic of faith the soul now puts on the second colour, which is a green vestment. By this, as we said, is signified the virtue of hope, wherewith, as in the first case, the soul is delivered and protected from the second enemy, which is the world. For this green colour of living hope in God gives the soul such ardour and courage and aspiration to the things of eternal life that, by comparison with what it hopes for therein, all things of the world seem to it to be, as in truth they are, dry and faded and dead and nothing worth. The soul now divests and strips itself of all these worldly vestments and garments, setting its heart upon naught that is in the world and hoping for naught, whether of that which is or of that which is to be, but living clad only in the hope of eternal life. Wherefore, when the heart is thus lifted up above the world, not only can the world neither touch the heart nor lay hold on it, but it cannot even come within sight of it.

And thus, in this green livery and disguise, the soul journeys in complete security from this second enemy, which is the world. For Saint Paul speaks of hope as the helmet of salvation[271]—that is, a piece of armour that protects the whole head, and covers it so that there remains uncovered only a visor through which it may look. And hope has this property, that it covers all the senses of the head of the soul, so that there is naught soever pertaining to the world in which they can be immersed, nor is there an opening through which any arrow of the world can wound them. It has a visor, however, which the soul is permitted to use so that its eyes may look upward, but nowhere else; for this is the function which hope habitually performs in the soul, namely, the directing of its eyes upwards to look at God alone, even as David declared that his eyes were directed, when he said: Oculi mei semper ad Dominum.[272] He hoped for no good thing elsewhere, save as he himself says in another Psalm: 'Even as the eyes of the handmaid are set upon the hands of her mistress, even so are our eyes set upon our Lord God, until He have mercy upon us as we hope in Him.'[273]

For this reason, because of this green livery (since the soul is ever looking to God and sets its eyes on naught else, neither is pleased with aught save with Him alone), the Beloved has such great pleasure with the soul that it is true to say that the soul obtains from Him as much as it hopes for from Him. Wherefore the Spouse in the Songs tells the Bride that, by looking upon Him with one eye alone, she has wounded His heart.[274] Without this green livery of hope in God alone it would be impossible for the soul to go forth to encompass this loving achievement, for it would have no success, since that which moves and conquers is the importunity of hope.

With this livery of hope the soul journeys in disguise through this secret and dark night whereof we have spoken; for it is so completely voided of every possession and support that it fixes its eyes and its care upon naught but God, putting its mouth in the dust,[275] if so be there may be hope—to repeat the quotation made above from Jeremias.[276]

Over the white and the green vestments, as the crown and perfection of this disguise and livery, the soul now puts on the third colour, which is a splendid garment of purple. By this is denoted the third virtue, which is charity. This not only adds grace to the other two colours, but causes the soul to rise to so lofty a point that it is brought near to God, and becomes very beautiful and pleasing to

Him, so that it makes bold to say: 'Albeit I am black, O daughters of Jerusalem, I am comely; wherefore the King hath loved me and hath brought me into His chambers.'[277] This livery of charity, which is that of love, and causes greater love in the Beloved, not only protects the soul and hides it from the third enemy, which is the flesh (for where there is true love of God there enters neither love of self nor that of the things of self), but even gives worth to the other virtues, bestowing on them vigour and strength to protect the soul, and grace and beauty to please the Beloved with them, for without charity no virtue has grace before God. This is the purple which is spoken of in the Songs,[278] upon which God reclines. Clad in this purple livery the soul journeys when (as has been explained above in the first stanza) it goes forth from itself in the dark night, and from all things created, 'kindled in love with yearnings,' by this secret ladder of contemplation, to the perfect union of love of God, its beloved salvation.[279]

This, then, is the disguise which the soul says that it wears in the night of faith, upon this secret ladder, and these are its three colours. They constitute a most fit preparation for the union of the soul with God, according to its three faculties, which are understanding, memory and will. For faith voids and darkens the understanding as to all its natural intelligence, and herein prepares it for union with Divine Wisdom. Hope voids and withdraws the memory from all creature possessions; for, as Saint Paul says, hope is for that which is not possessed;[280] and thus it withdraws the memory from that which it is capable of possessing, and sets it on that for which it hopes. And for this cause hope in God alone prepares the memory purely for union with God. Charity, in the same way, voids and annihilates the affections and desires of the will for whatever is not God, and sets them upon Him alone; and thus this virtue prepares this faculty and unites it with God through love. And thus, since the function of these virtues is the withdrawal of the soul from all that is less than God, their function is consequently that of joining it with God.

And thus, unless it journeys earnestly, clad in the garments of these three virtues, it is impossible for the soul to attain to the perfection of union with God through love. Wherefore, in order that the soul might attain that which it desired, which was this loving and delectable union with its Beloved, this disguise and clothing which it assumed was most necessary and convenient. And likewise to have succeeded in thus clothing itself and persevering until it should obtain the end and aspiration which it had so much desired, which was the union of love, was a great and happy chance, wherefore in this line the soul also says:

Oh, happy chance!

Chapter XXII

Explains the third[281] line of the second stanza.

It is very clear that it was a happy chance for this soul to go forth with such an enterprise as this, for it was its going forth that delivered it from the devil and from the world and from its own sensuality, as we have said. Having attained liberty of spirit, so precious and so greatly desired by all, it went forth from low things to high; from terrestrial, it became celestial; from human, Divine. Thus it came to have its conversation in the heavens, as has the soul in this state of perfection, even as we shall go on to say in what follows, although with rather more brevity.

For the most important part of my task, and the part which chiefly led me to undertake it, was the explanation of this night to many souls who pass through it and yet know nothing about it, as was said in the prologue. Now this explanation and exposition has already been half completed. Although much less has been said of it than might be said, we have shown how many are the blessings which the soul bears with it through the night and how happy is the chance whereby it passes through it, so that, when a soul is terrified by the horror of so many trials, it is also encouraged by the certain hope of so many and such precious blessings of God as it gains therein. And furthermore, for yet another reason, this was a happy chance for the soul; and this reason is given in the following line:

In darkness and in concealment.

Chapter XXIII

Expounds the fourth line[282] and describes the wondrous hiding place wherein the soul is set during this night. Shows how, although the devil has an entrance into other places that are very high, he has none into this.

'In concealment' is as much as to say 'in a hiding-place,' or 'in hiding'; and thus, what the soul here says (namely, that it went forth 'in darkness and in concealment') is a more complete explanation of the great security which it describes itself in the first line of the stanza as possessing, by means of this dark contemplation upon the road of the union of the love of God.

When the soul, then, says 'in darkness and in concealment,' it means that, inasmuch as it journeyed in darkness after the manner aforementioned, it went in hiding and in concealment from the devil and from his wiles and stratagems. The reason why, as it journeys in the darkness of this contemplation, the soul is free, and is hidden from the stratagems of the devil, is that the infused contemplation which it here possesses is infused into it passively and secretly, without the knowledge of the senses and faculties, whether interior or exterior, of the sensual part. And hence it follows that, not only does it journey in hiding, and is free from the impediment which these faculties can set in its way because of its natural weakness, but likewise from the devil; who, except through these faculties of the sensual part, cannot reach or know that which is in the soul, nor that which is taking place within it. Wherefore, the more spiritual, the more interior and the more remote from the senses is the communication, the farther does the devil fall short of understanding it.

And thus it is of great importance for the security of the soul that its inward communication with God should be of such a kind that its very senses of the lower part will remain in darkness[283] and be without knowledge of it, and attain not to it: first, so that it may be possible for the spiritual communication to be more abundant, and that the weakness of its sensual part may not hinder the liberty of its spirit; secondly because, as we say, the soul journeys more securely since the devil cannot penetrate so far. In this way we may understand that passage where Our Saviour, speaking in a spiritual sense, says: 'Let not thy left hand know what thy right hand doeth.'[284] Which is as though He had said: Let not thy left hand know that which takes place upon thy right hand, which is the higher and spiritual part of the soul; that is, let it be of such a kind that the lower portion of thy soul, which is the sensual part, may not attain to it; let it be a secret between the spirit and God alone.

It is quite true that oftentimes, when these very intimate and secret spiritual communications are present and take place in the soul, although the devil cannot get to know of what kind and manner they are, yet the great repose and silence which some of them cause in the senses and the faculties of the sensual part make it clear to him that they are taking place and that the soul is receiving a certain blessing from them. And then, as he sees that he cannot succeed in thwarting them in the depth of the soul, he does what he can to disturb and disquiet the sensual part—that part to which he is able to attain—now by means of afflictions, now by terrors and fears, with intent to disquiet and disturb the higher and spiritual part of the soul by this means, with respect to that blessing which it then receives and enjoys. But often, when the communication of such contemplation makes its naked assault upon the soul and exerts its strength upon it, the devil, with all his diligence, is unable to disturb it; rather the soul receives a new and a greater advantage and a securer peace. For, when it feels the disturbing presence of the enemy, then—wondrous thing!—without knowing how it comes to pass, and without any efforts of its own, it enters farther into its own interior depths, feeling that it is indeed being set in a sure refuge, where it perceives itself to be most completely withdrawn and hidden from the enemy. And thus its peace and joy, which the devil is attempting to take from it, are increased; and all the fear that assails it remains without; and it becomes clearly and exultingly conscious of its secure enjoyment of that quiet peace and sweetness of the hidden Spouse, which neither the world nor the devil can give it or take from it. In that state, therefore, it realizes the truth of the words of the Bride about this, in the Songs, namely: 'See how threescore strong men surround the bed of Solomon, etc., because of the fears of the night.'[285] It is conscious of this strength and peace, although it is often equally conscious that its flesh and bones are being tormented from without.

At other times, when the spiritual communication is not made in any great measure to the spirit, but the senses have a part therein, the devil more easily succeeds in disturbing the spirit and raising a tumult within it, by means of the senses, with these terrors. Great are the torment and the affliction which are then caused in the spirit; at times they exceed all that can be expressed. For, when there is a naked contact of spirit with spirit, the horror is intolerable which the evil spirit causes in the good spirit (I mean, in the soul), when its tumult reaches it. This is expressed likewise by the Bride in the Songs, when she says that it has happened thus to her at a time when she wished to descend to interior recollection in order to have fruition of these blessings. She says: 'I went down into the garden of nuts to see the apples of the valleys, and if the vine had flourished. I knew not; my soul troubled me because of the chariots'—that is, because of the chariots and the noise of Aminadab, which is the devil.[286]

At other times it comes to pass that the devil is occasionally able to see certain favours which God is pleased to grant the soul when they are bestowed upon it by the mediation of a good angel; for of those favours which come through a good angel God habitually allows the enemy to have knowledge: partly so that he may do that which he can against them according to the measure of justice, and that thus he may not be able to allege with truth that no opportunity is given him for conquering the soul, as he said concerning Job.[287] This would be the case if God allowed not a certain equality between the two warriors—namely, the good angel and the bad—when they strive for the soul, so that the victory of either may be of the greater worth, and the soul that is victorious and faithful in temptation may be the more abundantly rewarded.

We must observe, therefore, that it is for this reason that, in proportion as God is guiding the soul and communing with it, He gives the devil leave to act with it after this manner. When the soul has genuine visions by the instrumentality of the good angel (for it is by this instrumentality that they habitually come, even though Christ reveal Himself, for He scarcely ever appears[288] in His actual person), God also gives the wicked angel leave to present to the soul false visions of this very type in such a way that the soul which is not cautious may easily be deceived by their outward appearance, as many souls have been. Of this there is a figure in Exodus,[289] where it is said that all the genuine signs that Moses wrought were wrought likewise in appearance by the magicians of Pharao. If he brought forth frogs, they brought them forth likewise; if he turned water into blood, they did the same.

And not only does the evil one imitate God in this type of bodily vision, but he also imitates and interferes in spiritual communications which come through the instrumentality of an angel, when he succeeds in seeing them, as we say (for, as Job said[290]: Omne sublime videt). These, however, as they are without form and figure (for it is the nature of spirit to have no such thing), he cannot imitate and counterfeit like those others which are presented under some species or figure. And thus, in order to attack the soul, in the same way as that wherein it is being visited, his fearful spirit presents a similar vision in order to attack and destroy spiritual things by spiritual. When this comes to pass just as the good angel is about to communicate spiritual contemplation to the soul, it is impossible for the soul to shelter itself in the secrecy and hiding-place of contemplation with sufficient rapidity not to be observed by the devil; and thus he appears to it and produces a certain horror and perturbation of spirit which at times is most distressing to the soul. Sometimes the soul can speedily free itself from him, so that there is no opportunity for the aforementioned horror of the evil spirit to make an impression on it; and it becomes recollected within itself, being favoured, to this end, by the effectual spiritual grace that the good angel then communicates to it.

At other times the devil prevails and encompasses the soul with a perturbation and horror which is a greater affliction to it than any torment in this life could be. For, as this horrible communication passes direct from spirit to spirit, in something like nakedness and clearly distinguished from all that is corporeal, it is grievous beyond what every sense can feel; and this lasts in the spirit for some time, yet not for long, for otherwise the spirit would be driven forth from the flesh by the vehement communication of the other spirit. Afterwards there remains to it the memory thereof, which is sufficient to cause it great affliction.

All that we have here described comes to pass in the soul passively, without its doing or undoing anything of itself with respect to it. But in this connection it must be known that, when the good angel permits the devil to gain this advantage of assailing the soul with this spiritual horror, he does it to purify the soul and to prepare it by means of this spiritual vigil for some great spiritual favour and festival which he desires to grant it, for he never mortifies save to give life, nor humbles save to exalt, which comes to pass shortly afterwards. Then, according as was the dark and horrible purgation which the soul suffered, so is the fruition now granted it of a wondrous and delectable spiritual contemplation, sometimes so lofty that there is no language to describe it. But the spirit has been greatly refined by the preceding horror of the evil spirit, in order that it may be able to receive this blessing; for these spiritual visions belong to the next life rather than to this, and when one of them is seen this is a preparation for the next.

This is to be understood with respect to occasions when God visits the soul by the instrumentality of a good angel, wherein, as has been said, the soul is not so totally in darkness and in concealment that the enemy cannot come within reach of it. But, when God Himself visits it, then the words of this line are indeed fulfilled, and it is in total darkness and in concealment from the enemy that the soul receives these spiritual favours of God. The reason for this is that, as His Majesty dwells substantially in the soul, where neither angel nor devil can attain to an understanding of that which comes to pass, they cannot know the intimate and secret communications which take place there between the soul and God. These communications, since the Lord Himself works them, are wholly Divine and sovereign, for they are all substantial touches of Divine union between the soul and God; in one of which the soul receives a greater blessing than in all the rest, since this is the loftiest degree[291] of prayer in existence.

For these are the touches that the Bride entreated of Him in the Songs, saying: Osculetur me osculo oris sui.[292] Since this is a thing which takes place in such close intimacy with God, whereto the soul desires with such yearnings to attain, it esteems and longs for a touch of this Divinity more than all the other favours that God grants it. Wherefore, after many such favours have been granted to the Bride in the said Songs, of which she has sung therein, she is not satisfied, but entreats Him for these Divine touches, saying: 'Who shall give Thee to me, my brother, that I might find Thee alone without, sucking the breasts of my mother, so that I might kiss Thee with the mouth of my soul, and that thus no man should despise me or make bold to attack me.'[293] By this she denotes the communication which God Himself alone makes to her, as we are saying, far from all the creatures and without their knowledge, for this is meant by 'alone and without, sucking, etc.'—that is, drying up and draining the breasts of the desires and affections of the sensual part of the soul. This takes place when the soul, in intimate peace and delight, has fruition of these blessings, with liberty of spirit, and without the sensual part being able to hinder it, or the devil to thwart it by means thereof. And then the devil would not make bold to attack it, for he would not reach it, neither could he attain to an understanding of these Divine touches in the substance of the soul in the loving substance of God.

To this blessing none attains save through intimate purgation and detachment and spiritual concealment from all that is creature; it comes to pass in the darkness, as we have already explained at length and as we say with respect to this line. The soul is in concealment and in hiding, in the which hiding-place, as we have now said, it continues to be strengthened in union with God through love, wherefore it sings this in the same phrase, saying: 'In darkness and in concealment.'

When it comes to pass that those favours are granted to the soul in concealment (that is, as we have said, in spirit only), the soul is wont, during some of them, and without knowing how this comes to pass, to see itself so far withdrawn and separated according to the higher and spiritual part, from the sensual and lower portion, that it recognizes in itself two parts so distinct from each other that it believes that the one has naught to do with the other, but that the one is very remote and far withdrawn from the other. And in reality, in a certain way, this is so; for the operation is now wholly spiritual, and the soul receives no communication in its sensual part. In this way the soul gradually becomes wholly spiritual; and in this hiding-place of unitive contemplation its spiritual desires and passions are to a great degree removed and purged away. And thus, speaking of its higher part, the soul then says in this last line:

My house being now at rest.[294]

Chapter XXIV

Completes the explanation of the second stanza.

This is as much as to say: The higher portion of my soul being like the lower part also, at rest with respect to its desires and faculties, I went forth to the Divine union of the love of God.

Inasmuch as, by means of that war of the dark night, as has been said, the soul is combated and purged after two manners—namely, according to its sensual and its spiritual part—with its senses, faculties and passions, so likewise after two manners—namely, according to these two parts, the sensual and the spiritual—with all its faculties and desires, the soul attains to an enjoyment of peace and rest. For this reason, as has likewise been said, the soul twice pronounces this line—namely,[295] in this stanza and in the last—because of these two portions of the soul, the spiritual and the sensual, which, in order that they may go forth to the Divine union of love, must needs first be reformed, ordered and tranquillized with respect to the sensual and to the spiritual, according to the nature of the state of innocence which was Adam's.[296] And thus this line which, in the first stanza, was understood of the repose of the lower and sensual portion, is, in this second stanza, understood more particularly of the higher and spiritual part; for which reason it is repeated.[297]

This repose and quiet of this spiritual house the soul comes to attain, habitually and perfectly (in so far as the condition of this life allows), by means of the acts of the substantial touches of Divine union whereof we have just spoken; which, in concealment, and hidden from the perturbation of the devil, and of its own senses and passions, the soul has been receiving from the Divinity, wherein it has been purifying itself, as I say, resting, strengthening and confirming itself in order to be able to receive the said union once and for all, which is the Divine betrothal between the soul and the Son of God. As soon as these two houses of the soul have together become tranquillized and strengthened, with all their domestics—namely, the faculties and desires—and have put these domestics to sleep and made them to be silent with respect to all things, both above and below, this Divine Wisdom immediately unites itself with the soul by making a new bond of loving possession, and there is fulfilled that which is written in the Book of Wisdom, in these words: Dum quietum silentium contineret omnia, et nox in suo cursu medium iter haberet, omnipotens sermo tuus Domine a regalibus sedibus.[298] The same thing is described by the Bride in the Songs,[299] where she says that, after she had passed by those who stripped her of her mantle by night and wounded her, she found Him Whom her soul loved.

The soul cannot come to this union without great purity, and this purity is not gained without great detachment from every created thing and sharp mortification. This is signified by the stripping of the Bride of her mantle and by her being wounded by night as she sought and went after the Spouse; for the new mantle which belonged to the betrothal could not be put on until the old mantle was stripped off. Wherefore, he that refuses to go forth in the night aforementioned to seek the Beloved, and to be stripped of his own will and to be mortified, but seeks Him upon his bed and at his own convenience, as did the Bride,[300] will not succeed in finding Him. For this soul says of itself that it found Him by going forth in the dark and with yearnings of love.

Chapter XXV

Wherein is expounded the third stanza.

In the happy night, In secret, when none saw me, Nor I beheld aught, Without light or guide, save that which burned in my heart.

Exposition

The soul still continues the metaphor and similitude of temporal night in describing this its spiritual night, and continues to sing and extol the good properties which belong to it, and which in passing through this night it found and used, to the end that it might attain its desired goal with speed and security. Of these properties it here sets down three.

The first, it says, is that in this happy night of contemplation God leads the soul by a manner of contemplation so solitary and secret, so remote and far distant from sense, that naught pertaining to it, nor any touch of created things, succeeds in approaching the soul in such a way as to disturb it and detain it on the road of the union of love.

The second property whereof it speaks pertains to the spiritual darkness of this night, wherein all the faculties of the higher part of the soul are in darkness. The soul sees naught, neither looks at aught neither stays in aught that is not God, to the end that it may reach Him, inasmuch as it journeys unimpeded by obstacles of forms and figures, and of natural apprehensions, which are those that are wont to hinder the soul from uniting with the eternal Being of God.

The third is that, although as it journeys it is supported by no particular interior light of understanding, nor by any exterior guide, that it may receive satisfaction therefrom on this lofty road—it is completely deprived of all this by this thick darkness—yet its love alone, which burns at this time, and makes its heart to long for the Beloved, is that which now moves and guides it, and makes it to soar upward to its God along the road of solitude, without its knowing how or in what manner.

There follows the line:

In the happy night.

Footnotes

[1]Ascent, Bk. I, chap. i, sect. 2.

[2]Op, cit., sect. 3.

[3]Dark Night, Bk. 1, chap. iii, sect. 3.

[4]Op. cit., Bk. I, chap. i, sect. 1.

[5]Dark Night, Bk. 1, chap. viii, sect. 1.

[6]Op. cit., Bk. I, chap. viii, sect. 2.

[7]Ibid.

[8]Dark Night, Bk. I, chap. x, sect. 4.

[9]Op. cit., Bk. II, chap. iii, sect. 1.

[10]Op. cit., Bk. II, chap. i, sect. 1.

[11]Dark Night, Bk. II, chap. xi, sect. 1.

[12]Dark Night, Bk. II, chap. xvi, sect. 2.

[13][On this, see Sobrino, pp. 159-66.]

[14]Cf. pp. lviii-lxiii, Ascent of Mount Carmel (Image Books edition).

[15][It contains a series of paradoxical statements, after the style of those in Ascent, Bk. I, chap. xiii, and is of no great literary merit. P. Silverio reproduces it in Spanish on p. 302 (note) of his first volume.]

[16]The 'first friar' would be P. Antonio de Jesús, who was senior to St. John of the Cross in the Carmelite Order, though not in the Reform.

[17]The longest of these are one of ten lines in Bk. I, chap. iv, [in the original] and those of Bk. II, chaps. vii, viii, xii, xiii, which vary from eleven to twenty-three lines. Bk. II, chap. xxiii, has also considerable modifications.

[18]The chief interpolation is in Bk. I, chap. x.

[19]St. Matthew vii, 14.

[20][More exactly: 'purificative.']

[21]St. Luke xviii, 11-12.

[22]St. Matthew vii, 3.

[23]St. Matthew xxiii, 24.

[24][Lit., 'Presuming.']

[25][The original merely has: 'and are often eager.']

[26][Lit., 'a thousand envies and disquietudes.']

[27]St. Matthew xxv, 8. [Lit., 'who, having their lamps dead, sought oil from without.']

[28][Lit., 'to have.']

[29][Lit., 'these fervours.']

[30][Lit., 'into something of this.']

[31]The agnusdei was a wax medal with a representation of the lamb stamped upon it, often blessed by the Pope; at the time of the Saint such medals were greatly sought after, as we know from various references in St. Teresa's letters.

[32][The word nómina, translated 'token,' and normally meaning list, or 'roll,' refers to a relic on which were written the names of saints. In modern Spanish it can denote a medal or amulet used superstitiously.]

[33][No doubt a branch of palm, olive or rosemary, blessed in church on Palm Sunday, like the English palm crosses of to—day. 'Palm Sunday' is in Spanish Domingo de ramos: 'Branch Sunday.']

[34][Lit., 'recreation.']

[35][Lit., 'recreation.']

[36][Lit., 'of everything.']

[37]All writers who comment upon this delicate matter go into lengthy and learned explanations of it, though in reality there is little that needs to be added to the Saint's clear and apt exposition. It will be remembered that St. Teresa once wrote to her brother Lorenzo, who suffered in this way: 'As to those stirrings of sense. . . . I am quite clear they are of no account, so the best thing is to make no account of them' (LL. 168). The most effective means of calming souls tormented by these favours is to commend them to a discreet and wise director whose counsel they may safely follow. The Illuminists committed the grossest errors in dealing with this matter.

[38]St. John iii, 6.

[39][Lit. 'they even do it.']

[40][Lit., 'spiritual road.']

[41][Lit., 'these persons.']

[42][Lit., 'and treat this as their God.']

[43][The Spanish is impersonal: 'immediately this is taken from them,' etc.]

[44][Lit., 'and opinion.']

[45][Lit., 'anyhow.']

[46][Lit, 'the other boldnesses are.']

[47][Lit., 'they strive to obtain this, as they say, by the strength of their arms.' The phrase is, of course, understood in the Spanish to be metaphorical, as the words 'as they say' clearly indicate.]

[48][Lit., 'who are not influenced, neither act by reason, but from pleasure.']

[49][Lit., 'which we shall give.']

[50][áspero: harsh, rough, rugged.]

[51][Lit., 'against all the sweetlessness of self—denial.']

[52][Lit., 'causing them to enter.']

[53][Lit., 'and, as they say, their eye (el ojo) grows'—a colloquial phrase expressing annoyance.]

[54]1 Corinthians xiii, 6. The Saint here cites the sense, not the letter, of the epistle.

[55]St. Matthew xvi, 25.

[56][Lit., 'they are very weak for the fortitude and trial of perfection.']

[57]St. Matthew vii, 14.

[58][Lit., 'say.']

[59][Lit., 'say.']

[60][plática: the word is frequently used in Spanish to denote an informal sermon or address.]

[61][Lit., 'low'; the same word recurs below and is similarly translated .]

[62][Lit., 'to the better time.']

[63][Lit., 'And in this it is known very probably.']

[64]Numbers xi, 5-6.

[65][Lit., 'makes us to desire our miseries.']

[66][Lit., 'incommunicable.']

[67]Canticles vi, 4 [A.V., vi, 5].

[68][Lit., 'satisfactory and pacific.']
[69]Psalm lxxxiv, 9 [A.V., lxxxv, 8].
[70][The stress here is evidently on the transience of the distempers whether they be moral or physical.]
[71][Lit., 'spoiling themselves in the one.']
[72][Lit., 'because they seek their spirit.']
[73][Lit., 'without doing anything themselves.']
[74][Lit., 'which it may then wish to have.']
[75]Psalm lxxii, 21 [A.V., lxxiii, 21—2].
[76][Lit., 'livingness': cf. the quotation below.]
[77]Psalm xli, 3 [A.V., xlii, 2].
[78][Lit., 'and chance': the same word as in the verse—line above.]
[79]St. Matthew vii, 14.
[80]Genesis xxi, 8.
[81]Exodus xxxiii, 5.
[82][Job ii, 7-8].
[83][Lit., 'the deep heights.']
[84]Isaias lviii, 10.
[85]Isaias xxviii, 19. [The author omits the actual text.]
[86]To translate this passage at all, we must read the Dios cómo of P. Silverio (p. 403, 1. 20), which is also found in P. Gerardo and elsewhere, as cómo Dios.
[87]Isaias xxviii, 9.
[88]Habacuc ii, 1.
[89]St. Augustine: Soliloq., Cap. ii.
[90]Psalm lxii, 3 [A.V., lxiii, 1—2].
[91]Psalm xxxviii, 3 [A.V., xxxix, 2].
[92]Psalm lxxvi, 4 [A.V., lxxvii, 3—4].
[93]Psalm lxxvi, 7 [A.V., lxxvii, 6].
[94]Psalm l, 19 [A.V., li, 17]
[95][The 'spirit of giddiness' of D.V., and 'perverse spirit' of A.V., Isaias xix, 14.]
[96]Ecclesiasticus xxxiv, 9-10.
[97]Jeremias xxxi, 18.
[98][Lit., 'for certain days.']
[99][Lit., 'from a narrow prison.']
[100][i.e., between sense and spirit.]
[101]Psalm cxlvii, 17 [D.V. and A.V.].
[102]Wisdom ix, 15.
[103][Lit., 'Continues with other imperfections.']
[104][i.e., 'deadening of the mind.']
[105]Osee ii, 20.
[106]1 Corinthians xiii, 11.
[107][Ephesians iv, 24.]
[108]Psalm xcvi, 2 [A.V., xcvii, 2].
[109][Lit., 'not attaining.']
[110]Psalm xvii, 13 [A.V., xviii, 12].
[111]Job vii, 20.
[112]Psalm xxxviii, 12 [A.V., xxxix, 11].
[113]Job xxiii, 6.
[114]Job xix, 21.
[115][There is a reference here to Job vii, 20: cf. sect. 5, above.]

[116]Jonas ii, 1.
[117]Psalm xvii, 5—7 [A.V., xviii, 4—5].
[118]Psalm lxxxvii, 6—8 [A.V., lxxxviii, 5—7].
[119]Psalm lxxxvii, 9 [A.V., lxxxviii, 8].
[120]Jonas ii, 4—7 [A.V., ii, 3—6].
[121]Ezechiel xxiv, 10.
[122]Ezechiel xxiv, 11.
[123]Wisdom iii, 6.
[124]Psalm lxviii, 2—4 [A.V., lxix, 1—3].
[125][i.e., purgatory.]
[126]Job xvi, 13—17 [A.V., xvi, 12—16].
[127]Lamentations iii, 1-20.
[128]Job xii, 22.
[129]Psalm cxxxviii, 12 [A.V., cxxxix, 12].
[130][Lit., 'like to the dead of the world (or of the age).']
[131]Psalm cxlii, 3 [A.V., cxliii, 3—4].
[132]Psalm xxix, 7 [A.V., xxx, 6].
[133][Lit., 'and play his tricks upon it.']
[134]B. Bz., C, H. Mtr. all have this long passage on the suffering of the soul in Purgatory. It would be rash, therefore, to deny that St. John of the Cross is its author, [or to suppose, as P. Gerardo did, that he deleted it during a revision of his works]. An admirably constructed synthesis of these questions will be found in B. Belarmino, De Purgatorio, Bk. II, chaps. iv, v. He asks if souls in Purgatory are sure of their salvation. This was denied by Luther, and by a number of Catholic writers, who held that, among the afflictions of these souls, the greatest is this very uncertainty, some maintain that, though they have in fact such certainty, they are unaware of it. Belarmino quotes among other authorities Denis the Carthusian De quattuor novissimis, Gerson (Lect. I De Vita Spirituali) and John of Rochester (against Luther's 32nd article); these writers claim that, as sin which is venial is only so through the Divine mercy, it may with perfect justice be rewarded by eternal punishment, and thus souls that have committed venial sin cannot be confident of their salvation. He also shows, however, that the common opinion of theologians is that the souls in Purgatory are sure of their salvation, and considers various degrees of certainty, adding very truly that, while these souls experience no fear, they experience hope, since they have not yet the Beatific vision.

Uncertainty as to their salvation, it is said, might arise from ignorance of the sentence passed upon them by the Judge or from the deadening of their faculties by the torments which they are suffering. Belarmino refutes these and other suppositions with great force and effect. St. John of the Cross seems to be referring to the last named when he writes of the realization of their afflictions and their deprivation of God not allowing them to enjoy the blessings of the theological virtues. It is not surprising if the Saint, not having examined very closely this question, of which he would have read treatments in various authors, thought of it principally as an apt illustration of the purifying and refining effects of passive purgation; and an apt illustration it certainly is.

[135]Lamentations iii, 44.
[136][Lamentations iii, 9.]
[137]Lamentations iii, 9.
[138]Lamentations iii, 28.

[139][Lit., 'at the Divine things.']

[140]Psalm lxxii, 22 [A.V., lxxiii, 22].

[141]1 Corinthians ii, 10. [Lit., 'penetrates all things.']

[142]Wisdom vii, 24.

[143]2 Corinthians vi, 10.

[144][Lit., 'with a certain eminence of excellence.']

[145][Lit., '. . . sweetness, with great eminence.']

[146]Exodus xvi, 3.

[147]Wisdom xvi, 21.

[148][Lit., 'from every kind.' But see Tobias viii, 2. The 'deprived' of e.p. gives the best reading of this phrase, but the general sense is clear from the Scriptural reference.]

[149]Tobias viii, 2.

[150]Isaias lxiv, 4 [1 Corinthians ii, 9].

[151][Lit., 'be made thin.']

[152]Isaias xxvi, 17-18.

[153][Philippians iv, 7.]

[154][We have here split up a parenthesis of about seventy words.]

[155][Lit., 'and wept.']

[156]Lamentations iii, 17.

[157]Psalm xxxvii, 9 [A.V., xxxviii, 8].

[158][Lit., '. . . sees itself, it arises and is surrounded with pain and affliction the affections of the soul, that I know not how it could be described.' A confused, ungrammatical sentence, of which, however, the general meaning is not doubtful.]

[159]Job iii, 24.

[160]Job xxx, 17.

[161]Job xxx, 16.

[162]Lamentations iii, 17.

[163]Wisdom vii, 11.

[164]Ecclesiasticus li, 28—9 [A.V., li, 19—21].

[165][Lit., 'more delicate.']

[166][Lit., 'fury.']

[167][The sudden change of metaphor is the author's. The 'assault' is, of course, the renewed growth of the 'root.']

[168][Lit., '. . . from the soul, with regard to that which has already been purified.']

[169][Lit., 'not enlightened': the word is the same as that used just above.]

[170][The word translated 'over' is rendered 'gone' just above.]

[171][Lit., 'in loves'; and so throughout the exposition of this line.]

[172][Lit., 'cling,' 'adhere.']

[173][Lit., 'shut up.']

[174][Here, and below, the original has recogidos, the word normally translated 'recollected']

[175]Psalm lviii, 10 [A V., lix, 9].

[176]Deuteronomy vi, 5.

[177]Psalm lviii, 15-16 [A.V., lix, 14-15].

[178]Psalm lxii, 2 [A.V., lxiii, 1].

[179][Lit., as in the verses, 'in loves.']

[180][For cievro, hart, read siervo, servant, and we have the correct quotation from Scripture. The change, however, was evidently made by the Saint knowingly. In

P. Gerardo's edition, the Latin text, with cervus, precedes the Spanish translation, with ciervo.]

[181]Job vii, 2-4.

[182][No cabe: Lit., 'it cannot be contained,' 'there is no room for it.']

[183]Isaias xxvi, 9.

[184]Psalm l, 12 [A.V., li, 10].

[185][Lit., 'enamoured.']

[186]Lamentations i, 13.

[187]Psalm xi, 7 [A.V., xii, 6].

[188]The Schoolmen frequently assert that the lower angels are purged and illumined by the higher. Cf. St. Thomas, Summa, I, q. 106, a. 1, ad. 1.

[189][Lit., 'and softens.']

[190][More literally, 'is sick.']

[191]Psalm xxxviii, 4 [A.V., xxxix, 3].

[192][Lit., 'the beginnings.']

[193]The Saint here treats a question often debated by philosophers and mystics—that of love and knowledge. Cf. also Spiritual Canticle, Stanza XVII, and Living Flame, Stanza III. Philosophers generally maintain that it is impossible to love without knowledge, and equally so to love more of an object than what is known of it. Mystics have, however, their own solutions of the philosophers' difficulty and the speculative Spanish mystics have much to say on the matter. (Cf., for example, the Médula Mística, Trat. V, Chap. iv, and the Escuela de Oración, Trat. XII, Duda v.)

[194]St. John i, 5.

[195][Lit., 'the yearning to think of it.']

[196][The word translated 'estimation' might also be rendered 'reverent love.' The 'love of estimation,' which has its seat in the understanding, is contrasted with the 'enkindling' or the 'love of desire,' which has its seat in the will. So elsewhere in this paragraph.]

[197]St. John xx, 1 [St. Matthew xxvii, 62—6].

[198]St. John xx, 15.

[199][Lit., 'outskirts,' 'suburbs.']

[200]Canticles v, 8.

[201]Genesis xxx, 1.

[202]Ephesians iv, 4.

[203]Canticles viii, 1.

[204]St. Matthew x, 36.

[205][Lit., 'The line, then, continues, and says thus.' In fact, however, the author is returning to the first line of the stanza.]

[206][Lit., 'taste.']

[207]Some have considered this description exaggerated, but it must be borne in mind that all souls are not tested alike and the Saint is writing of those whom God has willed to raise to such sanctity that they drain the cup of bitterness to the dregs. We have already seen (Bk. I, chap. xiv, sect. 5) that 'all do not experience (this) after one manner . . . for (it) is meted out by the will of God, in conformity with the greater or the smaller degree of imperfection which each soul has to purge away, (and) in conformity, likewise, with the degree of love of union to which God is pleased to raise it' (Bk. I, chap xiv, above).

[208]Osee xiii, 9.

[209]Psalm xvii, 12 [A.V., xviii, 11].

[210]Psalm xvii, 13 [A.V., xviii, 12].

[211]Isaias v, 30.

[212]Psalm xxx, 21 [A.V., xxxi, 20].

[213]'Propter hoc Gregorius (Hom. 14 in Ezech.) constituit vitam contemplativam in charitate Dei.' Cf. Summa Theologica, 2a, 2ae, q. 45, a. 2.

[214]Jeremias i, 6.

[215]Exodus iv, 10 [cf. iii, 2].

[216]Acts vii, 32.

[217][Or: 'and they know not how to say it nor are able to do so.']

[218][Lit., 'to him that rules them.']

[219][Lit., 'that is set most far away and most remote from every creatures.']

[220]Baruch iii, 31.

[221]Psalm lxxvi, 19—20 [A.V., lxxvii, 18—19].

[222][Lit., 'of the roundness of the earth.']

[223]Job xxxvii, 16.

[224][Lit., 'rises to scale, know and possess.']

[225]Psalm lxxxiii, 6 [A.V., lxxxiv, 7].

[226]St. Luke xiv, 11.

[227]Proverbs xviii, 12.

[228]Genesis xxviii, 12.

[229][Lit., 'and annihilating oneself.']

[230]'Ut dicit Bernardus, Magna res est amor, sed sunt in eo gradus. Loquendo ergo aliquantulum magis moraliter quam realiter, decem amoris gradus distinguere possumus' (D. Thom., De dilectione Dei et proximi, cap. xxvii. Cf. Opusc. LXI of the edition of Venice, 1595).

[231][The word translated 'step' may also (and often more elegantly) be rendered 'degree.' The same word is kept, however, throughout the translation of this chapter except where noted below.]

[232]Canticles v, 8.

[233]Psalm cxlii, 7 [A.V., cxliii, 7].

[234]Psalm lxvii, 10 [A.V., lxviii, 9].

[235][Lit., 'to enter (upon).']

[236]Canticles iii, 2.

[237]Psalm civ, 4 [A.V., cv, 4].

[238]St. John xx.

[239][The word in the Spanish is that elsewhere translated 'step.']

[240]Psalm cxi, 1 [A.V., cxii, 1].

[241][Lit., 'makes in him this labour of eagerness.']

[242]Genesis xxix, 20.

[243][Lit., 'how much God merits.']

[244]Canticles viii, 5.

[245]Jeremias ii, 2.

[246]Psalm lxxxiii, 2 [A.V., lxxxiv, 2].

[247]Genesis xxx, 1.

[248][Lit., 'On this hungering step.']

[249]Isaias xl, 31.

[250]Psalm xli, 2 [A.V., xlii, 1].

[251]Psalm lviii, 5 [A.V., lix, 4].

[252]Psalm cxviii, 32 [A.V., cxix, 32].

[253]1 Corinthians xiii, 7.

[254]Exodus xxxii, 31—2.

[255]Psalm xxxvi, 4 [A.V., xxxvii, 4].

[256]Canticles i, 1.

[257]Canticles iii, 4.

[258][Lit., 'attain to setting their foot.']

[259]Daniel x, 11.

[260]'Dum Deum in ignis visione suscipiunt, per amorem suaviter arserunt' (Hom. XXX in Evang.).

[261][i.e., direct, not mediate.]

[262]St. Matthew v, 8.

[263]St. John iii, 2.

[264]St. John xvi, 23.

[265][Lit., 'that it dislocates the sight of all understanding.']

[266]1 St. Peter v, 9.

[267][Lit., 'a better undershirt and tunic.']

[268][Lit., 'this whiteness.']

[269]Osee, ii, 20.

[270]Psalm xvi, 4 [A.V., xvii, 4].

[271]1 Thessalonians v, 8.

[272]Psalm xxiv, 15 [A.V., xxv, 15].

[273]Psalm cxxii, 2 [A.V., cxxiii, 2].

[274]Canticles iv, 9.

[275]Lamentations iii, 29.

[276]Ibid. [For the quotation, see Bk. II, chap. viii, sect. 1, above.]

[277]Canticles i, 3. [A.V., i, 4.] [For 'chambers' the Spanish has 'bed.']

[278]Canticles iii, 10.

[279][Or 'health.']

[280]Romans viii, 24.

[281]i.e., in the original Spanish and in our verse rendering of the poem in The Complete Works of St. John of the Cross, Ed. by E. Allison Peers, Vol. II (The Newman Press, Westminster, Md.).

[282]i.e., in the original Spanish and in our verse rendering of the poem in The Complete Works of St. John of the Cross, Ed. by E. Allison Peers, Vol. II (The Newman Press, Westminster, Md.).

[283][The Spanish also admits of the rendering: 'remain shut off from it by darkness.']

[284]Matthew vi, 3.

[285]Canticles iii, 7-8.

[286]Canticles vi, 10 [A.V., vi, 11—12].

[287]Job i, 1-11.

[288]Such is the unanimous opinion of theologians. Some, with St. Thomas (Pt. III, q. 57, a. 6), suppose that the appearance which converted St. Paul near Damascus was that of Our Lord Jesus Christ in person.

[289]Exodus vii, 11—22; viii, 7.

[290]Job xli, 25.

[291][Lit., 'step.' Cf. Bk. II, chap. xix, first note, above.]

[292]Canticles i, 1.

[293]Canticles viii, 1.

[294]The word translated 'at rest' is a past participle: more literally, 'stilled.'

[295][Lit., 'twice repeats'—a loosely used phrase.]

[296]H omits this last phrase, which is found in all the other Codices, and in e.p. The latter adds: 'notwithstanding that the soul is not wholly free from the temptations of the lower part.' The addition is made so that the teaching of the Saint may not be confused with that of the Illuminists, who supposed the contemplative in union to be impeccable, do what he might. The Saint's meaning is that for the mystical union of the soul with God such purity and tranquillity of senses and faculties are needful that his condition resembles that state of innocence in which Adam was created, but without the attribute of impeccability, which does not necessarily accompany union, nor can be attained by any, save by a most special privilege of God. Cf. St. Teresa's Interior Castle, VII, ii. St. Teresa will be found occasionally to explain points of mystical doctrine which St. John of the Cross takes as being understood.

[297][Lit., 'twice repeated.']

[298]Wisdom xviii, 14.

[299]Canticles v, 7.

[300]Canticles iii, 1.

[301]Thus end the majority of the MSS. Cf. pp. lxviii—lxiii, Ascent of Mount Carmel (Image Books edition), 26-27, on the incomplete state of this treatise. The MSS. say nothing of this, except that in the Alba de Tormes MS. we read: 'Thus far wrote the holy Fray John of the Cross concerning the purgative way, wherein he treats of the active and the passive [aspect] of it as is seen in the treatise of the Ascent of the Mount and in this of the Dark Night, and, as he died, he wrote no more. And hereafter follows the illuminative way, and then the unitive.' Elsewhere we have said that the lack of any commentary on the last five stanzas is not due to the Saint's death, since he lived for many years after writing the commentary on the earlier stanzas.

Printed in the United States
207763BV00001B/159/P